Sunset

By the Editors of Sunset Books
Sunset Books • Menlo Park, CA 94025

Back Roads and Hidden Places

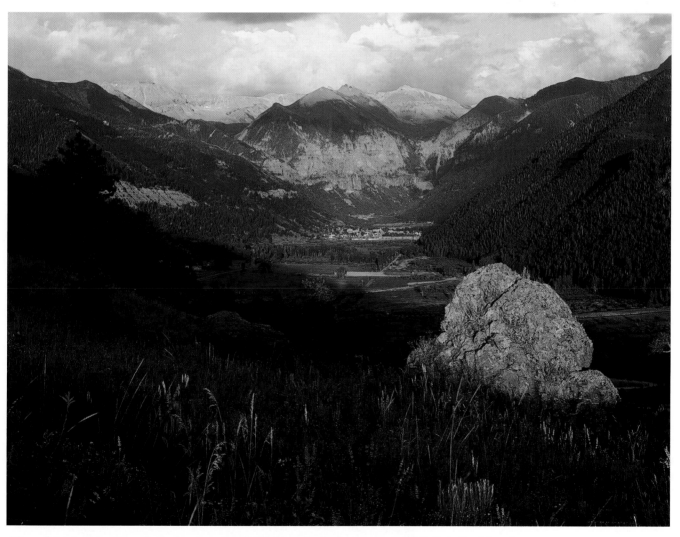

A former Colorado mining camp and current year-round resort, Telluride nestles in a box canyon among lofty Rocky Mountain peaks.

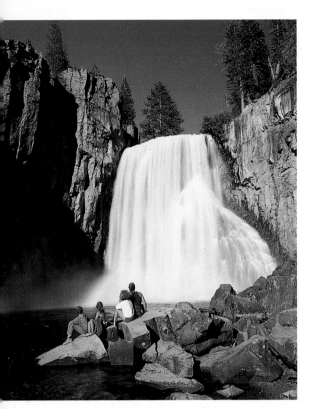

Rainbow Falls on the eastern flank of the Sierra Nevada.

First printing June 1999. Copyright © 1999 Sunset Publishing Corporation, Menlo Park, CA 94025. First edition. All rights reserved, including the right of reproduction in whole or in part in any form.

ISBN 0-376-05017-9
(Hardcover edition)

ISBN 0-376-05018-7
(Softcover edition)

Library of Congress Catalog Card Number: 99-61557

Printed in the United States.

For additional copies of *Back Roads and Hidden Places* or any other Sunset book, call 1-800-526-5111.

(Front Cover) Day hikers in California. Photography by Sean Arbabi.

{Back Cover} Arizona's cactus country. Photography by Scott Atkinson. Historic Silver City, Idaho. Photography by Ed Cooper. Sonoma County Vineyard. Photography by Larry Ulrich.

{Endpapers} Aspen leaves and pinecones carpet a forest floor. Photography by Claire Curran.

(Right) Merlot grapes in California's vine-filled Napa Valley.

Sunset Books

Vice President Sales: Richard A. Smeby

Editorial Director: Bob Doyle

Production Director: Lory Day

Art Director: Vasken Guiragossian

Staff for This Book:

Developmental Editor: Linda J. Selden

Book Editor: Barbara J. Braasch

Photo Editor: Joan Beth Erickson

Indexer: Teri Ann Johnson

Design: Mueller Design Interactive, Oakland

Cartography: Unless otherwise noted, all map design and cartography are by Reineck & Reineck, San Francisco

Production Coordinator: Patricia S. Williams

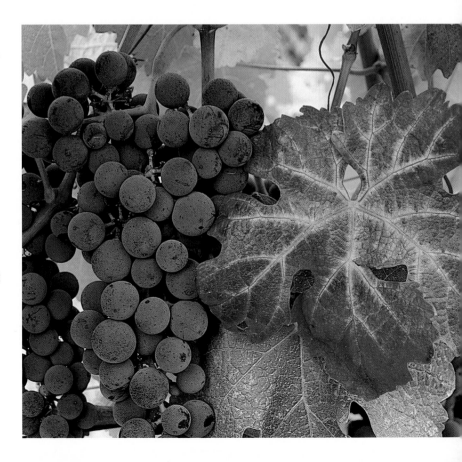

About this book...

We've rounded up 56 of the West's best back-road drives, from the Rocky Mountains States to the Pacific Coast. Many sites are truly off the beaten track; others are intriguing detours just off well-traveled routes. All start from major Western cities, making them good choices for travelers who want to add a few days to their itineraries. Even locals may find some discoveries in their own backyards. We know that things change, but attractions, hours, prices, telephone numbers, and highway designations are accurate as of press time. Maps are provided solely to highlight locations and are not intended to replace highway maps. Check automobile clubs, chambers of commerce, and visitor bureaus for more detailed route maps.

Research and Text:

Barbara J. Braasch
Kimberly Braasch
Mickey Butts
Carolyn Dobel
Joan Both Erickson
Jeanie Puleston Fleming
Bonnie Henderson
Susan Hauser
Edie Jarolim

Peter T. Jensen
David Lansing
Jena MacPherson
Caroline Patterson
Marcia Oxford
David L. Ryan
Kathie Selden
Nora Burba Trulsson

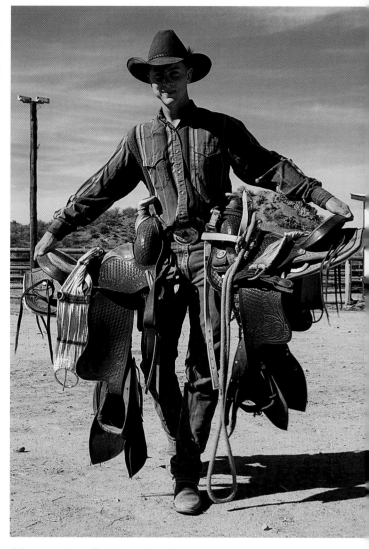

Arizona wrangler outfits dude ranch guests.

Photographers:

Wayne Aldridge/Borland Stock: 224. Sean Arbabi: 18 top, 62, 63, 70 bottom, 76, 155, 171. R. Valentine Atkinson: 59. Scott Atkinson: 24 top, 37, 169, 219. Larry A. Brazil: 46 top, 183 bottom. Jan Butchofsky-Houser: 28, 49 bottom, 67 bottom, 145, 152 bottom. Ed Callaert: 65. Carr Clifton: 38, 138, 198. Connie Coleman: 86, 87, 117, 122, 123, 124, 222 bottom, 233. Ed Cooper: 9, 60, 141, 172. Gary Crallé: 204, 205 bottom, 207, 208 top. Stephen Cridland: 82. Ben Davidson: 53, 64, 225. Mike Dobel: 134, 135, 136 bottom. Jack W. Dykinga: 202 bottom. Joan Beth Erickson: 177 top right, 235. David Falconer: 81, 110. C. Bruce Forster/Viewfinders: 83, 88, 90 top. Christopher Talbot Frank, 23, 221. Ken Gallard: 226. Mark E. Gibson: 3, 15, 21, 27, 33, 34 top, 56, 57 bottom, 69, 70 top, 74, 96, 98 bottom, 132, 166 top, 179. Jim Ginney: 72. Glenwood Springs Chamber Resort Association:

160, 161. Jeff Gnass: 6, 7, 73, 78, 80, 139, 140, 166 bottom, 185, 218. Thomas Hallstein/Outsight: 42 bottom, 51 bottom, 67 top, 103. Tony Hertz: 19. Dave G. Houser: 51 top, 54, 55, 147, 149, 151. Cynthia Hunter: 157, 158 top. Jerry Jacka: 177 bottom, 186 top, 88, 189 bottom, 191, 210, 216, 220. Peter Jensen: 31 bottom, 41 top. Susan Kaye: 163 bottom. Gill C. Kenny: 189 top, 190, 192, 194, 195, 196, 200. Dan Lamont: 114 bottom. Michael Lewis: 182, 228. J. D. Marston: 165. Curtis Martin: 2 bottom, 42 top, 180 top. Edward McCain: 183 top. Terrence McCarthy: 50. Michael Melford: 148, 150, 152 top. Terrence Moore: 186. David Muench: 1, 8 bottom, 44, 168, 201, 223. Marc Muench: 26, 227. Michael O'Leary: 108. George Olson: 230. Londie G. Padelsky: 2 top, 11 bottom, 22, 24 bottom, 36, 46 bottom, 202 top, 205 top. Jack Parsons: 162, 163

top. Larry Pierce/Steamboat Springs Chamber Association, Inc.: 158 bottom. Chuck Place: 10, 11 top, 12, 13, 14, 16, 31 top, 45, 49 top, 120 top, 170, 173 top, 175, 176, 177 top left, 208 bottom, 213, 215, 222 top. Bob Rink: 199. John A. Rizzo: 89, 101. Joel W. Rogers: 119, 120 bottom, 231. Rob Romig: 92, 94. David Ryan: 142, 143. Ed Selden: 173 bottom, 174. Kathie Selden: 156. Phil Schermeister: 8 top, 34 bottom. Gary Schimelfenig: 113. Phil Schofield: 90 bottom, 109, 111, 112, 126, 127, 130, 131, 136 top. Pete Stone: 98 top. James Tallon: 211, 214. Schmuel Thaler: 57 top. K. C. Thomas: 30. Larry Ulrich: 18 bottom, 20, 48, 100, 128, 236. Greg Vaughn: 41 bottom, 79, 84, 85, 97, 102, 104, 105. Greg Vaughn/Viewfinders: 93, 95, 114 top. Randy Wells: 180 bottom. Michael Wickes: 66. Doug Wilson: 116, 146, 234. Martha Woodward: 17. Wyoming Division of Tourism: 154.

Pacific Coast States 6

CALIFORNIA | OREGON | WASHINGTON

Southwest 168

NEW MEXICO | ARIZONA | UTAH | NEVADA

Travel Tips 218

Special Features

Pacific Co

CALIFORNIA | OREGON | WASHINGTON

Stat

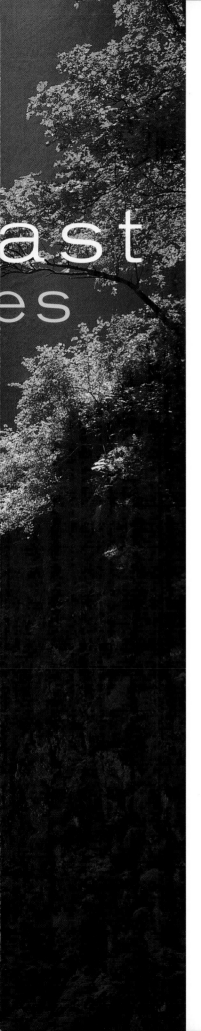

Though unified by the Pacific Ocean and defined by the mountain ranges that separate their sea-coasts from their interiors, California, Oregon, and Washington are distinctly different in appearance and appeal. Yet all three Pacific Coast states possess abundant natural resources and stunningly varied landscapes, ranging from snow-capped peaks to verdant valleys and unspoiled beaches.

The Pacific Coast states entered the 20th century with a history in which water was more important than land, from the time the original inhabitants drifted south after crossing the Bering Strait to the recent influx of immigrants from other Pacific Rim nations. Early explorers sailed across the Pacific, and even Yankee traders went around the Horn and up the coast to the mouth of the Columbia River long before Lewis and Clark journeyed overland.

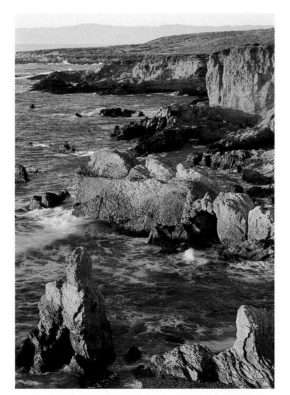

California

California stretches along the coast for more than 1,300 miles and expands inland for almost 300 miles at its widest point. It boasts some 30,000 miles of rivers and streams and more than 5,000 lakes. Almost 30 million acres of its diverse topography are protected in national and state parks and national forests.

Multnomah Falls (far left), the tallest cascade in Oregon, is a mere 25 miles east of downtown Portland.

The Pacific Coast's dramatic shoreline (left) extends for several thousand miles, from the border of Mexico to Canada.

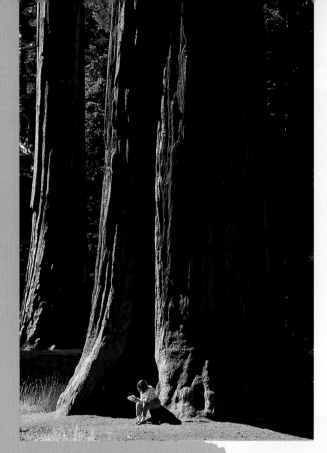

A person in the photo lends scale to California's mammoth Sequoia gigantea.

Washington's fertile Hood River Valley (below) bursts into spring bloom, providing a contrast to snowy Mt. Hood in Oregon.

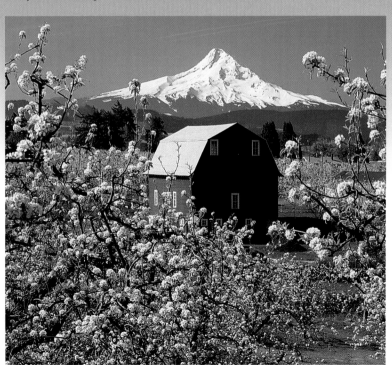

Tourists are drawn by the year-round mild climate, scenic splendors, last-frontier setting, and Hollywood-portrayed lifestyle. And smog, fog, traffic congestion, and the occasional earthquake aside, the Golden State satisfies their expectations. For starters, it contains one of the world's top visitor attractions (Disneyland), the country's favorite national monument (Cabrillo's landing site in San Diego outdraws even the Statue of Liberty), and best-loved national park (Yosemite), and North America's largest alpine lake (Tahoe). Here too are the world's tallest trees (coast redwoods), the most massive (giant sequoias), and the oldest (ancient bristlecone pines).

It also contains the highest and lowest points in the contiguous United States: lofty Mt. Whitney (14,494 feet) and, 85 miles away, Badwater in Death Valley (282 feet below sea level).

Oregon

Dense green forest, lofty mountains, driftwood-strewn ocean beaches, wheat-covered prairies, wilderness lakes and rivers, awesome desertlike plateaus—nature passed out scenery with a lavish hand in Oregon. The state boasts a dramatic 400-mile coastline. It is bordered on the north by the great artery of the Pacific Northwest—the Columbia River—and partially separated from Idaho to the east by mile-deep Hells Canyon, carved over eons by the waters of the Snake River.

Oregon's backbone is a majestic string of ice-capped dormant volcanoes—the Cascade Range. Most of the state's population lives on the moist, heavily forested western side; a broad high plateau stretches eastward to the Blue Mountains and the lonely land of the Great Basin. The Willamette River meanders through the broad, fertile Willamette Valley, whose focus is Portland, a center of urban activity.

Oregon's varying climes produce a landscape that is green and wet or high and dry. The tale of constant rainfall isn't true. What the state's northern latitude and 11,000-foot variation in elevation—from sea level to Cascade peaks—do trigger is a progression of delightful seasons. When spring or autumn arrives in Oregon, it's dramatic!

Washington

From cosmopolitan Seattle to the pastoral pleasures of the history-laden southeast, Washington enchants visitors. Crossing the Cascade Range from west to east is almost like crossing a national boundary. Seashores, forests, big cities, mountains, and legendary rainfall give way to grasslands, farm towns, river canyons, and a high desert climate.

Once the jumping-off spot for Alaska-bound prospectors, the northwest edge of the nation still maintains an air of frontier adventure, though the "frontier" now refers to Canada, its northern neighbor. Watching the ferries coming and going from Alaska, British Columbia, and the quiet backwaters of the San Juan Islands creates the urge to board—even if only to travel as far as Vancouver Island.

Before taking off, however, take time to roam around the state. Glacier-mantled Mt. Rainier (14,410 feet), 40 miles southeast of the Seattle–Tacoma metropolis, presides over the region, reminding everyone that rugged wilderness is only an hour away from major cities. If you prefer a more bucolic landscape, head across the Cascades to an almost-authentic Bavarian village and the state's major apple-growing area.

Whether you're looking for a stroll through fields of tulips, a walk on a lonely beach, a hike into an eerie green rain forest, or an alpine trek among wildflower-carpeted meadows and sparkling turquoise lakes, Washington satisfies.

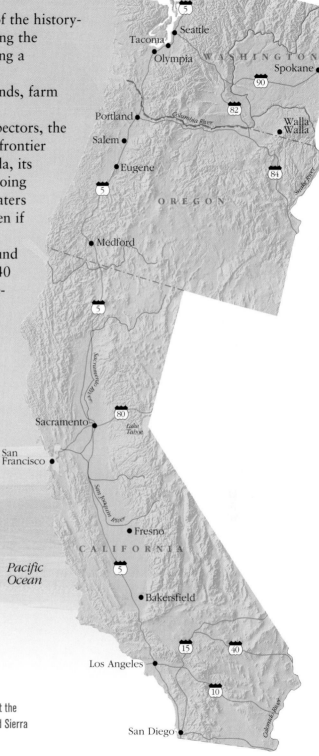

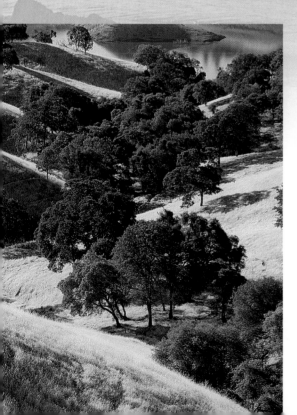

An autumn look at the rolling, oak-dotted Sierra Nevada foothills.

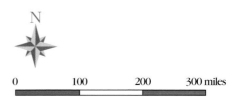

0   100   200   300 miles

Ojai & Santa Ynez
valleys

REGION		CALIFORNIA
Where	X	275-mile loop off U.S. Highway 101
When	X	Year-round destination

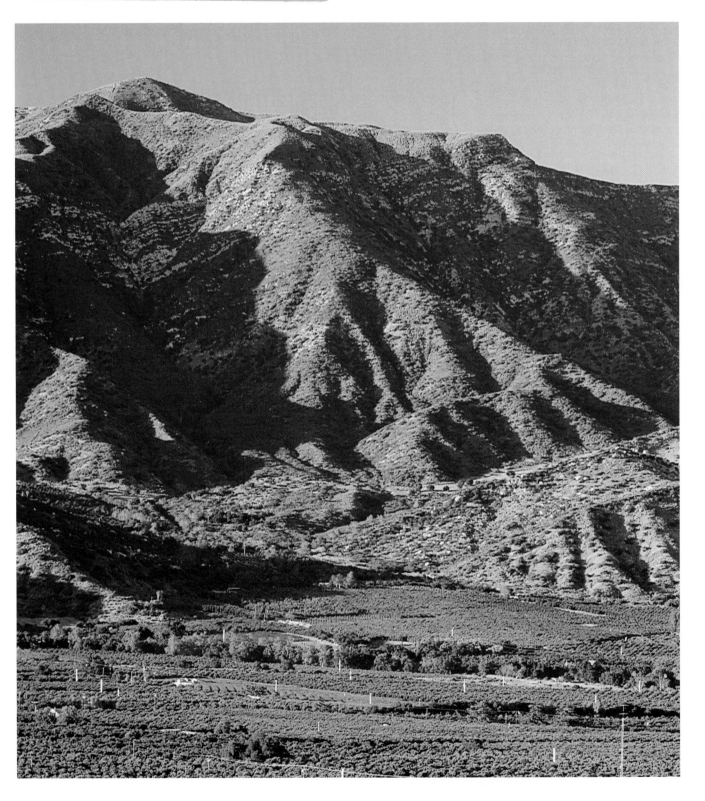

Many good reasons tempt travelers to get off coastal U.S. Highway 101 near Ventura and amble inland through the Los Padres National Forest and Santa Ynez Valley instead. Pretty little Ojai, the wine country through Foxen Canyon, and beautiful Lake Cachuma are only some of the lures along the way.

In fact, there are so many pleasures to sample that you may be tempted to extend your stay in restful Ojai Valley or soak up the Western ambience of Los Olivos and Ballard. But, if you complete this ambitious loop through Ventura and Santa Barbara counties, you'll be charmed by the rolling hills and quiet little communities that make this one of the most peaceful backcountry drives in Southern California.

Shangri-la in the Ojai Valley

From Ventura, drive 13 miles north on State Highway 33 past

Approaching the artists' colony of Ojai, roads run past acres of citrus and avocado orchards (left).

Miniature mare and foal (below) are from a local ranch; though most ranches are horse-oriented, they have been joined by llama and ostrich operations.

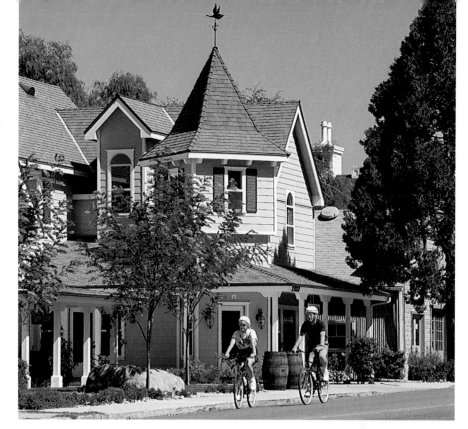

Cycling is one way to tour rural Santa Ynez Valley, home to award-winning wineries and horse ranches. These riders cruise the main street of Los Olivos, one of several small valley hamlets.

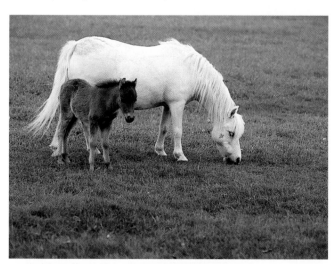

groves of citrus and avocado trees to Ojai, an artists' enclave and retreat that doubled as a Shangri-la location for the movie *Lost Horizon*. Since 1947, the town has hosted an acclaimed classical music concert in Libbey Park's Festival Bowl (late May or early June); if you miss that, there are free summer band concerts (8 p.m. on Wednesdays in July and August) at the same outdoor venue.

The road climbs up out of Ojai Valley along State 33 through the canyon of Matilija Creek, where, in May and June, you'll spot the elegant white blooms of matilija poppies blossoming on six-foot-tall bushes beside

the road. In about 6 miles, you'll come to Wheeler Hot Springs spa, where for a moderate price you can soak in private hot tubs situated in dense oak woodland. At the intersection with State Highway 166, turn west and drive 62 miles through the eroded badlands of Cuyama Valley to Santa Maria (for more on this farming town, see page 17).

Wine Country Around Los Olivos

On the southern edge of Santa Maria, exit on Betteravia Road and head east toward the wine country of Foxen Canyon. A number of tasting rooms have popped up along this country lane, which, 2 miles east of Santa Maria, becomes Foxen Canyon Road. You'll pass by Rancho Sisquoc (934-4332), Foxen (937-4251), Zaca Mesa (688-9339), and Fess Parker (688-1545), all with friendly, low-key tasting

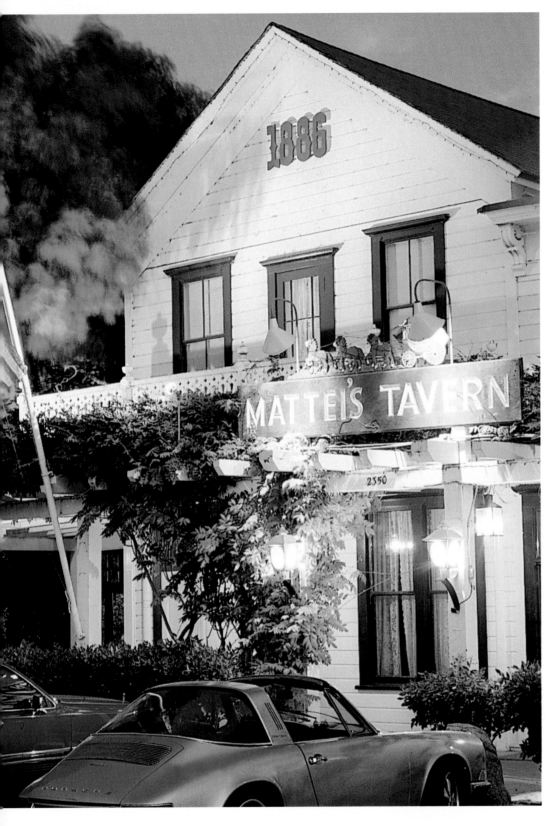

Porsches stop where stagecoaches used to call at Mattei's Tavern in Los Olivos. The venerable hotel and restaurant is popular with both locals and travelers.

old stagecoach route from Santa Barbara. Mattei's Tavern, a Los Olivos landmark, was built in 1886 as a hotel and restaurant to serve stage passengers; now it serves elegant dinners in a rustic setting. In town, a number of art galleries line Grand Avenue.

Unlike the Danish town of Solvang, which lies a few miles to the east, both Los Olivos and nearby Ballard (on Alamo Pintado Road) could be described as hamlets, loose groupings of ranches and homes centered on main streets or intersections too quiet for stoplights. Summers do get busy with tourists. But on weekdays and during the off-season, you'll have the area pretty much to yourself for browsing through galleries, tasting wine, and compiling classic California landscapes.

Back on State 154, the road crosses through the green meadows of Santa Ynez Valley before dropping down into heavy oak woodlands along scenic San

rooms. For a complete list of area wineries, pick up *Santa Barbara County Wineries*, a free guide available at most tasting rooms or from the Santa Barbara

County Vintners' Association (see address on next page).

Foxen Canyon Road meets State Highway 154 just west of Los Olivos, once a stop on the

Marcos Pass. You pass by a vast reservoir, Lake Cachuma, a favorite spot for bass fishers and bird-watchers (eagle tours are offered in winter). Halfway down the pass, take Stagecoach Road to historic Cold Spring Tavern, a good place to celebrate (or mourn) the end of your adventure. From the tavern, it's 10 miles to Santa Barbara and U.S. 101. Beautiful Santa

No museum piece, the little red schoolhouse in Ballard, dating from 1883, still serves local children.

Barbara is a favorite tourist stop. For tips on lodging, dining, and sightseeing, stop by the city's information center on Stearns Wharf.

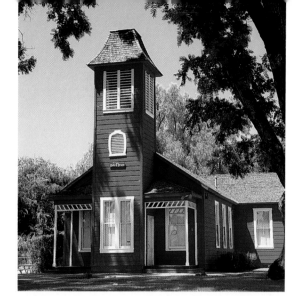

TRIP PLANNER

Unless otherwise noted, area codes are 805. Lodging rates for two people range from $ (under $100) to $$$ (above $250) per night.

WHERE

Ojai, 13 miles north of Ventura via State 33, can also be reached from Santa Barbara via the Casitas Pass (State Hwy. 150).

LODGING

The venerable **Ojai Valley Inn** (Country Club Rd., Ojai; 646-5511; $$$) is now a spa as well as a superb golf resort. More modest digs can be found at the **Theodore Woolsey House** (1484 E. Ojai Ave.; 646-9779; $-$$), a small country bed-and-breakfast just outside town. The **Los Olivos Grand Hotel** (2860 Grand Ave., Los Olivos; 800/446-2455; $$-$$$) mixes Victorian furnishings with Western art. The superb restaurant serves continental fare. **The Ballard Inn** (2436 Baseline, Ballard; 688-7770; $$), a charming country hostelry, has 15 rooms.

DINING

A good place for breakfast or lunch, the **Ojai Café Emporium** (108 S. Montgomery St., Ojai; 646-2733) has a reputation for vegetarian dishes, but it also offers hearty meals for meat eaters. If you end, rather than begin, your trip in Ojai, try the **Oak Grill** at the Ojai Valley Inn (see Lodging above) for nouveau California cuisine with a Southwest accent. **Mattei's Tavern** (State 154, Los Olivos; 688-4820) is a good place to sample local wines while dining on steak or prime rib. **Cold Spring Tavern** (5995 Stagecoach Rd. off State 154; 967-0066) is a rustic roadhouse with hearty fare.

ATTRACTIONS

Don't miss **Bart's Books** (corner of Matilija and Canada sts., Ojai; 646-3755), an open-air book mart designed around an old oak tree. It offers over 100,000 books, mostly used. For information about the annual **Ojai Music Festival** (held in late May or early June), call 646-2094. In addition to the many wineries in and around Foxen Canyon, there are two tasting rooms in downtown Los Olivos where you can sip a number of local wines. The best is the **Los Olivos Tasting Room and Wine Shop** (2905 Grand Ave.; 688-7406; daily 11-5:30), where you can sample wines from area vintners without their own tasting rooms.

FOR MORE INFORMATION

Ojai Valley Chamber of Commerce and Visitors Center (150 W. Ojai Ave., Ojai, CA 93024; 646-8126; open daily). Santa Barbara County Vintners' Association (P.O. Box 1558, Santa Ynez, CA 93460; 688-0881).

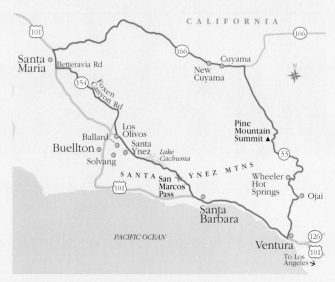

REGION		CALIFORNIA
Where	X	140 miles north of Los Angeles
When	X	Year-round destination; spring to early fall best

poking around
Lompoc

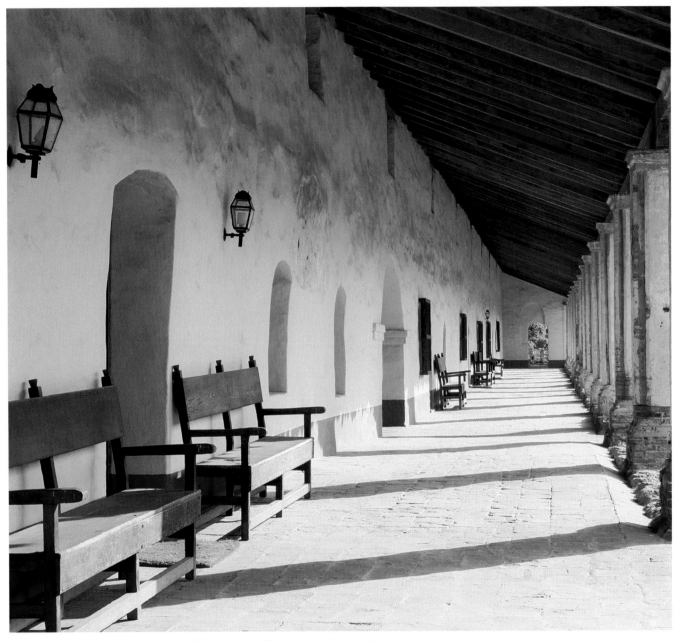

At La Purísima Mission, visitors may tour beautifully restored buildings and follow 25 miles of hiking trails.

More than half of the world's flower seeds are grown in bucolic Lompoc Valley, home to Vandenberg Air Force Base and a space shuttle launch complex.

From May to September, thousands of acres of hills surrounding the town of Lompoc are in gorgeous bloom, making it difficult to keep your eyes on the road. You'll see fields of marigolds, sweet peas, zinnias, asters, petunias, cornflowers, poppies, and more as you wander through this bucolic valley.

But flowers aren't the only attraction. Nearby is Mission La Purísima Concepcion, considered by many to be the most completely and authentically restored Franciscan mission in the California chain. A happy blend of climate and geology has been good not only for flowers but also for a burgeoning wine industry. Most of the grapes harvested around Lompoc are sold to wineries from Napa to Santa Barbara, but a couple of vineyards with tasting rooms are open to the public.

Flower Fields & a Pastoral Mission

The big event in Lompoc is the annual Flower Festival the last weekend in June. At that time, you can take a narrated bus tour into the surrounding hills and watch a parade of flower-decorated floats, among other activities. If you miss the festival, you can pick up a free self-guiding flower field tour brochure at the downtown chamber of commerce. The 19-mile tour guide tells you how to find the fields and what specifically grows in each one.

To get the best floral vista, head west from Lompoc on State Highway 246 (Ocean Avenue) to V Street, go left to Olive Avenue, and turn right. You'll soon come to a narrow lane, Bodger Road, opposite the Bodger Seeds company. Drive the short distance uphill to a panoramic lookout over acres and acres of bright flower fields. Bodger's greenhouses identify the varieties.

Back on State 246, drive 4 miles east of town until you see the sign to La Purísima Mission State Historic Park; turn left onto Mission Gate Road. This historic park, situated on 968 acres, includes a visitor center, hiking trails, picnic grounds, and the carefully restored mission, which is actually the second La Purísima settlement. An earthquake in 1812 destroyed the first mission in downtown Lompoc.

Valley Vineyards

Pick up a brochure at the mission's visitor center, which includes a small museum with dioramas and historical artifacts, to take a self-guided tour of the valley's vineyards. You can picnic in a shaded grove here or drive approximately 5 miles east on

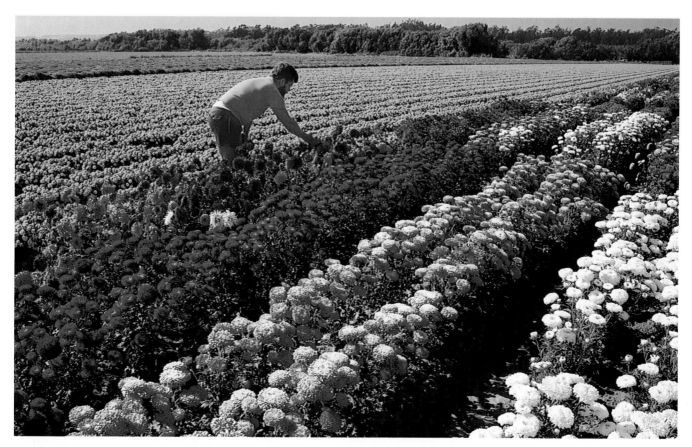

Blazing with brilliant color from May through September, acres of flower fields around Lompoc supply much of the world's flower seeds.

State 246 to Babcock Vineyards. Owners Walt and Mona Babcock and their son Bryan own 48 acres of vineyards, most of them planted to chardonnay grapes. Their tasting room is open Friday through Sunday.

Two other nearby vineyards worth a stop are Mosby Winery and Sanford Winery, both off Santa Rosa Road west of Buellton. To reach them from Babcock, continue east on State 246 to Santa Rosa Road, just off U.S. Highway 101, and go west back toward Lompoc.

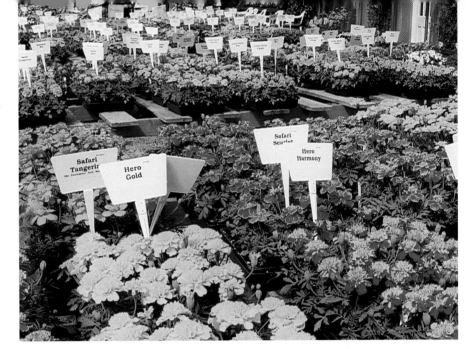
A good time to visit Bodger Seeds' greenhouses is during Lompoc's floral festival, held the last weekend in June.

⟸ TRIP PLANNER ⟹

Unless otherwise noted, area codes are 805. Lodging rates for two people range from $ (under $100) to $$$ (above $250) per night.

WHERE

Lompoc Valley is about 50 miles northwest of Santa Barbara between the Purísima Hills and the Santa Ynez Mountains. It's about 20 miles west of Buellton, crossroads to the Santa Ynez Valley and the "home of split pea soup."

LODGING

It's an easy day trip if you're staying in Santa Barbara, but the flower fields are at their most glorious first thing in the morning, so you might consider a stay in Lompoc. Reserve early for the flower festival. A number of reasonable hotels line H Street (State Hwy. 1), including **Best Western Flagwaver** (937 No. H St.; 736-5605; $) with 70 rooms. Closer to the flower fields is **Best Western Vandenberg** (940 E. Ocean Ave.; 735-7731; $), with 83 rooms. Rates

include a continental breakfast. A little more interesting (and costly) are the **Union Hotel** and the **Victorian Mansion** (both at 362 Bell St., Los Alamos; 344-2744; $ for hotel, $$$ for mansion) just north of Lompoc. These are themed rooms where you might sleep in a '56 Cadillac convertible or a gypsy wagon; call for details.

DINING

There are a number of simple eateries in Lompoc, including the **Outpost Oakpit BBQ** (124 E. Ocean Ave.; 735-1130), which serves hearty ribs and steaks for lunch and dinner (breakfast on Sundays). If the salty air makes you hanker for seafood, try **The Jetty** (304 W. Ocean Ave.; 735-2400). The **Union Hotel** in Los Alamos (see Lodging above) offers a family-style dinner in its antique-filled dining room on weekends only. Call to make sure they are open.

ACTIVITIES

The **Lompoc Valley Flower Festival** usually kicks off on the last Friday of June. Narrated bus tours of the fields during the festival cost about $5. For

information, call the Lompoc Valley Festival Association (735-8511). Almost as big an event is the **Mission Fiesta** at La Purísima Mission State Historic Park on the third Sunday in May, which features demonstrations of arts and crafts from the Spanish mission era. Call 733-3713 for more information.

FOR MORE INFORMATION

Lompoc Valley Chamber of Commerce (511 No. H St., Lompoc, CA 93436; 736-4567; open weekdays). Lompoc Museum (200 So. H St.; 736-3888; small fee) traces valley history.

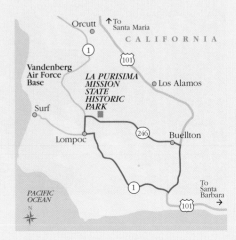

Nipomo Dunes *detour*

REGION		CALIFORNIA
Where	X	Midway between Los Angeles and San Francisco
When	X	Year-round route; often foggy in summer

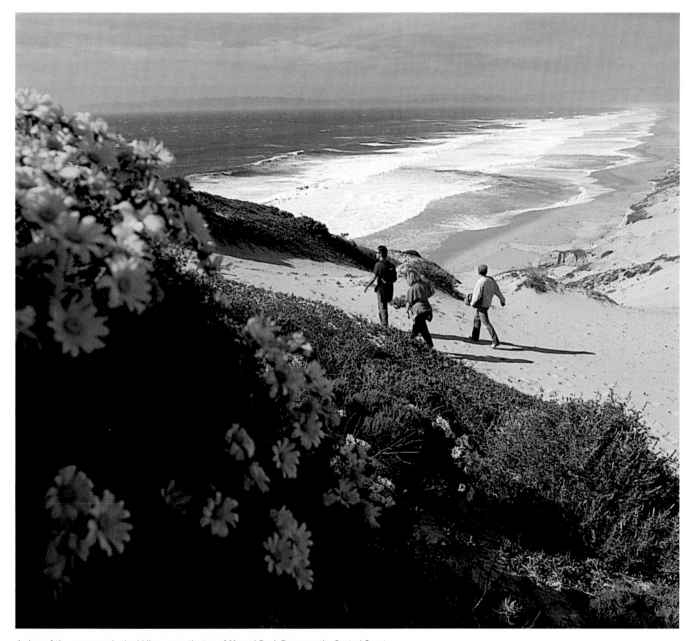

A view of the sea rewards tired hikers near the top of Mussel Rock Dunes on the Central Coast.

A quiet, unassuming curve of coastline between Santa Maria and San Luis Obispo on the Central Coast is often missed by visitors. The midpoint in this scenic stretch, Pismo Beach, gets its fair share of clam diggers and beach strollers, but a string of lesser-known towns—Guadalupe, Oceano, and Avila Beach—have their own charms and attractions. Mineral springs, rare dunes, and a historic covered pier all await travelers willing to take a weekend to explore short back roads.

This adventure begins in Santa Maria, a booming farming community known for its outlying vineyards and its tri-tip barbecue sandwiches. (Itinerant

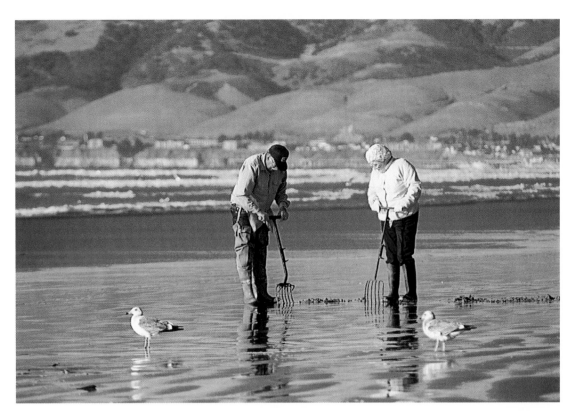

green bushes and, in spring, brilliant yellow flowers.

Clams & Fresh Fish

Back on State 1, continue north to Oceano, where you can explore more of the dunes in an all-terrain vehicle, which you can rent from B.J.'s ATV Rentals (481-5411). If the conditions are right, you can even drive your own car along a 5½-mile strip of beach, but call the Oceano Dunes State Vehicular Recreation Area

vendors patrol Broadway, the town's main drag, most weekends, grilling their flavorful meats over steel-drum barbecues.)

Nipomo Dunes & the City of the Pharaoh

From U.S. Highway 101, take the Main Street exit (State Highway 166) and drive west for about 9 miles to State Highway 1; then head north. Just outside Guadalupe, a tiny hamlet with some great Mexican restaurants, lies a strange Hollywood artifact: a buried stage set from Cecile B. DeMille's grandiose 1923 production, *The Ten Commandments*.

Here, on the southern edge of Nipomo Dunes, DeMille constructed a plaster City of the Pharaoh, with hieroglyphic-covered walls 100 feet tall flanked by four statues of Ramses II and 21 sphinxes, weighing 5 tons each. Continued excavation of the buried site makes it off-limits to visitors, but exhibits can be

seen at the Nature Conservancy Dunes Center (951 Guadalupe Street, Guadalupe; 343-2455).

Most of the rest of Nipomo Dunes is open to the public. One of the easiest, and prettiest, access points is Coreopsis Hill, midway between Guadalupe and Oceano. From State 1, go left on Oso Flaco Lake Road until it deadends, and then get directions from the Nature Conservancy's kiosk. The vast dunes are dotted with vibrant

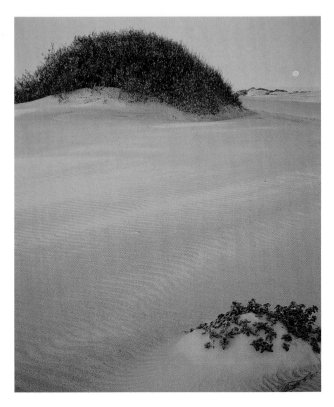

Moon sets over dunes near Oso Flaco Lake at Oceano Dunes State Vehicular Recreation Area.

(473-7230) first to make sure it's open. At The Livery Stable (1207 Silver Spur Place, Oceano; 489-8100) you can rent horses and go for a gallop along the surf's edge.

"The Clam Capital of the World," as Pismo calls itself, is a good stop for lunch or dinner. You'll find that just about every diner in town claims to serve the best clam chowder, but most locals say it can be found a block up from the pier at Splash Café.

State 1 and U.S. 101 merge here; take the first exit, Avila Beach Drive, and go northwest through groves of sycamores and open farmland. Two spas—Avila Hot Springs and Sycamore

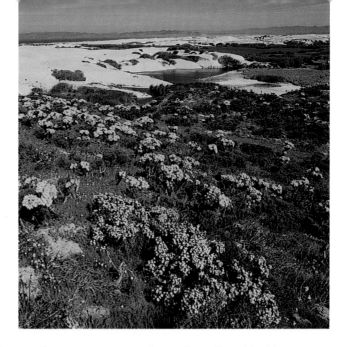

Brightly blooming Coreopsis Hill, midway between Guadalupe and Oceano, offers an easy—and pretty—access through Nipomo Dunes.

Mineral Springs Resort—will let you soak your tired muscles in hot sulfurous waters.

Continue along the road to Port San Luis harbor. At the end of the covered pier is the Olde Port Inn, which serves up freshly

caught rock cod and halibut as well as a hearty cioppino.

Take Avila Beach Drive back to State 1 and U.S. 101.

TRIP PLANNER

Unless otherwise noted, area codes are 805. Lodging rates for two people range from $ (under $100) to $$$ (above $250) per night.

WHERE

Santa Maria is 31 miles south of San Luis Obispo. To reach Avila Beach from the south, exit U.S. 101 at San Luis Bay Drive and follow the signs.

LODGING

Pismo Beach is a busy, popular beach resort, full of inexpensive hotels, motels, and inns. The best bargains can be found closer to the highways, but, if you prefer something a little quieter, try the **SeaVenture Resort** (100 Ocean View Ave.; 773-4994; $$-$$$), with 50 rooms right on the beach. Just north, **The Cliffs at Shell Beach** (2757 Shell Beach Rd., Shell Beach; 773-5000; $$-$$$) is a clifftop resort overlooking San Luis Obispo Bay. The rooms at **Sycamore**

Mineral Springs Resort (1215 Avila Beach Dr., Avila Beach; 595-7302; $$-$$$) all come with their own in-room hot tubs, or you can soak in a redwood tub beneath the sycamores.

DINING

Several restaurants along the Central Coast have been here so long they're practically institutions. **Jocko's** (corner of Tefft St. and Thomas Rd., Nipomo; 929-3686) is known for its great steaks and homemade salsa. Another favorite is **Splash Café** (197 Pomeroy Ave., Pismo Beach; 773-4653), an unpretentious surfers' stop that makes 10,000 gallons of clam chowder annually. A little more formal is the **Olde Port Inn** (Port San Luis pier, Port San Luis; 595-2515), known for its range of fresh fish specials.

ACTIVITIES

The **Nature Conservancy** leads occasional hikes to Coreopsis Hill and other popular dune sites, particularly during the fall. Call 545-9925 for

details. Pismo Beach has been sponsoring a **Clam Festival** and chowder cookoff in mid-October for over 50 years (773-4282).

FOR MORE INFORMATION

Contact the Nature Conservancy (above) for information on the Nipomo Dunes. Nipomo Chamber of Commerce (267 W. Taft, Nipomo, CA 93444; 929-1583). Pismo Beach Visitor Information Center (581 Dolliver St., Pismo Beach, CA 93449; 773-4382; open daily).

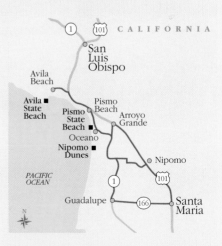

REGION		CALIFORNIA
Where	X	12 miles northwest of San Luis Obispo
When	X	Early fall through late spring; fog in summer

Morro Bay
backwaters

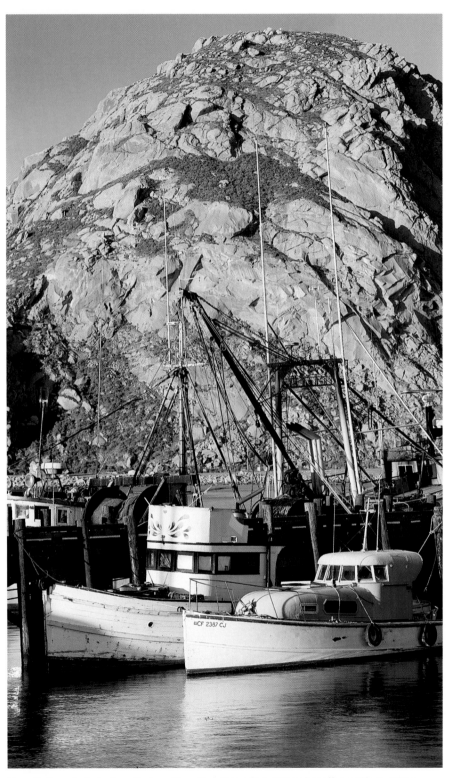

Dramatic Morro Rock stands sentinel over Morro Bay's fishing fleet. Boat cruises offer good harbor views.

From San Luis Obispo, State Highway 1 cuts through rolling farmland to an estuary where the waters are home to sea otters and seals and the land is a haven for blue herons and monarch butterflies. Travelers in a hurry to reach Hearst Castle in San Simeon often bypass—or are unaware of—the picturesque communities and unique natural areas south of Morro Bay.

Endangered peregrine falcons nest on Morro Rock, while great blue herons use a eucalyptus grove as a rookery. In fact, there are so many bird species along these unspoiled wetlands that the entire town is a bird sanctuary. In the nearby communities of Baywood Park and Los Osos, you'll find a reserve with peaceful trails wandering through ancient oaks, a woodsy park that becomes home to thousands of butterflies in the winter, and a hikers' haven known for its stunning views and blazing hills of wildflowers.

Following the Estuary

First stop is Morro Rock, just west of the Embarcadero at the end of Coleman Drive. Named by Portuguese explorer Juan Rodriguez Cabrillo, this monolith is a remnant of a prehistoric volcanic peak. You can't climb it, but you can get close enough for great views of The Rock as well

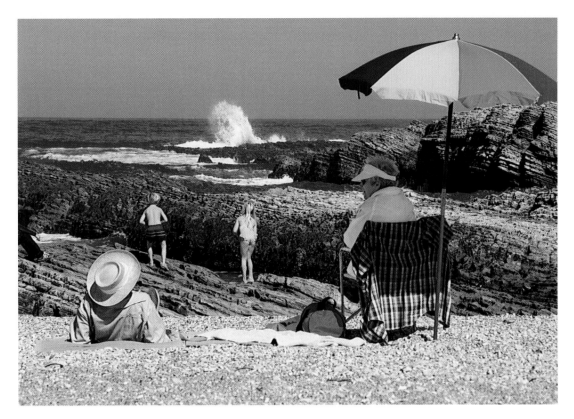

A lazy day at Montana de Oro State Park: many protected coves along the park's 7 miles of coastline offer space to sprawl.

...as of fishing boats, sea otters, and windsurfers heading in and out of the harbor.

Back on Embarcadero, head south through town, stopping in the colorful harbor areas where boats dock right behind the fish markets they service, and legions of noisy pelicans squabble over tasty tidbits. The road jogs left as it follows the shoreline, turning into Main Street and then Country Club Drive. Look for the Inn at Morro Bay on your right. Adjacent to the bayside hotel is a tall stand of eucalyptus trees where blue herons nest from January through June. A trail to the rookery is accessible from the Morro Bay Museum of Natural History, which focuses on the wildlife of the estuary.

Butterflies in South Bay

Past the museum, the road swings inland, cutting through Morro Bay State Park until it reaches Los Osos/Baywood Park Road. Turn right and follow the road into a little residential area of three quiet communities— Baywood Park, Los Osos, and Cuesta-By-The-Sea—known collectively as the South Bay. Just off Los Osos Valley Road as you drive into town, Los Osos Oaks State Reserve has a mile-long trail through a 90-acre grove of ancient, gnarled coast oaks.

Back on Los Osos Valley Road, go 1 mile west to 9th Street. Turn right, go 5 blocks to Ramona Avenue, and turn left. Just up ahead is tiny Sweet Springs Nature Preserve, where in winter you'll find thousands of colorful monarch butterflies clustered on the trunks and branches of eucalyptus trees.

Wildflowers by the Sea

Follow Los Osos Valley Road southwest toward Montana de Oro State Park, a 10,000-acre wildlife preserve whose Spanish name means "mountain of gold."

The gold in this case refers to the yellow and orange wildflowers, including California poppies, that carpet the hills in spring. Over 50 miles of hiking trails give you access to hidden coves and spectacular views of this wild coastline.

Stately pocket beaches and 7 miles of rocky coastline allow space for activities from tanning and tidepooling to swimming and kayaking.

Part of the reward of visiting Montana de Oro (often called one of the best parks on the Central Coast) is the grand vistas you receive from the coastal road. You get spectacular views of the town of Morro Bay, its long fingerlike sandspit, and huge Morro Rock.

If you plan to camp at one of the park's 50 sites, get there early; it's a very popular place. Information and a tour map are available at the park's tourist center.

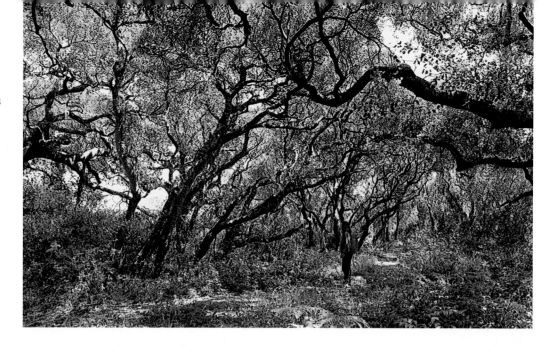

A mile-long trail threads among gnarled trees of 90-acre Los Osos Oaks State Reserve.

⟸ ⠿TRIP PLANNER⠿ ⟹

Unless otherwise noted, area codes are 805. Lodging rates for two people range from $ (under $100) to $$$ (above $250) per night.

WHERE

Morro Bay is 12 miles northwest of San Luis Obispo via State 1. If you want to do the trip in reverse, you can take Los Osos Valley Rd. off U.S. Hwy. 101, just south of the famed Madonna Inn, and go west about 15 miles to Los Osos.

LODGING

Situated right next to the blue heron rookery and a short walk from the Museum of Natural History, the **Inn at Morro Bay** (19 Country Club Rd.; 772-5651; $-$$) is an extremely convenient location from which to explore the county's South Bay. **The Back Bay Inn** (1391 2nd St., Los Osos; 528-1233; $) is on the water within walking distance of Baywood Park's small downtown area. **Baywood Bed & Breakfast Inn** (1370 2nd St., Los Osos; 528-8888; $-$$ includes breakfast) overlooks the bay and has individually decorated rooms.

Some campsites at **Morro Bay State Park** (State Park Rd., Morro Bay; 772-2560) offer marina views. Camping is permitted in designated areas at **Montana de Oro State Park**.

DINING

Perched on a bluff overlooking Morro Rock and the harbor, **Dorn's Original Breakers Café** (801 Market St., Morro Bay; 772-4415) is a casual favorite of both locals and visitors. Try the Boston clam chowder. The best meal in town, as far as we're concerned, is the well-prepared and varied fresh fish selection at **Hoppe's at 901** (901 Embarcadero, Morro Bay; 772-9012). The **Sculptured Egg** (1326 2nd St., Baywood Park; 528-0818) is known for its build-it-yourself omelets.

ACTIVITIES

Morro Bay Museum of Natural History (Morro Bay State Park; 772-2694; open daily; small fee) offers guided natural history hikes of the area. Some say **Morro Bay State Park**, with its 18-hole golf course and marina, is the most civilized park in the state system. At the opposite extreme is wild and rustic **Montana de Oro State Park** (Pecho Valley Rd., Los Osos; 528-0513), with its remote beaches and weather-sculpted shoreline. The shops along **Morro Bay's Embarcadero** are primarily of the souvenir type; elsewhere in town browsers will find several good galleries and a delightfully eclectic bookstore. **Baywood Park**'s art and crafts shops, though not numerous, are delightful to wander through.

FOR MORE INFORMATION

Morro Bay Chamber of Commerce (880 Main St., Morro Bay, CA 93442; 772-4467; open weekdays). Los Osos/Baywood Park Chamber of Commerce (781 Los Osos Valley Rd., Los Osos, CA 93402; 528-4884; open weekdays).

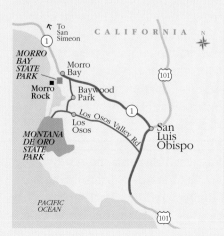

into

Owens Valley

REGION	CALIFORNIA	
Where	X	270 miles northeast of Los Angeles
When	X	Autumn or late spring drive

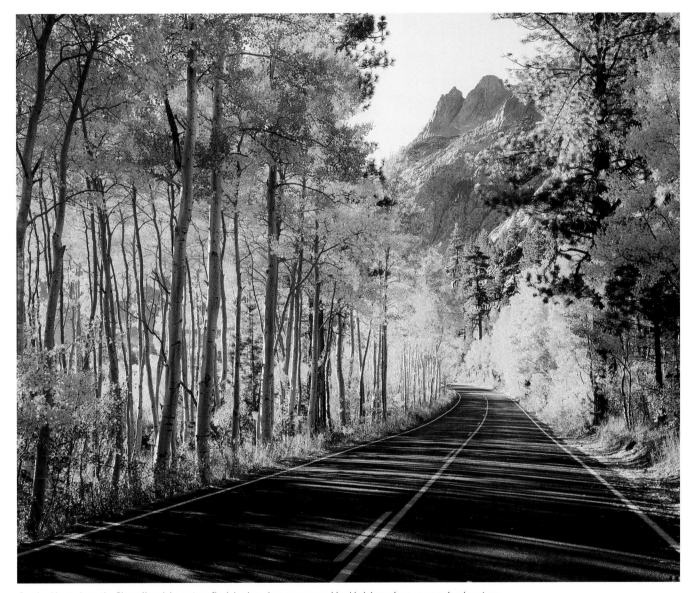

Scenic side roads on the Sierra Nevada's eastern flank lead up river canyons and beside lakes where aspens glow in autumn.

The eastern slope of the Sierra Nevada is a solemn testament to the dramatic forces that sculpted this land: the craggy granite peaks were created when the earth buckled and broke eons ago. U.S. Highway 395 parallels this spectacular mountain range, offering access to a number of natural wonders both east and west of the road between Bishop and Lee Vining, the eastern gateway to Yosemite National Park.

If it weren't for the popularity of the resort town of Mammoth Lakes, U.S. 395 might be the most lonesome highway in California. As it is, much of the traffic you are likely to encounter between Bishop and the Mammoth turnoff can be avoided by exploring the scenic side roads off U.S. 395 and passing up particularly heavy travel times

California 23

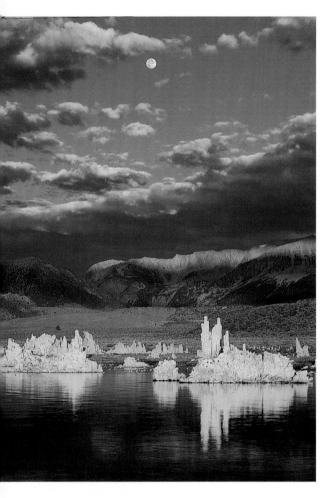

Dawn comes to Mono Lake, illuminating offshore tufa spires and the crest of the Sierras.

such as Sunday afternoons. You could drive this route in a day, but you would miss a lot. Better to plan two days or more, enjoying all the mountains afford and, if you're seeking fall color, drinking in the aspens' splendor along the way.

Entering Bishop

Bishop, the gateway town for those driving up from Southern California, still has a cowboy heritage. A good base for exploring surrounding country roads, it's well stocked with motels and restaurants. Don't miss a stop at Erick Schat's Bakery on Main Street, where there's always a line waiting to buy his still-warm sheepherder bread.

From Bishop it's a 42-mile climb north to the Mammoth Lakes region. The highway runs

like a boundary line between mountain and plain, with long, thin canyons clawing their way west into the high peaks of the Eastern Sierra. The most impressive fall color is found along creeks or around lakes in these canyons. Swatches of color can erupt in mid-September on the higher reaches and last well into October at the canyon mouths. Head up any of these canyons to hike, camp, fish, or picnic.

Along Mammoth's Scenic Loop

The turnoff to Mammoth Scenic Loop winds its way through forests of pines and aspens to the town of Mammoth Lakes. Stop by the visitor information center on State Highway 203 for information on biking, hiking, fishing, camping, and other outdoor activities. They also offer a free fall-color brochure.

Bishop, the gateway to Owens Valley, has a definite Old West flavor. It's not unusual to come across cowboys driving a herd along the road.

Back on the highway, the road climbs up to 8,036-foot Deadman Summit.

About 15 miles north of Mammoth Junction (State 395 and 203), you will see a sign for State Highway 158, the southern end of scenic June Lake Loop. This 16-mile detour leads through a quiet subalpine valley carved by an ancient glacier and past four sparkling lakes. For picture-perfect views of one of those spots called "Little Switzerland," stop at the appropriately named Oh! Ridge turnout overlooking June Lake.

Lunch or breakfast can be found at the modest Silver Lake Resort General Store.

From the north end of the loop, it's just 5 miles to Lee Vining and access to Northern California via State Highway 120 over Tioga Pass (closed winters).

Mono Lake

That strange, glassy-surfaced body of water to the east of Lee Vining is Mono Lake Tufa State Reserve. Fed by underground springs and the runoff from five streams, it is three times more saline than the ocean. Not a dead sea, the lake is filled with brine

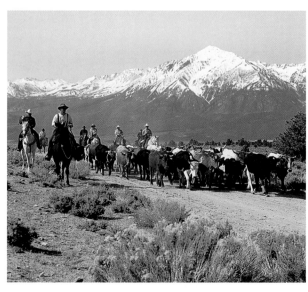

shrimp, making it a copious food bank for thousands of nesting and migrating birds.

An impressive visitor center, just off the highway, will fill you in on the lake's natural history. A

1-mile interpretive trail named for Mark Twain, an early visitor, skirts the tufas spires offshore.

⇄ TRIP PLANNER ⇒

Unless otherwise noted, area codes are 760. Lodging rates for two people range from $ (under $100) to $$$ (above $250) per night.

WHERE

Owens Valley is most easily accessible from Los Angeles. U.S. 395 branches off I-15 near Victorville.

LODGING

In Bishop, the **Best Western Creekside Inn** (725 N. Main St.; 872-3044; $-$$ includes continental breakfast) has nicely landscaped grounds and a rushing creek. Or try the antique-filled **Chalfant House Bed and Breakfast** (213 Academy St.; 872-1790; $).

Mammoth Lakes has become an all-season town in the last few years as the ski resort focuses on mountain biking and other summer activities once the snow melts (skiing usually continues into July). Its large concentration of rooms and central location make it a good place for an overnight stop. The **Tamarack Lodge Resort** (Twin Lakes Rd. off Lake Mary Rd.; 934-2442; $-$$$) has 25 tidy cabins tucked among the pines and 11 rooms in the vintage-1924 main log building. **Mammoth Mountain Inn** (One Minaret Rd.; 800/222-2244; $$-$$$) sits conveniently across from the ski resort's main lodge.

Farther north, **Silver Lake Resort** (June Lake Loop, across from Silver Lake; 648-7525; $-$$) offers 16 rustic cabins, but you need to book early. Forest Service campgrounds in the area stay open summers until

mid-to late-October. Contact the Forest Service Visitor Center on State 203 in Mammoth Lakes (934-2505).

AUTUMN LEAF-PEEPING

Good canyons for viewing fall color lie between Bishop and Mammoth. From south to north **South Lake Road** (State 168), exit for **Toms Place** and **Rock Creek** (two good campgrounds among the aspens). **Hilton Creek** exit, **McGee Creek Road**, and **Convict Lake** turnoff.

DINING

Whiskey Creek, with outlets in both Bishop (524 N. Main St.; 873-7174) and Mammoth Lakes (State 203; 934-2555), is known for its choice steaks and barbecued ribs. **Roberto's Café** (271 Old Mammoth Rd.; 934-3667) serves up cheap and tasty Mexican food, while nearby **Giovanni's** (Minaret Village Mall, Old Mammoth Rd.; 934-7563) does the same with pizza and pasta.

ANNUAL EVENTS

Bishop marks the seasons with two bookend events: **Mule Days** over the Memorial Day weekend and the **Wild West Rodeo** over Labor Day weekend. Both emphasize the town's cowboy roots. **Fourth of July** in Mammoth Lakes includes a downtown parade followed by spectacular fireworks over Crowley Lake.

FOR MORE INFORMATION

Bishop Chamber of Commerce (690 N. Main St., Bishop, CA 93514; 873-8405). Mammoth Lakes Visitors Bureau (State 203, P.O. Box 48, Mammoth Lakes, CA 93546; 934-2712).

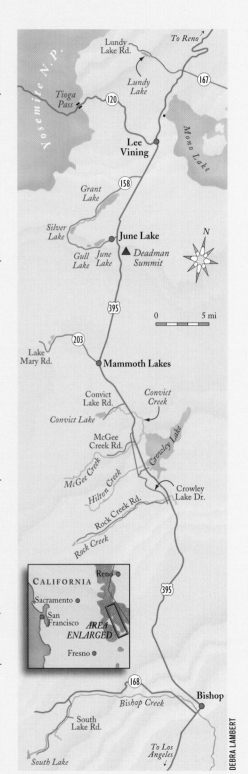

DEBRA LAMBERT

REGION	CALIFORNIA
Where	X	20 to 40 miles north of downtown San Diego
When	X	Less crowded from late fall through early spring

the slow way to
San Diego

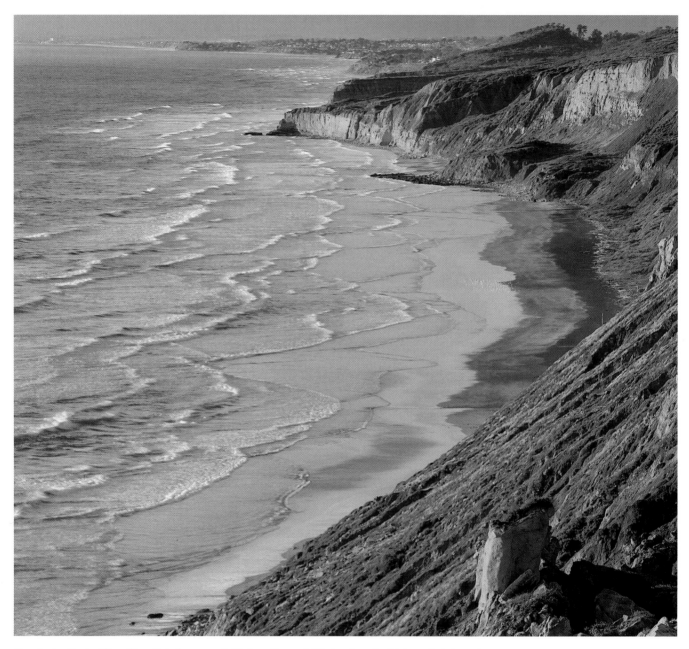

Towering headlands of Torry Pines State Reserve mark drive's southern end. Hike here for splendid views of whales and waves.

Once it was difficult—except on foot—to travel along northern San Diego County's coast. Low bluffs edged with wind- and wave-carved sandstone cliffs plowed into the sea. The sucking mud of broad lagoons and estuaries, fanning out every few miles at the mouths of seasonal rivers, routed horseback and wagon travel several miles inland. From the Mission era until the late

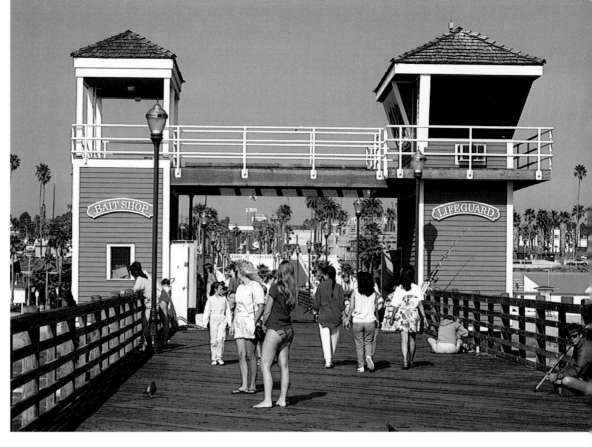

Promenading along the Oceanside pier is a tradition. Rewards include good views of coast and surfers plus seafood snacks.

1800s, the coast was a series of quiet, isolated hilltop farming towns.

Today most travelers bent on reaching San Diego from Los Angeles still parallel the coast a few miles inland on Interstate 5, which cleaves through chaparral-clad mesas with hardly an ocean view. What motorists miss is a 20-mile-long string of funky but often charming beach towns that, though nearly moribund for a decade following I-5's debut, bounced back with an eclectic collection of shops, restaurants, small hotels, and resorts.

Residents also gained new respect for what's left of the natural landscape surrounding them. Swimmers and surfers have long loved the region's beaches, but the five remaining lagoons were once reviled as smelly swamps, of little use to anyone. Now these vital wetlands attract hikers and bird-watchers.

You can travel this route in either direction; we started at the north end, in Oceanside. Twenty miles isn't far, but if you stop often, you'll need at least two days to explore leisurely.

From Rollers to Ranunculuses

Take a morning walk to the tip of Oceanside's pier, the longest on the West Coast; it dances a little when the big winter "rollers" steam in beneath it. From here, either drive through quiet neighborhoods on Pacific Street to the south end of town, or visit the Oceanside Museum of Art, a fine civic center, and a popular breakfast spot, The Longboarder Café (Pier View Way at N. Coast Hwy.).

"Longboard" is surfer terminology for any surfboard over about nine feet long. For many, these boards symbolized a golden age of surfing here in Oceanside (and up and down the California coast): a time in the 1960s and 1970s when "hanging ten" and "gremmie" entered the language. To explore some of that history, visit the California Surf Museum (223 N. Coast Hwy.), located in a storefront not far from the pier.

After passing through a lather of unsightly commercial development, keep an eye out for a left turn (just before you cross a wetland on a causeway) into Buena Vista Nature Center, where you'll find interesting displays of wetland ecology.

The road stretches out a bit as you enter Carlsbad and cross Agua Hedionda Lagoon (Spanish for "stinking water") before it splits at Palomar Airport Road (Route S12). Detour inland to visit the region's famous flower fields in spring or see the Legoland park. The fields recall an era when much of the region

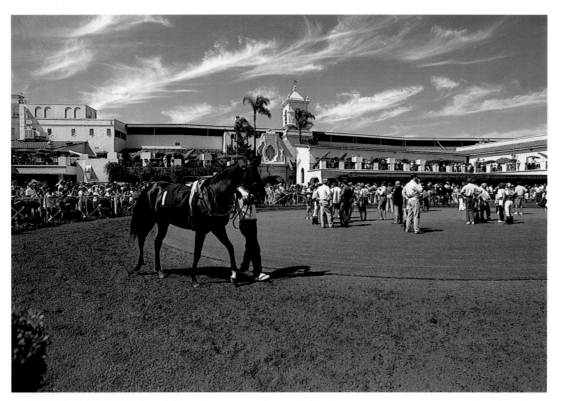

Wily bettors view steeds before each race, then take their seats to see the exciting—and perhaps profitable—outcome. The Del Mar Fairgrounds also host an annual county fair in late June.

was agricultural; today this working farm produces a harvest of ranunculus corms (the huge displays of delicate, multicolored flowers are never cut). Carlsbad's village center hides one of the coast's best antique-dealer districts and some good eateries.

South to Del Mar

From Carlsbad south, you'll see a more upscale stretch of coastal development. You pass beneath an immense eucalyptus windbreak in Leucadia before entering Encinitas and a 1-mile detour inland to Quail Botanical Gardens. Because of the mild coastal climate, more exotic plants from different countries and climes grow at Quail than you'd find almost anywhere else in the world.

As you pass the lotus flower–shaped rooftops of a spiritual retreat at the south end of Encinitas, look west for the entrance to what local surfers call "Swami's"—a blufftop view spot officially named Seacliff Park. Then the highway follows the very edge of the cliff for a mile to Cardiff-by-the-Sea.

Below the bluffs of Solana Beach, San Elijo Lagoon offers hiking and bird-watching. In town, visit Fletcher Cove Beach Park, a pocket beach with sandstone cliffs on each side. Cedros Avenue is an exciting souk of designer shops in what once was an industrial district by the railroad tracks.

Consider staying in Cardiff, Solana Beach, Del Mar, or at Torrey Pines Mesa, with its famous 36-hole municipal golf course that rambles along a cliff high above the Pacific. Reserve your second day for explorations of Del Mar.

The town is best known for a racetrack founded in the 1930s by Bing Crosby and his Hollywood friends. Its village atmosphere and long beaches

that stretch south to Torrey Pines State Reserve have long made it a popular spot. The reserve's trails lead past rare pine trees (they grow only here and on one of the Channel Islands off Santa Barbara) to vista points high above the surf.

If your visit coincides with a low or minus tide in the afternoon, don't miss taking a long walk on the reserve's beach, from the entry kiosk south to Flat Rock or beyond. Flat Rock, also known as Bathtub Rock, juts into the waves but is accessible at low tide. On its tidepool-divoted top, you'll find a deep, square, bathtub-size hole filled with crystal-clear seawater. The hole's origin remains somewhat of a mystery, although it's rumored to have been the exploratory excavation of a Welsh miner looking for coal.

From here, deeply furrowed cliffs of sandstone run down to a still-wild coast. As if sensing that even a road can't defeat these cliffs, Route S21 turns inland, terminating at the interstate east of La Jolla.

Unless otherwise noted, two area codes cover the coast: 760 from Oceanside to Cardiff-by-the-Sea; 619 from Cardiff to Del Mar. Lodging rates for two people range from $ (under $100) to $$$ (above $250) per night.

WHERE

Locals refer to Route S21 as the "Coast Highway" despite street sign names that change from town to town. End your journey where S21 rejoins I-5 in San Diego near the University of California campus.

LODGING

You'll find many lodging options, from budget motels to luxury resorts. Two major 5-star resorts located east of I-5 in Carlsbad lie inland, and golfers will enjoy **La Costa Resort and Spa** (Costa Del Mar Rd.; 438-9111; $$$) or **Four Seasons Resort Aviara** (7100 Four Seasons Pt., Batiquitos Lagoon; 603-6800; $$$).

Cardiff-by-the-Sea Lodge (142 Chesterfield; 944-6474; $$-$$$ includes breakfast) hides in a small town near San Elijo State Beach. **Courtyard by Marriott** (717 S. Hwy. 101, Solana Beach; 792-8200; $$) is near a secret stairway to a cliff-guarded beach. **L'Auberge Del Mar** (1540 Camino Del Mar; 259-1515; $$$) offers the best resort-town ambience and luxury along your drive. Also in Del Mar, **Stratford Inn** (710 Camino Del Mar; 755-1501; $$) provides a lower-cost alternative. High on a bluff beside Torrey Pines State Reserve, **The Lodge at Torrey Pines** (11480 N. Torrey Pines Rd.; 453-4420; $$) caters to both golfers and hikers. **Sheraton Grande Torrey Pines** (10950 N. Torrey Pines Rd.; 558-1500; $$$) also attracts golf and tennis aficionados.

Two state beaches offer clifftop campgrounds above great swimming and tidepool-rich shorelines: **San Elijo State Beach** in Cardiff-by-the-Sea and **South Carlsbad State Beach** in Carlsbad. Make reservations through ParkNet (800/444-7275).

DINING

Eating on the coast is about view and location. If you want to eat beside the waves, best bets are **Charlie's By The Sea** (2526 S. Hwy. 101; 942-1300), **The Beach House** (2530 S. Hwy. 101; 753-1321), and **The Chart House** (2588 S. Hwy. 101; 436-4044), all just south of Cardiff. **Jake's** (1660 Coast Blvd.; 755-2002) in Del Mar has great dinner specials in the bar before 6.

In Solana Beach, you can sit in the pepper tree-shaded patio of hip **Café Zinc** (132 S. Cedros Ave.; 793-5436) and enjoy excellent pastries, light breakfasts, and creative sandwiches. The terrace or main room at **Il Fornaio** (Del Mar Plaza; 755-8876) looks over the ocean. From the open kitchen come excellent fowl, seafood, and Italian specialties—and the coast's best bread. For make-your-own taco dinners and sunset views, try lively **Taco Auctioneers** (1951 San Elijo Ave.; 942-8226) in Cardiff.

ATTRACTIONS

To get close to coastal lagoon bird life, bring your binoculars and visit Oceanside's free **Buena Vista Lagoon Nature Center** (2202 S. Coast Hwy.), where rush-lined trails lead to hidden patches of open water. Hikers' best bets are **Torrey Pines State Reserve and Beach** just south of Del Mar and **San Elijo Lagoon County Park & Ecological Reserve** in Solana Beach. To reach San Elijo Lagoon's trailhead, take Lomas Santa Fe Dr. east to Rios Ave., then go left about 1 mile to the lagoon.

In March and April, **The Flower Fields at Carlsbad Ranch** (just east of I-5 on Palomar Airport Rd. at Paseo Del Norte; 10 to dusk daily; small fee) open their vast, multicolored flower fields for one of the West's great flower spectacles. Nearby, **Legoland California** (Palomar Airport Rd.) features miniature Lego-made townscapes, rides, and attractions geared to children under 12. Trails at **Quail Botanical Gardens** (230 Quail Gardens Dr., Encinitas) wind among rare bamboo, exotic fruits, cacti, and thousands of diverse specimen plants from around the world.

SHOPS

Carlsbad's numerous antique dealers cluster around State St. and Carlsbad Village Dr. **Solana Beach Cedros Design District** is just off the coast route via Lomas Santa Fe. **Del Mar Plaza** fits upscale shops, galleries, and restaurants into an Italian hill-town design; enjoy a glass of wine in the main plaza at sunset.

FOR MORE INFORMATION

Oceanside Chamber of Commerce (928 N. Hill St., Oceanside, CA 92054; 722-1534). Del Mar Chamber of Commerce (1104 Camino Del Mar #214, Del Mar, CA 92014; 755-4814).

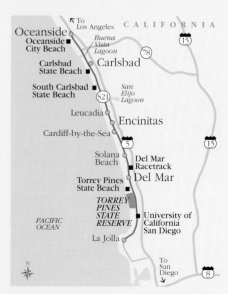

REGION	CALIFORNIA
Where X	50 miles north of San Diego
When X	Year-round, but hot in summer

Drive *to* the Stars

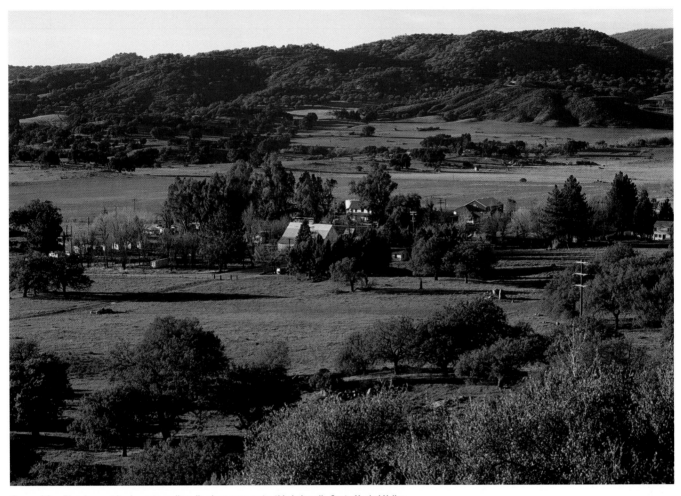

Some of San Diego's great backcountry valleys lie along your route: this is bucolic Santa Ysabel Valley.

In the hidden valleys beneath one of the world's best-known astronomical observatories, bucolic vistas still seem lifted from an old fruit-crate label. Sunny citrus groves stretch for miles to the base of purple-hued mountains sometimes dusted with snow. Winding State Highway 76 unfurls along the sycamore-shaded banks of San Luis Rey River.

Here in Pala and Pauma valleys, a turn-of-the-century Southern California still exists.

Guarded by the rugged scarp of Agua Tibia and Palomar mountain ranges, the region's climate teeters between searing desert heat and cooling ocean zephyrs threading in from a foggy seacoast only 25 miles away.

Several bands of Native Americans found these valleys first, and they still own much of the region. In August 1795, Father Juan Mariner left the San Diego Mission on horseback to explore the backcountry. He

soon returned with reports of fertile alluvial lands and abundant water. Although too far inland to be part of the main mission chain, the Asistencia of San Antonio de Pala became an important first step in a plan (later abandoned) to establish an inland chain of assistance or support missions.

As you head east on State 76 from Interstate 15, Pankey Farms fruit stand sits on a little hill in the midst of its own orchards. In

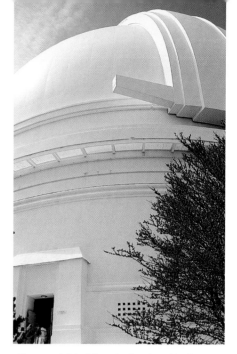

fall or winter, the smell of peeled tangerines fills your car as you continue past steep hillsides bearded with avocado trees. Gray-and-white mottled trunks of native sycamores line the roadside. In a few places in the riverbed, mining dredges move mountains of sand.

For Whom the Bell Tolls

About 5½ miles along your route, you enter the Pala Indian Reservation by turning off on a side street (Pala Mission Road) and following it to the small mission, founded in 1816. The long, unusually narrow chapel's floor is a wavy carpet of original adobe tile. A quadrangle 181 by 236 feet shelters a peaceful garden; off the gift shop, a small museum holds original church vestments and other artifacts.

In the 19th century, this area became famous for tourmaline gemstones, and several mines shipped many carats of the pink mineral to clients around the world, including the Empress of China. Today Gems of Pala allows tourmaline lovers to search through fresh buckets of "mine run" diggings for a steep $50, but searchers often find gems the size of a pencil eraser.

To the Mountaintop

After 21 miles along State 76, turn up the mountain for the climb to Palomar Mountain State Park and the world-famous observatory. Views on your way up make it hard to keep your eyes on the road. On a clear day after a storm or when Santa Ana winds rake in from the desert, even Mexico's Coronado Islands are visible southwest of the tiny towers of downtown San Diego, 40 miles away.

Soon signs warn "Unlawful To Throw Snowballs At Vehicles," proof (along with the pines) that you're approaching 5,000 feet in elevation. In the park's picnic areas, don't miss the acorn grinding rocks or the

After your visit to Palomar's gleaming white dome, don't miss the Greenway Museum gallery and gift shop nearby.

many trails through oak and cedar woods into surprisingly broad meadows.

No visit to Palomar is complete without a look at the dome and telescope operated by the California Institute of Technology. Even in daytime (the facility closes at night), the sense of breakthrough discovery and exploration here is palpable. No other earthbound instrument has contributed as much to the definition of the universe as we know it. The museum gallery features stunning shots of outer space.

From here "it's all downhill"—so much so that an odd sport has developed called the "Palomar Plunge," in which you coast 16 miles (vertical drop 5,000 feet) on rented bicycles back to the valley. Continue on State 76 past the broad grasslands surrounding Lake Henshaw, headwaters area for the San Luis Rey River, and finish your trip at the little crossroads town of Santa Ysabel. From here, you can return to San Diego.

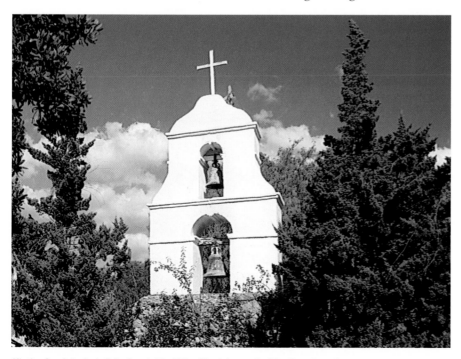

Mission San Antonio de Pala, founded in 1876, still retains much of its 19-century charm.

Unless otherwise noted, area codes are 760. Lodging rates for two people range from $ (under 100) to $$$ (above $250) per night.

WHERE

State 76 heads east from I-15 along the San Luis Rey River past citrus groves, fruit stands, and a historic mission, then climbs a broad valley beneath high mountains and a vast tract of Cleveland National Forest. An especially scenic side trip on County Roads S6 and S7 takes you up and back down Mt. Palomar. End your trip at Santa Ysabel on State 79 (about 70 miles to this point) and return to San Diego, or continue on for a stay in the mountain town of Julian (see San Diego's Backcountry, page 33).

LODGING

Few hostelries serve this well-traveled but surprisingly undeveloped area; however, **Lazy H Ranch** (on State 76 just west of County S6 junction; 742-3669; $) hides rooms and a pool in several rambling but homey buildings in the citrus groves and eucalyptus trees of Pauma Valley, about 16 miles from I-15.

Basic rooms and cabins at **Palomar Mountain Lodge** (22228 Crestline Rd. off County S6; 742-8744; $) serve visitors to the mountaintop, but a nearby hodgepodge of travel trailers and outbuildings breaks the forest spell.

CAMPING

Campsites at popular 2,000-acre **Palomar Mountain State Park** (742-3462; small day-use fee per vehicle; overnight camping via ParkNet, 800/444-7275) nestle amid stone walls and fireplaces under gnarled oaks and shaggy cedars. **La Jolla Indian Reservation** offers day-use picnic sites, a waterslide park (Sengme Oaks), inner-tubing through the river's shallow pools and riffles, and campsites (State 76, 4 miles east of County S6; 742-1297; fee for vehicles).

DINING

The low-ceilinged, garden-view restaurant at **Lazy H Ranch** (see Lodging above) brings in locals as well as occasional tourists for breakfast, lunch, and dinner. On Palomar Mountain near the state park, the big breakfasts at **Mother's Kitchen** (junction County S6 and S7) draw world-class competitive cyclists as well as motorcyclists. For lunch, try the lasagna or a veggie burger at this all-vegetarian restaurant.

Closer to Palomar Observatory, the unroofed porch with stone fireplace at **Palomar Mountain Lodge** (see Lodging above) entices travelers to sip a beer or an iced tea outside on a nice day or inside at dusk in front of a blazing fire.

For decades, motorists from all over the county have made **Dudley's Bakery** in Santa Ysabel (at the junction of State 78 and 79) their destination for a huge variety of fresh-baked breads, including their famous dark brown bread and jalapeño loaves. Also in tiny Santa Ysabel, **Julian Pie Company** restaurant can be a good stop for dinner before driving back to San Diego.

SHOPPING

Santa Ysabel Gallery (intersection of State 78 and 79), located in a small white house with creaky wood floors, warrants a stop. The gallery features the work of mountain-dwelling artist James Hubbell, internationally known for his stained glass, organic architectural design, and wood and metal sculpture. Next door, a bent-willow furniture maker, housed in a historic gas station, is noted for his rustic craftsmanship.

ATTRACTIONS

An observation area inside **Palomar Observatory**'s massive white dome affords a free glimpse of the huge telescope (end of County S6; open daily 9-4; 742-2119).

Deep in the backcountry, **Mission San Antonio de Pala** (5½ miles east of I-5 on Pala Mission Rd.; open Tuesday-Sunday; church and grounds free, small fee for museum) still reflects its early-1800s heritage, although an Indian gaming casino may be built near here.

Located in a rundown cluster of trailers, **Gems of Pala** (about 7 miles east of I-15 at Magree Rd.; 742-1356; open Thurs.-Sun.) offers a surprisingly fine collection of gemstones and minerals for sale, with an emphasis on tourmaline from the nearby Stewart Mine. Spend an hour and sift your own 70-lb. bucket of tourmaline "mine run" (not tailings) material for $50.

Gravity Activated Sports (16220 State 76, Pauma Valley; 742-2294) offers 16-mile downhill "Palomar Plunge" cycling rides daily at 10:30.

FOR MORE INFORMATION

Cleveland National Forest, Palomar Ranger District (1634 Black Canyon Rd., Ramona, CA 92065; 788-0250).

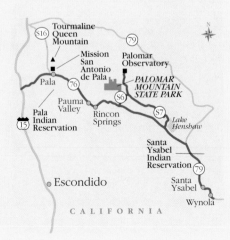

San Diego's
backcountry

REGION	CALIFORNIA
Where X	34 miles east of San Diego
When X	Best in spring and fall

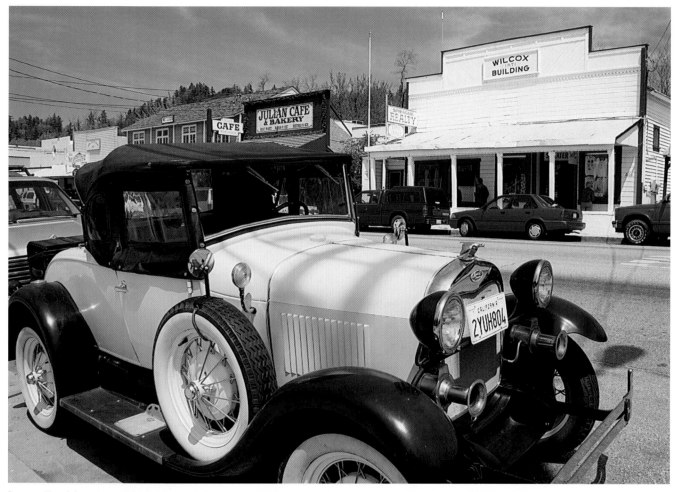

Once a gold rush boom town, Julian retains many 19th-century storefronts and plenty of character. It is popular with antique car drivers out for a Sunday tour.

Mention back roads in San Diego, and the first destination you'll hear is Julian. For generations this small hard-rock mining town, founded during a prosperous gold rush in 1869, has been the ultimate Sunday drive destination for San Diegans. In fall, during the height of apple season, the town swells with thousands of visitors until the streets and shops feel as packed as the sliced apples piled under the flaky crusts of the region's famous pies.

In a rush to get there, however, travelers sometimes miss the ultimate pleasure of driving through Cuyamaca Rancho State Park and on the aptly named Sunrise Highway, a snaky ribbon clinging to the crags above Anza-Borrego Desert. Here the sun first strikes San Diego County each day, spreading its warmth across the desert and up Mt. Laguna.

Leaving Interstate 8 on State Highway 79, you pass through a small valley sheltering the quiet community of Descanso, then begin your ascent up the south flanks of Oakzanita Peak on a series of hairpin turns. Once a vast cattle ranch dating back to the days of the California Spanish dons, Cuyamaca Rancho State Park changes its botanical capes many times as you gain elevation, from chaparral to oak to Methuselah-girthed pine and cedar on its mountaintops. Stop at park headquarters to get an overview and pick up a guide to hiking and camping options.

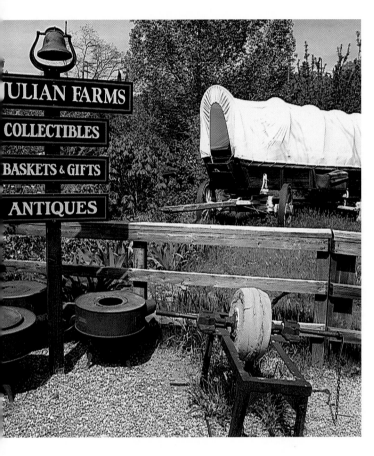

Prowl Julian's cluttered antique shops for treasures, and don't miss their fine little historical society museum.

Perhaps the most popular hike in the park is the climb to Stonewall Peak (5,730 feet), a surprisingly easy one-hour walk with a 1,000-foot elevation gain up a switchback trail to a throne-like granite summit. In fall, black oaks arched over another trail, called Milk Ranch Road, will remind you of a Vermont hillside ablaze with fiery golds and reds.

Gold Rush to Pie Stampede

After State 79 skirts meadows around Lake Cuyamaca (a popular fishing spot), it climbs again into Julian. Weekend parking is difficult, so time your trip for a weekday. Despite the crowds, the town gets quiet once you're a block or two off Main Street or climb the hill to the pioneer cemetery. To really experience the region's pioneer roots, take the casual but informative tour of the Eagle Mine.

Leaving Julian on Farmers Road, you'll take the secret back door to Wynola, a route few tourists use as they speed homeward along State 78 and 79 just west of town. At Wynola Road, detour to Menghini Winery and its adobe tasting room. Local hikers know that nearby Volcan Mountain offers a beautiful climb through oak woodlands and meadows high above Julian. Pick up a picnic lunch in town and bring plenty of water.

Apple orchards cover several hundred acres of the rolling hills and valleys beneath Volcan Mountain. At 4,200 feet, the orchards get enough cold snaps to set good fruit, and the area's hot summers make tart apples somewhat higher in sugar content. In Wynola, poke around some of the shops and fruit stands, then return to Julian.

On the Desert's Rim

To return to I-8, take County Route S1 where it veers southeast from State 79 at Lake Cuyamaca. Not as winding as State 79, it enters, after 10 miles, a broad meadow called Little Laguna.

Pull into El Prado or Laguna campgrounds to view the meadow. An easy, level trail skirts Little Laguna on its opposite side; in spring, the intense green meadow, ringed with purple lupine and vast patches of goldfields, becomes an Oz-like setting where your boot toes will be dusted with pollen. If you have time, hike on to Big Laguna, another lake and meadow habitat, where successions of blooms create bands of color around the receding lake in late spring.

At Mt. Laguna—site of picnic grounds, a desert viewpoint, and a scientific observatory—the road bends west again, rejoining I-8 after 9 miles. If you have a little extra time, turn right just before I-8 and follow Old Hwy. 80 through Guatay back to your starting point near Descanso.

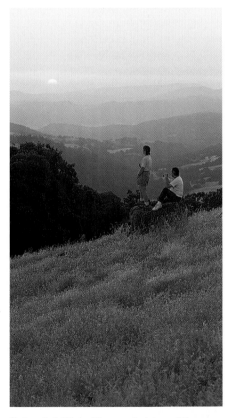

On top of ol' Volcan, hikers can look toward the ocean or across the desert.

Unless otherwise noted, area codes are 760. Lodging rates for two people range from $ (under $100) to $$$ (above $250) per night.

WHERE

State 79 climbs northward 29 miles from I-8 into the heart of San Diego's Laguna Mountains backcountry. At the historic gold-mining town of Julian, drivers have the option of continuing on to Anza-Borrego Desert State Park or returning to I-8 via scenic County S1, the "Sunrise Highway."

LODGING

Julian's dozens of bed-and-breakfasts are a thriving cottage industry. To stay in a gold rush-era hotel, try 1897 **Julian Gold Rush Hotel** in the heart of town (2032 Main St.; 765-0201; $-$$ with full breakfast). The region's one resort is **Orchard Hill** (2502 Washington St.; 765-1700; $$). To get a feel for the woods and local living, try **The Artist's Loft** bed-and-breakfast (4811 Pine Ridge Ave.; 765-0765; $$). In addition to 2 rooms, they also rent 2 cabins—historic **Big Cat Lodge**, a retreat with large stone fireplace, wood-burning kitchen stove, and sleeping porch (newly renovated), and **Strawberry Hill**, a redwood bungalow deep in the forest. The owners are excellent cooks.

CAMPING

Oak groves shade campsites amid lichen-covered boulders in **Cuyamaca Rancho State Park** (15027 Hwy. 79 south from Julian; 765-0755 for park information; for campsite reservations, 800/444-7275; $12). Two main campgrounds, Paso Picacho (85 sites) and Green Valley Falls (81 sites), lie close to many hiking trails.

Green Valley has beautiful (but dangerous) slick-rock wading pools.

William Heise County Park (619/694-3049 for information; for campsite reservations, 619/565-3600; day use, camping fees) is set in a deep forest on Julian's west side. From State 78/79, go 1 mile west of Julian to Pine Hills Rd., then south 2 miles to Frisius Rd., and east on Frisius 2 miles to the park entrance.

DINING

For a small town, Julian is packed with eateries. Apple pie is the big attraction; you'll find the freshest and best tasting at **Mom's Pies** (2119 Main St.). Lines may be long, but they move quickly. **Julian Pie Company**'s (2225 Main St.) fruit usually comes from their own orchard; try the crumb topping apple pie.

Eateries favored by locals include **Romano's Dodge House** (2718 B St.; 765-1003; lunch and dinner), **Julian Tea and Cottage Arts** (2124 Third St.; 765-0832; afternoon tea), **Julian Grille** (2224 Main St.; 765-0173; lunch and dinner), and **The Old Firehouse** (2128 Fourth St.; 765-2130; breakfast, lunch, and dinner, with biscuits and gravy that may rival your Southern grandmother's).

On State 79 near I-8, **Descanso Junction Restaurant** (8306 State 79; 445-0964) has a front door almost on the main road and a loyal clientele for breakfasts and burgers.

SHOPS, STANDS & WINERIES

Julian's compact downtown allows you to see all the shops in town on a short stroll. For local fruit, however, you may have to range out onto the roadsides. **Meyer Orchard** fruit stand (3962 State 78, Wynola) features many familiar and unusual varieties. Others include **Apple Lane Orchards** (2641 Apple Ln., Julian),

Sun Mountain Orchards (Wynola and Farmer rds.), and **Farmers Mountain Vale Ranch** (4510 State 78, Wynola). In town, don't miss **Julian Cider Mill** (Main at B) for apple cider, local honey, and gifts.

In Guatay just east of Descanso, look for **Trynn Woodworking** on the north side of Old Hwy. 80. The hand-carved wooden spoons and other kitchen utensils are sinuous works of art. Wineries and tasting rooms for a small but growing wine industry include **Codarossa** (4510 State 78; 765-1195), **Menghini Winery** (1150 Julian Orchards Dr.; 765-2072), and **Witch Creek** (2000 Main St.; 765-2023).

ATTRACTIONS

For an underground look at mining, visit **Eagle & High Peak Mines** (end of C St., $1/4$-mile outside of Julian; 765-0036; fee). In **Julian Pioneer Museum** (2811 Washington; 765-0227; tiny fee), the aisles are crowded like a country store with displays, antiques, and memorabilia. **Volcan Mountain Nature Preserve** (trailhead on Farmers Rd. north of town) offers guided hikes.

FOR MORE INFORMATION

Julian Chamber of Commerce (2129 Main St., Julian, CA 92036; 765-1857).

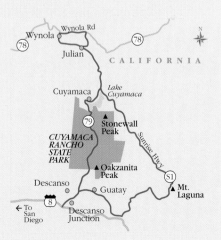

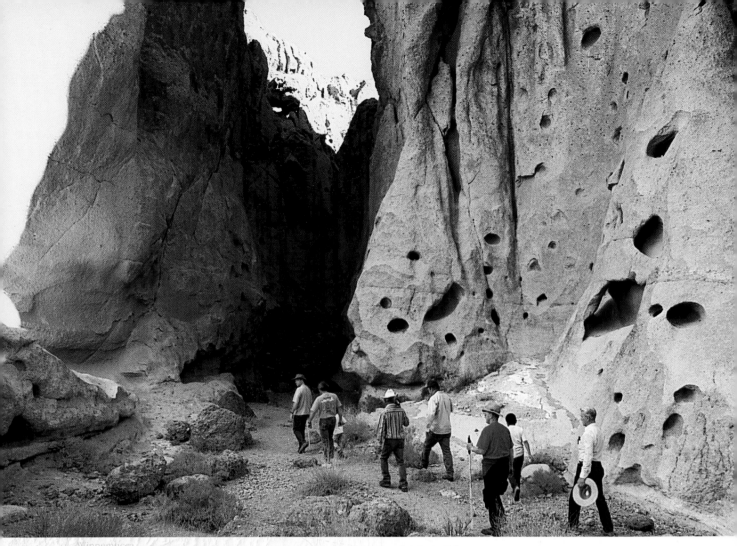

Deep in bubble-packed lava flows, hikers enjoy the volcanic wonder aptly named Hole-in-the-Wall.

California's Desert Discoveries

"I once more take you far beyond the wire fence of civilization to those places (unhappily few now) where the trail is unbroken and the mountain peak unblazed," wrote desert wanderer John C. Van Dyke in 1901. Today the search for those same unblazed places (and their protection) has led to the California Desert Protection Act of 1994 and its two most notable destinations: Joshua Tree National Park (once a national monument) and Mojave National Preserve.

Seeing these areas is problematic. Three interstates traverse Southern California's vast desert lands, but the through-the-windshield view seems harsh to travelers bent only on reaching the Colorado River or beyond. The answer lies in immersing yourself in the desert's own ripples of rock and sand, broken often by its most distinctive totem, the spiky Joshua tree. From Joshua Tree National Park northward via back roads, this region unveils an overwhelming array of wild and weird topography, climate zones from fiery to freezing, and the many creatures and plants that adapt with an encyclopedic array of water-saving ingenuities and survival skills.

A myriad of delights awaits the wanderer, from climbing singing sand dunes and inspecting a train station in the middle of nowhere to descending into cool caverns and camping under a blanket of stars. Wildlife is abundant, though only rarely visible: antelope, mule deer, bighorn sheep, kit foxes, coyotes, and desert tortoises, to mention only a few.

Golden Boulders in the Sun

Many travelers think of the desert as a mostly low-lying region. Some of it is, particularly in the Salton Sink region and deep in Death Valley. But the presence of Joshua trees, the characteristic plant of the Mojave Desert, tells a different story. Whenever you see a Joshua tree (*Yucca brevifolia*), you know you're probably at a much higher elevation than most novice desert travelers realize: 2,500 to 4,500 feet. Hence the appellation "high desert."

These elevations make the Mojave somewhat cooler in summer than the Colorado Desert, and downright cold (or even snowy) in winter. Plan your trip for March or April when days are mild, the wildflowers are out, and the Joshua trees are in bloom. Or venture out in fall when the region cools off after the searing summer heat.

Begin your journey with a loop drive through the sculptural landscape of Joshua Tree National Park. The most direct route from the Los Angeles area is to head east on Interstate 10, turning north on State Highway 62 just past the Palm Springs turnoff to the south. The main park entrance is in the town of Twentynine Palms, although there are several other portals.

Wind and water have molded most granite formations here into giant egg-shaped nodules and domes that dwarf rock climbers clinging to their rough fissures and ledges. Deep in rock gardens, isolated spring-fed ponds ("wells" or "tanks" in desert parlance) provide year-round water and invite hikers to stretch their legs to reach these cooler picnic sites.

Nowadays the park is abuzz all winter long with the clink and cries ("Belay on!") of rock climbers. Bring binoculars, pull a camp chair out of the trunk, and sit down

Mountains are giant rock piles sculpted by water freezing and expanding in boulder cracks. Yucca, often called the "Lord's Candles," rise from their prickly nests.

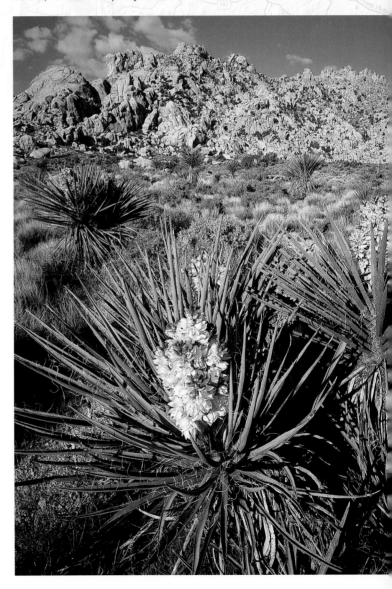

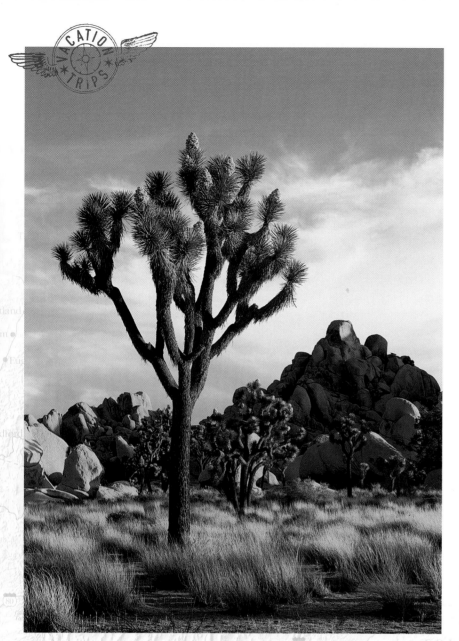

Joshua Tree National Park shelters one of the world's strangest species. Searing heat is the summer norm, but snow is not uncommon in winter—this is high desert.

southern edge of the base serve both soldiers and tourists. Twentynine Palms has tried to add to its ambience with a citywide mural project, but, regrettably, most of the route here is lined with one fast-food franchise or chain motel after another.

Some gems hide off the main route, however, like Roughley Manor, a 1928 stone house now taking guests. Wherever you stay, be sure to spend some time each night under the stars. You'll never identify more constellations whirling around the Pole Star than here, and shooting stars are particularly easy to spot.

On to Amboy

After a 50-mile drive through the park and environs, drive north over Sheep Hole Pass on Amboy Road. Note the canals and salt-works etched into dry Bristol Lake, and keep an eye out to the west for Amboy Crater, a black cinder cone well worth the climb to its summit. Wear sturdy boots and gloves; the glasslike pumice is extremely abrasive. From the crater rim, hikers look down on several petticoats of lava that spread across the desert floor approximately 10,000 years ago.

Amboy is located on a bent-arm–shaped vestige of original Route 66 and the Atchison, Topeka & Santa Fe rail line. A few old buildings, motels, and other artifacts of the route's glory days before the advent of the interstate highway system will keep photographers busy. Many place

along the roadside pullouts to watch awhile; their acrobatics are a slow ballet on a vertical stone stage. The park has become so popular in winter that campgrounds are full from late fall through spring on weekends, so plan any overnight stay for a weekday.

Desert at War

General George Patton trained WW II troops in the Mojave, toughening them to face the rigors of North Africa by sending men and equipment into mock battle. In many places, tank and Jeep tracks are visible today. U.S. Marines still train on a base adjacent to Twentynine Palms, and several towns strung out along State 62 at the names are unforgettably improbable: Klondike, Siberia, and Bagdad.

To the Singing Kelso Dunes

Some of Mojave National Preserve's most dramatic terrain lies on either side of Kelbaker Road, which runs almost 100 miles northwest from Interstate 40 to the town of Baker on Interstate 15. Heading north you'll pass between Granite and Providence mountains. Pavement gives way beneath your tires to well-graded gravel. A huge "Devils Playground" stretches to the northwest, home of Kelso Dunes and their astonishing pyramidal summit, about 600 feet higher in elevation than the surrounding countryside. An access road leads west from Kelbaker Road to the south edge of the dunes. The high dunes are only 1½ miles from the parking lot.

Where does the sand come from? Ancient river and lake beds cleave and dimple the Mojave's crust on a massive scale, and hikers can easily see the forces of geology and climate that result in sand being lifted daily from Afton Canyon, the Mojave River, and Devil's Playground, then pushed to Kelso until high winds butt and eddy against the scarp of the Providence Mountains. Confused, the gales drop their granular cargo in a dune system that literally changes before your eyes on most days, sweeping away footprints not long after you make them, redefining the dunes' most spectacular feature: long ridges falling off to either side like great shimmering curtains.

To hike to the summit, head cross-country toward a saddle on the right, then traverse a knife-edge of sand leading to the top. Listen for the "singing" sound made when

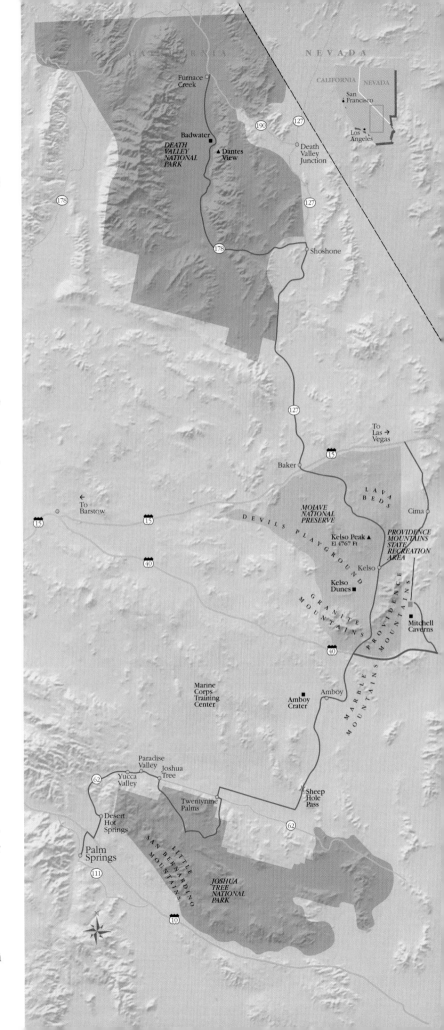

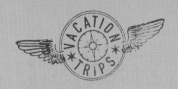

Classic Desert Oases

California's desert is nothing if not about extremes, provoking disparate reactions from first-time visitors. People either rush through the apparent desolation before them, or they take time to examine the landscape, finding inspiration in its wide diversity. Those who linger may choose to camp among the creosote and cacti or opt for accommodations nearby, returning each evening to civilization after a day in the wilderness.

Today, some of the most notable examples of desert architecture are the hotels and inns that opened the terrain to early travelers looking for creature comfort where hitherto there had been only creatures. These two desert oases were instant classics that set the standard for their time and continue to do so today.

Two Bunch Palms (67-425 Two Bunch Palms Trail, Desert Hot Springs, CA 92240; 800/4724334; $$-$$$) has villas by their mineral-water hot pools. Midweek spa packages include lodging, meals, and spa treatments. The resort is about 45 miles southeast of Joshua Tree National Park off State 62.

For travelers continuing on to Death Valley, **Furnace Creek Inn** (P.O. Box 1, Death Valley National Park, CA 92328; 760/786-2345; $$$) is a stylish choice. It brought luxury to Death Valley when it opened in 1927—and it's still a delightful option for those who prefer amenities like fine dining, a pool, and a golf course.

molasses-like flows of sand dislodged by your feet set up a resonating "hum" as they slide down each steep face. Equally interesting on the lower dunes are the circular patterns scribed by grass tips; winds swirl into this valley from every direction. The way down is easy—run straight toward the bottom! A round-trip hike takes one to two hours.

In Kelso, only minutes beyond the dunes, wander along the arched loggia of a magnificent Mission Revival-style train station built in the 1920s by Union Pacific. (The National Park Service plans to convert the station to a visitor center.) The town of Kelso originally became a stop on the Los Angeles–to–Salt Lake City route thanks to a nearby source of water for steam trains. It's difficult to envision now, but with the railroad and local mining activity the town was once home to 2,000 people.

Now you face a difficult choice; whether to head northeast past Cima Dome, with its ancient petroglyphs and the desert's most significant stand of Joshua trees, or northwest past cinder cones and lava beds. Some of the flows look as if they stopped just short of the road only a few decades ago. If time allows, you can loop over both routes by including the stretch of Interstate 15 east of Baker. Be sure to stop in at that city's Desert Information Center (under the giant thermometer) for advice on everything from hikes to camping in the open desert.

Campgrounds & Caverns

Camping in the desert lures both kinds of outdoorsperson—the experienced "desert rat," who never met a dirt road he or she didn't like (firmly subscribing to the old saying that bad roads make good wildernesses), and the more casual "tailgate camper," who loves the freedom to drive in, unload the gear right beside the car, and be watching the sunset, chilled aperitif in hand, within the hour.

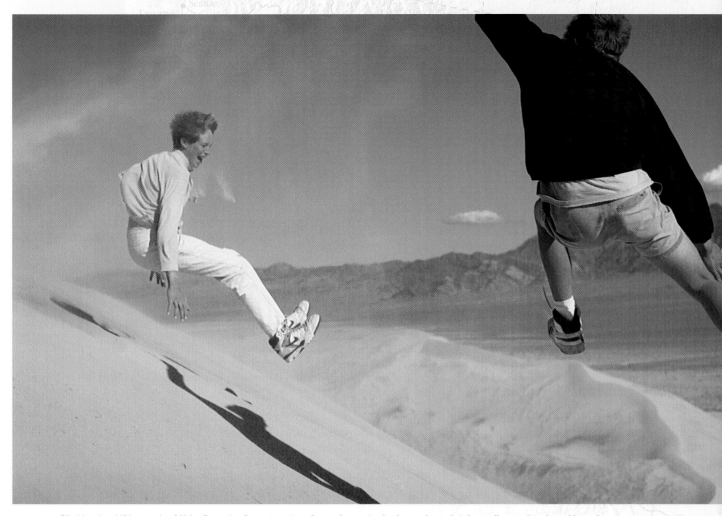

Climbing the shifting sands of Kelso Dunes is often a two-steps-forward, one-step-back experience, but descending can be a hop, skip, and a leap. On your way up the dunes, watch for abundant animal and insect tracks.

The desert accommodates both. Like Anza-Borrego Desert State Park, its low-desert cousin far to the south, Mojave National Preserve allows camping in primitive areas. Pull off anywhere you see a previously used informal campsite; don't cre-

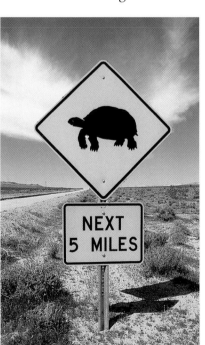

Warning signs alert drivers that rare desert tortoises and cars don't mix.

ate any new disruption to desert habitat, especially by driving off-road. Campfires are allowed, but bring your own wood and use existing, park-installed fire rings (these are found only in developed campgrounds) or enjoy a blaze contained in your own device, such as a metal pan or three-legged brazier. Never build a fire on the desert floor, and leave no trace, not even ashes.

Weather changes can be sudden and extreme in winter and spring. Snow flurries are not uncommon as late as the first week in April, but they soon pass and create some of America's most glorious scenery, such as the sight of the Providence Mountains cloaked in white high above the Kelso Dunes.

Wildflowers are a spring attraction in the high desert, and grand displays occur about once every ten years, with varying

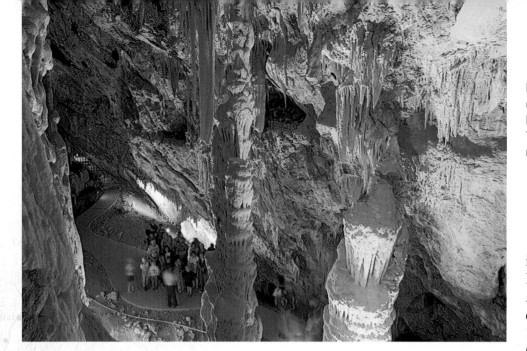

Mitchell Caverns once housed early man and some Pleistocene-era mammals. Today the cave is a cool respite not far from the interstate.

degrees of bloom during the interim years, all a result of a subtle combination of winter rains and temperatures. Some years, alas, there may be virtually no blooms, for seeds can remain dormant for several seasons. Call desert information centers for up-to-date wildflower reports. Because of the Mojave's higher altitude, the yearly bloom in the Cima Dome area usually occurs in early April.

Another of the park's major attractions, reached by returning to the Cima Dome region and heading east up Cedar Canyon through Mid Hills to Black Canyon Road, is the east side of the Providence Mountains. Here you'll find the weird hobgoblin caves of Hole-in-the-Wall's lava flows as well as Mitchell Caverns, deep limestone caves once inhabited by Pleistocene sloths as well as ancient tribespeople. Old mines dot the area, making this site a favorite with rockhounds. This is also the setting for the area's two developed campgrounds, Mid Hills and Hole-in-the-Wall.

At Mitchell Caverns, the visitor center seems to hang off the mountainside, affording spectacular views to the east. From September through May, rangers lead 90-minute trips into the caverns weekdays at 1:30, weekends and holidays at 10, 1:30, and 3. Other times of the year, guided tours are offered at 1:30 weekends only. In addition to seeing the caverns, hike the interpretive Mary Beal Nature Trail. Also worth the effort is the steeper 1-mile climb on the Crystal Spring Trail, which leads up a rocky canyon to an outlook affording panoramic views.

Six campsites near the caverns let you greet the sunrise before returning to Interstate 40 and the long drive toward either Las Vegas or Los Angeles—a demanding haul best attempted in the morning with a fresh cup of coffee close at hand.

If time permits, you might consider lengthening your desert stay by retracing your steps to Baker on Interstate 15 and taking a back road (State Highway 127) north about 55 miles to State Highway 178, a southern entry into legendary Death Valley National Park.

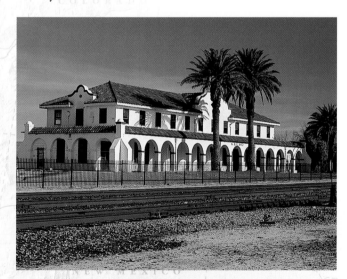

Rail passengers once disembarked at Kelso for a good meal. Today the grand station awaits a new life as the national preserve's visitor center.

Hundreds of miles of well-graded dirt and gravel roads lace the Mojave area (heavy rains may cause damage). Many are passable to passenger cars. All vehicles must stay on designated roads. Be sure to fill your tank before entering the region, carry plenty of drinking water, and check on weather and road conditions in advance. Be prepared to camp a night or two to avoid long drives over unpaved roads. Also be prepared for snow flurries from December to early April.

Unless otherwise noted, area codes are 760. Lodging rates for two people range from $ (under $100) to $$$ (above $250) per night.

WHERE

Total mileage for this epic desert drive will be at least 300 miles, not including your mileage to Joshua Tree National Park, where your trip begins, or home from Mojave National Preserve. After about 50 miles spent exploring Joshua Tree's loop road and side routes, continue north from Twentynine Palms on Amboy Rd. almost 50 miles to Amboy, and jog east 6 miles to Kelbaker Rd. Go north 11 miles to I-40, where you enter Mojave National Preserve.

On Kelbaker Rd., it's 21 miles to Kelso and another 73 miles to Baker and I-15. If time allows, drive east 26 miles on I-15 to Cima Rd.; go south 22 miles through the preserve to Cedar Canyon Rd. Go east 6 miles to Black Mountain Rd., then south 20 miles through a region highlighted by Mid Hills, Hole-in-the-Wall, and Mitchell Caverns in the Providence Mountains. Leave the preserve by traveling south 10 miles on Essex Rd., rejoining I-40.

LODGING

Travelers to this remote region have a few lodging options north of Joshua Tree, some of them unusual. Be prepared to camp a night or two to avoid long drives over unpaved roads. Near Joshua Tree and the north edge of Mojave National Preserve, you'll find several bed-and-breakfasts, as well as numerous motels.

In Twentynine Palms, **Roughley Manor Bed & Breakfast** (74744 Joe Davis Rd.; 367-3238; $-$$) occupies a large 1928 stone house set in a grove of rustling Washingtonia palms. Four cottages are scattered about the grounds, which include 107 rose bushes and two great horned owls. Motels include a large **Best Western Gardens Motel** (7487 Twentynine Palms Hwy.; 367-9141; $-$$ includes breakfast). At **Homestead Inn** bed-and-breakfast (call for directions to 74153 Two Mile Rd.; 367-0030; $-$$), you'll get a feel for desert living (and a telescope for viewing night skies) well off busy State 62.

At the north edge of Mojave National Preserve, **Bun Boy Motel** (State Hwy. 127 at I-15, Baker; 733-4363; $) is a reliable respite before the long drive west to Los Angeles or east to Las Vegas. Or stay in the new section of the **Wills Fargo Motel** (52252 Baker Blvd.; 733-4477; $), and enjoy the pool.

In Amboy, on an original stretch of Route 66, the partly renovated **Amboy Hotel** (733-4263; $) is little changed from the legendary highway's glory days.

CAMPING

Of 9 campgrounds in **Joshua Tree National Park**, 6 are open on a first-come, first-served basis (free), while reservations must be made at the other 3 (small fee) through DESTINET at 800/365-2267.

Developed campgrounds (fee) at Mid Hills and Hole-in-the-Wall in **Mojave National Preserve** are open year-round.

DINING

The owner/chef at **Twentynine Palms Inn** (73950 Inn Ave.; lunch and dinner only; 367-3505) often puts her own home-grown vegetables on the menu and bakes all breads. This fairly elegant establishment has been in business over 70 years. Triple-stacked hamburgers at **Don's American Barbecue** (72183 Twentynine Palms Hwy.; 367-0301; lunch and dinner) have local U.S. Marines betting whether they can take a bite.

Don't let its hodgepodge of signs dismay you; **The Mad Greek** (Baker Hwy. and State 127, Baker; 733-4354), with its lamb and beef pitas, is a welcome break from usual hard-by-the-interstate road food.

ATTRACTIONS

For tour details or reservations for **Mitchell Caverns**, write P.O. Box 1, Essex, CA 92332, or call 928-2586. There is a small charge to tour the caverns and a small fee for reservations.

DESERT MUSEUMS

For an educational overview of the desert and other travel questions, visit **Hi-Desert Nature Museum** (57116 Twentynine Palms Hwy., Twentynine Palms, CA 92277; 369-7212), **Mojave Desert Information Center** (Baker, under the giant thermometer; 733-4040), and **California Desert Information Center** (831 Barstow Rd., Barstow, CA 92311; 255-8760).

FOR MORE INFORMATION

Joshua Tree National Park (74485 National Park Dr., Twentynine Palms, CA 92277-3597; 367-5522), Mojave National Preserve (222 E. Main St., Barstow, CA 92311; 733-4040).

REGION	CALIFORNIA
Where X	One hour north of San Francisco
When X	Year-round destination; best weather in spring and fall

West Marin's
hidden roads

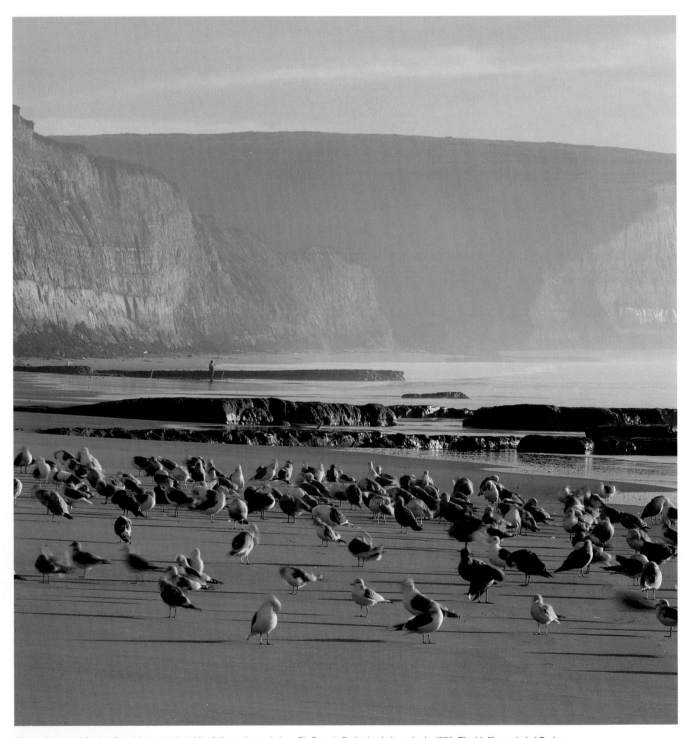

The landscape of Drakes Beach has remained blissfully unchanged since Sir Francis Drake landed nearby in 1579. The bluffs reminded Drake of the white cliffs of Dover in his native England.

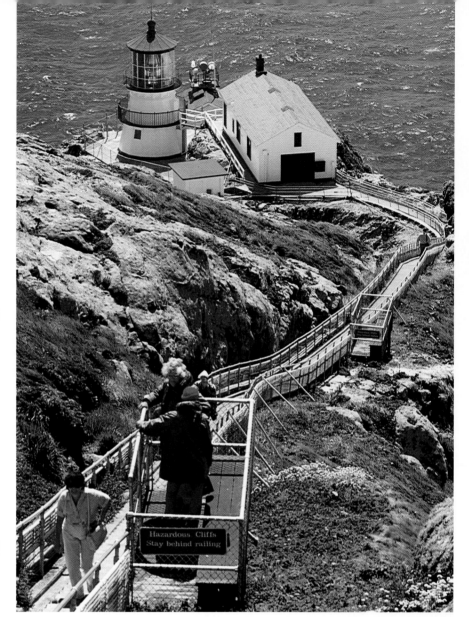

If the time is right, visitors who brave the 300 steps down to Point Reyes Lighthouse might be treated to some of the best whale-watching on the West Coast.

Every year from January to April, gray whales pass the Marin County coast on their 10,000-mile migration north from the waters off Baja, Mexico, to the Bering Sea of Alaska. Point Reyes National Seashore—whose hammer-shaped 85,000 acres jut 10 miles out into the Pacific Ocean—is a good place to watch their progress. From the Point Reyes Lighthouse, whales can be spotted breaching. Often all you'll see is a whale "spyhopping" with its nose just above the waterline, which biologists speculate could be the creature's way of charting its course by means of familiar landmarks.

Whales aren't the only mammals that can't keep their eyes off the west Marin coastline. Each year millions of tourists ride the county's roller-coaster coastline roads, climbing from sandy beaches, pristine marshes, and rolling ranchland up to sheer cliffs that free-fall into the powerful surf below.

To the Lighthouse

One of the most pleasant and least crowded ways to get to the Marin coast is by way of Lucas Valley Road, which begins 20 miles north of the Golden Gate Bridge off U.S. Highway 101 at the Lucas Valley Road exit, past San Rafael. This route to Point Reyes Station meanders 20 miles along forest and creeks (near George Lucas's off-limits Skywalker Ranch) until the coun-

tryside opens up into rolling hills at the town of Nicasio.

To reach the town, turn right on Nicasio Valley Road for about a mile. The tiny village is really just a pleasant bend in the road, but it's worth a stop to see the all-white St. Mary's Church and the fire-engine-red Nicasio schoolhouse (now a private residence). Continuing on, you pass the Nicasio Reservoir.

To reach the town of Point Reyes Station, take a left at Point Reyes–Petaluma Road, and another left at State Highway 1. Either Point Reyes Station or nearby Inverness makes a pleas-

ant stop for browsing and buying picnic supplies before venturing along the national seashore. Stop by the Bear Valley Visitor Center near Olema (Bear Valley Road; open daily) to learn more about the area's natural history and to stock up on maps and guides to the park's numerous outdoor activities.

You could spend more than a week exploring the seashore and still only scratch the surface. The 4.1-mile (one-way) Bear Valley Trail, perfect for hiking or cycling, winds through Douglas fir and bay trees before it dead-ends at a spectacular ocean over-

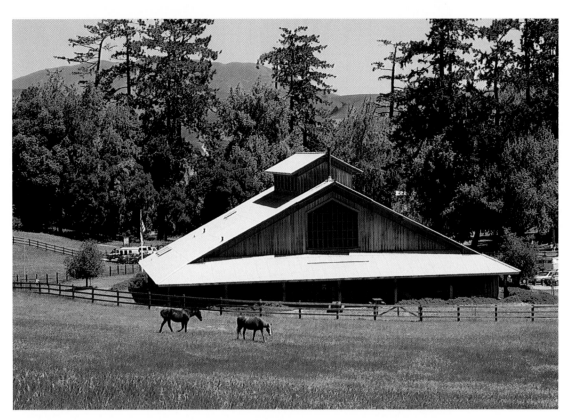

Bear Valley Visitor Center is an excellent starting point for your exploration of the Point Reyes National Seashore.

look at Arch Rock. From historic Pierce Point Ranch at the end of Pierce Point Road, you can walk down to the tidepools at McClures Beach, hike the Tomales Point Trail (10 miles round-trip), or just quietly observe the area's 500 head of tule elk.

On the other side of Point Reyes, at Drakes Beach, you can stroll beneath the white cliffs and then catch a shuttle (weekends and holidays, late December to mid-April) to Point Reyes Lighthouse (open Thursday through Monday, 10-5).

You walk down 300 steps to reach the lighthouse, located at the windiest and foggiest spot on the West Coast. But on a clear day the whalewatching is excellent. (Less crowded and equally scenic is nearby Chimney Rock, another good tidepool spot.)

You'll hate to leave, but when the time comes, make your way back to San Francisco along twisting State 1, passing Stinson and Muir beaches and jaw-dropping ocean vistas before heading inland and connecting again with U.S. 101.

Side Trip

You'll swear you're in Ireland when you drive the little-traveled back roads of west Marin in winter. For a lovely afternoon drive, set off with a good map from Point Reyes Station on Point Reyes–Petaluma Road. Continue 10 miles to Hilson Hill Road, then take a left and drive 3 miles.

You can return through Marshall by taking a left on Marshall–Petaluma Road, or continue on by taking a right, driving 3 miles, and taking a left on Chileno Valley Road. You pass 10 miles of peaceful, rolling ranchland before turning left on Tomales–Petaluma Road. Drive 5 miles until the road intersects with State 1.

The towns of Tomales and nearby Dillon Beach make pleasant stops. Continue south on State 1 for 16 miles to Point Reyes Station past oyster farms along the quiet shores of Tomales Bay.

Park rangers brought rare tule elk back from near extinction at Tomales Point.

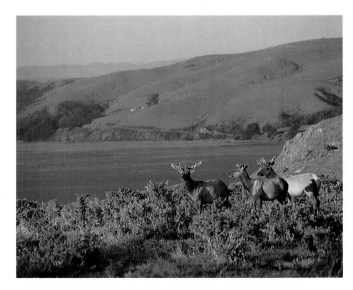

Unless otherwise noted, area codes are 415. Lodging rates for two people range from $ (under $100) to $$$ (above $250) per night.

WHERE

It's about 50 miles from San Francisco to Point Reyes Station. You can reach Point Reyes National Seashore from U.S. Hwy. 101 via State Hwy. 1 (Sir Francis Drake Blvd.) as well as by scenic Lucas Valley Road.

LODGING

West Marin offers travelers a range of accommodations from funky to tony — and always very "Marin" in spirit. The owners of the **Chileno Valley Ranch B & B** (5105 Chileno Valley Rd.; 707/765-6664; $$) rescued from near-death this Victorian Italianate gem, the centerpiece of a 600-acre cattle ranch set amid a peaceful valley along the Marin-Sonoma county line.

Blackthorne Inn (266 Vallejo Ave., Inverness Park; 663-8621; $$) is a fanciful treehouse nestled in a quiet wooded canyon, featuring the Eagle's Nest, an octagonal, all-windows room high among the branches (be warned that its bathroom is located outside across a footbridge). **Hotel Inverness** (25 Park Ave., Inverness; 669-7393; $$) is a genteel restored hotel built in 1906 that offers 5 boldly decorated rooms, some with decks that overlook a rare stand of bay laurels on Inverness Ridge. **Rosemary Cottage** (75 Balboa Ave., Inverness; 663-9338; $$) is a hideaway along the edge of Point Reyes National Seashore. Rosemary's sister cottage, **The Ark** (180 Highland Way, Inverness; 663-9338; $$), is a budget-minded throwback to '70s Marin.

Visitors to the **Point Reyes Seashore Lodge** (10021 State 1, Olema; 663-9000; $-$$) can literally walk out the doors of their rooms and into the park. Many of the 21 rooms feature creek views and whirlpool baths.

These referral services will help you book a stay in one of the area's many other inns and cottages: **West Marin Network** (663-9543), **Inns of Marin** (663-2000), **Inns of Point Reyes** (663-1420), and **Point Reyes Lodging** (663-1872).

DINING

Experience west Marin's finest upscale dining at **Manka's Inverness Lodge** (30 Callendar Way off Argyle St., Inverness; 669-1034; lodging $$-$$$), a 1917 hunting lodge.

Tomales Bay Foods (680 Fourth St., Point Reyes Station; 663-9335) is a shrine to the agricultural bounty of west Marin, showcasing a world-class sampling of artisan cheeses at the Cowgirl Creamery, local organic produce, and an inexpensive café that serves delicious sandwiches, soups, salads, coffee, and desserts.

Debra's Bakery (12301 Sir Francis Drake Blvd., Inverness Park; 669-7312) serves homemade pastry, breads, and light lunch fare. It's run by a former owner of the popular **Bovine Bakery** in downtown Point Reyes Station (663-9420).

Olema Inn (10000 Sir Francis Drake Blvd. at State 1; 663-9559; lodging $-$$) offers moderately priced seafood and homey American fare in an airy country inn built in 1876. Sir Francis Drake would have welcomed the sight of the **Pelican Inn** (State 1 at Muir Beach; 383-6000; lodging $$), an authentic Elizabethan-style country inn with a restaurant and pub downstairs that serves hearty, well-priced English food and drink.

Taste some of the most delicious bivalves on the West Coast along State 1 at the **Hog Island Oyster Company** (663-9218) and the **Tomales Bay Oyster Company** (663-1242), both near Marshall.

SHOPS

Point Reyes is home to a number of unique shops, including **Shaker Shops West** (5 Inverness Way, Inverness; 669-7256), **Spirit Matters** (12307 Sir Francis Drake Blvd., Inverness Park; 663-8699), **Black Mountain Weavers** (11245 Main St., Point Reyes Station; 663-9130), and **Nita Collage** (65 Third St. #17, next to Tomales Bay Foods; 663-1160).

ACTIVITIES

Tamal Saka Tomales Bay Kayaking (Marshall; 663-1743) rents individual kayaks and leads excellent paddling tours of Tomales Bay.

FOR MORE INFORMATION

Point Reyes National Seashore (Point Reyes, CA 94956; 663-1092). West Marin Chamber of Commerce (663-9232).

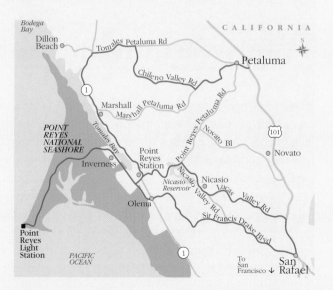

REGION	CALIFORNIA
Where	X	50 miles north of San Francisco
When	X	Best autumn through spring

rambling through Sonoma County

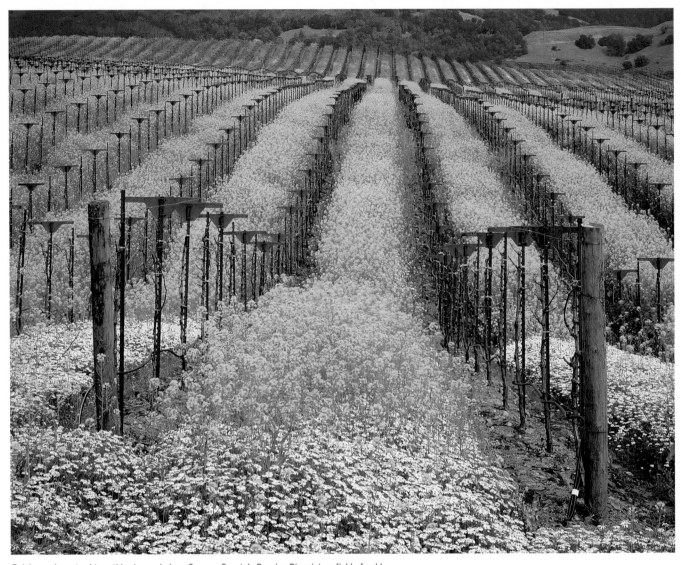

Daisies and mustard turn this vineyard along Sonoma County's Russian River into a field of gold.

With bountiful vineyards, bucolic scenery, and blue-ribbon agricultural products, Sonoma County rewards visitors with an idyllic experience in any season. However, avoiding summer crowds and heat will make touring wineries more of a delight. Spring and fall showcase the region's natural beauty, while in winter vintners are less pressed for time and eager to discuss the vine-to-wine process with devotees of the grape.

Considered the birthplace of the California wine industry, Sonoma's valleys are lined with thousands of acres of vineyard lands that serve well over 100 wineries of all sizes.

Comparisons with its showier neighbor, Napa Valley, often leave Sonoma playing the part of country cousin. Don't be fooled into translating its down-to-earth reputation into dreary motels and functional dining, for Sonoma easily equals Napa in elegant lodgings and inspired cuisine.

The best of the county remains a secret to casual visitors, who gravitate toward more accessible wineries and larger towns. Driving tours of three valleys between the Coast Range and the Mayacamas Mountains —Sonoma (Valley of the Moon), Russian River, and Dry Creek— get you out into the countryside to explore wine cellars, produce stands, and restaurants off the main roads.

Valley of the Moon

This tour begins at the historical center of the town of Sonoma, where Franciscans erected California's last mission in 1823 to mark the northern end of "The King's Highway," or El Camino Real, which connects all of the California missions. Twelve years later, General Mariano Vallejo established Sonoma's plaza and presidio, the site of the short-lived Bear Flag Revolt in 1846.

Explore the square's historic buildings and verdant gardens, try to catch a glimpse of the friendly mission ghost, and then stop by the visitors bureau (453

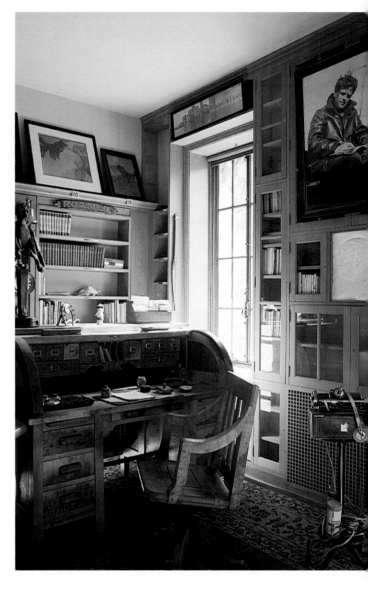

A look at author Jack London's studio is only one of the attractions at the state historic park in Glen Ellen that bears his name.

First Street E.) to pick up a Farm Trails map of local ranchers and farmers from whom you can buy goods directly. After sampling tangy aged jack during the cheese-making tour at Vella Cheese Company (315 Second Street E.), pick up other picnic fare at the Sonoma Cheese Factory (2 Spain Street) and drive north out of town on Arnold Drive.

En route to Glen Ellen, stop for the scenic tram tour at Benziger Family Winery (1883 London Ranch Road) before heading up the road to the former ranch of author Jack London. Now a state historic park,

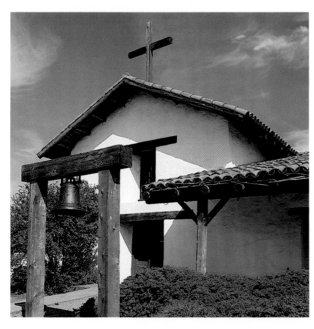

Mission San Francisco Solano, founded July 4, 1823, contains an outstanding museum collection.

the 800-acre property includes the author's two-story home, his grave, and the ruins of Wolf House, a 26-room mansion that mysteriously burned to the ground shortly before London and his wife were to occupy it. The park offers 9 miles of hiking trails, one of which leads to the top of Sonoma Mountain, a perfect spot for breaking out a picnic basket.

Upon arriving in timeless Glen Ellen, prowl among dusty volumes at the Jack London Bookstore (14300 Arnold Drive), then cross the street to visit the tasting room and historic center at Glen Ellen Winery. The 3-ton grinding wheel next door marks the Olive Press, a converted winery that has become an oil-pressing facility and shop offering premium olive oils and other olive-based products.

Continue north on State Highway 12 to Kenwood, home of several fine wineries, including Kenwood Vineyards (9592 Sonoma Highway), Stone Creek Wines (9380 Sonoma Highway), and Chateau St. Jean (8555 Sonoma Highway).

The Wine Room (9575 Sonoma Highway) allows you to sample the offerings from smaller, prestigious wineries, such as Adler Fells and Kaz, and to talk with some of the winemakers. With advance notice, Adler Fells (5325 Corrick Lane, Santa Rosa; 539-3123) also welcomes visitors to drink in the magnificent views from their winery, perched high on a ridge overlooking the valley.

Other spectacular views, and notable picnic spots, can be found northeast of Kenwood in Sugarloaf Ridge Park (2605 Adobe Canyon Road), part of the Mayacamas Mountains. Views from the park's lofty elevation include Sonoma and Napa valleys, San Francisco Bay, and the distant Sierra Nevada.

Backtracking on State 12, you'll find Carmenet (1700 Moon Mountain Drive; 996-5870), another family-owned winery requiring prior notice from visitors. Progress slowly along the narrow mountain road, keeping an eye out for deer and quail. While touring this intriguingly designed winery, note the aging caves drilled into volcanic rock. You can hike above the secluded complex to enjoy the scenery before returning to Sonoma.

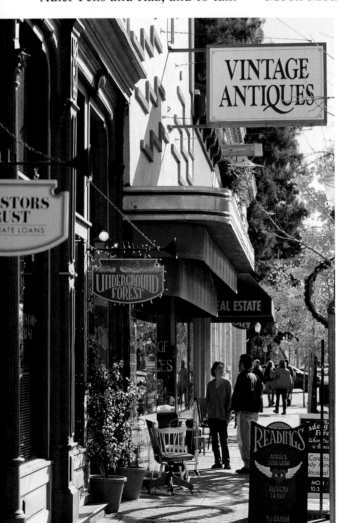

Healdsburg's heart is its well-preserved square, a pleasant mix of antique shops, boutiques, bookstores, and other businesses.

Once you arrive back in town, pamper yourself with an aromatherapy massage at luxurious Sonoma Mission & Spa (18140 Sonoma Highway, Boyes Hot Springs; 938-9000, 800/862-4945; reservations required) before making a dinner selection from a valley restaurant.

Russian River Valley

Start this tour from Santa Rosa, driving north on U.S. Highway 101 to River Road. Heading west, you'll come to family-owned Martinelli Winery (3360 River Road), a good place to stock up on picnic supplies and locally made products. A few miles farther on, the road reaches the meandering Russian River, where the temperature drops as coastal fog and old-growth redwoods blot out the sun.

The area's cooling influences nurture grapes used in sparkling wines and explain why three brothers from Bohemia chose this site in 1882 to found Korbel Champagne Cellars (13250 River Road). Today, guided tours explore the champagne cellars and Korbel's latest development, the Russian River Brewing Company microbrewery. An on-site market and delicatessen sells four varieties of premium-quality ales. From May to October, visitors can also tour Korbel's antique rose garden.

North of the one-time logging camp of Guerneville lies Armstrong Redwoods State Reserve (17000 Armstrong Woods Road). If the day is warm, cool off along the easy nature trail through stately redwoods that reach heights of over 300 feet.

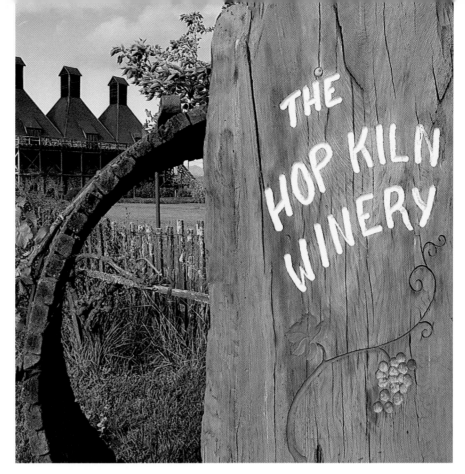

Signs mark the turnoff to Hop Kiln Winery in the Russian River Valley.

Leaving Guerneville, angle southeast on State Highway 116, climbing slightly out of the river gorge and up into farmland and orchards. Near the small town of Forestville, home to numerous berry farms, lies local landmark Kozlowski Farms (5566 Gravenstein Highway N.), worth a stop to peruse the produce and over 60 homemade food products, including vinegars, jams, and pies.

In summer and fall, the white farmhouse at Foxglove Farm (5280 Gravenstein Highway N.), north of the apple-growing town of Sebastopol, doubles as a produce stand and a Christmas shop. Depending on the time of year, fill up the backseat with pumpkins or handmade ornaments before circling back to Santa Rosa.

Russian River Valley

If you arrive on a Saturday from May through December, make the farmers' market in

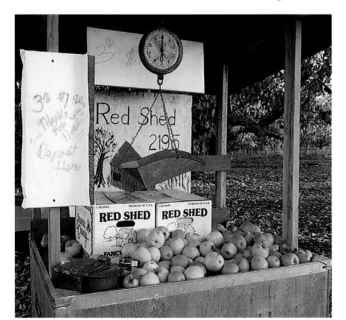

Healdsburg (West North and Vine streets) your first stop on this loop. On any day, schedule a quick trip to the Downtown Bakery and Creamery (308A Center Street) for wonderful sticky buns and the Oakville Grocery (124 Matheson Street) for picnic supplies. Tear yourself away from the small shops bordering the town's historic plaza and pick up a Farm Trails map at the Healdsburg Chamber of Commerce (217 Healdsburg Avenue) to find out which seasonal produce

Back-road travelers in Sonoma County will pass many roadside markets, such as this fruit stand near Sebastopol.

and flower stands are open as you head south of town along Westside Road.

On a bank above the Russian River lies distinctive Hop Kiln Winery (6050 Westside Road), a 1905 barn converted to a winery in 1974. With its impressive stonemasonry, picnic grounds, and bird sanctuary, this winery is a favorite spot for those touring the region by bicycle as well as car.

Retracing your route, drive north on Westside until it becomes West Dry Creek Road. At this point the road offers turnoffs for several vineyards with uncrowded tasting rooms, such as Dry Creek Vineyard (3770 Lambert Bridge Road), Ridge/Lytton Springs Winery (650 Lytton Springs Road; closed Tuesday through Thursday), and Quivira Vineyards (4900 West Dry Creek Road). At the head of the valley, sample hallmark Zinfandel at Preston Vineyards

(9282 West Dry Creek Road), which also produces olive oils and hearth-baked breads.

Looping over Yoakim Bridge Road and heading south on Dry Creek Road brings you to the outstanding Ferrari-Carano Vineyards and Winery gardens (8761 Dry Creek Road), where flower-lined paths wander along a stream, by a waterfall, and into a water garden. After sampling wines in the Italian villa–style tasting room, close the loop by returning to Healdsburg.

⸬TRIP PLANNER⸬

Unless otherwise noted, area codes are 707. Lodging rates for two people range from $ (under $100) to $$$ (above $250) per night.

WHERE

Sonoma Valley is about a 45-minute drive from San Francisco. Go north on U.S. 101, then east on State Hwy. 37 until its intersection with State Hwy. 12, which heads north to the town of Sonoma.

LODGING

The region offers many charming bed-and-breakfasts and inns that generally offer lower room rates from late autumn to early spring.

In Healdsburg, **Honor Mansion** (14891 Grove St.; 800/554-4667; $$-$$$ includes a sumptuous breakfast) is a restored Victorian mansion on a quiet street; rooms have antique decorations and private baths. In Guerneville, **Applewood Inn** (13555 Hwy. 116; 800/555-8509; $$-$$$ includes full breakfast) is set deep in the redwoods; comfortable rooms, some with fireplaces and patios or balconies. Set among Santa Rosa vineyards, **Vintners Inn** (4350 Barnes Rd.; 800/421-2584; $$-$$$ includes deluxe continental breakfast) offers 44 rooms decorated in a country French style.

In Glen Ellen, **Gaige House Inn** (13540 Arnold Dr.; 800/935-0237; $$-$$$ includes full breakfast) has a lovely garden, pool, Jacuzzi tub, and small deck overlooking a creek. In Sonoma, a great location and friendly staff mark **Thistle Dew Inn** (171 W. Spain St.; 800/382-7895; $), with 6 rooms, most with fireplaces and decks, in two period houses. **El Pueblo Inn** (896 W. Napa St.; 996-3651; $) is a modern motel a mile from the plaza.

RVs up to 24 feet can camp at **Sugarloaf Ridge State Park** (2605 Adobe Canyon Rd., Kenwood, CA 95452; 833-5712; reservations required Mar. 15-Oct.; 800/444-7275).

DINING

As befits a region renowned for fine wines and farm-fresh foods, many restaurants stand out for their focus on local labels and ingredients. As hours (and menus) vary widely, call ahead for times and reservations

In Healdsburg, check out trendy **Bistro Ralph** (109 Plaza St.; 433-1380) for stylish, savory meals and mouth-watering crème brûlée. Or sample fresh and imaginative concoctions at tiny restaurant **Ravenous** (117 North St.; 431-1770), a long-time local favorite.

Outside Santa Rosa, unassuming **Willowside Cafe** (3535 Guerneville Rd.; 523-4814) consistently offers memorable dishes in a country tavern setting, while rustic and secluded **John Ash and Co.** (4330 Barnes Rd.; 527-7687) designs great pizzas and offers an extensive wine list.

In Sonoma, **Babette's** (464 First St. E.; 939-8921) makes excellent use of local produce for its French menu; cafe/wine bar; formal dining room. Diners at **The General's Daughter** (400 W. Spain St.; 938-4004) sip wine on the veranda before ordering from an ever-changing menu inside the restaurant's Victorian rooms.

FOR MORE INFORMATION

Sonoma Valley Visitors Bureau (453 First St. E., Sonoma, CA 95476; 996-1090). Sonoma County Tourism Program (2300 Country Center Dr., Ste. B-260, Santa Rosa, CA 95403; 800/576-6662). Healdsburg Chamber of Commerce (217 Healdsburg Ave., Healdsburg, CA 95448; 433-6935). Russian River Chamber of Commerce (16209 First St., Box 331, Guerneville, CA 95446; 869-9000).

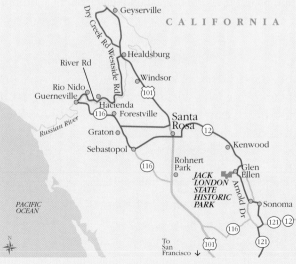

Anderson Valley
sampler

REGION		CALIFORNIA
Where	X	100 miles north of San Francisco
When	X	Year-round rural retreat

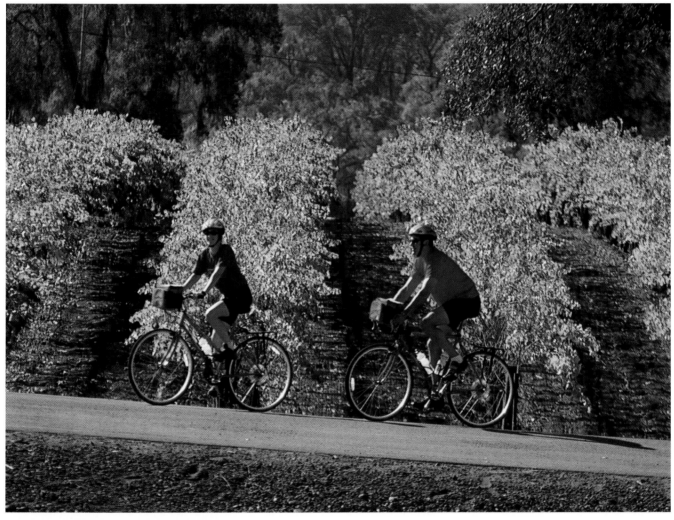

Pick up picnic supplies in Boonville before heading out for a ride; Anderson Valley vintners usually offer tables plus sips of their vintages.

State Highway 128, a two-lane country road, winds through bucolic Anderson Valley on its way to the Mendocino coast 30 minutes away. But the scenic area through which it passes is filled with so many tempting treats, from respected wine cellars and apple farms to cozy bed-and-breakfasts and pleasantly unpretentious restaurants, that many travelers succumb to the valley's leisurely charms and decide to stay awhile.

The heart of the broad valley embraces the hamlets of Boonville, Philo, and Navarro, and is known mainly for apple growing, winemaking, and sheep ranching. In spring, colorful wildflowers accent the rolling green hillsides; in autumn, the valley's vineyards turn color, its apples grow crisp and winy, and the air takes on a beautiful clarity.

Tasting—Wine, Beer & Apple Cider

The valley's misty mornings, sunny afternoons, and cool nights seem to favor slow-maturing wine varietals such as Chardonnay, Pinot Noir, Gewürztraminer, and Riesling. A score of wineries, many clustered

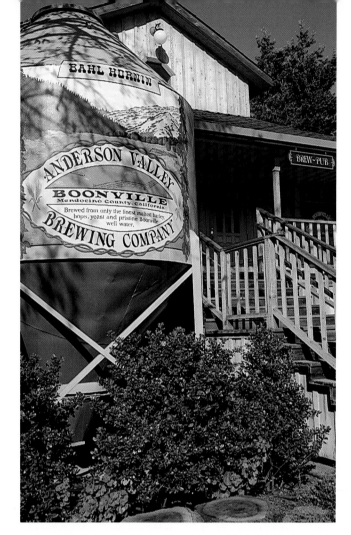

Brewing company started making brews in the basement of the old Buckhorn Saloon, still a popular place to taste their wares.

juices, and other tantalizing products. Don't pass up a visit to The Apple Farm (18501 Greenwood Road, Philo), particularly in autumn. They feature hard-to-find varieties and offer an orchard walk and cider-pressing samples. The farm's weekend cooking classes require prior arrangements, but their produce stand, stocked with jams, jellies, chutneys, syrup, vinegar, apple juice, cider, and dried fruit, is open year-round.

Other Options

With so many good things in nearby orchards and fields, it's no wonder the valley has attracted top-notch chefs to a growing culinary scene. Reservations are deservedly required for dinner at The Boonville Hotel restaurant, which serves appealing California cuisine in a setting that attracts locals as well as tourists. A more casual taqueria lunch is served Wednesday through Sunday.

If a leisurely picnic seems the best idea, select a table in a well-landscaped winery setting or head for Hendy Woods State Park (day-use fee), along the Navarro River near Philo. The park's stands of old-growth redwoods are blessedly quiet, tour bus–free, and disabled–accessible—good places to dodge the heat of an Indian summer afternoon or walk off a wine tasting or two.

Fortunately, the valley is still free of souvenir-type shops. You will find the works of many fine artists and craftspeople at galleries and shops. Boonville's Rookie-To Gallery is one pleasant place to browse, and All That Good Stuff sells cards and gifts in a fine old general store.

At the turn of the century, the valley residents developed a lingo of their own to amaze and amuse visitors. A few words of "Boontling" you might see or hear include *bahl gorms* (good

around Philo, open daily for tasting. You can sample sophisticated sparkling wine facilities at Scharffenberger and Roederer, and also enjoy the down-home hospitality of smaller family-run wineries like Navarro Vineyard, with a devoted following who stock up on recent releases. Cellars like Pepperwood Springs and Husch have an added attraction—lofty valley views.

Popular Anderson Valley Brewing Company started making outstanding beers in the basement of the old Buckhorn Saloon on Boonville's main drag. Even though the company moved into a larger plant, the laid-back saloon and restaurant is still the best place to taste their wares.

Several stands sell the valley's acclaimed apples, ciders, organic

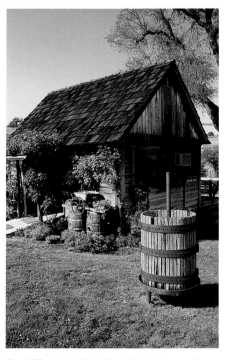

Husch Winery is well worth a visit to taste premium wines and to enjoy pleasant picnic sites and grand valley views.

food), *buckey walter* (pay phone), and *horn of zeese* (cup of coffee).

To learn more about this linguistic phenomenon, visit the free Anderson Valley Historical Society Museum (open 11–4, Fri.–Sun. May–Oct., 1–4 rest of the year) housed in the Little Red School House between Boonville and Philo.

Beyond Navarro, State 128 wanders through the Navarro River Redwoods State Park on its 15-mile route to the coast. It's a pretty drive with an impressive stand of redwoods rising between the road and the river.

The road meets State Highway 1 south of the tiny town of Albion.

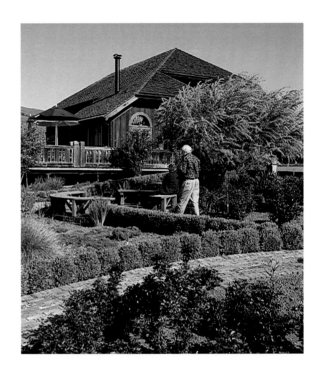

Repeat visitors at Navarro Vineyard in Philo know that production never matches demand for the winery's new releases.

TRIP PLANNER

Unless otherwise noted, area codes are 707. Lodging rates for two people range from $ (under $100) to $$$ (above $250) per night.

WHERE

Anderson Valley lies about 2 1/2 hours north of San Francisco. To reach State 128 from the Bay Area, exit U.S. Hwy. 101 at Cloverdale.

LODGING

Valley lodging is somewhat limited, so it's wise to have reservations. In addition to Boonville's small hotel, travelers will find one motel in Philo and a handful of bed-and-breakfasts between Boonville and Navarro.

The Boonville Hotel (895-2210; $-$$ includes continental breakfast) has 8 second-floor rooms and suites and 2 child- and pet-friendly suites in a separate building. Among the small bed-and-breakfasts in Boonville are **Anderson Creek Inn** (Anderson Valley Rd.; 895-3091; $-$$), with in-room fireplaces and an outdoor pool,

and **The Apple Farm's** "Room With a View" (895-2461; $).

In Philo, **Philo Pottery Inn** (State 128; 895-3069; $-$$) offers tidy rooms with baths in a handsome century-old farmhouse. The secluded **Pinoli Ranch Country Inn** (get detailed directions when you call; 895-2250; $$) has a suite with a view of the rose garden. Amenities include wine, evening dessert and drinks, and a lavish breakfast.

DINING IN DOWNTOWN BOONVILLE

The dining room at **The Booneville Hotel** (see Lodging above) has the best food in town. The **Buckhorn Saloon** restaurant is a good place for a drop-in supper of meat-and-potatoes fare. For a light lunch, try the **Boont Berry Farm Store**'s deli area and **Biscotti Notti**, which serves coffees, homemade biscotti, and pasta-type lunch and salad plates. Or grab a burger at the **Redwood Drive-In**. In addition to lunch and dinner, the **Horn of Zeese** is popular for its large country breakfasts.

SPECIAL EVENTS

Among the annual events at the Boonville fairgrounds are a free **Spring Wildflower Show** on the last Sunday and Monday of April and an old-fashioned **County Fair & Apple Show**, featuring a rodeo, sheep dog trials, square dancing, and a parade, in mid-September.

FOR MORE INFORMATION

Anderson Valley Chamber of Commerce (P.O. Box 275, Boonville, CA 95415; 895-2379). Mendocino Winegrowers Alliance (P.O. Box 11409, Ukiah, CA 95482-1409; 744-1363).

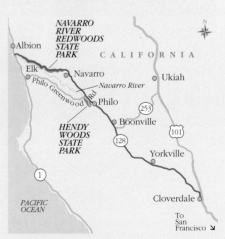

REGION	CALIFORNIA	
Where	X	120 miles south of San Francisco
When	X	Year-round destination

Carmel Valley
hideaways

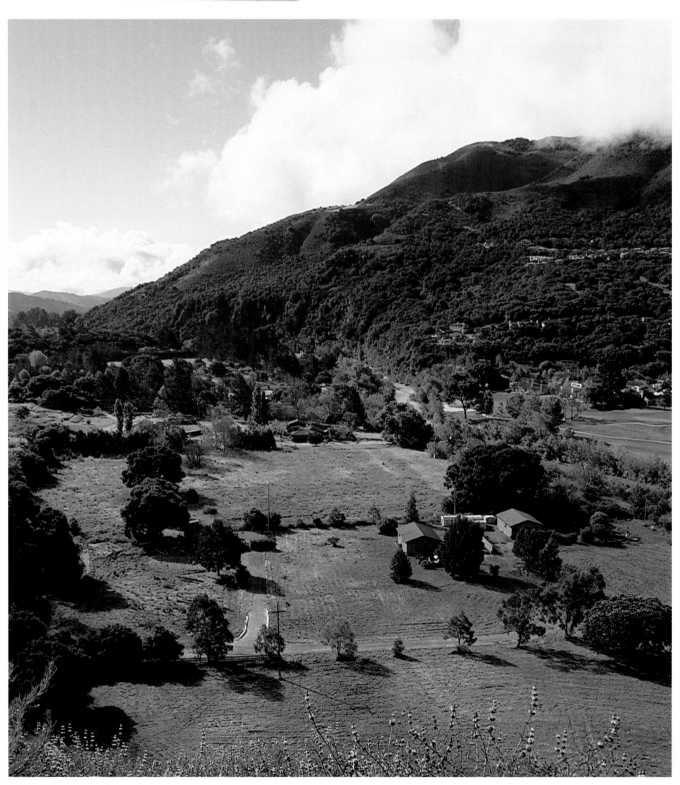

When coastal resorts are socked in by fog, rural Carmel Valley, which stretches inland for some 20 miles, makes a sunny alternative.

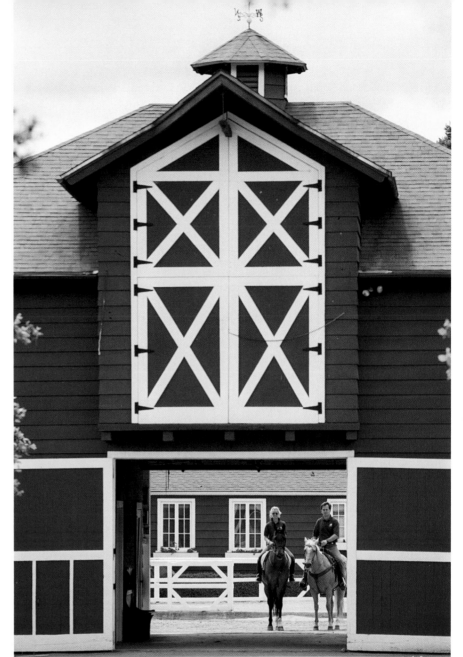

Even the barn looks good at Stonepine Estate Resort, a former Crocker mansion and one of the valley's most upscale havens.

With its wealth of natural and manmade attractions, the Monterey Peninsula draws hordes of visitors year-round. But Carmel Valley, tucked away to the south of its more famous neighbors, offers discriminating travelers fewer people, less traffic, and plenty of places for browsing, dining, and overnighting. At summer's peak, when the coastal towns of Monterey and Carmel are socked in by fog, the sunny valley beckons. So turn away from the traffic jamming State Highway 1 and head inland on Carmel Valley Road (County G16) for a lazy detour.

Despite championship golf courses, world-class tennis clubs, award-winning wineries, well-known resorts, and small shopping centers, the big steep-walled valley surrounded by the Santa Lucia Mountains is still a rural retreat, with working ranches, produce markets, and organic gardens. Carmel Valley Road (the main artery) has only two stoplights, and the valley's population of some 4,000 is thinly scattered over its 13-mile length. The affluent village of Carmel Valley remains unincorporated, and a huge chunk of open space nearby looks much as it did during the days of Spanish land grants.

From Wineries to Woodlands

Orchards, flower fields, and vegetable farms share the valley with vineyards. Though the Carmel Valley appellation is one of the state's smallest wine districts, seven wineries (several with tasting rooms) feature prize vintages. The first winery you'll see is striking Chateau Julien, the valley's largest. About 5 miles inland, the attractive French-style

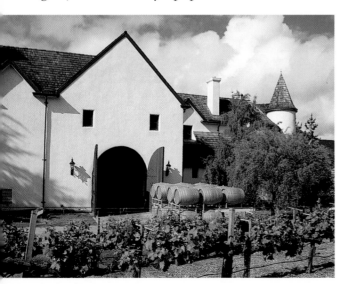

Attractive Chateau Julien Winery, the valley's largest vintner, is also the first one reached on Carmel Valley Road from the west.

facility provides a solid introduction to Monterey County wines. In the cobblestone courtyard and gardens outside the tasting area, picnic benches invite visitors to linger.

You can sample Carmel Valley wines with a meal at posh Quail Lodge Resort & Golf Club, just off Carmel Valley Road north-west of Chateau Julien. Stop for lunch at the informal Golf Club restaurant, or treat yourself to a sumptuous dinner at The Covey.

Continue up winding Carmel Valley Road to Garland Ranch Regional Park (8.5 miles east of State 1). Loll by the river's rocky shores or hike on a 20-mile network of trails. Pick up a map and bird checklist at the park's small visitor center.

The Village

In the village you can poke around art galleries, antique shops, and the small historical museum. Two tasting rooms let you sample local offerings from some small valley vintners.

⠿TRIP PLANNER⠿

Unless otherwise noted, area codes are 831. Lodging rates for two people range from $ (under $100) to $$$ (above $250) per night.

WHERE

Carmel Valley Village is about a 25-mile round trip from State 1 on Carmel Valley Rd. Turn onto the road at the Carmel Rancho shopping center, which fronts The Barnyard shops. End your journey in the village or continue through rolling hills a slow 40 miles to eventually join U.S. Hwy.101 south of Soledad.

LODGING

What with the quiet and the quail, an overnight in Carmel Valley feels like a weekend in the country—albeit a very civilized country with prices to match. In addition to posh resorts, several smaller secluded lodges, all on or near Carmel Valley Rd., offer a feeling of yesteryear retreats.

Carmel by the River RV Park (27680 Schulte Rd.; 624-9329; $) has full hookups for campers.

Quail Lodge Resort & Golf Club (8205 Valley Green Dr.; 624-1581; $$-$$$) and **Carmel Valley Ranch** (One Ranch Rd.; 625-9500, 800/422-7635; $ to $$) welcome golfers; the ranch also has horses.

John Gardiner's Tennis Ranch (114 Carmel Valley Rd; 659-2207; $$$ includes meals) caters to racket-carrying guests. **Los Laureles Lodge** (313 W. Carmel Valley Rd.; 659-2233; $-$$), the 1930s home of Muriel Vanderbilt, and **Robles del Rio Lodge** (200 Punta del Monte; 659-0170; $$ to $$$) are historic charmers. **Valley Lodge** (Carmel Valley and Ford rds.; 659-2261, 800/641-4646; $ to $$) has fireplaces and a big pool. Flower fanciers enjoy the lush gardens of **Hidden Valley Inn** (102 W. Carmel Valley Rd.; 659-5361, 800/367-3336; $$). Pricey **Stonepine Estate** (150 E. Carmel Valley Rd.; 659-2245; $$$), a former Crocker banking family mansion with stables, pool, and tennis courts, sits among 330 forested acres.

DINING

Lugano's Swiss Bistro, in The Barnyard (see directions below), offers crisp salads, superb onion soup, and fondues. In the village, assemble picnic makings at **Carmel Valley Market** in the shopping center or enjoy lunch at **Bon Appetit** (7 Delfino Pl.; 659-3559) or **Sole Mio Caffe Trattoria** (3 Delfino Pl.; 659-9119). For grand valley views, drive up to **The Ridge Restaurant** at **Robles del Rio Lodge**. Steak fanciers flock to **Will's Fargo Dining House & Saloon** (Carmel Valley Rd. in the Village; 659-2774) for dinner.

SHOPS

For a free horticultural tour of plantings throughout The Barnyard's multi-level collection of upscale shops and restaurants, meet in front of the **Thunderbird Book Shop and Café** at noon Sundays in summer. Don't overlook **Succulent Gardens & Gifts** at the center's north end, with its large display of weather vanes, table-top fountains, garden statuary, and planters. To reach The Barnyard, turn right on Carmel Rancho Blvd. and right again on Carmel Rancho Ln.

FOR MORE INFORMATION

Carmel Valley Chamber of Commerce (Box 288, Carmel Valley, CA 93924; 659-4000). Their office on Carmel Valley Rd. is in the heart of the village opens 1-5 Tues.-Thurs.

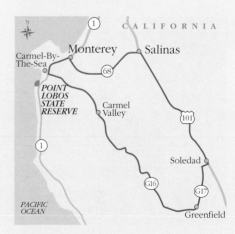

a Sierra Sampler

REGION	CALIFORNIA
Where X	4 to 5 hours southeast of San Francisco
When X	Summer to early-autumn destination

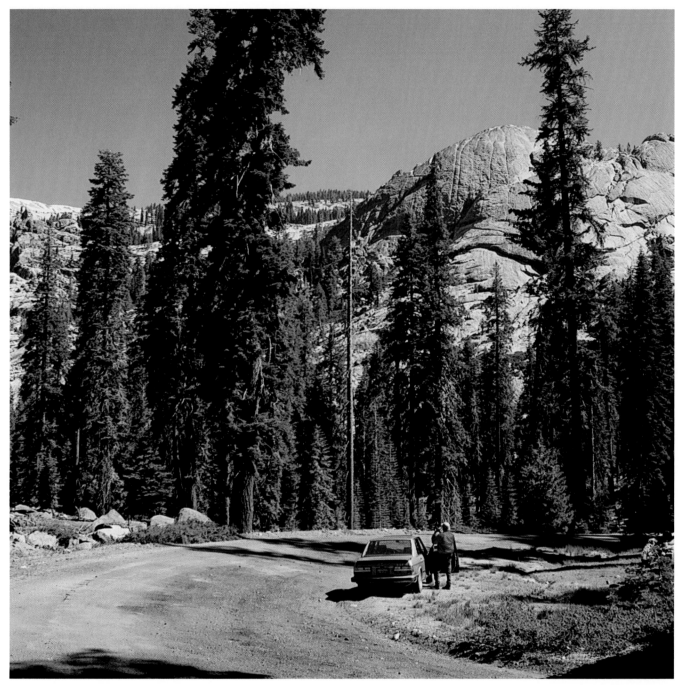

The Sierra Vista Scenic Byway is aptly named, as one traveler—taking advantage of a wide spot in the road—can attest.

The foothill town of Oakhurst is either the southern terminus of the Gold Country or a gateway to Yosemite National Park, depending on whether you are coming from the north or south. It's also the starting point to the Sierra National Forest's Sierra Vista Scenic Byway, a 100-mile loop that dips down along the northern shore of Bass Lake before heading northeast to the edge of the Ansel Adams Wilderness.

This is high country, topping out at the 7,308-foot Cold Spring Summit. Most of the drive is along paved roads, though the top of the loop takes you along a gravel stretch of about 5 miles. Your reward for sticking with it is a panoramic view of the Minarets, Mt. Ritter, and Mammoth Mountain, plus wide-open meadows ablaze with wild-flowers late into summer.

Talking Grizzly & Bass Lake Turnoff

Make a stop at the Southern Yosemite Visitor Center just off State Highway 41 (follow the

Oakhurst plaque marks the southern terminus of State Highway 49, which winds 310 miles north through the heart of the Gold Country.

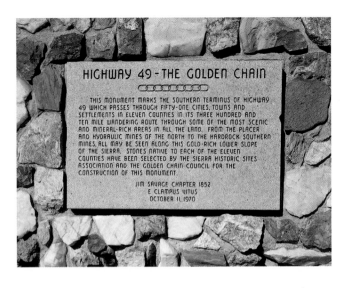

sign) in Oakhurst. Ask them about weather and road conditions, and be sure to pick up a copy of the free "Sierra Vista Scenic Byway" brochure, which outlines your tour. Before leaving town, look for the talking grizzly statue downtown at the intersection of State 41 and County Road 426. He'll give you a rundown of the many attractions at Bass Lake.

Take State 41 north to County Road 222, turn right, and follow signs to Bass Lake. As you near this popular resort, bear left on County Road 274 and stop at the Pines Resort area for sand-

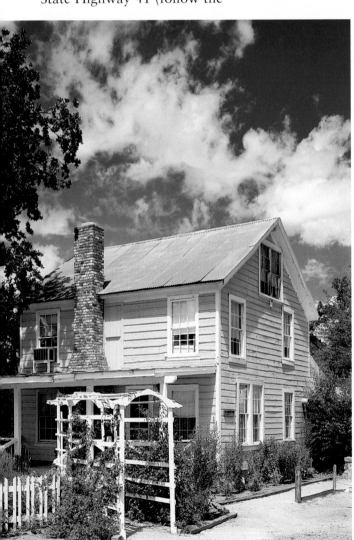

Built in 1870, the Laramore-Lyman House is one of a collection of historic buildings that make up Fresno Flats Historical Park in Oakhurst.

wiches and other picnic goodies. Just beyond the Pine Resort, head north on Beasore Road, which climbs gently through a mixed forest of old oaks and towering pines. Your eyes might be drawn to sunny meadows filled with crimson columbine or showy lupine, both of which bloom into August. Enjoy their beauty, but remember that picking flowers in national forests is illegal.

Just past the Cold Springs Summit, the scenery changes. Yellow pines give way to a dense forest of white fir, and all around you are the granite plugs and chiseled boulders left by glaciers that gouged the valley some 60,000 years ago. Here the pavement ends and the road gets a little bumpy, but don't worry—it's only for a few miles. This might be a good spot to take a break and enjoy lunch. There are several level areas with stunning views nearby.

Heavenly Vistas & an Indian Museum

At the Minarets Road (Forest Service Road 81) junction, turn right, following signage for Mammoth Pool Reservoir. If you feel like doing a little fishing, veer east on Mammoth Pool Road, or continue ahead until you get to the turnout for Mile High Vista, a spectacular overlook into the Ansel Adams, John Muir, and Kaiser wilderness areas.

At this point, the road begins to descend, passing two Forest Service campgrounds before turning into County Road 225. Just before reaching the junction of County 274 and the little town of North Fork, you'll come to the Sierra Mono Indian Museum. This cultural center for the Mono people, known for their fine basketry, displays various tribal crafts.

To finish the drive, take County 274 back along Bass Lake's northern shore, then County 222 and State 41 on to Oakhurst. To extend your stay in the southern Sierra foothills, head north from Oakhurst on State 49 to explore the Gold Country (see page 72).

TRIP PLANNER

Unless otherwise noted, area codes are 209. Lodging rates for two people range from $ (under $100) to $$$ (above $250) per night.

WHERE

Oakhurst is a 90-minute drive south from Yosemite. It can be reached via State Hwy. 41 from Fresno. From the San Francisco Bay Area, you can also take State Hwy. 140 east from Merced to Mariposa, and State Hwy. 49 south to Oakhurst.

LODGING

A number of inexpensive, family-style hotels line busy State 41 in Oakhurst. The most luxurious accommodation in and around the Yosemite Valley also is located here: the lavishly appointed, antique-filled **Chateau de Sureau** (P.O. Box 577, Oakhurst, CA 98644; 683-6860; $$$). Don't pop in without a reservation.

Sporting 20 lakefront suites—each with fireplace and deck—**Ducey's on the Lake** (North Shore Dr.; 800/350-7463; $$), at Bass Lake, looks like one of those impressive wood-and-stone lodges found along the shores of North Lake Tahoe. Ducey's is part of the **Pines Resort**, which also operates the **Pines Chalets** (North Shore Dr.; 800/350-7463; $$), cozy, two-story units with full kitchens, living rooms, and decks.

DINING

Every bit as elegant as the adjoining inn, the Chateau du Sureau, and just as pricey, is **Erma's Elderberry House** (48688 Victoria Ln., Oakhurst; 683-6800), which offers a daily 6-course prix fixe menu from around $65 per person. In Bass Lake, **Ducey's on the Lake** (see Lodging above) includes a waterside restaurant serving everything from pasta to several excellent fresh fish dishes.

ACTIVITIES

Sierra Mono Indian Museum (near North Fork via County 247; 877-2115; hours vary) sponsors a festival in early August with authentic dancing and crafts demonstrations. And if you'd rather do the scenic byway by bike than by car, an annual 100-mile ride, known as the **Grizzly Century**, takes place the first weekend of October; call 877-2218.

FOR MORE INFORMATION

Eastern Madera County Chamber of Commerce (corner of State 41 and County 426, behind the talking grizzly; 683-7766; open weekdays). Bass Lake Chamber of Commerce (P.O. Box 126, Bass Lake, CA 93604; 642-3676; open weekdays).

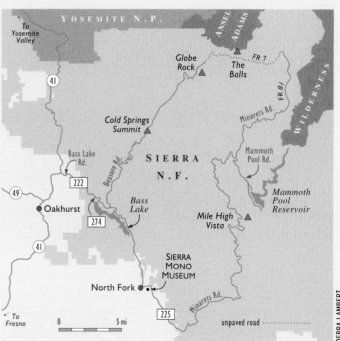

DEBRA LAMBERT

REGION	CALIFORNIA
Where X	3 hours north of Sacramento
When X	Best in spring for blossoms; late autumn for waterfowl

up the Sacramento River

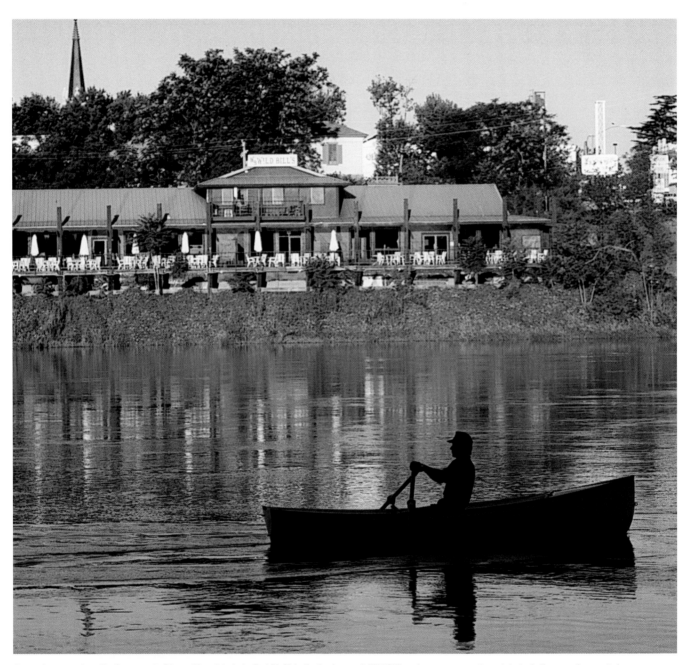

A morning row where the Sacramento River widens into Lake Red Bluff. In the background, Wild Bill's, where you can get a quiet steak dinner and a great view.

The upper Sacramento Valley has two fine examples of river towns: Redding and Red Bluff. Both look onto the big Sacramento River and have large trees, gracious buildings, and a sleepy pace. Instead of taking Interstate 5 or State Highway 99 from Sacramento, you might enjoy a ramble through quiet country towns on small roads that follow the levees.

Start your drive at Woodland, northwest of Sacramento on State Highway 113. This former mining camp, established in 1861, brims with turn-of-the-century architectural gems. Farther north lies Knights Landing, a small community somewhat reminiscent of hamlets along Mark Twain's Mississippi. Turn left here onto Fourth Street to reach State Highway 45. As the road angles northwest across open farmland, note the rice "checks"—flooded paddies surrounded by low-lying levees.

Colusa, 5 miles to the north, is a popular swimming and waterskiing center. Three miles southwest of town lies one of a series of Sacramento National Wildlife Refuges, winter homes for millions of migratory wildfowl. For a 3-mile self-guided auto tour or a 1-mile walking tour, get maps at the center.

State 45 continues north 23 miles to Hamilton City. From here, turn west to reach I-5 at Orland, 30 miles south of Red Bluff.

Touches of History

Red Bluff is a pleasant spot to take a downtown walking tour (maps at the chamber of commerce). Many of the handsome old buildings now hold antique stores: the most impressive may be the old I.O.O.F. Building, at Washington and Oak streets. At Washington and Ash streets, the 1880s Italianate Kelly-Griggs house serves as a museum devoted to Red Bluff's past.

More history lies just north of town at William B. Ide Adobe State Historic Park. Ide was the first (and only) president of California's short-lived Bear Flag Republic, in 1846, and for decades this humble adobe was said to have been his home. Though the adobe dates from his era, there's no proof Ide owned it. Still, the park provides a glimpse into life on an early California rancho as well as tables for picnics.

Around Redding

Turtle Bay Museums and Arboretum rises along a bend of the Sacramento River. It's the start of an ambitious dream that in time will encompass three museums and 500 acres of grounds. The first segment, Paul Bunyan's Forest Camp, honors the region's logging days. Outside, a miniature Sacramento River pours off a model Mt. Shasta. A suspension bridge will eventually replace the boardwalk that leads to the real river and

Friends enjoy an afternoon horseback ride around Redding. Mt. Shasta looms in the distance.

will link the site with an arboretum on the opposite riverbank.

The Sacramento River Trail, one of the prettiest riverside walks anywhere, begins a mile to the west. The route runs along the Sacramento's south bank, crosses over the river on a pedestrian bridge, and then leads you east to Caldwell Park. You can cross Diestlehorst Bridge (also pedestrian) back to your start, or linger awhile and explore the park's two small museums—the Redding Museum of Art & History and the Carter House Natural Science Museum. Both museums are open daily except Mondays.

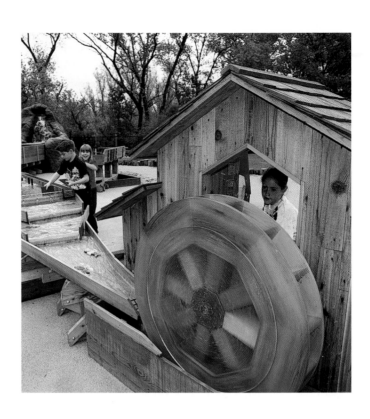

Paul Bunyan's Forest Camp, part of the Turtle Bay Museums and Arboretum complex, celebrates the region's logging days.

⇦ TRIP PLANNER ⇨

Unless otherwise noted, area codes are 530. Lodging rates for two people range from $ (under $100) to $$$ (above $250) per night.

LODGING

Redding has a full range of chain motels alongside I-5. Red Bluff's Victorian neighborhoods support a number of gingerbread-trimmed B&Bs: **Faulkner House** (1029 Jefferson St.; 800/549-6171; $) is a nicely restored 1890s Queen Anne, and **Jeter Victorian Inn** (1107 Jefferson St.; 527-7574; $-$$) dates from 1881.

DINING

Hatch Cover (202 Hemsted Dr., Redding; 223-5606) offers surf and turf with a view of the Sacramento River. **Jack's Grill** (1743 California St., Redding; 241-9705) doesn't look like much from the outside—or the inside.

But the steaks are superb, and the joint is a Redding tradition. The **Green Barn** (5 Chestnut Ave., Red Bluff; 527-3161) is another good steak house. **Wild Bill's Rib, Steakhouse & Saloon** (500 Riverside Wy., Red Bluff; 529-9453) has more great steak and a deck overlooking the river.

MUSEUMS

Hayes Antique Truck Museum (2000 E. Main St., Woodland; 666-1034; open daily Mar.-Oct., Thurs.-Tues. rest of year; small fee) has more than 1,000 vintage vehicles. **Kelly-Griggs Museum** (311 Washington St., Red Bluff; 527-1129; donations) is open 1-4 Thurs.-Sun. **William B. Ide Adobe State Historic Park** (21659 Adobe Rd., Red Bluff; 529-8599; parking fee) is open daily 8-dusk. **Paul Bunyan's Forest Camp** at Turtle Bay (800 Auditorium Dr., Redding; 243-8850) opens 10-5 Tues.-Sun.; small admission fee

includes entry to the Caldwell Park museums.

FOR MORE INFORMATION

Redding Convention & Visitors Bureau (777 Auditorium Dr.; 800/874-7562). Red Bluff Chamber of Commerce (100 Main St.; 527-6220).

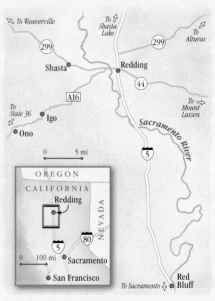

Trinity Alps
country

REGION	CALIFORNIA
Where X	5 hours northeast of Sacramento
When X	Best from spring through fall

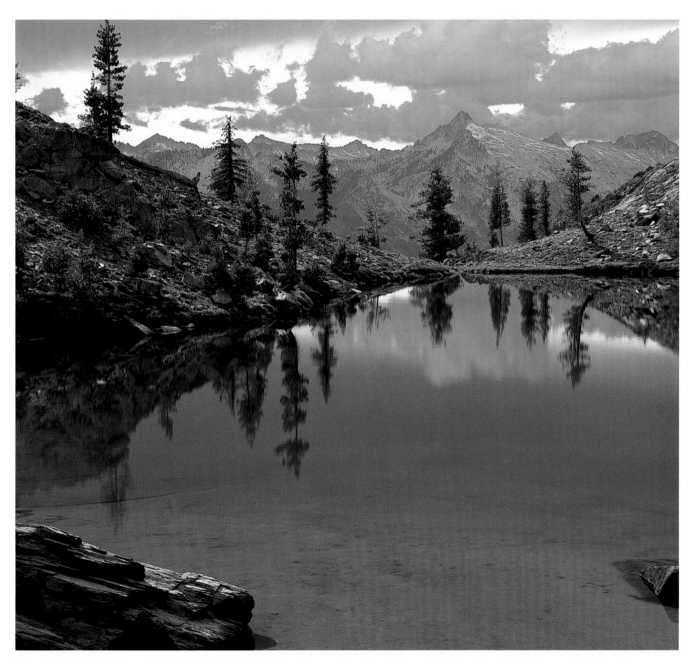

Viewed from the Siligo Peak area of the Trinity Alps, the Sawtooth Mountain seems to spring out of a rockbound tarn. Over a half-million acres of pristine wilderness await hardy travelers to the region.

Rugged and saw-toothed, Northern California's Trinity Alps are camouflaged by lower mountains. You scarcely notice them from Redding on Interstate 5, and even their easy approach from State Highway 299 has never brought the peaks much heavy traffic. Two roads explore their southern and eastern perimeters and link historic old gold towns. The main road, State 299 from Redding, parallels the Trinity Trail, famous as an Indian path, pioneer trail, and

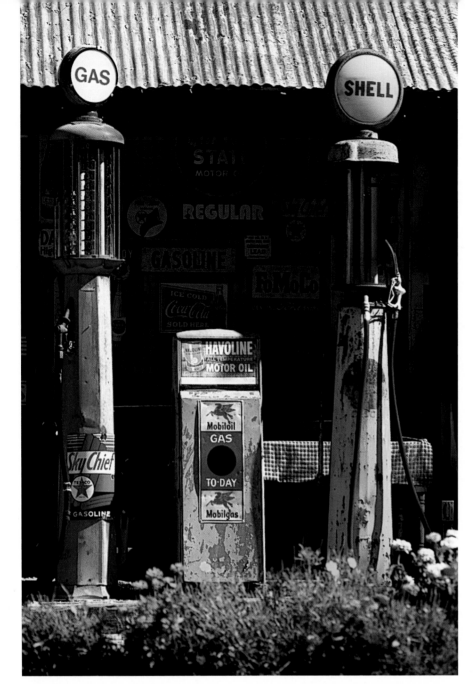

Antique gas pumps fuel Lewiston's historic image; the former gold camp contains a collection of antiques.

Litch Store is filled to the rafters with dry goods from the mining era.

Continuing along the highway, you'll pass Whiskeytown Lake. At the National Park Service visitor center at the east side of the lake (open daily 9-5 in summer; varies rest of year), you can stock up on information about this popular fishing, boating, waterskiing, scuba diving, and swimming spot.

Beyond Whiskeytown Lake, State 299 climbs over Buckhorn Summit (3,200 feet) before reaching the turnoff to the little hamlet of Lewiston. Drive 4 miles north and turn left on Deadwood Road to reach the funky collection of antique shops lining the road, including the Country Peddler with its relics from days gone by rusting out front. The one-lane Lewiston Bridge spans the Trinity River, which runs right beside the road. Here you'll find some of the state's best catch-and-release fly-fishing for salmon, steelhead, and trout.

Returning to State 299, it's another 15 miles to reach Weaverville, gateway to the Alps and seat of Trinity County. This former boom town at the junction of State 3 and State 299 came to life in 1851, when gold brought a flood of miners—including some 2,500 Chinese immigrants. Brick facades and exterior spiral staircases remain almost unchanged along Main Street. Drop by the chamber of

gold rush road. State Highway 3 from Weaverville through peaceful Scott Valley to Yreka was part of the old Oregon Wagon Road. In the 1850s, a gold rush brought thousands of miners to every river and gully in these parts.

There's still gold in these hills. Recreational panning is permitted in the Whiskeytown unit of the national recreation area. But today most visitors come to enjoy mountain wildflowers and dogwood in spring, the hot, lazy days of summer, and the brilliant show of fall colors.

Along the Trinity Byway

From Redding, head west 4 miles on State 299 to reach Shasta, the "Queen City of the North" during the 1850s and now a mere ghost of its former regal self. Today the crumbling brick ruins are protected as a state historic park. The old courthouse and jail are now a museum, and the refurbished commerce (210 N. Main Street) for a self-guided walking tour of the town's quaint stores, pleasant homes, and old churches. The free J. J. "Jake" Memorial Museum (508 Main Street; open daily April through November) contains mementos of the town's gold roots: a stamp mill, blacksmith shop, and miner's cabin.

Not to be missed is the Joss House State Historic Park (Oregon and Main streets), a lovely legacy of the area's often-persecuted Chinese. Built in 1853, "The Temple Among the Forest Beneath the Clouds" is a perfectly preserved Taoist temple, complete with hand-carved wooden altar. The temple (small fee) is open daily in midsummer, Wednesday–Sunday in spring and fall, and Saturday year-round.

Into Scott Valley

From Weaverville, State 3 roams north along the edge of Trinity Lake through maple, dogwood, fir, and pine trees as it begins its twisting ascent over Scott Mountain Pass into peaceful Scott Valley. Numerous hiking trails turn off a patchwork of gravel roads, including the popu-

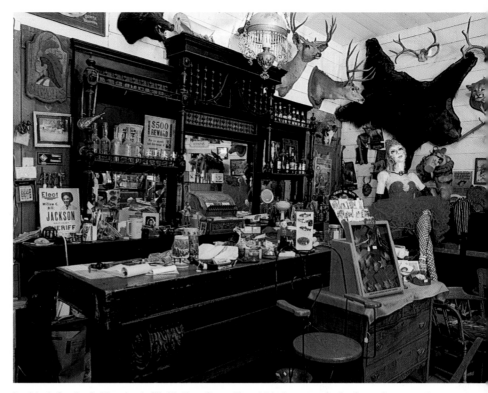

Lewiston's Country Peddler shop is filled to the rafters with an intriguing array of relics from a bygone past.

lar Lake Eleanor, Tangle Blue, Pacific Crest, Boulder Lake, and Stoddard Lake trails.

After 29 miles, you reach the turnoff to Trinity Center, relocated after the Trinity Dam flooded the old town in the 1960s and created the 25-mile-long Trinity Lake. The Scott Museum on Airport Road (open Tuesday–Saturday afternoons in midsummer; donations accepted) gives you an idea of how it was to live in the early mining days. Coffee Creek, 8 miles

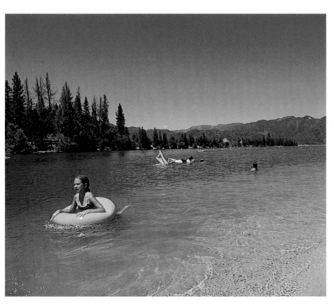

Whiskeytown Lake, a popular summer spot, is the jewel of the Whiskeytown-Shasta-Trinity National Recreation Area north and west of Redding.

beyond Trinity Center, is home to numerous summer resorts among the glacier-carved Alps.

Coming down from the mountain, you pass the almost deserted, block-long village of Callahan, a former trading center for miners and ranchers with a few century-old buildings lining the boardwalks. Tiny Etna, 15 miles to the north, appears almost a metropolis by contrast. Leave your car behind and walk the quiet streets of this picture-perfect village, once known as Rough and Ready. Pick up a free copy of the town's self-guided walking tour at the Scott Valley Drug Store with its old-fashioned soda fountain (511 Main Street).

Leaving Etna, another 15-mile drive past rustic barns and rolling farmland brings you to the sleepy little town of Fort Jones, the former site of an old army outpost. Another 15 miles and you've reached Yreka and

I-5, the end of your journey. Wild West lawlessness, Chinese tong wars, and an 1871 fire were not enough to destroy this tough town. Though the area is booming, some fine old restored 1850-era buildings still stand on Miner Street. The Siskiyou County Courthouse (311 Fourth Street) exhibits nugget and placer gold, and museum (910 S. Main Street) contains other displays. In summer, the Blue Goose Steam Train offers a 3-hour scenic tour. Call (842-4146) for details.

⇐ TRIP PLANNER ⇒

Unless otherwise noted, area codes are 530. Lodging rates for two people range from $ (under $100) to $$$ (above $250) per night.

WHERE

Two major highways wind through the Alps: State 299 (Trinity Scenic Byway) from Redding to the coast at Eureka and State 3 (Trinity Heritage National Scenic Byway) from Weaverville to Yreka. Allow at least 3 days to get the most out of this loop off I-5.

LODGING

Brigadoon Castle (9036 Zogg Mine Rd., Igo, near Redding; 888/343-2836; $$-$$$), tucked away on 86 secluded acres beside a roaring creek, resembles a Scottish castle. Amenities include a great hall with vaulted ceiling, a hot tub, and sumptuous breakfasts and dinners. The **Old Lewiston Inn** (Deadwood Rd., Lewiston; 800/286-4441; $), located on a prime fly-fishing stretch of the Trinity River, is a haven for anglers and seclusion-seekers. Fishing packages available. **Weaverville Victorian Inn** (1709 Main St.; 623-4432; $-$$) is a clean, no-frills motel with 67 rooms (cable TV, pool, some rooms with hot tubs) in the center of town. **Carrville Inn Bed and Breakfast** (Carrville Loop Rd. off State 3, Carrville; 266-3511; open mid-March through Oct.; $$) is a historic inn high in the Trinity Alps along the former

California-Oregon stagecoach route filled with antiques and featuring a menagerie of exotic farm animals, including llamas and emus. Cabins and resorts around Coffee Creek include **Ripple Creek Cabins** (Coffee Creek Rd.; 266-3505; $) and **Bonanza Creek Resort** (Coffee Creek Rd.; 266-3305; $). Both have 1-week minimum stays in summer.

DINING

At the **Lewiston Hotel** (Deadwood Rd., Lewiston; 778-3823), you can toss back a few beers with the locals and enjoy one of the biggest steaks you'll ever see at this one-of-a-kind, moderately priced restaurant and bar. **LaGrange Café** (315 N. Main St., Weaverville; 623-5325), open for lunch, dinner, and Sunday brunch, is known far and wide for its buffalo burgers, steaks, seafood, and wild game entrees. **Pacific Brewery** (401 S. Main St., Weaverville; 623-3000) has been a purveyor of ales since gold rush days. It has a full selection of microbrews and moderately priced breakfasts, lunches, and dinners. Stop by **Forest Café** (Manns Rd. off State 3; 266-3575), Coffee Creek's only year-round restaurant, for inexpensive home-style breakfasts, lunches, and dinners, or visit **Seng Thong** (434 Main St.; 467-5668) in Etna for expertly prepared, moderately priced Thai-Vietnamese cuisine that has been featured in *Bon Appétit*.

OTHER ATTRACTIONS

Highland Art Center (503 Main St., Weaverville; 623-5211), housed in a

century-old building, displays the works of local artists. **Alpen Cellars** (East Fork Rd. near Coffee Creek; call 266-3363 for an appointment) nestled in a remote mountain valley, features White Riesling, Pinot Noir, Gewürztraminer, and Chardonnay wines.

For hiking, backpacking, and mountain-biking maps, day-use permits, and other information, contact the Shasta-Trinity National Forest ranger station (State 299, Weaverville; 623-2121).

FOR MORE INFORMATION

Trinity County Chamber of Commerce (315 Main St., P.O. Box 517, Weaverville, CA 96093; 800/487-4648). Shasta Cascade Wonderland Association (1699 State 273, Anderson, CA 96007; 800/474-2782).

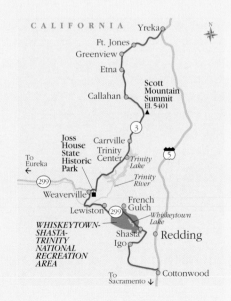

crossing California's
Lonely Corner

REGION	CALIFORNIA
Where	X	350 miles from Oregon to Nevada
When	X	Spring through autumn route

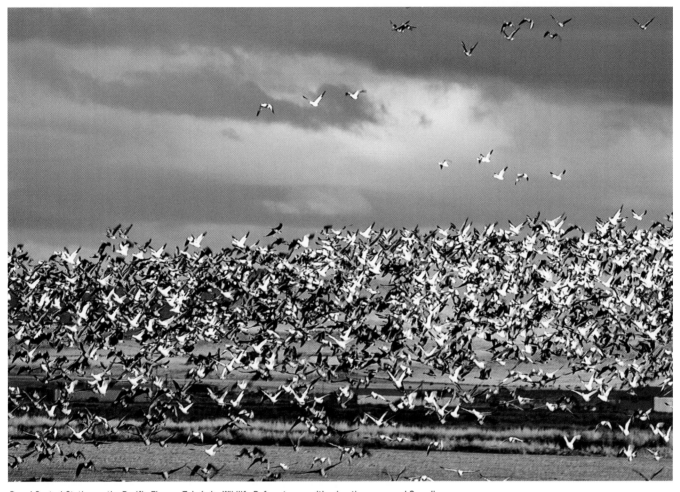

Grand Central Station on the Pacific Flyway, Tule Lake Wildlife Refuge teems with migrating snow and Canadian geese.

Over vast shallow lakes, migrating geese swirl in honking formations. Under brooding black lava flows, a honeycomb of caves awaits explorers who find themselves behind a windshield one minute, then crawling on their knees in pitch darkness the next, a flashlight beam their only guide. On a rippling landscape of sagebrush that gives way to alkaline flats, the earth's curvature becomes almost tangible. Each

car seems a tiny boat sailing on a huge and lonely sea before returning to a glittering port.

Welcome to the "Lonely Corner"—or "corners" in this case. California and Nevada meet in a northern region where forested mountains kneel to desert, where rainfall gives way to searing summer heat and aridity, and where twisting roads straighten and stretch for miles like a cold snake uncoiling.

Most travelers experience the region via mountain-skirting U.S. Highway 395, the route of choice between Southern California and the Pacific Northwest before Interstate 5. But U.S. 395 misses the heart of historic Modoc country and its battlefield, Lava Beds National Monument, as well as Nevada's sagebrush country and two famous deserts, Black Rock and Smoke Creek.

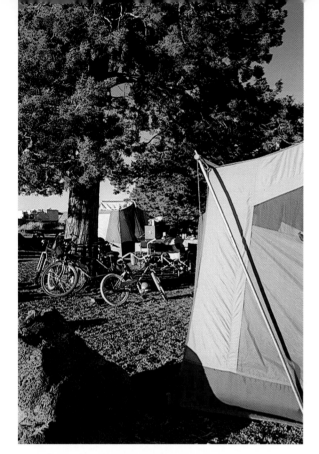

Travelers camp at Lava Beds, a seldom-full campground in the shadow of Caldwell Butte, site of some ice caves.

Captain Jack Country

Begin your journey in Klamath Falls, Oregon, a historic lumber town 61 miles east of I-5. As you head south on State Highway 39 through farmlands along the Lost River, you enter one of the most significant wetland regions on the Pacific Flyway—the migratory route taken by a majority of the West's waterfowl, including regal Canadian geese.

Entering California near Tule Lake Wildlife Refuge, turn off State Highway 139 at Homestead to skirt the refuge (overlooks and trails help you spot bird life) and enter Lava Beds National Monument.

Site of fierce battles in 1872 between a faction of Modoc Indians and the U.S. government, Lava Beds is a rugged natural redoubt. Here hundreds of caves (over 400 now known) and lava flows hid Indian Chief Captain Jack and his band during their last bitter struggle for freedom. "Nobody will ever want these rocks. Give me a home here," pleaded Captain Jack. He was denied (later hanged), but today the flows and tubes are one of the world's best volcanic parks, as well as a legacy to his pride and battle skills.

Continuing through Modoc National Forest, the route follows the Pit River into Alturas. The quiet town center's historic storefronts string out near the "skyscraper" landmark of its day: the 3-story Niles Hotel, an early 1900s survivor.

Heading east through patchy pine, sagebrush, and juniper, the road crests at scenic Cedar Pass and drops down into Cedarville (a good spot to spend the night) and Surprise Valley. A log-cabin trading post, built in 1865 and now located in Cedarville Park, is the oldest building in Modoc County. Early settlers were surprised to find lake beds here, hence the valley's name.

Ancient Lake Lahontan once inundated the large alkali lake beds that herald your entrance into a region of the Great Basin. This huge ice-age lake, fed by melting glaciers, covered much of northwestern Nevada.

Trail of the Wild Mustang

Herds of feral horses, progeny of steeds that escaped from early explorers and ranchers, roam much of Nevada's sagebrush country. Now known more romantically as wild mustangs, the herds can sometimes be glimpsed in the distance as you continue southeast about two hours across low rolling hills on a secondary highway, State 447.

At Gerlach, the road crosses a rail line and the gap between the Smoke Creek and Black Rock deserts, site of a 1990s world land-speed record. The BLM allows access to the dry lake-bed flats northeast of town, one of the West's best places to watch unusual sports like amateur rocket launchings and three-wheeled sail-craft as well as simply feel the immensity of the desert.

With a "bump hat" and a battery-operated lantern on loan from ranger headquarters, you can explore Lava Beds National Monument's fascinating wormlike holes on your own.

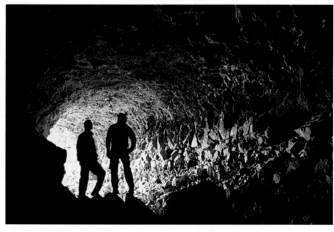

South of Gerlach on State 447, you pass a gypsum mine, then skirt dry Winnemucca Lake until you see Pyramid Lake, terminus of the Truckee River from California's Lake Tahoe. From Nixon, go west on State Highway 446 along the lake, where you can stop to fish or camp. Head south on State Highway 445 to pass the Wild Horse and Burro Center. Take a look at the BLM's busy corrals. Soon the Reno/Sparks metropolis swallows the last of the road's remoteness with an ever-expanding collection of housing developments.

⇐ TRIP PLANNER ⇒

Unless otherwise noted, area code 530 covers northeast California; area code 775 covers most of Nevada. Most towns are so small you won't need street addresses. Lodging rates for two people range from $ (under $100) to $$$ (above $250) per night.

WHERE

From Klamath Falls, Oregon, go south approximately 45 miles on State Hwys. 39 and 139 to California's Lava Beds National Monument. Continue on State 139 through the Modoc National Forest to State Hwy. 299 into Alturas, then cross the Warner Mountains and Cedar Pass to historic Cedarville, California. Gerlach and Reno lie to the south. Carry plenty of water on this trip.

LODGING

You'll want to spend at least one night (perhaps two or three) on this drive. You can camp in seldom-crowded Lava Beds National Monument, or choose from several small motels and bed-and-breakfasts in three stopovers along the way: Alturas, Cedarville, and Gerlach. Camping is also available on BLM-administered dry lake-beds near Gerlach and Pyramid Lake.

Lava Beds National Monument (667-2282; 41 campsites; fee) welcomes campers and RV owners on a first-come, first-served basis. Located on busy U.S. 395, Alturas has a number of motels and one large historic hostelry, the **Niles Hotel** (Main St.; 233-3261; $), with 10 antique-furnished rooms and baths.

For more of a back-road experience, stay in Cedarville's clean and neat **Sunrise Motel** (on State 299; 279-2161; $) or drive 7 miles to a working ranch bed-and-breakfast, **Cockrell's High Desert Lodging** (Star Route 11A, Cedarville, CA 96104; 279-2209; $).

In Gerlach, the eclectic, very basic **Bruno's Country Club** has 40 rooms (P.O. Box 70, Gerlach, NV 89412; 557-2220; $) but can be booked solid during nearby world land-speed record attempts.

DINING

You'll find few choices from Klamath Falls to Alturas. In Alturas, try popular **Nipa's** (233-2520), which serves good, big-portioned Thai and American food from a converted gas station that is a decorating and gardening triumph, complete with noisy cockatoos. **Niles Hotel** (see Lodging above) features seafood and prime rib dining in a historic setting.

In Cedarville, the owner/chef at **Country Hearth** (on State 299; 279-2280; open daily for breakfast, lunch, and dinner) rises early each morning to do all her baking. Locals especially enjoy the daily specials.

"Desert rats" have made **Bruno's Country Club** (see Lodging above) and Bruno's own ravioli into something of a legend, but the bar here is really its most popular feature in a land with few watering holes.

FOR MORE INFORMATION

Lava Beds National Monument (P.O. Box 867, Tulelake, CA 96134; 667-2282). Palomino Valley Corral mustang program of the Bureau of Land Management (775/475-2222). Bureau of Land Management (Winnemucca, NV, office; 623-1500). Modoc National Forest (441 N. Main St., Alturas, CA 96101; 233-5811).

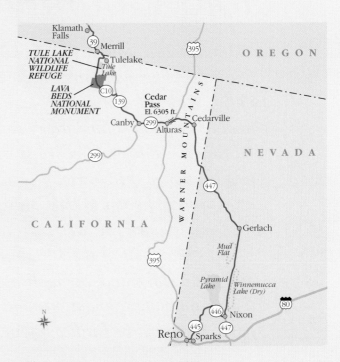

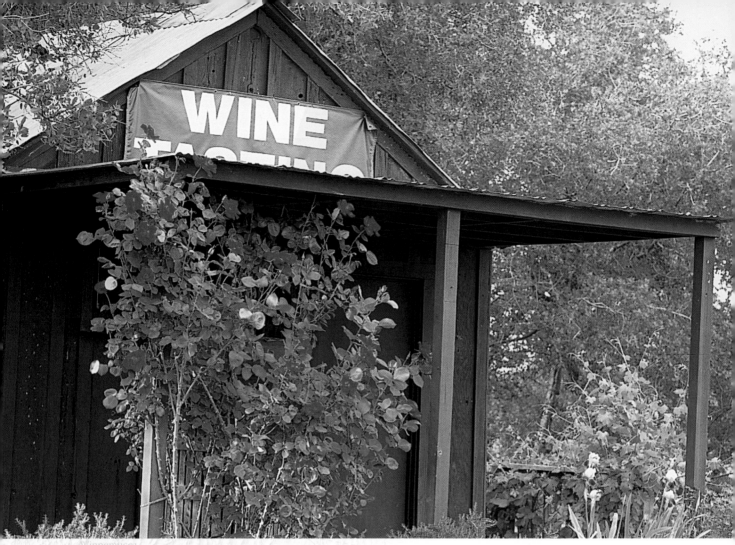

A onetime ranch bunkhouse now sees duty as the tasting room for Story Winery, one of more than a dozen Amador County wineries in Shenandoah Valley.

Gold Country Byways

"*Monday 24th this day some kind of mettle was found in the tail race that looks like goald first discovered by James Martial, the boss of the mill.*" *With this barely legible diary entry, Henry W. Bigler, a workman at Captain John Sutter's sawmill on the American River in Northern California, recorded the moment in January 1848 that would change the course of history. James Marshall's find focused the attention of the world on California and spawned a great migration that would open the West.*

Less than half of the 500 mining camps spawned between 1848 and 1860 still stand. Some disappeared entirely; others are little more than crumbling foundations and names on signposts. State historic parks preserve the former boom towns of Columbia and North

Bloomfield and Sutter's reconstructed sawmill at Coloma.

Appropriately named State Highway 49 winds through the Sierra Nevada foothills. You could probably drive its 310 twisting miles in a day or two, but it takes more time to investigate attractions along the highway and follow side roads often missed by visitors.

No matter where you wander, look for crumbling stone walls, scarred hillsides, mine tailings and headframes, rusted equipment, and overgrown cemeteries. These may be the only remnants of a once boisterous and prosperous settlement. Tombstones often tell terse tales of a prospector's unfulfilled dreams.

Southern Gold Camps

Travelers often miss the region between Oakhurst (the southern terminus of State 49) and Sonora, although it produced millions in gold. Oakhurst's New England–style church (now crowning a knoll in the cemetery) was built in 1891 when the town was called Fresno Flats; other survivors are gathered into Fresno Flats Historical Park off Highway 41.

Mariposa, 29 miles to the north, has served as a county seat since 1850, and its handsome courthouse is California's oldest. A 276-pound bell in the cupola has tolled the hours since 1866. Also of interest are the state's mining museum and a fine history museum.

A loop off State 49 leads to Hornitos, a one-time raucous, lawless site rich in history. Follow Old Toll Road (6 miles north of Mariposa) west 12 miles, returning to State 49 on Bear Valley Road. Hornitos was supposedly the haunt of Joaquin Murieta, certainly early California's most storied outlaw. Founded by Mexican miners who had been voted out of neighboring Quartzburg by an American law-and-order committee, Hornitos reflects Mexican influence more than any other Gold Rush settlement. (Incidentally, Quartzburg failed to survive despite its self-righteousness, or perhaps because of it.) The town's name is Spanish for "little ovens," possibly because of the unusual oven-shaped tombstones in the graveyard below St. Catherine's Church. Stroll past the jail and other buildings— many marked with bullet holes.

Back on State 49, stop by Coulterville for a look at the restored Hotel Jeffery, built in 1851 as an inn for stagecoach passengers. The adjoining Magnolia Saloon boasts an impressive 60-foot wooden bar. In front stand the local "hangin' tree" and the Whistling Billy steam engine, once used to haul ore from the rich Mary Harrison Mine. The 1851 Sun Sun Wo store is an adobe remnant of a large Chinese settlement.

Old Groveland is on State Highway 120, the northern route into Yosemite

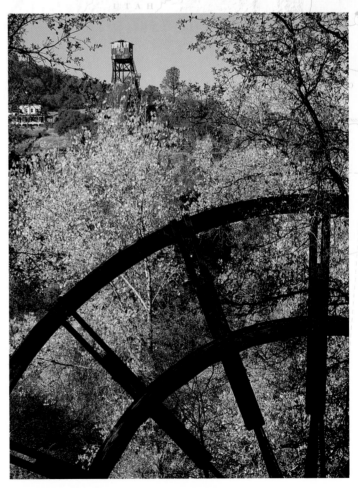

From this tailing wheel site, you look across rolling hills to the main buildings of Jackson's former mile-deep Kennedy Mine.

National Park. (Take Priest Road from Coulterville to State Highway 120, and turn east 3 miles.) Originally called Garrote in honor of the hanging of a horse thief in 1850, a later, presumably saner, populace changed the name. The carefully restored 1849 Groveland Hotel is popular with rafters who run the Tuolumne River. The Iron Door Saloon nearby, built in 1852, claims to be the state's oldest watering hole.

Back on State 49, head for Jamestown, 3 miles west of Sonora. The town may look familiar: it has appeared as a backdrop in many TV and movie Westerns. A local merchant describes it now as "two blocks of shops with a ton of collectibles." He forgot to add good restaurants and inns. Children (and adults) will enjoy panning at Gold Mining Camp on Main Street. When panning palls, ride behind a steam engine at Railtown 1897 State Historic Park (weekends only), tour the roundhouse, or enjoy a picnic in the park.

Murphys & Beyond

Take a 9-mile detour east on State Highway 4 from Angels Camp to charming Murphys. On your way, you'll see signs for two nearby caverns. The large stand of Sierra redwoods that makes up Calaveras Big Trees State Park, 20 miles beyond Murphys, was first seen by John Bidwell in 1841.

Murphys was settled in 1848 by John and Daniel Murphy, who came west in 1844 with the first wagon train to cross the Sierras. By 1849, the Murphys made their fortune and left town. But others stayed, prospered, and erected the substantial brick and limestone buildings you see today. Among the names in the Murphys Hotel register are Mark

Twain, U. S. Grant, Henry Ward Beecher, J. Pierpont Morgan, and Horatio Alger. Notorious stagecoach robber Black Bart signed in as "Charles Bolton, Silver Mountain." Seven wineries offer tours and tasting. Milliaire is downtown, others only minutes away. For sheer entertainment value, don't miss Kautz Ironstone Vineyards (Six Mile Road; 728-1251; open 11-5 daily).

Daffodils & Grinding Rocks

State Highway 88 intersects with State 49 at Jackson. Follow it east a few miles to the Pine Grove-Volcano Road turnoff for photogenic Volcano. Along the road, you pass Chaw'se Indian Grinding Rock State Historic Park, with a limestone outcropping so impressive that a replica resides in the Smithsonian Institution.

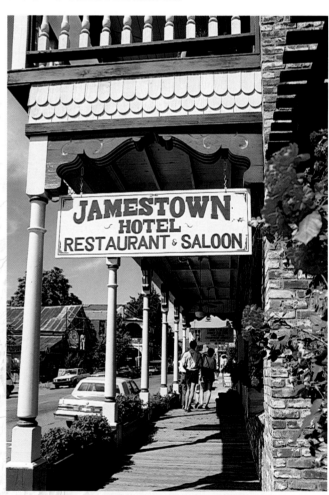

A profusion of antique shops, boutiques, restaurants, and small hotels lines Jamestown's main street.

Volcano's early residents were a lively bunch, as intent on developing their little town as they were in digging gold. At the height of its prosperity, the town boasted a public library, debating society, little theater, and astronomical observatory. Perhaps the most unusual souvenir is Old Abe, a cannon wheeled out during the Civil War by Union volunteers to put down a threatened maneuver by Confederate sympathizers.

Every spring, acres of golden daffodils carpet the slopes of a pioneer homestead 3 miles north of Volcano. Known as Daffodil Hill, the site is lovingly tended by descendants of the original settlers, who open it to the public during blooming season, mid-March to early April.

Wine & Music

At Plymouth, 9 miles north, a turn east onto Shenandoah Road from Fiddletown Road leads to Shenandoah Valley, Amador County's wine country. More than a dozen award-winning wineries, most with tasting rooms and picnic areas, lie on or near the road. Sobon Estate (14430 Shenandoah Road), housed in an 1856 winery, turned the original cellar into a free museum.

Fiddletown, 6 miles east of Plymouth, is a sleepy, tree-shaded village with a few 19th-century structures. It got its name when a member of the founding Missouri party chastised the younger men for "always fiddling around." (The town still hosts an annual fiddling contest.) Fiddletown once had the largest Chinese community outside of San Francisco; a rammed-earth adobe, built in 1850 as an herb shop, testifies to those days.

Georgetown Road

The 28-mile detour to Georgetown on State Highway 193 north of Placerville is worth the drive simply for the views you receive as the road twists, turns, and dips into the canyon of the South Fork of the American River at Chili Bar, a favorite put-in spot for rafters. Georgetown got its start

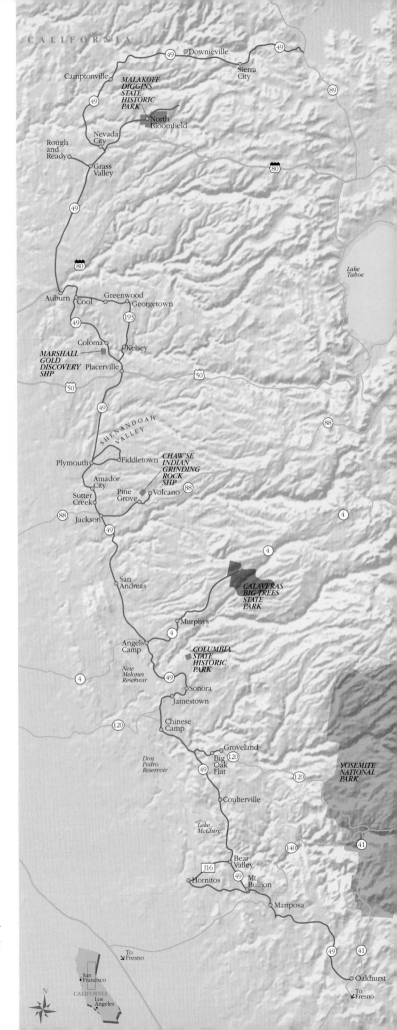

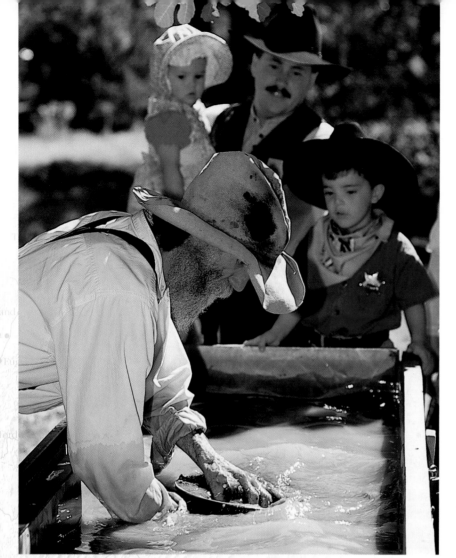

An oldtimer shows his avid audience exactly how to swirl a gold pan without losing the precious metal.

Around the Northern Mines

In autumn, gold still gleams on hillsides along the northernmost stretch of State 49—in the tinted leaves of aspen, cottonwood, liquidambar, and maple. On the 75 miles from Grass Valley to the highway's northern terminus at Vinton, State 49 climbs to 5,700 feet at Yuba Pass, crossing the Yuba River several times.

Malakoff Diggins State Historic Park, site of the world's largest hydraulic mine, is 16 miles northeast of Nevada City on North Bloomfield Road. The mine operated from 1866 to 1884, carving a canyon and flushing silt down as far as San Francisco Bay. Hiking trails in the 3,000-acre preserve give the best views of the gorge. The heart of the park is the remnant of once-bustling Bloomfield; 30 original buildings remain.

Between Nevada City and Downieville, 43 miles north, State 49 passes several small Gold Rush towns. Downieville nestles in a natural wooded amphitheater surrounded by lofty, pine-clad mountains. Though the population has dwindled considerably since the Gold Rush, and fire and flood have done their best to destroy this settlement, it is still one of the region's most true-to-life gold towns.

State 49 follows the old stage road on its way to Sierra City, overshadowed by the towering Sierra Buttes. A mile east of town, the Kentucky Mine Park and Museum allows a good look at a hard-rock gold mine that operated from the 1850s to the 1950s.

in 1849 when a group struck it rich while working the stream below the town. After a fire leveled the original city in 1852, it was rebuilt with the inordinately wide streets you see today. In 1855, some 3,000 people enjoyed the cultural life of the town. A few buildings from that era still stand. The two-story Georgetown Hotel was built on the site of an even earlier hostelry. The Shannon Knox House, the town's oldest residence, was constructed with lumber shipped around the Horn.

Greenwood, west of Georgetown on State 193, began in 1848 when trapper John Greenwood and his two sons set up a store to provide supplies to the hungry miners. The town grew to a respectable size in those early years, but little remains save the Pioneer Cemetery. Georgetown Road rejoins State 49 at Cool, a former stage stop on the Auburn-Georgetown route.

The Gold Country has two area codes: 209 south of Placerville; 530 to the north. Lodging rates for two people range from $ (under $100) to $$$ (above $250) per night.

WHERE

The Gold Country lies in the Sierra Nevada foothills east of Sacramento.

LODGING

The historic, 3-story **Hotel Jeffery** (1 Main St., Coulterville; 878-3473; $-$$) offers 21 rooms, a dining room, and an Old West saloon. The refurbished **Groveland Hotel** (18767 Main St., Groveland; 962-4000, 800/273-3314; $$-$$$) has 17 rooms and an acclaimed restaurant. **Jamestown Hotel** (18153 Main St., Jamestown; 984-3902; $$) has a nice bar and restaurant as well as rooms. **Dunbar House, 1880** (271 Jones St., Murphys; 728-2897; $$), an attractive inn with garden, lies a block from downtown.

A long-time favorite, the 18-room **Sutter Creek Inn** (79 Main St., Sutter Creek; 267-5606; $$) is close to shops but nicely shielded from traffic by lovely grounds. In Amador City, the **Imperial Hotel** (14202 State 49; 267-9172; $$) provides 6 whimsically decorated rooms, bar, and fine restaurant. **Coloma Country Inn** (345 High St., Coloma; 622-6919; $$), a 7-room country retreat, is nestled on shady lawns just outside the park.

Nevada City is noted for its inns, including two 19th-century charmers: **Emma Nevada House** (528 E. Broad St.; 265-4415; $$) and **Marsh House Bed & Breakfast Inn** (254 Boulder off Broad St.; 265-5709; $$). Downieville's **Sierra Shangri-La** (P.O. Box 285; 289-3455; $$; open Apr.-Dec., weather permitting) has 3 bedrooms in the lodge and 8 cottages, all on the Yuba River.

DINING

For exotic fare such as grilled elk, dine at **Bella Union** (18242 Main St., Jamestown; 984-2421; dinner Tues.-Sun., weekend lunch). Among other offerings, **Grounds** (402 Main St., Murphys; 728-8663) serves a tasty quesadilla sparked with fresh salsa.

Choices on Sutter Creek's main street include **Zinfandel's** (267-5008), **Sutter Creek Palace** (267-1300), and **Caffe Via d'Oro** (267-0535), the last is also open for lunch.

Posh Nosh (318 Broad St., Nevada City; 265-6064) is a local favorite for sandwiches and microbrews. **Cirino's** (309 Broad St., Nevada City; 265-2246) is a landmark, with traditional Italian dishes (seafood, pasta, veal) done well.

ATTRACTIONS

Fresno Flats Historical Park (49777 Rd. 427 off State 41, Oakhurst; 683-6570; small fee), an outdoor museum of weathered treasures, is open Wed.-Sat. afternoons. **California State Mining and Mineral Museum** (Mariposa County Fairgrounds south of town; 742-7625; small fee) opens daily Wed.-Sun. year-round, and Mon. in summer. **Mariposa County Museum and History Center** (12th and Jessie sts.; 966-2924; donation) opens daily Mar.-Oct., weekends year-round except Jan. **Railtown 1897** (5th Ave., Jamestown; 984-3953; tour, train charges) has daily roundhouse and shop tours, 1-hour train rides on weekends, Apr.-Oct.

Spelunkers will enjoy **Mercer Caverns** (1 mile north of Murphys off Sheep Ranch Rd.; 728-2101; fee) and **Moaning Cavern** (2 miles south of Vallecito off Parrotts Ferry Rd.; 736-2708; fee). **Calaveras Big Trees** (State 4, Arnold; 795-2334) provides a venue for camping, hiking, picnicking, swimming, fishing, and winter cross-country skiing in addition to 6,000 acres of *Sequoiadendron giganteum*. **Chaw'se Indian Grinding Rock** (Pine Grove–Volcano Rd., Pine Grove; 296-7488) has a fine Native American museum and shady campground.

Empire Mine (10970 E. Empire St., Grass Valley; 273-8522; fee), open daily in summer, weekends rest of the year, offers tours and hiking, cycling, and picnicking areas. **Malakoff Diggins** (off Tyler Foote Crossing Rd.; 265-2740, cabin reservations; Parknet at 800/444-7275, camping reservations) has ranger-led tours of the town. The **Sierra County Museum** (Main St., Downieville; 289-3423; donations) 1852 building is as interesting as the displays: it once housed a Chinese store and gambling den. **Kentucky Mine Park & Museum** (1 mile northeast of Sierra City; 862-1310; fee) has walking tours of the stamp mill and museum.

FOR MORE INFORMATION

Mariposa County Visitors Bureau (5158 State Hwy. 140, Mariposa, CA 95338; 888/554-9013). Murphys Business Association (P.O. Box 2034, Murphys, CA 95247; 800/225-3764). Amador County Chamber of Commerce (P.O. Box 596, 125 Peek St., Jackson, CA 95642; 800/649-4988). Nevada City Chamber of Commerce (132 Main St., Nevada City, CA 95959; 800/655-6569).

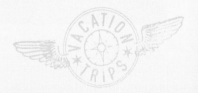

Columbia River Gorge
detours

REGION		OREGON
Where	X	Starts 15 miles east of Portland
When	X	Summer through fall destination

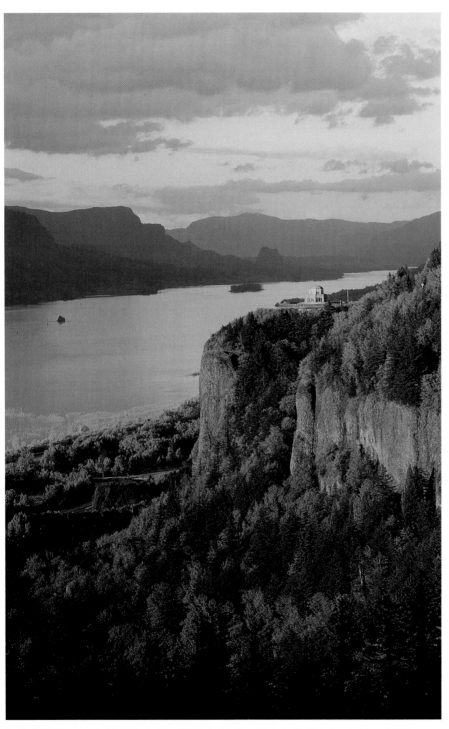

Anchoring the west end of the Oregon side of the Columbia River Gorge is the Vista House at Crown Point, a stone structure built in 1918 as a stopping place for early motorists.

There is no place on earth quite like the Columbia River Gorge. For 70 miles the powerful river cuts through towering volcanic rock formations on its route to the Pacific Ocean. Layers of basalt from scores of molten lava floods are visible in ancient cliffs that rise as high as 4,000 feet. More than 70 waterfalls, the greatest concentration in North America, cascade down cliff faces.

Long a transportation corridor for explorers, trappers, and pioneers, the gorge became a tourist destination after construction of the Columbia River Highway in 1913–15. The first major paved road in the Northwest, it was then considered an engineering marvel. Although it has long since been replaced by Interstate 84, remnants of the historic highway, old U.S. Highway 30, can still be traveled by car or on foot.

A 22-mile stretch between Troutdale and Ainsworth State Park is a particularly beautiful drive. The narrow highway winds along the basalt cliffs, offering extraordinary views and access to seven waterfalls, including 620-foot Multnomah Falls, Oregon's top tourist attraction.

High above the river along the old highway, you'll find calendar

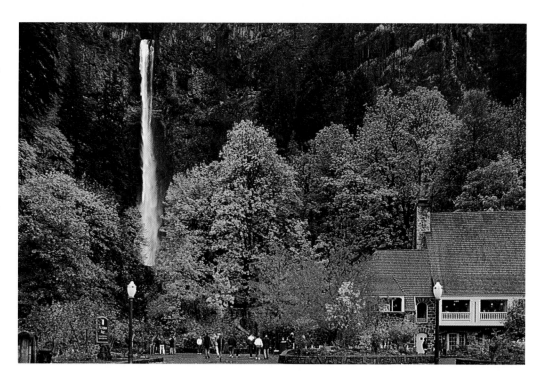

It could be a pretty fall postcard: Multnomah Falls Lodge at the base of the 620-foot-high cascade. The old lodge is now a restaurant and visitor center.

and postcard scenes from Women's Forum State Park. At Crown Point State Park, enjoy a panorama of the gorge from the upper level of the 1918 Vista House, an octagonal structure built from basalt stone as a rest stop for early motorists.

The Gorge Act

Builders of this highway put preservation before other considerations when they planned the route. Impact on the environment was to be minimal, and impact on the senses monumental. The idea was to make the beauty of the gorge accessible to all and to impress upon visitors the necessity of protecting it for the future.

Basically, that is the philosophy behind the 1986 Gorge Act, which created the Columbia River Gorge National Scenic Area. The act seeks a delicate balance between conservation and development in a 292,500–acre area along the Oregon and Washington shores of the Columbia River between the Sandy River, near Troutdale, and the Deschutes River, east of The Dalles, Oregon.

The act stipulated that federal money would help build interpretive and conference centers, one in Oregon and another in

Washington. In 1993, Skamania Lodge, a mountain resort and conference center, complete with 18-hole golf course, tennis courts, and nature trails, opened in Stevenson, Washington. Thanks to its excellent river–view restaurant, it quickly became a popular destination for both tourists and diners. Just a short walk away from the lodge is the Columbia Gorge Interpretive Center, with historical, geological, and cultural exhibits.

In 1997, the Columbia River Gorge Discovery Center in The Dalles opened. The center is linked by a lobby to the Wasco County Historical Museum. The high-ceilinged lobby is designed to represent the gorge itself, with 30-foot-high Douglas fir tree trunks along a black granite replica of the Columbia River. Its walls are jigsaw patterns of basalt rock, mounted in layers like the basalt flows that formed the gorge's walls.

The center is another good place to learn about the gorge's

geology, history, economy, and culture. Displays teach everything from Native American lore to practice in riding a sailboard. Visitors can mount an actual board and watch themselves riding the Columbia River waves on a video monitor. In recent years, the town of Hood River, Oregon, has become an international windsurfing center. Winds in the gorge create a sort of wind tunnel effect, which lures windsurfers from around the world. On warm summer days, their colorful sails look like butterflies flitting across the choppy river.

Roll On, Columbia

There's no better way to get acquainted with the mighty Columbia River than to ride its waves. At Cascade Locks, you can board the triple-decked Columbia Gorge sternwheeler for a two-hour cruise, with a running commentary on the river and its history by the captain.

Heading downstream toward Bonneville Dam, the boat passes

under the Bridge of the Gods. Built in 1926, the graceful, silver cantilever bridge linking Oregon and Washington is part of the Pacific Crest Trail that stretches from Canada to Mexico. The original Bridge of the Gods, which figures in Indian legends, resulted from an ancient landslide that changed the river's course. Reminders of that slide are still visible in the scarring of nearby mountains.

Another natural attraction on the Washington shore is Beacon Rock. Jutting up 848 feet, it is the core of an extinct volcano and, next to the Rock of Gibraltar, the world's second largest monolith. Lewis and Clark named it when they passed this way in 1805. They sent a scout scrambling to the top to determine if the Pacific Ocean was visible. (It's not.) Now there's a trail up the rock. Even without the ocean, the view is spectacular.

Powerhouses & Fish Ladders

Bonneville Dam, built in 1936, has visitor centers on both the Oregon and Washington sides of the river. Both are worth visits. In fact, next to Multnomah Falls, the dam is the gorge's most popular draw.

Visitors are welcome every day at Bradford Island Visitor Center, which is reached by driving over the gate of the navigation lock and across the top of the first powerhouse. The navigation lock has its own small visitor center. Visitors are also welcome at the turn-of-the-century fish hatchery, just down the road from the lock. The entire area on the Oregon side of the river is listed on the National Register of Historic Places.

To reach the Washington Shore Visitor Complex and get up close and personal with the immense generators, drive 3 miles east to cross Bridge of the Gods, then 2 miles west on State Highway 14. An escalator rising 113 feet gives visitors a bird's-eye view of the eight generators, and a walkway just above floor level allows a stroll to the surface of a generator and a peek inside at the spinning turbine. The vibrating floor is an eerie reminder that just below your feet immense amounts of water are crashing past, making turbine blades whir to produce electricity.

At both visitor centers you get good views of the variety of fish that pass through the dam, which is becoming more fish-friendly since the introduction of fish screens and newly designed turbines. But fish are still counted the way they have been since 1938—by people.

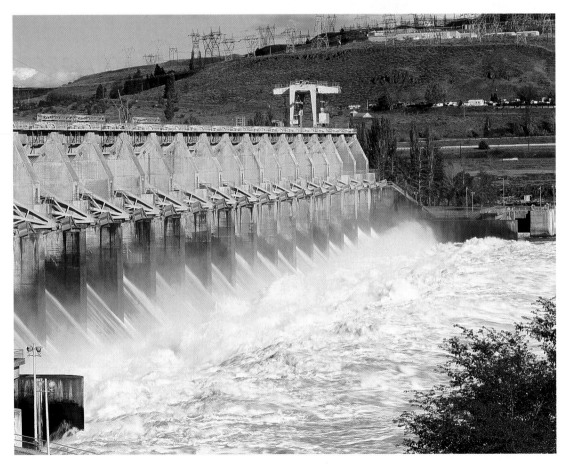

The Dalles Dam, at the eastern end of the gorge, spills water to aid in the wild salmon recovery program.

You can also watch fish at the Bonneville Fish Hatchery, built in 1909. Its grounds are beautifully landscaped with stone-lined viewing ponds and woodsy trails. Immense trout are close enough to touch, and sturgeon look absolutely prehistoric, which they are.

Gorgeous Gorge

But the main attraction of the Columbia River Gorge will always be its sheer beauty. For the full sensual experience, follow one of the many hiking trails into the hills and around the water-falls. Many hiking guides are available at area bookstores.

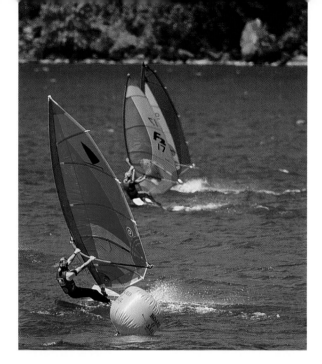

The Columbia River at the mouth of the Hood River is windsurfing central.

⇐ TRIP PLANNER ⇒

Unless otherwise noted, area codes are 541. Lodging rates for two people range from $ (under 100) to $$$ (above $250) per night.

WHERE

The Columbia River Gorge National Scenic Area begins about 15 miles east of Portland on I-84 and extends about 70 miles, past The Dalles.

LODGING

In Cascade Locks, the **Best Western Columbia River Inn** (735 SW WaNaPa St.; 374-8777, 800/595-7108; $-$$) has river views and an indoor pool, spa, and exercise room. Across the river in Stevenson, WA., the **Skamania Lodge** (1131 Skamania Lodge Dr.; 509/427-7700, 800/221-7117; $$-$$$) is an elegant mountain resort, complete with 18-hole golf course and a highly rated restaurant. The elegant **Columbia Gorge Hotel** (4000 Westcliff Dr., Hood River, OR; 386-5566, 800/345-1921; $$-$$$), built in 1921 and renovated in the 1970s, offers great river views and a fine restaurant.

DINING

Both the **Skamania Lodge** and the **Columbia Gorge Hotel** (see Lodging above) have excellent restaurants. The dining room of the historic **Multnomah Falls Lodge** is open from 8 a.m.–9 p.m. for meals (503/695-2376). For more casual fare, try the **Charburger** (714 SW WaNaPa St., Cascade Locks, OR; 374-8477). Indian and pioneer arti-facts decorate the spacious restau-rant, which has a good river view.

ATTRACTIONS

The **Columbia River Gorge Discovery Center** and the **Wasco County Historical Museum** (The Dalles, OR; 296-8600) are open 10-6 daily; there is an admission charge. The **Columbia Gorge Interpretive Center** (Stevenson, WA; 509/427-8211) opens daily 10-7 in the summer, 10-5 in the winter; admission is charged.

The Columbia Gorge sternwheeler, operated by **Columbia River Cruises** in Cascade Locks, makes three 2-hour cruises daily during the summer. Call 374-8427 for information.

Bonneville Dam's **Bradford Island Visitor Center** and the **Washington Shore Visitor Complex** (374-8820) are open daily 9-5.

FOR MORE INFORMATION

The Columbia River Gorge Visitors Association (404 W. Second St., The Dalles, OR 97058; 800/984-6743) has maps and other information.

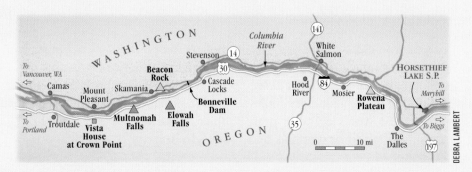

REGION	OREGON	
Where	X	90-mile loop from Portland
When	X	Spring through fall

Willamette Valley *sampler*

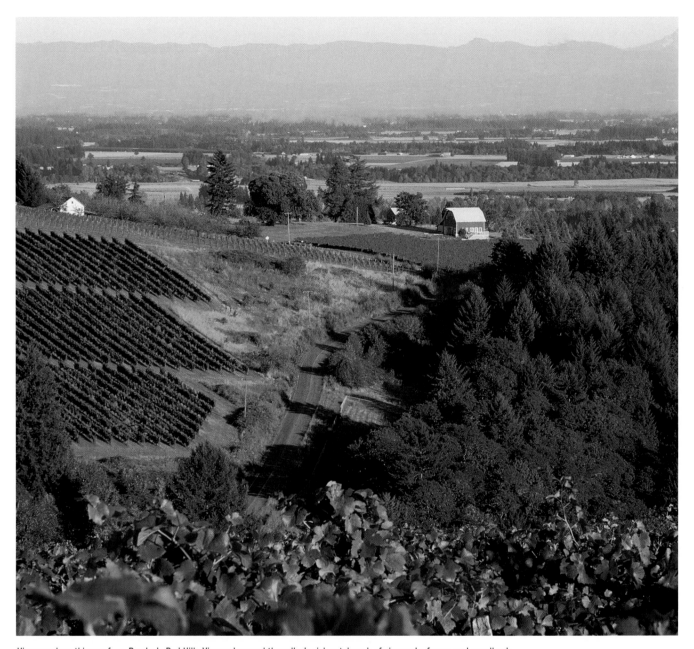

Views such as this one from Dundee's Red Hills Vineyards reveal the valley's rich patchwork of vineyards, farms, and woodlands.

Graced with elegant oaks and evergreens, a fish-thick river, grasslands, rolling hills, and an Old World sensibility, the green Willamette Valley is one of the West's legendary destinations—a fabled land of milk and honey. Weary Oregon Trail pioneers were sustained by dreams of making a wonderful new life here, and the valley didn't disappoint them. Amazingly, it's even more of an Eden today.

There's staggering abundance, especially in summer and early fall when vastly diverse crops—from hops to hazelnuts and countless fruits in between—are at their peak, flower fields bloom, crisply verdant vineyards stretch for miles, and tasting rooms stay open longer as wineries offer new releases.

Add historic small towns, specialty gardens, and plenty of back roads to explore, and abundance also becomes the challenge for travelers. Our route samples the valley's best offerings on a loop through its northern end.

End of the Oregon Trail

We begin southeast of Portland, at End of the Oregon Trail Interpretive Center (1726 Washington Street) in Oregon City. Emigrants arrived here in the mid-1800s and camped on Abernathy Green before making permanent homes in the valley. Large replicas of wagons contain exhibits, hands-on 19th-century activities, and performance space. The center opens most days at 9, the first tour is at 10. (For tour hours, call 657-9336; admission is charged.)

From here, follow State Highway 99 E southwest to the

historic communal town of Aurora. History buffs will want to explore the furniture, quilt, and textile exhibits in the Old Aurora Colony Museum (corner of 2nd and Liberty streets) or take in the antique stores.

Bells, Bearded Iris & a Bridge

Approach the German farming community of Mt. Angel at noon or 6 p.m. and you'll hear the bells of Mt. Angel Abbey. Built in 1883 by Benedictine monks, it crowns a hill overlooking the town. Visit for its architecture, especially the beautiful library, and the panoramic view. A clear day offers heavenly profiles of mounts Hood, St. Helens, Adams, and Rainier to the north.

Walking maps are available in the gift shop. For information on private retreats at the abbey, contact the Retreat House (845-3025).

Two miles south of town on old State Highway 214, you'll see signs for one of the valley's three dozen covered bridges, The Gallon House Bridge, named during Prohibition when a German farmer sold gallon jugs of bootlegged schnapps here.

The classic small town of Silverton is home to the Oregon Garden, destined to be one of the Northwest's grand display gardens; its 60-acre first phase opens in 2000. From early May through mid-June, myriad tones of bearded iris bloom on 250 acres at Cooley's Gardens (11553 Silverton Road S.E.;

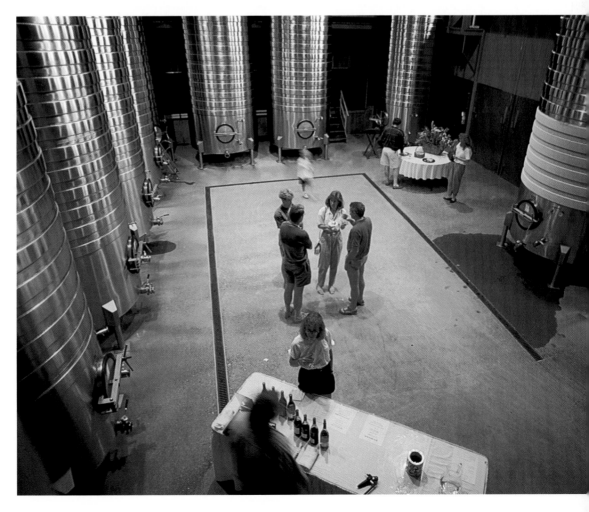

Rex Hill Winery is a popular spot for tastings and a cool stop for summer travelers, who often bring a lunch to enjoy at the winery's picnic sites.

873-5463); peak bloom is May 15–30. In season, 5 acres of beds and garden spaces are open daily.

Continue your valley drive by going west on the Silverton Road (State Highway 213), crossing Interstate 5, and passing through the state capital of Salem. If you have time, take a 30-mile loop southeast from Silverton on State Highway 214 to see 10 beautiful waterfalls at Silver Falls State Park. State 214 loops back and meets State Highway 22 east of Salem.

When the irises are in peak bloom (around the end of May), take a detour to Schreiner's Iris Gardens near Salem (call 800/419-4747 for directions) for a self-guided tour of the flower fields or for a picnic on the grounds. Plants, cut flowers, and gifts are also available.

Along Highway 99W

About 10 miles west of Salem, turn north on State Highway 99W, the wine country's thoroughfare. Signs along the highway point out most wineries. Many are easily accessible, some tucked away in the hills down long winding roads; a map is a necessity.

Follow State 99W north to Amity. You'll see signs leading to the Lawrence Gallery/The Oregon Wine Tasting Room (19702 S.W. Highway 18; 843-3787), where you'll find a changing selection from over 50 Oregon wineries (including those without tasting rooms). The restaurant here is a good choice for lunch.

Two elegant country inns offer panoramic valley views: Wine Country Farm, near Dayton, is also an Arabian horse farm. (The Joel Palmer restaurant, specializing in wild mushroom cuisine, is nearby.) Youngberg Hill Vineyard & Inn,

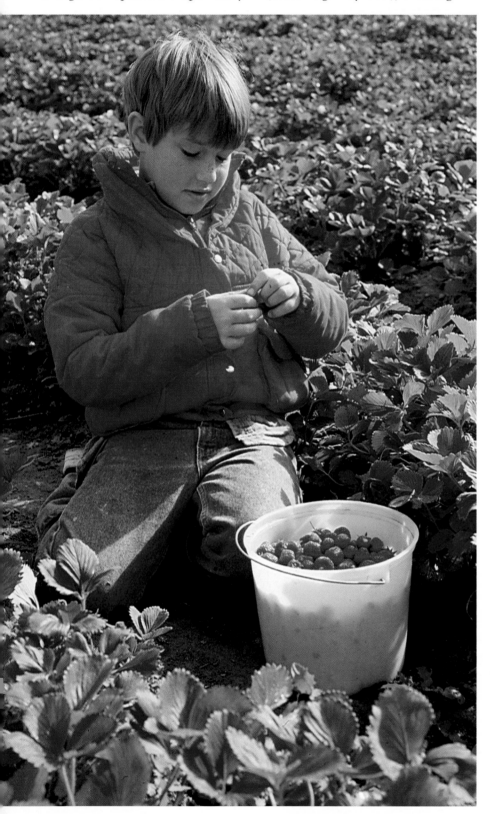

Youngster samples garden-fresh strawberries, just one of the valley's many succulent berry varieties.

outside the growing town of McMinnville, has its own wine label.

McMinnville is famous for the prestigious International Pinot Noir Festival held each summer on the grounds of picturesque Linfield College. It's always a sellout; call early for details on getting tickets (800/775-4762).

From here north, Highway 99W gets busier as it leads you to Newberg and Yamhill, the bustling southwest suburbs of Portland.

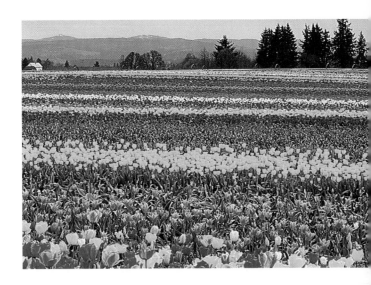

Spring fields of tulips at the Wooden Shoe Tulip Company near Mt. Angel.

▚TRIP PLANNER▞

Unless otherwise noted, area codes are 503. Lodging rates for two people range from $ (under $100) to $$$ (above $250) per night.

WHERE

Interstate 5 and the Willamette River provide parallel spines for the over-100-mile-long valley. It's 50 miles wide in some places, and lies between the state's two largest cities, Portland to the north and Eugene to the south.

LODGING

Two farmhouse bed-and-breakfasts between Mt. Angel and Silverton offer quaint rural settings: **Abiqua Creek Farms B&B** (11672 Nusom Rd.; 873-6878; $) and the **Egg Cup Inn B&B** (11920 Sioux St.; 873-5497; $).

Elegant country inns offer panoramic valley views. **Youngberg Hill Vineyard & Inn** (10660 S.W. Youngberg Hill Rd.; 472-2727, 888/657-8668; $$), outside McMinnville has French country décor. **Wine Country Farm** (6855 N.E. Breyman Orchards Rd.; 864-3446, 800/261-3446; $-$$) is near Dayton.

Many of the valley's several dozen bed-and-breakfast options—always a great way to get back-road insider tips—can be found in the **Border to Border Bed & Breakfast Directory**; call (800) 841-5448 for details.

DINING

Two Dundee restaurants offer a small-town setting. Popular appetizers at **Tina's** (760 Highway 99W; 538-8880) include pan-fried oysters with lemon-caper mayonnaise and warm chèvre rolled in hazelnuts with roasted garlic. **Red Hills Provincial Dining** (276 Highway 99W; 538-8224), a cozy Craftsman-style restaurant, is known for its Dungeness crab cakes with sun-dried tomato aïoli, home-made breads, and ice creams.

WINERY TIPS

Many wineries are family-owned, making only a few thousand cases per year that are primarily consumed in-state—a great reason to visit. Most wineries offer free samples; a few charge a small fee, often good toward a purchase. Oregon Wine Advisory Board's free brochure, *Discover Oregon Wineries*, (800) 242-2363, provides details and comprehensive maps.

PRODUCE STANDS

Firestone Farms, an elaborate road-side stand south of Dundee, sells produce plus a vast array of Northwest cottage industry products. Summer berries—including strawberries, logan-berries, gooseberries, red and black raspberries, Marionberries, and boy-senberries—are here fresh in season, and in sauces and preserves. Their berry or peach milkshakes are reason enough to stop.

FOR MORE INFORMATION

For a Silver Falls Tour Route brochure with information on Mt. Angel and Silverton, call 845-6882; you will also receive information on Mt. Angel's Oktoberfest.

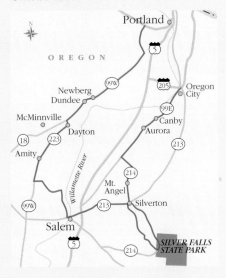

REGION	OREGON
Where	X	100 miles northwest of Portland
When	X	Year-round destination

Astoria's
quirky charm

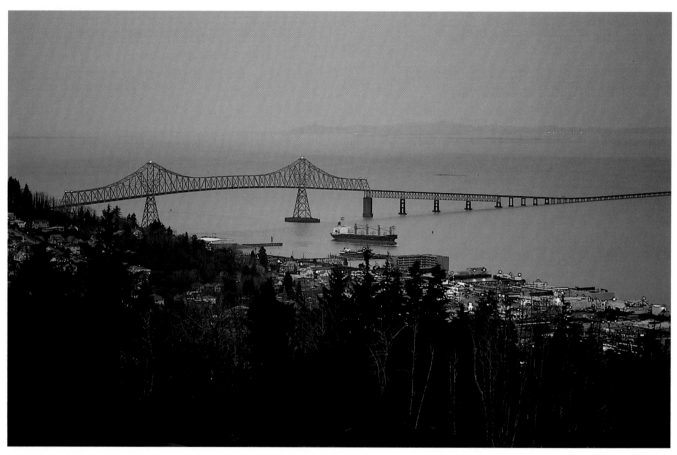

The 4-mile-long Astoria-Megler Bridge spans the Columbia River to join Oregon and Washington; you can enjoy this view from the Astoria Column.

Astoria has always looked to the river for good things: fish, most of all, but also ships to carry those fish—as well as a fortune in fur and lumber—to buyers around the globe. But recent years have been hard on this historic town, the oldest American outpost in the western U.S. The fishing and logging industries declined, leaving Astoria to hunker down and look to the future.

The wait was worthwhile as better times have come for its downtown. Cafés, galleries, and shops of all descriptions are opening, and business is up everywhere. Once again, the good fortune has come from the Columbia River.

Museum Walks

Cruise ships have discovered this great western river and the town just a few miles from its mouth. From spring through fall, both day trips out of Portland and week-long cruises up the Columbia now regularly include a stop at Astoria. The ships approach the foot of 17th Street, dropping anchor next to the old lightship *Columbia* outside the Columbia River Maritime Museum, and release their passengers for several hours of shore leave, just enough time for a brief introduction to this eminently walkable town. An overnight stay gives you time to linger.

Start your exploration where the tour passengers do—at the nationally acclaimed waterfront maritime museum. If history is your main interest, head up the street to the Heritage Museum. (A side trip 5 miles southwest of town to Fort Clatsop National Memorial, site of the Lewis and Clark expedition's 1805–1806 winter quarters, and to the Civil War–era military installations at nearby Fort Stevens State Park is another worthwhile outing.)

City Walks

Otherwise, from the 17th Street Pier, head west on the waterfront walkway, a footpath on the old rail bed that's been paved and spruced up with benches and streetlights. The walkway extends to Sixth Street, with plenty of distractions along the

Be sure to drop anchor at the renowned Columbia River Maritime Museum, which hosts tours at its historic lightship, Columbia.

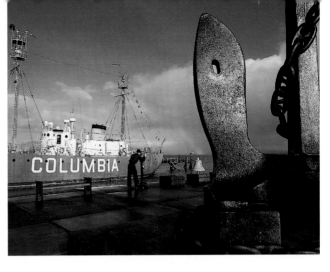

way, from shops at Pier 11 and eateries to such traditional waterfront denizens as Englund Marine Supply and Fergus-McBarendse Co., a stellar fresh seafood market.

At Sixth Street (or before), follow any of the numbered streets south into downtown, where you'll find a characteristically Astorian mix of the quirky and the conventional. Walk along Marine Drive or Commercial Street back to the 17th Street Pier.

TRIP PLANNER

Unless otherwise noted, area codes are 503. Lodging rates for two people range from $ (under $100) to $$$ (above $250) per night.

WHERE

Astoria is on U.S. Hwy. 101 in Oregon, 10 miles inland from the mouth of the Columbia River. From Portland, take U.S. Hwy. 26 northwest 75 miles to U.S. 101 and head north. Alternatively, follow U.S. Hwy. 30 north and west along the Columbia River into Astoria.

LODGING

Astoria's older neighborhoods are dominated by dazzling Victorian homes, nearly a dozen of which have been turned into bed-and-breakfasts. Among them, **Clementine's Bed and Breakfast** (847 Exchange St.; 325-2005, 800/521-6801; $) has 5 guest rooms, each exquisitely decorated with antiques and overlooking either the river or the lush garden. **Rosebriar Hotel** (636 14th St.; 325-7427, 800/487-0224; $-$$), with 11

rooms, has been restored to its 1902 elegance. Reserve a campsite at **Fort Stevens State Park** by calling 800/452-5687.

DINING

Ira's (915 Commercial St.; 338-6192) serves innovative meals, from a 10-greens salad to original preparations of local seafood. The **Columbian Café** (1114 Marine Dr.; 325-2233) is a favorite with locals; expect the unexpected. The **Cannery Café** (1 Sixth St.; 325-8642) sits at the water's edge; the menu is Italian-leaning, the interior Tuscan-toned. **Rio Café** (125 Ninth St.; 325-2409) turns out homemade tortillas, salsa fresca, and other regional Mexican fare. **Shark Rock Café** (1092 Marine Dr.; 325-7720) serves unusual combos; try the salmon club sandwich.

MUSEUMS

The **Columbia River Maritime Museum** (1792 Marine Dr.; 325-2323) is open daily. Call the **Heritage Museum** (1618 Exchange St.; 325-2203) to check hours there and at its

sister museums, **Uppertown Firefighters Museum** (housed in an 1896 firehouse at 30th and Marine Dr.) and **Flavel House Museum** (441 Eighth St.). **Fort Clatsop National Memorial** (5 miles south of town off U.S. 101; 861-2471) is open daily except Christmas.

FOR MORE INFORMATION

Astoria-Warrenton Area Chamber of Commerce (Box 176, Astoria, OR 97103; 325-6311, 800/875-6807).

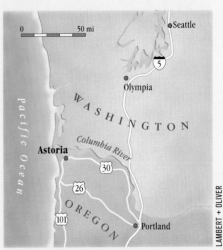

REGION	OREGON	
Where	X	230-mile northeastern Oregon loop
When	X	June through October destination

wandering through the Wallowas

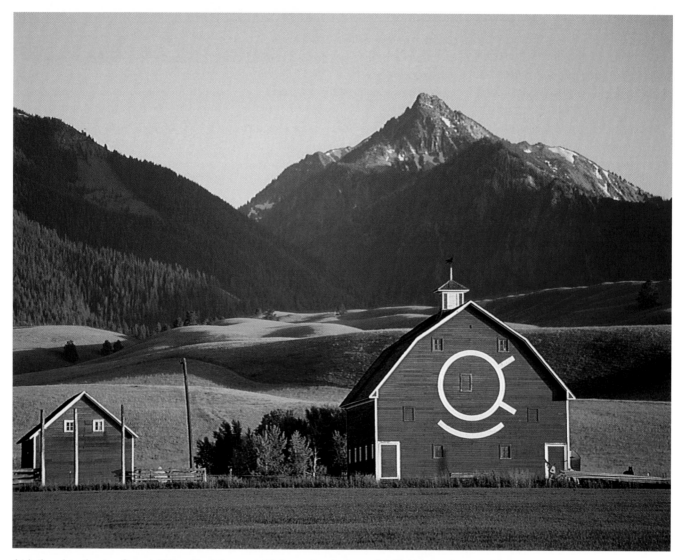

A trip through northeastern Oregon's Wallowa Mountains reveals tidy farms, charming towns, fish-filled lakes, and rugged wilderness terrain.

The mountainous landscape between Interstate 84 and Hells Canyon in northeastern Oregon bears witness to a history of collisions. Tectonic plates met here violently, rearranging part of the Great Basin into a jumble of 9,000–foot granite peaks and the deepest gorge in North America. Here too a clash occurred between an advancing nation hungry for gold and cattle pasture and the Nez Perce tribe. The clash was fueled by the ultimately irreconcilable ideas of nonviolence and geographical sovereignty.

To the contemporary visitor to this remote corner of Oregon, these dramas seem far distant, remembered mostly in museums and roadside plaques. Paved roads now encircle the Wallowa (wuh-LAU-uh) Mountains, skirting the rim of Hells Canyon and passing through towns whose architecture and unhurried ways hark back to their 19th-century origins. Lodging ranges from campsites to alpine chalets.

Scenic Highlights

This route along what the U.S. Forest Service has dubbed the Hells Canyon National Scenic Byway could be driven in a day, but you would do most of your sightseeing through car windows. Instead, plan a three-day weekend or longer to visit major attractions such as Wallowa Lake, the view from the top of 8,256-foot Mt. Howard via the Wallowa Lake Tramway, Hells Canyon Overlook, and the National Historic Oregon Trail Interpretive Center. This will leave time for even more memorable opportunities: a picnic beside an icy mountain stream, a hike to an alpine lake, the discovery of a "must–have" sculpture in a gallery in Joseph, and an hour's bookstore browse near the town square in Enterprise.

Trip Route to Joseph

For a clockwise tour, begin in the town of La Grande, off I-84. Follow State Highway 82 as it winds into the mountains through the small towns of Elgin, Wallowa, Enterprise, and Joseph.

At the north end of Wallowa Lake, Joseph is a popular jumping-off spot for trips into the mountains. More recently, it has evolved into something of an art colony, with bronze foundries and galleries, most dedicated to Western art. Browse the shops and galleries on your own, or hook up with a tour of a foundry to learn about bronze lost-wax casting and see new sculptures—from palm-size to monumental—in the making.

At the south end of the 4-mile-long lake is Wallowa Lake State Park. The campground is not too appealing (almost no vegetation between campsites), but access to the lake for boating and windsurfing and to trails for horsepacking and hiking is superb. Nearby lodging choices range from rustic cabins to a historic lodge.

The lake's south end is also the starting point for four–passenger gondola rides 3,200 vertical feet up to the top of Mt. Howard. From the top, a network of short trails loops around the summit, offering views of the mountains and deep gorges of four states. Summit trails aren't connected with any wilderness trails; for that, you'll need to take the tram back down and hike, or horse-pack, up to one of several creek valleys leading into the high country.

Most trails heading up into the Wallowas and their centerpiece, the Eagle Cap Wilderness, start at either Wallowa Lake or Hurricaine Creek, the next valley to the west. Aneroid Lake is a popular and, at 12 miles round-trip, ambitious day-hike destination from Wallowa Lake. For an alternative hike, walk about 3 miles up Hurricane Creek to reach the cool falls at Slick Rock Creek.

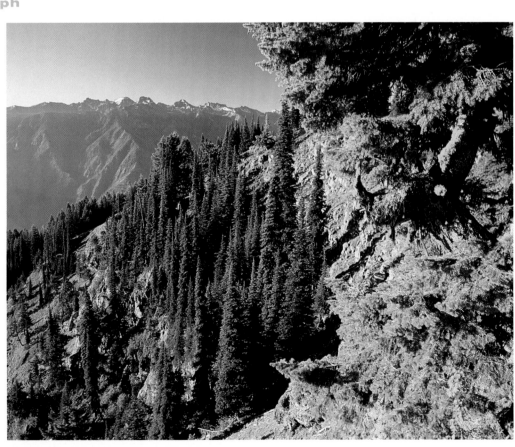

Roads through the Wallowa National Forest lead visitors to overlooks along the Oregon side of Hells Canyon.

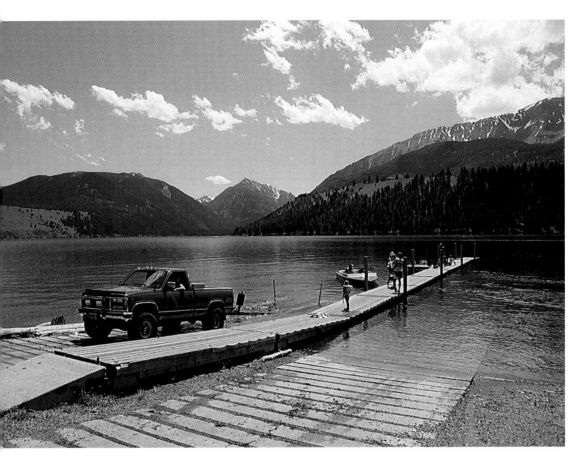

Wallowa Lake's ramp makes it easy for vacationers to get their boats in and out of the water.

remote and timeless. If your time is short, consider a day trip by jet boat.

Heading east, State 86 takes you past the ranches and farms of the foothills. About 5 miles east of I-84 and Baker City, the route passes Flagstaff Hill and the National Historic Oregon Trail Interpretive Center, which re-creates the emigrant experience with multimedia exhibits of interest to

Into the Wilderness

From Joseph, drive east 8 miles on County Road 350, then turn right onto Forest Service Road 39, skirting Eagle Cap Wilderness. Just before crossing the Imnaha River, you'll pass a couple of quiet, primitive Forest Service campgrounds. A detour up Road 3960, along the river, leads to more choices.

Watch for signs to Hells Canyon Overlook, a 3–mile side trip on a paved road, where picnic tables come with a view into the canyon to the Snake River and across to the Seven Devils Mountains in Idaho. There are other viewpoints down into the canyon, notably Hat Point to the north, but they require longer drives on rough roads. Road 39 meets State Highway 86 about 10 miles east of the town of Halfway, a good jumping-off point for jet boat and raft trips

down the Snake River or horse–, llama–, or backpacking trips up into the Wallowas. Most Snake River float trips start just below Hells Canyon Dam, 22 miles north of the town of Oxbow. Major rapids on this portion of the Snake River are few but memorable, clustered as they are in the first 17 miles below the dam. From then on, the lure is the dramatic, steep-walled canyon itself,

Bronze foundries and galleries in Joseph specialize in Western subjects. This one stands atop a museum on the main street.

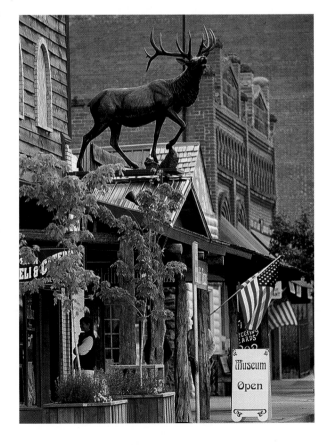

all ages. Allow plenty of time not only to walk through the indoor displays, but also to explore the outside trails that wind through the sagebrush to 150-year-old wagon ruts.

From Baker City, complete the route loop by taking I-84 north to La Grande.

⠿ TRIP PLANNER ⇒

Unless otherwise noted, area codes are 541. Lodging rates for two people range from $ (under $100) to $$$ (above $250) per night

WHERE

La Grande is off I-84, 260 miles east of Portland and 170 miles northwest of Boise. The Wallowas are dramatic in winter and summer, but snow closes Rd. 39 by mid-November most years; it reopens around Memorial Day.

LODGING

Chandler's Bed, Bread, and Trail Inn (700 S. Main St.; 432-9765, 800/452-3781; $) is a bit like an alpine chalet in downtown Joseph; an inside log staircase climbs to 5 guest rooms, 3 with private baths. Breakfasts are generous, and a shared kitchenette gives guests the option of fixing their own dinners. **Wallowa Lake Lodge** (60060 Wallowa Lake Hwy., Joseph; 432-9821; $-$$), at the south end of the lake, is tall on historic ambience but a bit tight on space; cabins are a good choice for families.

The 1889 **Geiser Grand Hotel** (1996 Main St., Baker City; 523-1889; $-$$) was once the finest hotel between Salt Lake City and Portland; it is again, after extensive restoration completed in 1997. Period furnishings, ornate restored mill-work, and a suspended stained-glass ceiling in the downstairs Palm Court have helped make the hotel the centerpiece of the downtown historic district.

Pine Valley Lodge (163 Main St., Halfway; 742-2027; $) is a genuine find. Owners Dale and Babette Beatty bought and refurbished a collection of buildings on both sides of Main Street to create this engaging hostelry. Eclectic and arty furnishings, exquisite food, and gracious service enhance any stay.

In the mountains, primitive **Forest Service campgrounds** are on a first-come, first-served basis. Reserve a campsite at **Wallowa Lake State Park** by calling 800/452-5687.

DINING

Mamacita's (110 Depot St., La Grande; 963-6223) is a hometown favorite for inexpensive Mexican fare in a friendly atmosphere. There is no bar, but wine margaritas are available along with Mexican beers. Special menu for children.

Vali's Alpine Deli and Restaurant (59811 Wallowa Lake Hwy., Joseph; 432-5691) features Hungarian-German specialties for dinner, homemade doughnuts in the morning. Call ahead for a reservation, and bring a big appetite. Both the dining room and the more informal saloon at Baker City's **Geiser Grand Hotel** (see Lodging above) feature steak plus pasta, fresh fish, and a good wine and microbrew selection.

INTO THE BACKCOUNTRY

Call the U.S. Forest Service's Wallowa Mountains Visitor Center (426-4978) or drop by the center, on the western edge of Enterprise off State 82, for information on hiking, horse-packing, or llama-packing in **Eagle Cap Wilderness** and elsewhere in Wallowa-Whitman National Forest. The center also has information on rafting and hiking in **Hells Canyon**. In summer, it's open 8 to 5 daily (from noon Sundays).

Wallowa Lake Tramway operates summers only; for hours and fare information, call 432-5331.

FOR MORE INFORMATION

Baker County Visitors Bureau (490 Campbell St., Baker City, OR; 523-3356, 800/523-1235). La Grande-Union County Visitors Bureau (1912 Fourth St., #200, LaGrande, OR; 963-8588, 800/848-9969). Wallowa County Chamber of Commerce (107 S.W. First St., Enterprise, OR; 426-4622, 800/585-4121).

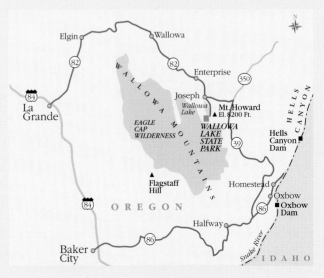

REGION	OREGON	
where	X	2 to 3 hours south of Portland
when	X	Summer and fall best seasons

romancing
Oregon's Covered Bridges

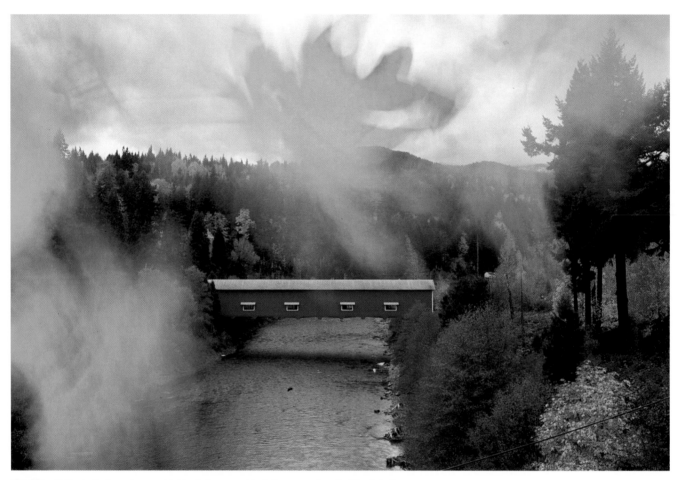

The Office Bridge is the longest covered bridge in Oregon and just steps away from the Westfir Lodge.

You don't have to go all the way to Madison County, Iowa, to see enough covered bridges to fill a book. Oregon boasts an ample collection of these romantic, rustic reminders of a bygone era. There are 52 in all, but the best assortment can be found in just two neighboring counties. In fact, the covered bridges of Lane and Linn counties, 28 in all, outnumber those of any state west of the Mississippi. In fall, the area looks like New England.

Covered bridges span creeks and rivers all over western Oregon, but the Willamette Valley counties surrounding Albany and Eugene hold the greatest number and variety. There are long ones, short ones, red ones, and white ones. Most are listed on the National Register of Historic Places.

Umbrellas for Bridges

In the early years of the 20th century, covered bridges in western Oregon numbered about 450. And, as anyone ever caught in a sudden explosion of Oregon's "liquid sunshine" can understand, they served a practical purpose. Roofs were raised over the bridges' wooden floors to shield them from rain and prevent them from rotting.

Fortunately for Sunday drivers, many of the bridges are in clusters, a short distance from one another. On a sunny summer or fall day, pack a picnic and follow one or more of these covered-bridge loops. Don't forget to bring the camera to capture vibrant fall foliage framing bright red or white clapboard bridges.

A Bridge Roster

In Linn County, east of Albany and near the town of Scio, you can follow Covered Bridge Tour Route signs to take in five bridges, most dating from the late 1930s. The Shimanek Bridge over Thomas Creek, however, was built later, in 1966. Four predecessors at this site, dating from 1891, fell victim to flood or storm damage. Bright red with white trim and louvered windows, it's one of the county's most picturesque bridges.

Save your picnic for Larwood Bridge, built in 1939 near where the Roaring River meets Crabtree Creek. The white, open-sided span can be admired from Larwood Wayside, an inviting picnic spot on the bank of the creek with picnic tables, barbecues, and a restroom, all shielded by huge, colorful, maple trees.

In and around Cottage Grove in Lane County, there are six covered bridges. Two of them, Centennial (1987), a pedestrian bridge, and Chambers (1936), a railroad bridge, are right in the middle of town. The oldest covered bridge in the county, Mosby Creek Bridge (1920), is the only one of the six that's still open to vehicular traffic. A one-lane road of wooden planks runs through the white wooden structure.

About 12 miles east of Cottage Grove, the 105-foot Dorena Bridge, built in 1949 to accommodate logging traffic over the Row River, sits in disuse next to a modern highway bridge. Recently restored and given a fresh coat of white paint, the older and more majestic bridge still gets plenty of foot traffic. Picnickers stop at the wayside for a peaceful view of the river, and neighbors have claimed the bridge as the perfect place for weddings and other community gatherings.

East of Eugene, four covered bridges dot an area near the town of Lowell. Except for the Lowell Bridge (1945), sitting in neglect and disrepair next to a concrete span, they are all treasures in the woods, nestled in lush, colorful foliage. As you drive through the Parvin (1921), Pengra (1938), and Unity (1936) bridges, listen to the sounds of tires thumping over wooden planks and the water of the creek rushing underneath.

The great beauty of them all is farther east, in the town of Westfir. The 180-foot-long Office Bridge, built in 1944 to connect a lumber company's mill with its office across the North Fork of the Willamette River, is the longest covered bridge in Oregon and the only one with a connected walkway. Bright red, with white trim and flower boxes, it becomes more festive at Christmas, when townspeople decorate it and line its portals and windows with colored lights. Look for Santa Claus himself at the annual lighting ceremony.

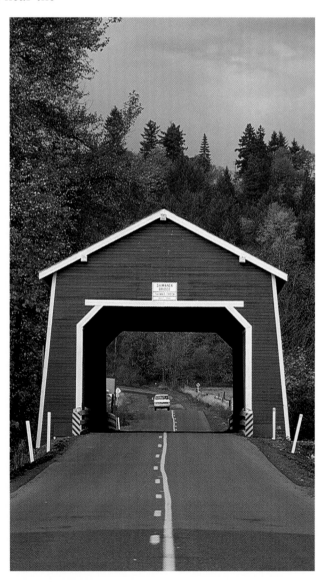

Shimanek Covered Bridge crosses over Thomas Creek in Linn County near the town of Scio.

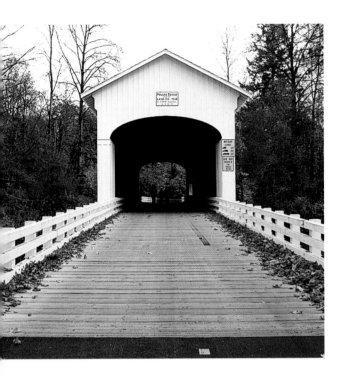

Pengra Bridge, built in 1938, is just east of Eugene, off State Highway 58.

Covered Bridge Central

The perfect ending to a covered bridge outing is seeing the Office Bridge at sunrise, then sitting down to a full English breakfast. Conveniently, the building that once housed the office of the Westfir Lumber Co. is now a delightful bed-and-breakfast inn, the Westfir Lodge. It sits directly across the street from the bridge, tucked behind a white picket fence and rambling gardens.

Hosts Gerry Chamberlain and Kenneth Symons have turned their lodge into Covered Bridge Central. Among the antique furnishings in the comfortable Victorian parlor is a plethora of books, videos, and scrapbooks about Oregon's covered bridges. Somehow the guests' evening conversation over tea and cake almost always turns to bridges.

⇐ ∷TRIP PLANNER∷⇒

Unless otherwise noted, area codes are 541. Lodging rates for two people range from $ (under $100) to $$$ (above $250) per night.

WHERE

Interstate 5 is the convenient jumping-off place for many of the covered bridges in Linn and Lane counties. To follow the loop around Scio, take State Hwy. 226 east of Albany; visit the two covered bridges in Cottage Grove, then go east on Mosby Creek Rd. or Row River Rd. to see others. Take State Hwy. 58 south of Eugene and east to Lowell; continue east to Westfir to see the Office Bridge.

LODGING

Unfortunately, Covered Bridge Country doesn't boast lodging nearly as lovely as the bridges. One exception is the **Westfir Lodge** (47365 1st St.; 782-3103; $).

For other lodging in the Eugene-Cottage Grove area, call the Eugene/Springfield Convention and Visitors Bureau (484-5307, 800/547-5445). For lodging in the Albany area, call the Albany Visitors Assn. (928-0911, 800/526-2256).

DINING

Rosalina's (47720 School St., Oakridge; 782-5589) is the best bet near Westfir. The Mexican food is delicious and authentic, and the service is stellar (lunch and dinner daily).
Novak's Hungarian Paprikas (2835 Santiam Hwy. SE, Albany; 967-9488) has long been the place to eat in Albany. The owners left Hungary as refugees in 1956, but they haven't forgotten how to prepare delicious Hungarian specialties and desserts. Open for dinner daily.

FOR MORE INFORMATION

"Covered Bridges in Lane County, Oregon" brochure & map (Lane County Public Works Dept., 3040 N. Delta Hwy., Eugene, OR 97401; 341-6900). "Cottage Grove Covered Bridges" brochure & map (Cottage Grove Area Chamber of Commerce P.O. Box 587, 710 Row River Rd., Cottage Grove, OR 97424; 942-2411). "Covered Bridge Country" brochure & map (Albany Visitors Assn., 435 W. First Ave., Albany, OR 97321; 926-1517).

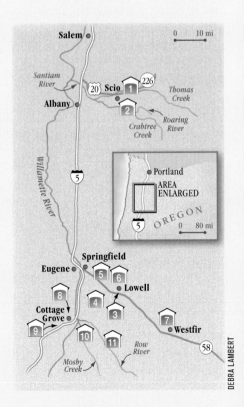

the new
Newport

REGION		OREGON
Where	X	114 miles southwest of Portland
When	X	Year-round destination; whale watching March–April

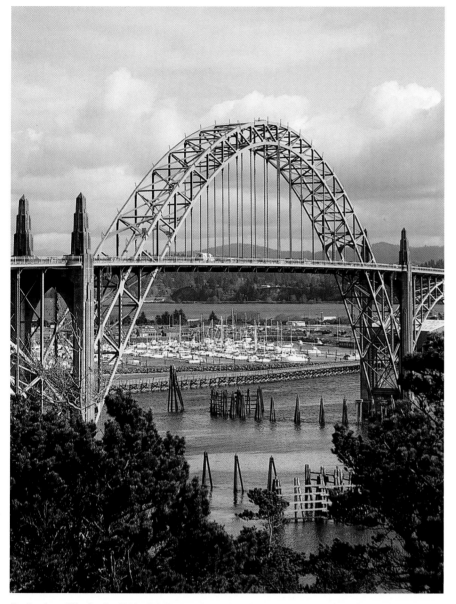

Steel arches of Yaquina Bay Bridge link the aquarium and marine science center at South Beach with Newport's bustling bayfront and, to the north, Yaquina Head.

Newport used to be easy to see in a day: a few hours at South Beach or Agate Beach flying kites and tossing the Frisbee, a little bayfront browsing, a visit to the octopus at Hatfield Marine Science Center, and home.

Now it's hard to do justice to this central coast town in even a three-day weekend. The opening of the Oregon Coast Aquarium in the early 1990s added a good half-day to a visit here, and the $5.5 million renovation of the public wing at the marine science center next door brings it up to a full day. Adding a visit to Yaquina Head and a naturalist-led boat trip to see whales off-shore, and your itinerary is full before you've even hit the broad beach.

Where to begin? The bayfront is a good choice. With everything from fine art to kites and coastal kitsch, a wax museum, and a resident collection of noisy sea lions lounging at the water's edge, even kids enjoy browsing here. If the weather is damp, you're never far from a bowl of clam chowder.

The bayfront is also the starting point for whale-watching trips. Motor out of Yaquina Bay into the open ocean; your best chances to see whales are during spring migration (March and April) and in summer. You'll find a variety of whale-watching tours. Marine Discovery Tours' 65-foot boat is always staffed with a naturalist and loaded with on-board labs to enhance the experience.

South Beach

Drive across Yaquina Bay Bridge to reach South Beach, home of the Oregon Coast Aquarium and Hatfield Marine Science Center. There's plenty to see in the aquarium: moon jellies, an ocher octopus curled in its cave, Aialik the sea otter, tufted puffins underwater and overhead, and,

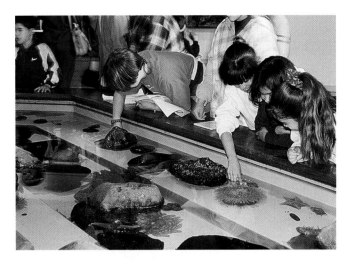

Children and parents gravitate to the science center's touch pool, where textured sea stars and squishy anemones tolerate gentle handling.

by summer 2000, a walk-through open ocean exhibit.

Next door, the marine science center now serves as a hands-on showcase for marine research. A please-touch pool with sea urchins, hermit crabs, and other tidal creatures appeals to children—and adults. You'll gain a few new perspectives in the research gallery—say, of a limpet's raspy tongue or the tube feet of sea stars—in the center's tidepool exhibit.

Yaquina Head

Yaquina Head could occupy the better part of a day. The 127-year-old lighthouse is open summer mornings for guided tours. From a viewing platform, you can watch for whales and nesting seabirds. Stairs lead down the bluff to rich tidepools.

TRIP PLANNER

Unless otherwise noted, area codes are 541. Lodging rates for two people range from $ (under $100) to $$$ (above $250) per night.

WHERE

Newport is on U.S. Hwy. 101 about 2½ hours from either Portland or Eugene. Wander along U.S. 101 from the north or south, or take U.S. Hwy. 20 west from Interstate 5 at Corvallis (the most direct route).

LODGING

When you leave the kids at home, reserve a room in the Nye Beach neighborhood. Pack your walking shoes in case it's too cool for bare feet on the beach, a scarf to dress up your sweater, and jeans if the Newport Performing Arts Center's schedule entices. You can always catch the aquarium on your next trip.

Each room at the **Sylvia Beach Hotel** (267 N.W. Cliff St.; 265-5428; $-$$) at Nye Beach reflects the mood of an individual author; the attached **Tables of Content** restaurant serves elegant, family-style meals. Next door, **Nye Beach Hotel** (219 N.W. Cliff St.; 265-3334; $-$$) is a laid-back favorite. **Embarcadero Resort** (1000 S.E. Bay Blvd; 800/547-4779; $$) offers kitchenettes and bay views. **Ashley Inn** (2633 S. Pacific Way; 888/427-4439; $-$$) is near the aquarium.

Reserve a campsite at South Beach or another nearby state park by calling 800/452-5687.

DINING

Canyon Way Restaurant (1216 S.W. Canyon Way; 265-8319) feeds body and soul with an attached bookstore and excellent clam chowder. No fried clams at **Sharks Seafood Bar & Steamer Co.** (852 S.W. Bay Blvd.; 574-0590); everything's steamed. Cozy as an old wooden yacht, **Whale's Tail** (Bay Blvd. and Herbert St.; 265-8660), is a favorite with locals and visitors. The food at **Cosmos Café** (740 W. Olive St.; 265-7511), across the street from the performing arts center, is fresh and original; browse the attached gallery.

EXPLORING

Oregon Coast Aquarium (2820 S.W. Ferry Slip Rd.; 867-3474). **Hatfield Marine Science Center** (2030 Marine Science Dr.; 867-0100). **Yaquina Head Interpretive Center** (750 Lighthouse Dr.; 574-3100). **Marine Discovery Tours** (345 W. Bay Blvd.; 800/903-2628). **Newport Performing Arts Center** (265-2787).

FOR MORE INFORMATION

Greater Newport Chamber of Commerce (555 S.W. Coast Hwy.; Newport, OR 97366; 265-8801, 800/262-7844).

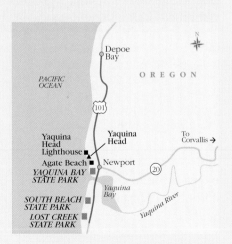

Oregon's Lake District

REGION	OREGON	
Where	X	3 hours southeast of Portland
When	X	June through October best time

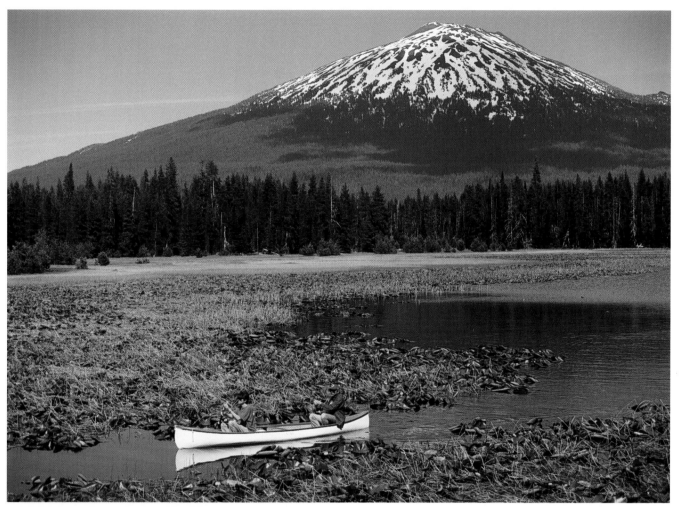

Mt. Bachelor looms over central Oregon's Hosmer Lake, one of a dozen major lakes on the Cascade Lakes Highway and a magnet for summer canoeists and anglers.

There's nothing else quite like it in the Northwest: a first-class paved road that begins in a major town and leads within minutes into the heart of the high Cascades. What began as a 100-mile circuit of wagon roads—hence its original name, Century Drive—is now an 87-mile loop joining U.S. Highway 97 south of Bend with Forest Service Road 46, better known as the Cascade Lakes Highway, tracing the edge of Three Sisters Wilderness.

Along the way, the road winds among glacier-draped dormant volcanoes, over two rivers, through forests of Douglas fir and lodgepole pine, and past a dozen major lakes and hundreds of little ones. Visit in summer for the best hiking and canoeing weather or in fall when the fish are biting and the slow pace of the region's rustic lakeside resorts is even slower.

Do drop by Bend's charming downtown before you head out of town. Two decades ago, the Bend area was rustic and little known outside the Northwest. Now the hills around Bend are dotted with million-dollar

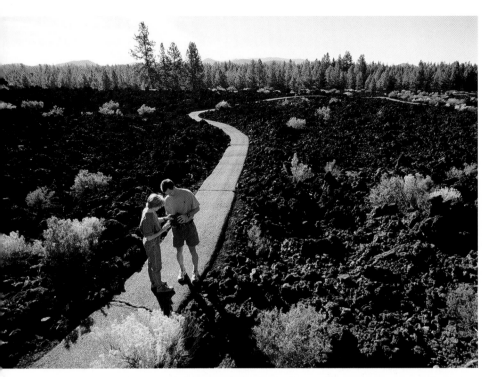

A paved path leads through volcanic rock at Newberry National Volcanic Monument's Lava Lands Visitor Center 11 miles south of Bend off U.S. 97.

homes. Not surprisingly, the town has filled up with shops and restaurants catering to this new upscale clientele.

Summer Fun

Resorts at the east end of the Cascade Lakes loop drive offer all the usual amenities—golf, swimming, tennis, and so on. Mt. Bachelor ski area offers summer chairlift rides to the summit through Labor Day. Otherwise, recreation along the Cascade Lakes Highway is unpackaged. Hiking is one big appeal, with options ranging from a level stroll around Todd Lake to an ascent of 10,358-foot South Sister peak. In between, consider a day hike into any of several wilderness lake basins. Canoeing and fishing are big; boat rentals are available at several lakes. Bring your road bike to tour on the highway and paved side roads. For off-road

exploring, use a mountain bike on one of the many designated forest trails. Bike shops in Bend and Sunriver (and, in summer, at Mt. Bachelor) sell maps and rent bikes.

A Lake Loop

From Bend, follow signs to Mt. Bachelor ski area, 22 miles to the west on Cascade Lakes Highway. Road 46 continues west past Todd, Sparks, and Devils lakes, then curves south to Elk Lake, peaceful with canoes and other non-motorized craft, where a resort rents both cabins and boats. Here motorboats are allowed, but at speeds of 10 mph or less to maintain a tranquil atmosphere. Atlantic salmon in Hosmer Lake, just to the east, is a big draw for anglers (fly fishing only).

Motorists have several options for looping back to U.S. 97, including picking up Forest Road

40 south of Lava Lake. But if you do you'd miss several choice lakes: Cultus, lively with water-skiers in summer; Crane Prairie Reservoir, popular with anglers; tranquil, tiny North and South Twin Lakes; and Wickiup Reservoir, which, like Cultus, allows motorboats to cut loose. Forest Road 42, between Crane Prairie and the Twin Lakes, can return you to U.S. 97 about 4 miles south of Sunriver.

Detour north up U.S. 97 a few miles past Sunriver to learn more about the geologic processes that formed this landscape and the critters that live here. Stop at Lava Lands Visitor Center, the information headquarters for Newberry National Volcanic Monument, where interpretive exhibits and dioramas explain how lava oozing from Newberry Crater 1,500 years ago led to caves, cones, and fields of lava

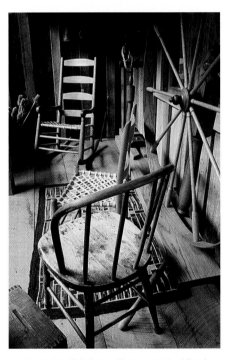

Don't miss the High Desert Museum south of Bend. The intriguing complex is crammed with objects from the area's pioneering past.

throughout the region. Rangers can point you toward such nearby volcanic attractions as the Obsidian Flow, Lava River Cave, and Lava Cast Forest.

North another 5 miles is the High Desert Museum, where elegant indoor galleries and 20 acres of outdoor exhibits introduce you to the natural and human history of the region. Inside, take a "walk through time" that brings history to life, and peruse galleries featuring Native American and Western art. Outdoors, you'll find a river otter pool (watch from above or under the water) and have opportunities to get personal with porcupines and birds of prey. Exhibits at a sheepherder's wagon and settler's cabin vividly detail the rigors of early life on the high plateau.

TRIP PLANNER

Unless otherwise noted, area codes are 541. Lodging rates for two people range from $ (under $100) to $$$ (above $250) per night.

WHERE

Bend is at the junction of U.S. Highways 97 and 20. From Portland, take U.S. Highway 26 past Mt. Hood to U.S. 97 at Madras and continue south.

LODGING

Sunriver (off U.S. 97, 15 miles south of Bend; 593-1000, 800/547-3922; $$-$$$) is a logical—and luxurious—choice for a Cascade Lakes base camp; options range from guest rooms to whole houses. **Inn of the Seventh Mountain** (18575 S.W. Century Dr., Bend; 382-8711, 800/452-6810; $$-$$$) and **Mt. Bachelor Village** (19717 Mt. Bachelor Dr., Bend; 389-5900, 800/452-9846; $$) are both full-service resorts.

Accommodations are also available at three rustic lakeside resorts. Cabins at both **Elk Lake Resort** (Rd. 46; 317-2994; $-$$) and **Cultus Lake Resort** (Rd. 4635 off Rd. 46; 389-5125; at the tone, dial 037-244; $-$$) are pretty bare bones; most have kitchens. Most appealing of the three is **Twin Lake Resort** (Rd. 4260 off Rd. 42; 593-6526; $-$$), with log cabins overlooking quiet South Twin

Lake. Make reservations as far in advance as possible; sometimes phone communication with the remote resorts is difficult.

Campers can choose among more than a dozen primitive **Forest Service campgrounds** in the area. The campground at privately owned **Lava Lake Lodge** (382-9443) offers full hookups. (The lodge offers no other accommodations.)

DINING

Grab a bite at Mt. Bachelor's **Café Blue at Sunrise Lodge** (see Other Attractions at right for Mt. Bachelor phone number) or at a lunch counter at one of the lakeside resorts on Cascade Lakes Hwy.; otherwise, bring a picnic or your own groceries for cooking at your cabin.

Sunriver has lots of dining options, from pizza and pasta to the elegant **Meadows at the Lodge** restaurant (see Sunriver lodging above). In Bend, **Broken Top Club** (61999 Broken Top Dr.; 383-8210) offers original Northwest cuisine and spectacular mountain views. If it's your first visit to Bend, don't miss **Pine Tavern Restaurant,** a local favorite for 50-plus years (967 Brooks; 382-5581). The food at **Deschutes Brewery and Public House** (1044 N.W. Bond St.; 382-9242) is tasty, and the brew—from Obsidian Stout to Bachelor Bitter—is central Oregon's best.

OTHER ATTRACTIONS

Take a chairlift to the summit, ride mountain bikes on Nordic ski trails, or grab burgers and brew at **Mt. Bachelor** (382-2442, 800/829-2442).

You could spend hours at the complex that comprises the **High Desert Museum** (3½ miles south of Bend at 59800 S. U.S. 97; 382-4754; open daily). Volcanoes shaped central Oregon's landscape, a fact attested to by a stop at **Lava Lands Visitor Center** (11 miles south of Bend off U.S. 97; 388-5664).

FOR MORE INFORMATION

Deschutes National Forest (1645 E. U.S. 20, Bend, OR 97701; 388-2715). Central Oregon Visitors Association (63085 N. Hwy. 97, #107, Bend, OR 97701; 382-3221, 800/905-2363).

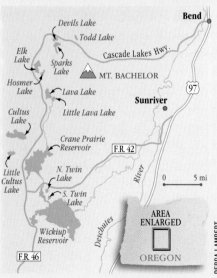

REGION		OREGON
Where	X	260 miles south of Portland
When	X	Best in summer

Old Stage Road
through Jacksonville

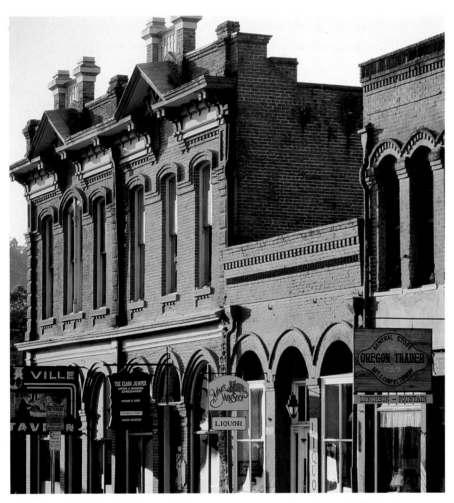

California Street, like other streets in downtown Jacksonville, is lined with 19th-century buildings that now house businesses, shops, restaurants, and inns.

Driving along Interstate 5 south of Grants Pass, the heavy truck traffic and a sea of motorists going somewhere fast may make you forget that travelers in this region once took time to look around. In fact, as horseback riders or stagecoach passengers appreciated sumptuous valley views and mountains in all direc-tions, they may have uttered these immortal words: "There's gold in them thar hills!"

Appropriately enough, Gold Hill is the ideal place to exit the freeway to get a better feel for those days of prospectors and pioneers. Linking the town of Gold Hill with Jacksonville, its more famous Gold Rush neigh-bor 12 miles to the south, is another early Oregon artifact, Old Stage Road.

It was built as a wagon route in 1853, not long after gold was discovered near what was to become the thriving town of Jacksonville, and later carried stagecoaches bound from Jacksonville to Roseburg. A seg-ment of the road just south of Gold Hill was later part of the Applegate Trail, which brought Oregon Trail pioneers to south-ern Oregon. Over the years, Old Stage Road carried gold miners, adventurers, and farmers to the riches of the Rogue River Valley.

Saving a Road

In 1993, the rolling road was in danger of losing much of its his-toric character when Jackson County officials announced they would widen and straighten it. In response, the Westside Neighbors Association was formed to pro-tect and preserve Old Stage Road. The county modified its plans and even helped the associ-ation get the road named a Jackson County Historic Landmark in 1998.

In time, neighbors will erect interpretive signs pointing out historic features of the route. For now, it's a peaceful, slow-paced alternative to the freeway. Mean-dering along its curves, dips, and rises, you can almost hear the creaking wheels of the wagons and the clip-clop of the horses that traveled the route.

Just before Jacksonville, Old Stage Road becomes Oregon Street. When it intersects with California Street, you know you're in the heart of this well-preserved town, another artifact of the Gold Rush era. Most of the wood and brick structures lining the streets are original buildings that sprang up during the town's gold boom. In 1966, Jacksonville became the first town in the U.S. to be named a National Historic Landmark. More than 80 of its buildings are

listed on the National Register of Historic Places.

Walking the streets is an experience in itself, but be sure to get the full story at the Jacksonville Museum, housed in the 1883 county courthouse. Next door, in the 1910 jailhouse, is a delightful Children's Museum. If you believe that dead men do tell tales, another fascinating part of Jacksonville's story is told on the gravestones at the Jacksonville Cemetery, which dates from 1859. At the top of a hill, the cemetery also offers lovely views over the town to the golden Siskiyou Mountains in the distance.

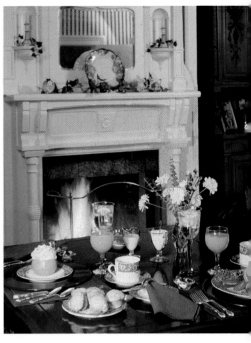

Guests enjoy a cozy breakfast in front of the fire at this charming Jacksonville inn.

TRIP PLANNER

Unless otherwise noted, area codes are 541. Lodging rates for two people range from $ (under $100) to $$$ (above $250) per night.

WHERE

Driving south on I-5, take the Gold Hill exit and drive south on Old State Road. Driving north on I-5, exit at Medford and follow State Hwy. 238 7 miles west to Jacksonville.

LODGING

Jacksonville abounds with bed-and-breakfasts in its historic homes. To really get a feel for Old Stage Road, try the **Touvelle House Bed & Breakfast** (455 N. Oregon St.; 899-8938, 800/846-8422; $-$$) at the southern end of town. It's a 1916 Craftsman mansion built on a hill under spreading oaks. There are 6 rooms with private baths, a pool/spa, and gourmet meals.

The **Jacksonville Inn** (175 E. California St.; 899-1900, 800/321-9344; $$-$$$) was built from brick in 1861. There are 8 guest rooms with antique canopy beds on the second floor, 1 with a whirlpool tub, and 3 honeymoon cottages.

DINING

The **Jacksonville Inn** (see Lodging above) has a two-level dining room and lounge that is packed with locals and visitors who keep coming back for the exceptional continental cuisine. The **McCully House Inn** (240 E. California St.; 899-1942), a bed-and-breakfast in an 1860 home, is also renowned for gourmet dining.

ATTRACTIONS

The **Jacksonville Museum**, (206 N. 5th St., 773-6536) is open daily 10-5 Memorial Day through Labor Day, 10-5 Wednesday-Sunday in winter. The **Children's Museum** next door features an old school, bank, barbershop, and vintage toys.

The **Britt Festivals**, a summer-long concert series featuring world-class performers in classical, jazz, folk/country, musical theater, and dance, is held in an outdoor amphitheater on the estate of Peter Britt, Jacksonville's pioneer photographer. Ticket information: P.O. Box 1124, Medford, OR 97501; 779-0847, 800/882-7488.

FOR MORE INFORMATION

Visitor Information Center (P.O. Box 33, Jacksonville, OR 97530; 899-8118).

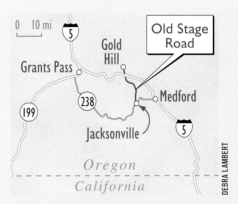

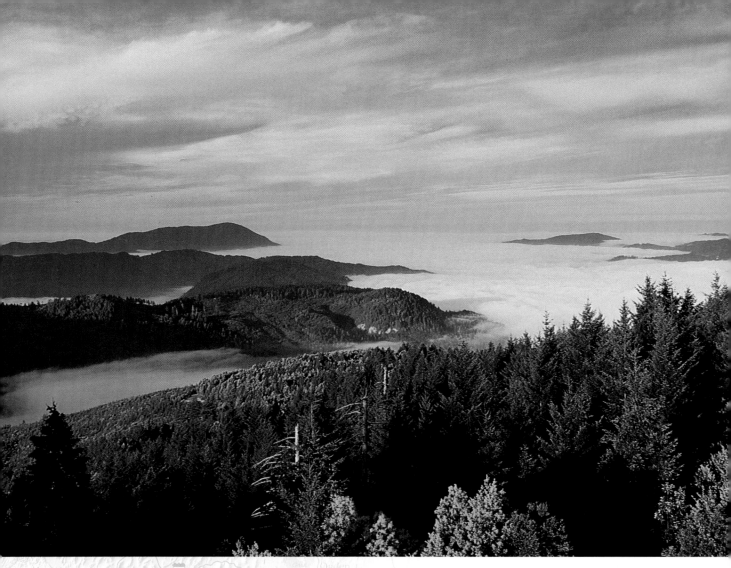

Morning fog fills Siskiyou Mountain valleys, seen from atop Quail Prairie Lookout northeast of Brookings. The Siskiyous contain western Oregon's oldest rocks and its most botanically diverse forests.

Adventures in the Siskiyous

Venerable and wizened, not ingratiating like the Cascades and Sierra—those are the words naturalist David Rains Wallace uses to characterize the Siskiyous, that wild and remote realm of mountains in southwestern Oregon and northwestern California. "Their canyons," he writes in The Klamath Knot, "…seem to drop down forever, slope after forest-smothered slope, to straitened, boulder-strewn bottoms so noisy with waters and shadowed by vegetation that they may bring startling dreams and uneasy thoughts to campers."

One's thoughts may indeed be uneasy here at times: when you're halfway down the wild Illinois River, for example, with spring rain pelting your gray raft and no way out but through the froth and rock of a rapids known as the "Green Wall." But more often are the sweet memories of charmed days and nights in the Siskiyous. An evening dip in a sapphire Smith River swimming hole, the day's heat held still in the steep-walled canyon. A walk alongside the Chetco River in autumn, the season captured in the spicy bay leaves crunching underfoot and in the palette of colorful leaves reflected in the still water. A spring raft trip down the Rogue, the perfume of wild azaleas sweetening the air well before their pastel blooms come into view.

"The clutches of hell"—that's how a sheriff's deputy described one corner of the Siskiyous north of the Kalmiopsis Wilderness after it swallowed up an experienced backpacker (he eventually found his way out). That's not where, or how, newcomers should start their exploration of these mountains. Instead, take U.S. Highway 101 or Interstate 5, then follow a river: the Rogue, the Smith, or the Chetco. Here are three routes that can give you a taste of the Siskiyous without requiring you to give up civilization entirely—or even a little.

Following the Rogue

The Rogue River might be described as a pool-drop river with plenty of white-water excitement, threading a wilderness area dotted with rustic lodges accessible only by boat or trail. Details like this have made a float down, a hike alongside, or a jet boat trip up the Rogue one of the West's classic vacations.

From Grave Creek west of Grants Pass, take three or more days to float through the wild section of this designated wild and scenic river. Help paddle a raft, paddle your own inflatable kayak, or stay high and dry in a classic drift boat. Camp along the river, or stay overnight at one of several rustic riverside lodges offering hot showers, clean sheets, and hearty family-style meals in the midst of the wilderness.

The same territory is accessible via a 40-mile hiking trail along the river's north bank; start at either end, or cut your trip short by starting at the remote pioneer community of Marial. Carry a tent and sleeping bag, or stay at riverside lodges, carrying only a light pack (lodges can provide breakfast, dinner, and a sack lunch for the trail). Spring is the best season to hike the Rogue Trail; from summer through September, the trail can be hot and dusty, and campsites and lodges filled with rafting parties and steelhead anglers. April through June, the canyon is the quiet province of hikers and a handful of early-season boaters.

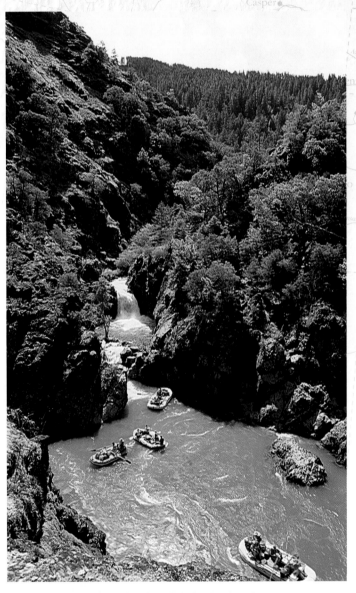

Rogue River rafters gather at Stair Creek Falls, floating above deep pools where salmon congregate in summer.

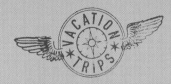

Overnight at a Lookout

To feel like you're on the top of the world, spend the night at a lookout. Sunsets are slow and late, dawns early. In between are all the little adventures that result from half-camping, half-lodging on a mountaintop: dramatic weather changes, supper cooked on a wood-burning stove, a parade of visitors—most of them four-legged or winged.

Three lookouts and a handful of forest cabins in the Siskiyous are available for overnight rental ($); accessible via passenger car, all require reservations, sometimes months in advance (although you could luck into a cancellation). Tiny (15 by 15 feet) lookouts best accommodate couples, four or five people at most; consider a forest cabin for larger groups, or Bear Basin Lookout, which is rented with adjacent Pierson Cabin.

Off U.S. 191. Northeast of Brookings are two lookouts (Quail Prairie and Snow Camp) plus ground-level Packer's Cabin; no children under age 12 at Quail Prairie. Call Chetco Ranger District (541/469-2196) for prices and reservations.

Off U.S. 199. East of Crescent City are Bear Basin Lookout and Pierson Cabin. Call Smith River NRA (707/457-3131) for details.

Plan to spend about 5 days to traverse the entire trail; on a weekend, backpackers can hike a few miles in and back out. For a one-way hike, take an hour-long jet boat ride upriver from Gold Beach or Foster Bar, then spend at least two days walking back out. Go prepared. Wood ticks can be a problem on the trail in spring and summer; check clothing and skin periodically. Also be on guard for the canyon's ubiquitous poison oak.

Don't have three or four days to while away on the Rogue? Outfitters in Grants Pass and Galice can get you on the river in a raft or inflatable kayak for a few hours or all day, with or without a guide. The stretch of river between Grants Pass and Grave Creek isn't as remote as the lower

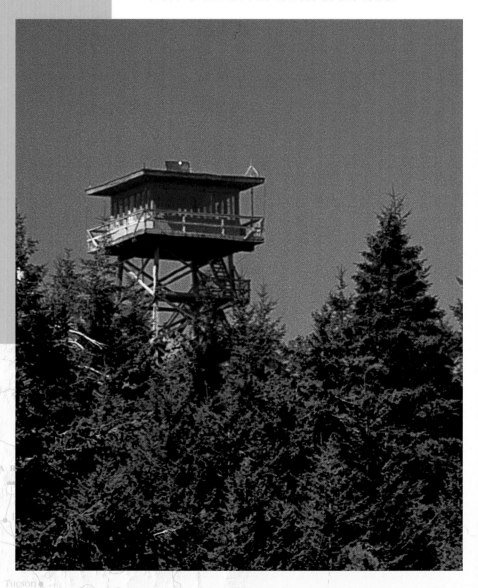

Square tower-mounted lookout tops the trees on Quail Prairie Mountain. Built in 1963, it is one of several lookouts and ground-level cabins available for overnight rental in the Siskiyous.

canyon, but it's still plenty scenic, with enough bouncy rapids (including a pass through steep-walled Hellgate) to keep things lively.

For a driving vacation, leave I-5 at Merlin (north of Grants Pass) and take Merlin-Galice Road west. Spend a night at county-run Indian Park or at a riverside lodge. In Galice, pick up Bear Camp Road (Forest Service Road 23) for a slow, scenic drive over the Siskiyous to the coast (snow closes it in winter). Spend the night at a woodsy, primitive campground, at an oceanside motel in Gold Beach, or at one of the lower Rogue's lodges, all accessible by road.

Rogue River mail boats have been carrying letters and freight to isolated upstream settlements since 1895. They still carry the mail, but today's 30- to 60-passenger hydro-jets operate mainly as tour boats through the scenic lower canyon. Tours originate in Gold Beach and run as far as Blossom Bar Rapids, just above

Paradise Lodge. Trips range from 64 to 104 miles round trip and generally include a lunch or dinner stop at a riverside lodge. Jet boat tours of the river above or below the wild section are available from Grant Pass or Gold Beach.

Following the Chetco

Erratic in spring on its upper reaches, the Chetco is for the most part an easy-going river: intimate, gentle, its banks lush with vegetation. Fishing is popular here in winter. More recently, one outfitter has begun sharing the river's spring and summer pleasures on scenic floats in inflatable kayaks.

Late spring brings the azalea bloom; visit Azalea City Park near the river's mouth in Brookings. The Siskiyous' unusual geologic history is reflected in the colorful beach rocks— from polished pebbles to offshore monoliths—at Harris Beach State Park, just north of Brookings, and at McVay Rock State Recreation Site, south of town.

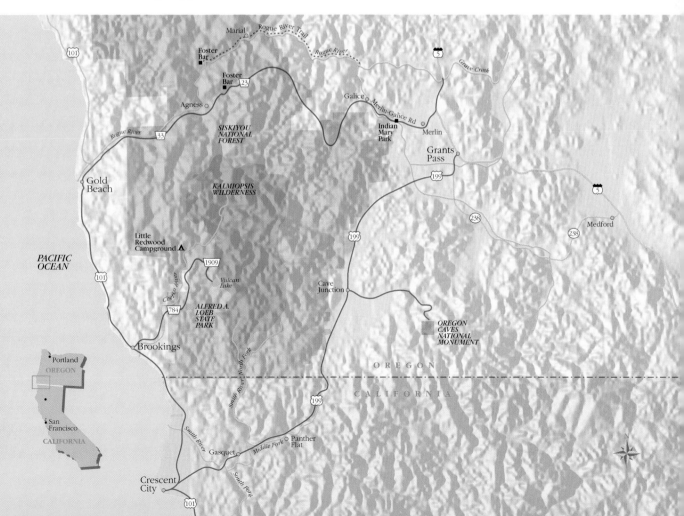

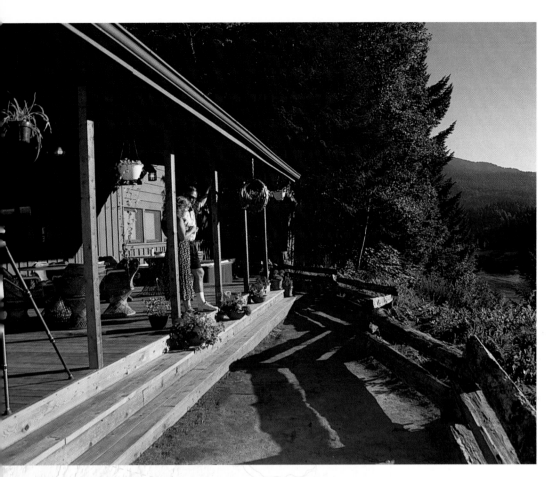

The Santa Anita Lodge offers a little sunshine and Rogue River views with its morning coffee.

Monument; watch for signs to two wineries along this route, both open to the public for tasting. At the caves, tour guides lead walks through an underground maze of fantastic calcite sculptures. A four-year, $1.3-million restoration project was completed here in 1998. Aboveground trails invite hiking here as well. Visitors can stay overnight at the lodge or at two appealing creekside primitive campgrounds on the road to the caves.

Drive up the Chetco along the river's north bank for camping at Alfred A. Loeb State Park, smaller Little Redwood Campground, or one of the scattered primitive campsites along the river. Near Loeb State Park, you can hike among the world's northernmost coastal redwoods on the Redwood Nature Trail, a lovely 1-mile loop. For more serious hiking, continue up the road into Siskiyou National Forest and, eventually, Kalmiopsis Wilderness. It's a long rocky drive to the trailhead, but the 1.8-mile hike to Vulcan Lake is a gem.

Following the Smith

U.S. Highway 199 between Grants Pass and Crescent City slices through the heart of the Siskiyous, its narrow twists and turns frustrating hurried drivers. For travelers who take the time to explore, U.S. 199 grants access to several wonders of the West, from marble caves to some of the West's premiere swimming holes.

At Cave Junction, turn off U.S. 199 toward Oregon Caves National

Southwest of the Oregon state line, U.S. 199 follows the serpentine route of the Middle Fork Smith River, with plenty of access points for wading, picnicking, or swimming. Drive off the main road into the mountains or up the South Fork to reach trailheads for hikes. Wildflowers peak here April through June. Guided whitewater raft trips on the free-flowing forks of the Smith are generally available March through June, when water levels are high and weather inviting. Swimming holes are many, but the best, most secluded spots are along the South Fork; look for river access signs along the road. Three campgrounds are perched along the Middle Fork Smith River, just off U.S. 199; each has its charms, but Panther Flat, with hot showers and flush toilets, is the top pick.

Unless otherwise noted, area codes are 541. Lodging rates for two people range from $ (under $100) to $$$ (above $250) per night.

WHERE

Grants Pass, gateway for trips down the Rogue and the northern end of U.S. 199, is off I-5 about 250 miles south of Portland. Crescent City, CA, at the southern end of U.S. 199, is about 350 miles north of San Francisco on U.S. 101. Brookings is 25 miles north of Grants Pass, Gold Beach another 30 miles north.

LODGING

A night or more in a lodge by the Rogue River is an experience not to be missed. Just outside Grants Pass is **Morrison's Rogue River Lodge** (8500 Galice Rd., Merlin; 476-3825, 800/826-1963; $-$$); anglers and others keep returning for the food, the view, and the hospitality. On the lower Rogue, rustic 1930s **Santa Anita Lodge** (36975 Agness-Illahe Rd., Agness; 247-6884) combines African trophies, a huge stone fireplace, a four-course dinner, and wonderful views. Downstream, outside of Gold Beach is the elegant, exquisitely sited **Tu Tú Tun Lodge** (96550 N. Bank Rd., Gold Beach; 247-6664, 800/864-6357; $$), frequently featured in world's-best-lodge listings.

In Brookings, the 1917 Craftsman-style **South Coast Inn** (516 Redwood St.; 469-5557, 800/525-9273; $-$$) is just off U.S. 101; accommodating hosts are happy to hook you up with an outfitter, make a dinner reservation, or point you toward good hiking trails. Upriver, **Chetco River Inn** (21202 High Prairie Rd.; 670-1645; $$) is a dream of a fishing lodge—whether or not you fish. Hand-stitched quilts accent 4 guestrooms in this contemporary home fronting the river; lunch and dinner are available by request, in addition to a generous breakfast.

Off U.S. 99, **Oregon Caves Lodge** (20000 Caves Hwy., Caves Junction; 592-3400; $-$$) is charming and rustic, just what you would expect of a 1934 mountainside hotel. Sheathed in bark, the lodge rises like a tree six stories above the creek, which runs through the dining room. **Patrick Creek Lodge** (13950 U.S. 199; 707/457-3323; $-$$), 8 miles east of Gasquet, has been catering to travelers since 1926. To reserve a campsite at **Panther Flat**, call 800/280-2267.

DINING

Riverside lodges pride themselves on their food; many (including **Morrison's** and **Tu Tú Tun**) serve passersby as well. If you're in Grants Pass at dinnertime, consider **Hamilton House** (344 N.E. Terry Ln.; 479-3938) in the owner/chef's elegant family home. In addition to a dining room, **Oregon Caves Lodge** has a memorable 1930s-style soda fountain. Time a trip down U.S. 199 to hit the nearly endless Sunday brunch buffet at **Patrick Creek Lodge** (see Lodging above). Best south coast dinners are at **Chives** (1025 Chetco Ave., Brookings; 469-4121).

ON THE RIVER

Most rafting and kayaking on the Chetco and Smith rivers take place from late winter through spring and into June, a time when water levels are high. The Rogue is raftable spring through fall.

Each of these rivers is well known for its anadromous fish runs; with some skill and in the right season, you could well hook a steelhead or salmon. Chinook salmon run late fall and winter, with smaller runs in spring; steelhead run spring and fall. In spring or summer, try your hand at trout (catch-and-release only in some areas). Sporting goods or specialty fishing shops in Grants Pass, Brookings, or Crescent City can get you organized with gear, point you to some good fishing holes, and outfit you with proper permits. But if you're new to the territory and your time is limited, hire a guide.

A call to **Smullen Visitor Center** (479-3735) can provide you with information on guided raft, drift boat, or hiking trips down the Rogue and on the river's remote lodges accessible only by boat or on foot. To hook up with a fishing guide on the Chetco River, call **Chetco Ranger District** (469-2196). **Wilderness Canyon Adventures** (888/517-1613) offers 1- to 5-day spring trips on the boisterous upper river (some start in the Kalmiopsis Wilderness) and 1-day floats on the lower river beginning in May or June, all in inflatable kayaks. The **Smith River National Recreation Area** (707/457-3131) can provide names of outfitters for fishing or floating that river, as well as suggestions for hikers and swimmers.

FOR MORE INFORMATION

Grants Pass Visitors & Convention Bureau (1995 N.W. Vine St.; 476-7717, 800/547-5927) and Gold Beach Chamber of Commerce (29279 Ellensburg #3; 247-7526, 800/525-2334) have information on lodging, float trips, jet boat trips, and other Rogue River attractions. For south coast information, contact Brookings-Harbor Chamber of Commerce (P.O. Box 940, Brookings; 469-3181, 800/535-9469). A Siskiyou National Forest map is helpful for touring along the Rogue and Chetco rivers; call their headquarters (471-6500). For information on Oregon Caves, call 592-3400.

REGION		WASHINGTON
Where	X	130 miles southwest of Seattle
When	X	Year-round destination

Washington's Winter Secret

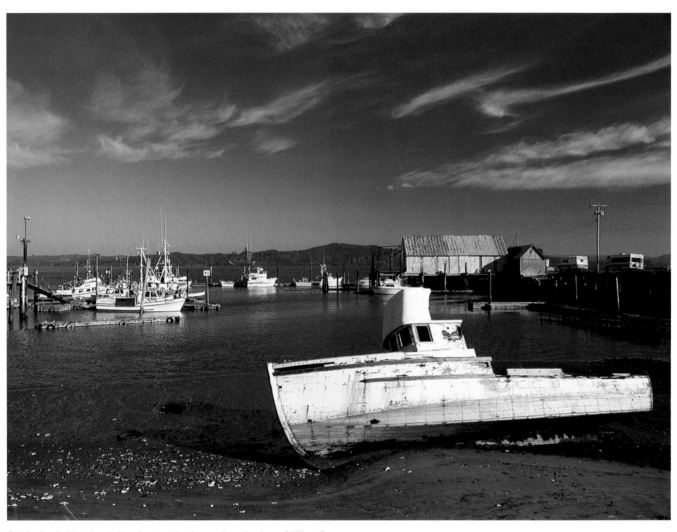

Tokeland's placid harbor shelters boats—old and new—along the shore of Willapa Bay.

Whatever the weather, one overlooked stretch of Washington's shoreline never fails to satisfy—even in winter. Extending from Grays Harbor to Willapa Bay, the coastline is dotted with driftwood-littered beaches, picturesque harbors, and pleasant places to eat and spend the night. You can explore all of them on a weekend on an easy loop drive off U.S. Highway 101 between the towns of Aberdeen and Raymond.

Along the way, roadside seafood markets sell fresh oysters, so bring a cooler to carry a pint or two back to your lodgings. If you're a bird-watcher, carry binoculars to get a good look at the many species that inhabit the bays and beaches.

Westport

From Aberdeen, State Highway 105 follows the south shore of Grays Harbor to Westport, dubbed the "Sports Fishing Capital of the World." If you'd like to try your luck for coho salmon or bottomfish, such as greenling, halibut, lingcod, and rockfish, reserve a spot on one of the charter boats that go out year-round, weather permitting. In summer, daily passenger ferry service connects Westport with the popular resort area of Ocean Shores, which sits on a peninsula separating Grays Harbor from the Pacific Ocean.

For a pleasant stroll, walk the waterfront along Westhaven Drive. At the south end of the dock area, the Westport Maritime Museum is housed in the old Coast Guard station, a Colonial Revival-style clapboard complete with watchtower and widow's walk. Displays include marine mammal skeletons and vintage photos of old Westport residences and coastal defense patrol activity during World War II. There's also a fine collection of Northwest tribal baskets. Historians and lighthouse buffs will enjoy the light and Fresnel lens that were first installed in the 1890s at Destruction Island Lighthouse, 40 miles north of Westport. When the lighthouse was updated with state-of-the-art electronics in 1995, the light and lens were moved to the museum, which recently added a building to display them.

Just south of the dock area is Westhaven State Park. A mile-long trail leads through the dunes along the ocean to the 107-foot-tall Grays Harbor Lighthouse, built in 1897. (Tours of the lighthouse can be arranged through the museum.) Offshore, you may even spot a gray whale; whale-watching season officially runs from March through May.

More Beaches & Birds

South of Westport, State 105 winds along the Pacific for about 12 miles, offering numerous turnoffs to broad sandy beaches framed with driftwood and fringed by dunes. Twin Harbors State Park, about 4 miles south of Westport, has a wide, gently sloping beach that's a favorite with surf-fishers, kite fliers, and agate hunters. Grayland Beach State Park, at the south end of the town of Grayland, seems to be the destination for a dramatic repository of driftwood.

Both parks offer trails, picnic areas, campsites, and an abundance of shorebirds, including long-billed curlews, marbled godwits, black-bellied plovers, whimbrels, and willets. Shimmering strands of dunlins and sandpipers swoop across the sky. Watch for waterfowl, too, including scoters diving for fish and large flocks of pintails and wigeons. The peregrine falcon, an endangered species, is reappearing along this coast.

Turn off the main road to explore the tiny towns of Grayland and North Cove.

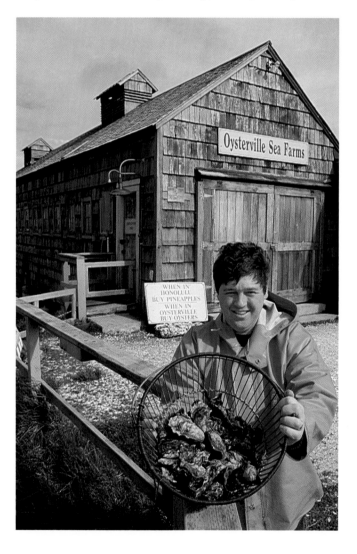

Oysterville Sea Farms harvests a bountiful crop of delicious Willapa Bay oysters.

These hamlets are dotted with turn-of-the-century houses and beach shacks. Cranberry bogs around the area bloom in June and are harvested in October. You'll see cranberries featured on restaurant menus.

Poke Around Tokeland

Tokeland, one of the state's oldest resorts, sits at the north end of Willapa Bay. Home to some 200 people in winter (a figure that doubles in summer), the town has no gas stations and just a few stores, including The Pregnant Onion Antiques (open at the owner's whim).

A great place to shop for fresh crab, shrimp, canned tuna,

smoked sturgeon, and other fish delights is the Nelson Crab Cannery. In fall, the Department of Fish and Wildlife opens a fishery for views of one of the coast's best salmon runs.

According to locals, Tokeland has the most beautiful beach on the coast, primarily because there is never anyone on it.

From Tokeland, State 105 turns east and takes you back to U.S. 101.

This delivery of roses goes into the mailbox at 133 on a country road near Grays Harbor.

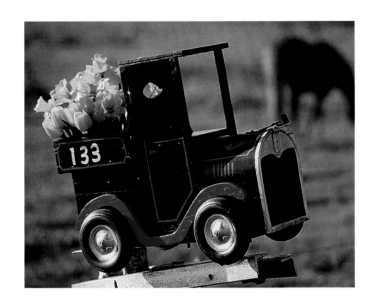

TRIP PLANNER

Unless otherwise noted, area codes are 360. Lodging rates for two people range from $ (under $100) to $$$ (above $250) per night.

WHERE

Beach towns lie along State 105, a 50-mile loop drive off U.S. 101 between Aberdeen and Raymond. Westport is the only town along this coast with a gas station.

LODGING

Westport and Grayland have a number of small family-owned motels offering reasonably priced rooms (some with kitchenettes), a few houses that rent nightly or weekly, and several RV parks. For resort-style lodging overlooking the ocean, check into **Chateau Westport** (710 W. Hancock St.; 800/255-9101; $ including continental breakfast). Over 100 attractive rooms, a heated pool, and a hot tub make it ideal for families. The stately 17-room clapboard **Tokeland Hotel and Restaurant** (100 Hotel Rd.; 267-7006; $ including breakfast) first opened for business in 1889. Set on

a grassy promontory overlooking Willapa Bay, it offers small, comfortable, charmingly furnished rooms and a dining room open daily for breakfast, lunch (except Sunday), and dinner. Save room for the special Sunday dinner treat, cranberry pot roast cooked with cloves and cinnamon and smothered with whole cranberries in sauce.

DINING

Anthony's (280 E. Dock St., Westport; 286-1609) serves tasty Greek dishes, such as beef and prawns souviaki. **Inn of the West Wind** (2119 Nyphus St., Westport; 268-0677) cooks what people in town like, home-style American cuisine.

MUSEUMS

In winter, **Westport Maritime Museum** (2201 Westhaven St.;

268-0078) is open from noon to 4 Wed.-Sun.; call for tours of **Grays Harbor Lighthouse**. Donations are requested.

FOR MORE INFORMATION

Westport/Grayland Chamber of Commerce (2985 S. Montesano St., Westport, WA; 266-9422). Tokeland North Coast Chamber of Commerce (276-7006).

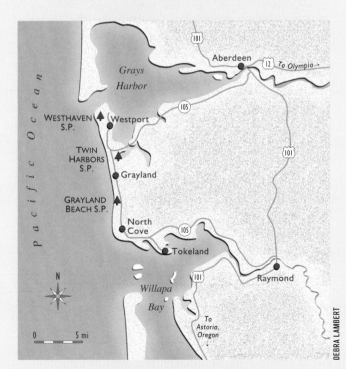

to the top of
Mt. Baker

REGION		WASHINGTON
Where	X	145 miles northeast of Seattle
When	X	Summer or winter

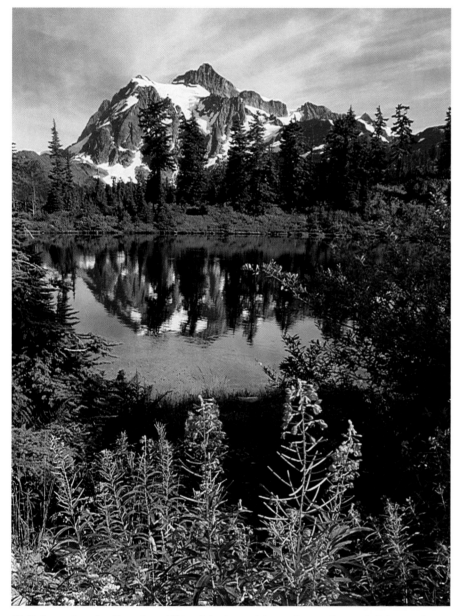

Mt. Shuksan, mirrored on the surface of Picture Lake, is one of the state's most photographed views on the road to the top of Mt. Baker.

On a clear day, snow-capped Mt. Baker claims the eye of travelers all over northwest Washington and southwest British Columbia. A favorite of downhill skiers and snowboarders, it offers Washington's longest ski season—from November to May. In warmer months, hikers, fishers, and sightseers are drawn by the area's awe-inspiring beauty, just as miners were drawn here by gold in the late 1800s. One of the state's prettiest drives, 55-mile Mt. Baker Highway and Scenic Byway (State Highway 542) from Bellingham to the top of the mountain, got its start from those miners' dreams. Today it offers a bonanza of views and recreation options.

From Vineyards to Heather Meadows

The road meanders along the Nooksack River through verdant farming and forest land. In summer, you'll see signs to U-pick berry farms. Mount Baker Vineyards, halfway between Nugent's Corner and Deming, offers vineyard and mountain views and picnic tables; their tasting room is open year-round. Beyond here, the road turns north. Near Maple Falls, Silver Lake County Park is a good stop for boaters and fishers.

Glacier, just inside the boundary of Mt. Baker/Snoqualmie National Forest, has a general store, eateries, and lodging. It is your last chance for services. Stop at the public service center, a mile east of town, for maps, hiking tips, and information on mountain conditions. Six miles east of Glacier, Nooksack Falls can be viewed safely from a fenced overlook just a half-mile from the road. Four miles beyond the falls, watch for a grove of towering old-growth Douglas firs.

Narrowing with switchbacks, the road climbs 3,200 feet in the last 10 miles as you reach the heart of Mt. Baker Ski Area. You pass White Salmon Day Lodge, a handsome log complex built in 1996. A mile beyond is the entrance to beautiful Heather Meadows, an alpine area usually open by mid-July. A highlight here is Picture Lake. Trails around the lake lead through summer wildflowers of lupine and fireweed. Stop at Austin Pass Picnic Area and Heather Meadows Interpretive Center for terrific views of Bagley Lakes and mountain ridges dotted with bonsai-like silver fir and 500-

Crafted from sturdy stone and wood, Heather Meadows Interpretive Center, built as a warming hut in 1940, now houses displays and a gift shop.

year-old mountain hemlock.

A short wheelchair–accessible trail offers easy exploration; longer trails also leave from here.

The road ends at a parking lot, usually accessible by late July, at 5,140-foot Artist Point

viewpoint. The name speaks for itself. You will have stunning views of 10,778-foot Mt. Baker, 9,038-foot Mt. Shuksan, and 5,628-foot Table Mountain.

TRIP PLANNER

Unless otherwise noted, all area codes are 360. Lodging rates for two people range from $ (under $100) to $$ (above $250) per night.

WHERE

Take exit 255 from Interstate 5 in Bellingham; Mt. Baker is 55 miles to the east.

LODGING

Near Maple Falls, 411-acre **Silver Lake Park** encompasses a former private resort and early homestead. Seven cabins are available for rental year-round (call 599-2776 well in advance to reserve; $); there are also 73 campsites. The **Glacier Creek Motel & Cabins** (Mt. Baker Hwy. at Glacier; 800/719-1414, 599-2991; $) has pleasant, basic accommodations with kitchenettes just off Mt. Baker Hwy.

Mt. Baker Lodging (7500 Mt. Baker Hwy. at Maple Falls; 599-2453,

800/709-7669; $$-$$$) and **Mt. Baker Chalet** (9857 Mt. Baker Hwy., Milepost 33, at Glacier; 599-2405; $-$$$) are reservation services representing area houses, cabins, and condos. Specify whether you're interested in a rustic cabin or a modern house.

FOOD & DINING

Mount Baker Vineyards (Mt. Baker Hwy.; 592-2300) opens daily 11-5 for tasting. A short detour from the winery, eclectic **Everybody's Store** (State Hwy. 9, Van Zandt; 592-2297) sells everything from Northwest native art and hiking books to sandwiches made with local cheeses and sausages. **Milano's Market and Deli** (Mt. Baker Hwy., Glacier; 599-2863)

offers hearty pastas and sandwiches; it's a good stop for families.

FOR MORE INFORMATION

U.S. Forest Service Glacier Public Service Center (599-2714) is open May through October (599-2714). For winter information on Mt. Baker ski area, call 734-6771. Bellingham-Whatcom County Convention and Visitors Bureau (904 Potter St., Bellingham, WA 98226; 800/487-2032 voice mail, 671-3990) has a main office just off I-5 at exit 253.

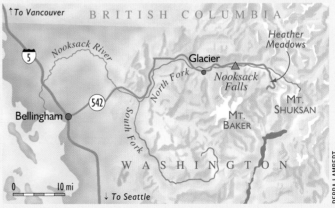

Leavenworth—
alpine village in apple country

REGION		WASHINGTON
Where	X	120 miles northeast of Seattle
When	X	All-season destination

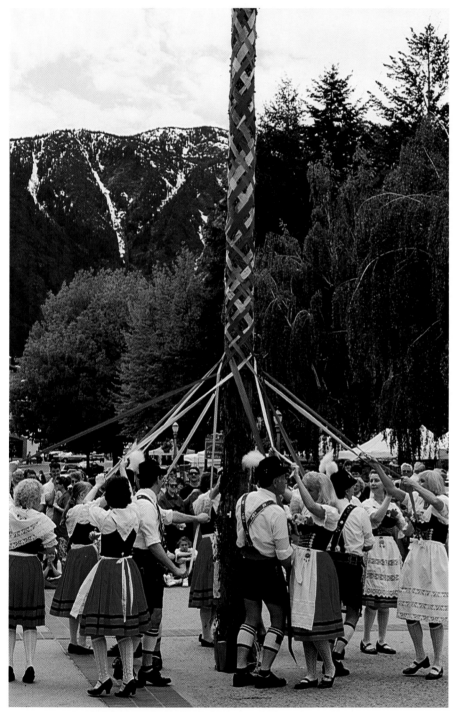

Wearing traditional costumes (lederhosen and dirndl), Bavarian dancers in Leavenworth weave ribbons around a maypole at the annual May celebrations.

Postcard-perfect mountain peaks, abundant year-round recreation, and a prime spot on a popular route between western and eastern Washington earn Leavenworth high marks from travelers. The self-styled Bavarian village feels authentic. Though it may be jam-packed during festivals—Maifest, Autumn Leaf, and Christmas Lighting are a few of more than a dozen events held annually—it also offers the serenity of an alpine retreat at other times.

Come here in summer to hike nearby mountain trails, go fishing, or simply soak up the sunshine. In autumn, savor colorful foliage; Tumwater Canyon, a scenic 9-mile stretch of U.S. Highway 2 west of Leavenworth, is brilliant with fall color. A visit in winter or spring showcases the area's most magical seasons. Snow or a profusion of apple and pear blossoms can transform the Wenatchee Valley with a veil of white.

For Fun in the Snow & Valley Music

Cross-country skiing is a popular winter pastime around Leavenworth. Two unique, off-the-beaten-path lodgings put you in the thick of ski trails. At the west edge of town, you'll see signs for Icicle Creek Road.

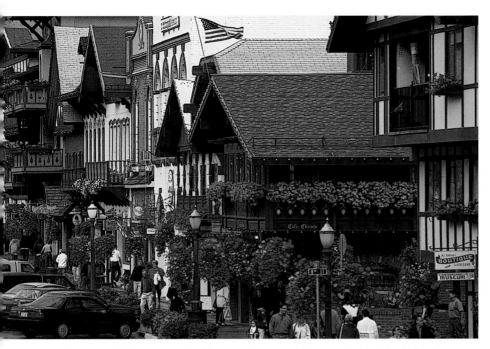

Front Street, a 3-block-long promenade of Bavarian-style stores and restaurants, forms the heart of town, drawing shoppers and strollers.

Follow this 2¹/2 miles to Sleeping Lady Conference Center, a 67-acre retreat with accommodations tucked in amid towering Ponderosa pines. Adjacent to the center's entrance, you'll see signs for the Leavenworth Winter Sports Club hut; a small fee gives you access to miles of groomed trails (509/548-5115). Sleeping Lady is also home to the Icicle Creek Music Center, a performance setting for a resident chamber group and musicians from around the country.

East of town, 3 miles up a primitive winding road traversed only by snowcats and snowmobiles in winter, is Mountain Home Lodge. It's a favorite with cross-country skiers and those simply seeking a mountain hideaway with gourmet food.

Spring Blooms & Back Roads

The 18 miles between Leavenworth and Wenatchee, the area's bustling center of commerce to the east, are flanked with apple and pear orchards that burst into blossom in late April and early May. A handful of tiny communities, connected by meandering back roads, lie in between. Prey's Fruit, a mile east of Leavenworth on U.S. 2, not only sells fruit but also offers spring orchard tours by appointment (509/548-5771). Nearby, Smallwood Harvest (509/548-4196) sells fruit and also gives hints for driving tours.

Watch for the exit to Peshastin, just east of these fruit stands. Follow the road as it ambles west

Apples-on-your-honor at Feil Fruit Stand near Wenatchee. Popular valley varieties include Red and Golden Delicious, Fuji, Gala, and Jonathan.

several miles back toward Leavenworth; take the Chumstick Road north and west to the small community of Plain. Stop and browse in the hardware store before circling back to Leavenworth via Lake Wenatchee.

You can also follow country roads east from Peshastin and, when you emerge again on U.S. 2, go a few miles farther east to the town of Cashmere. Liberty Orchards (117 Mission Street; 509/782-4088) makes the popular Aplets and Cotlets as well as other fruit candies at their headquarters here. Their shop, open daily, offers samples of fruit candies; 20-minute guided kitchen tours are given on weekdays. Get a quick history lesson on the settlement of Central Washington by visiting Cashmere's Pioneer Village (600 Cotlets Way; 782-3230; admission fee), a block from the highway (take the second Cashmere exit). It's open daily except Monday from March to October.

The village includes a schoolhouse, blacksmith shop, saddle and print shops, jail, saloon, and an assay office from nearby

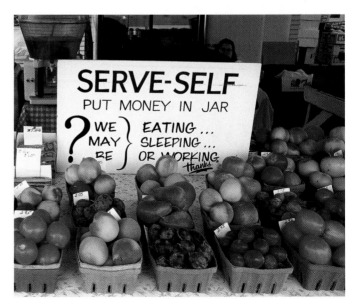

Blewitt Mines—20 buildings in all. The church is the only replica; the others are original dwellings from Chelan and Douglas counties. Most were built by pioneers before 1892, the date when the Great Northern Railway started service in the region.

An 1891 reconstructed waterwheel stands beside the museum on the Wenatchee River. It once provided irrigation water to a nearby farm. The museum itself is packed with area memorabilia, including a rare Native American gut basket from the Wenatchee people.

⁞⁞TRIP PLANNER⁞⁞⇨

Unless otherwise noted, area codes are 509. Lodging rates for two people range from $ (under $100) to $$$ (above $250) per night.

WHERE

Leavenworth lies in the eastern foothills of the North Cascades, a few hours northeast of Seattle, along U.S. Hwy. 2.

LODGING

Many hideaways are convenient to town yet seem worlds away. Your choices range from in-town bed-and-breakfasts to rustic cabins and elegant mountain retreats. **Sleeping Lady** (7375 Icicle Creek Rd.; 548-6344, 800/574-2123; $$-$$$ including meals) has cabin complexes decorated with natural fabrics and locally crafted iron accents. Don't miss the outdoor glass icicle sculpture by Dale Chihuly near the dining room. **Mountain Home Lodge** (Mountain Home Rd.; 548-7077, 800/414-2378; $$-$$$; winter rates include food) is a modern inn with mountain-style décor set 3 miles from and 1,000 feet above town. In summer, the area surrounding it is a hiker's dream. **Run of the River Inn** (9308 E. Leavenworth Rd.; 548-7171, 800/288-6491; $-$$), a country-style retreat on the Icicle River, has a very special setting overlooking wetlands between two bird refuges. The inn offers hiking and biking tips. Cabin and house rentals around Plain are plentiful.

DINING

Restaurant Österreich (633 A Front St.; 548-4031) serves gourmet Austrian fare including a mouth-watering apple strudel. **Viscontis** (548-1213) serves rustic Italian fare in a spot overlooking **The Leavenworth Brewery** (636 Front St.; 548-4545). The Whistling Pig wheat beer, known as "The Pig," is a favorite.

Ask to see the wood-fired ovens and pick up fragrant cinnamon rolls at **Homefires Bakery** (13013 Bayne Rd., off Icicle Creek Rd.; 548-7362). Streusel-topped apple pies and rustic Normandy Farm bread—a light rye made with apple cider—are specialties of **Anjou Bakery** (1 mile east of Cashmere; you'll see signs from the highway; 782-4360).

ATTRACTIONS

Hummel figurines, cuckoo clocks, lederhosen, and music boxes are just a few of the Teutonic curiosities you'll find along Front St. Be sure to check out the Old World carving at **The Woodcarver** (715-B Front St.; 548-2064). **The Gingerbread Factory** (828 Commercial St.; 548-6592) makes holiday-themed cookies and has a gift shop. You'll find everything from vintage snowshoes to Pendleton blankets at **Cabin Fever Rustics** (923 Commercial St.; 548-4238). The **Nutcracker Museum** (735 Front St.; 548-4708, 800/892-3989) displays over 3,000 different kinds of nutcrackers; it's open May-Oct. from 2-5 (small fee).

FESTIVAL

Wenatchee's **Washington State Apple Blossom Festival** coincides with peak bloom. Call the Wenatchee Area Visitor & Convention Bureau (662-2116, 800/57-APPLE) for information and dates. The **Washington Apple Commission Visitors Center** (2900 Euclid Ave., Wenatchee; 663-9600), open weekdays year-round and also weekends beginning in May, gives blossom information, provides apple displays, and offers free samples.

FOR MORE INFORMATION

The Leavenworth Chamber of Commerce (894 U.S. 2, Leavenworth, WA 98826; 548-5807) and the Wenatchee Area Visitor & Convention Bureau (2 S. Chelan Ave., Wenatchee, WA 98807-0850; 662-2116) offer lodging and travel information.

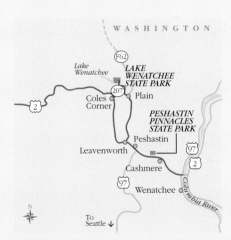

REGION	WASHINGTON	
Where	X	Two hours from Seattle/Tacoma
When	X	Spring through fall destination

Port Townsend—
a Victorian seaport

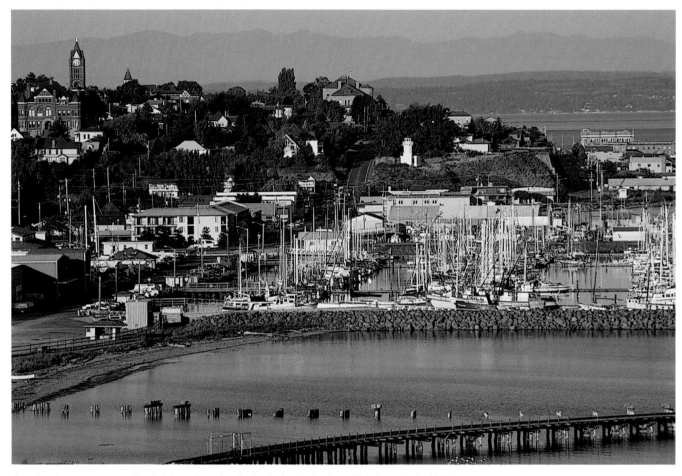

On a clear day you can survey the whole town, from shop-lined waterfront to handsome Victorians atop the bluff.

One of only three Victorian seaports in the U.S. on the National Historic Register, Port Townsend blends the best of past and present. The town is a lively mixture of historic waterfront and blufftop Victorian residential area, with expansive Fort Worden State Park nearby. For centuries the S'Klallam tribe lived around the harbor they called Kah Tai, plying the waters of Puget Sound in large dugout canoes. In 1792, Captain George Vancouver gave the anchorage its English name in honor of the Marquis of Townshend.

In the 19th century, the outpost became a city of 7,500. Riches from lumber, plus speculation that Port Townsend's position as a seaport would make it a North American railroad terminus, caused a building boom. The tracks stopped in Seattle, and Port Townsend fell into an economic depression. But poverty can be a great preserver. The buildings stood, many of them empty and badly in need of repair, until the 1960s, when tourists discovered Port Townsend. In the past three decades, the city has been returned to its former splendor, brick by brick.

Plan to spend at least two days to explore the town's granite, brick, and wood-framed

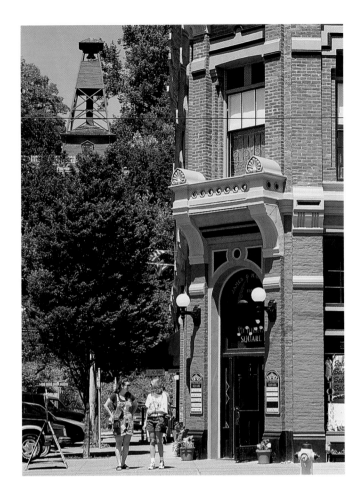

Antique shops, restaurants, and galleries fill the interiors of elegant old buildings along Water Street.

structures that stand defiantly on this northeast corner of Washington's Olympic Peninsula. The charming town and its wild beaches, which jut into both Puget Sound and the Strait of Juan de Fuca, present a dramatic contrast.

A One-time Boom Town

Handsomely facaded former saloons and bordellos lining Water and Washington streets downtown are filled today with antique shops, eateries, and galleries, some devoted to the work of local artists and craftspeople. The lucrative trade in tourist junk has been largely bypassed, although you'll find a T-shirt shop or two.

At the far northeast end of Water Street is the Jefferson County Historical Society

Museum and Library (210 Madison Street), housed in the 1891 city hall and jail. According to local legend, Jack London unwillingly spent the night here in 1897 en route to the Yukon. A few blocks southeast is the dock for Washington State Ferries, which sails to and from Keystone on Whidbey Island. Trips take about 30 minutes; boats accommodate pedestrians, cyclists, and motorists.

Climb the staircase at Taylor Street to reach the high bluff rearing above the once-bawdy waterfront. On this plateau looking south over Puget Sound, polite society lived graciously in

Mother and daughter enjoy tea on the porch of the beautifully restored James House, the Northwest's first bed-and-breakfast.

large Victorians with broad verandas. Ancient monkey puzzle trees, Monterey cypress, lilacs, tamarisks, and Irish and English yews are living proof of this gentility; these exotic horticultural fashions were imported more than a century ago. Considering the view and setting, it's not surprising that many of the old houses have been converted into bed-and-breakfasts.

Stretching through the center of the bluff lies Lawrence Street, where you'll find Aldrich's Grocery (940 Lawrence Street), built in 1887 as part of the business district established so that bluff homeowners could avoid the bordellos and raucous sailors on the lower streets along the wharf. The venerable store features a variety of gourmet foods usually available only in urban centers. Sally's, the deli space, serves hot soups, sandwiches, and other goodies. An upstairs apartment has been featured on the town's historical homes' tour.

Where Sound & Strait Meet

North of Port Townsend, a lighthouse at Point Wilson marks the meeting of Puget Sound and the Strait of Juan de Fuca. Fort

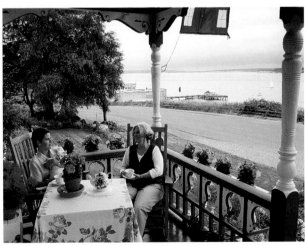

Worden was built on this strategic location in 1902. Used by the military until 1953, it became a state park 20 years later. With 434 acres of wide beaches, picnic facilities, a boat launch, forest trails, and deserted gun batteries, the fort is easily worth a day's exploration. The parade grounds remain, and the Centennial Rhododendron Garden contains more than 1,100 plants.

⋙ TRIP PLANNER ⋙

Unless otherwise noted, area codes are 360. Lodging rates for two people range from $ (under $100) to $$$ (above $250) per night.

WHERE

To reach Port Townsend from Seattle, drive south to Tacoma and follow State Hwy.16 to Hood Canal Bridge on State Hwy. 104. Cross the bridge and turn north on State Hwy. 19. Or take the Washington State Ferries from Seattle to Bainbridge Island and State Hwy. 305 to State Hwy. 3 north to the Hood Canal Bridge. For ferry information in-state, call (800) 843-3779; out of state, call (888) 8008-7977 or (206) 464-6400.

LODGING

In a place where Victoriana reigns, choosing a place to sleep can be a delightful decision. Photo-worthy inns promise a trip back in time—with modern amenities. One of the most majestic is the ornate **Ann Starrett Mansion** (744 Clay St.; 800/321-0644; $-$$), built by a ship captain and contractor as a wedding gift for his wife. The impeccably restored, 12-room **James House** (1238 Washington St.; 385-1238; $-$$) has the most commanding view on the bluff. It was built for the city's first land trader and stands as an example of the town's great wealth. Painted in its original bright colors, the **Old Consulate Inn** (313 Walker St. at Washington St.; 800/300-6753; $-$$ includes a seven-course breakfast), a

former German consulate, was built in the Queen Anne style. The imposing two-story porch of the sparkling white, shingled **Quimper Inn** (1306 Franklin St.; 385-1060; $-$$) looks as much Deep South as Northwest. **Manresa Castle** (7th and Sheridan sts.; 800/732-1281; $-$$), a grand old 1892 house on the southwest end of town, is now a small hotel. The mansion was built for the town's first mayor in 1892, expanded by the Jesuit Order in 1925, and converted in the mid-1970s into a 40-room hotel and restaurant (dinner only).

To reserve a three- to six-bedroom house on Officer's Row at **Fort Worden State Park**, or for camping information, call 385-4730, ext. 433. For hostel information, call 385-0655.

DINING

Port Townsend's 18 restaurants cater to every taste. Locals laud **Lonny's** (2330 Washington St.; 385-0700; dinner daily except Tuesdays), noted for organic produce, free-range chickens, sea-fresh fish, and attention to detail. The **Silverwater Café** (237 Taylor St.; 385-6448; lunch and dinner daily) elevates Northwest cuisine to its most sublime. Don't miss the raspberry-white chocolate cheesecake. **Jake's Original Grill** (600 Sims Wy.; 385-5356; lunch and dinner daily except Sunday) serves a "Gorgonzola hamburger to die for," according to one local.

FESTIVALS

The 5-day **Victorian Festival** in late March includes a bus tour in the historic residential area. A ticket to the **Taste of Townsend**, held around Veterans' Day, lets you sample such delectables as citrus-glazed salmon and almond-crusted halibut. The entertaining **Wooden Boat Show,** in September, draws more than 300 old wooden sailboats and boat fans.

FOR MORE INFORMATION

Port Townsend Visitor Information Center (2437 E. Sims Way; 385-3722 in-state, 888/365-5978 out of state) is open daily.

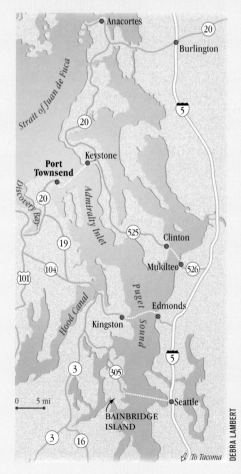

Olympic Coast
sanctuaries

REGION		WASHINGTON
Where	X	3 to 4 hours west of Seattle
When	X	Spring through fall best seasons

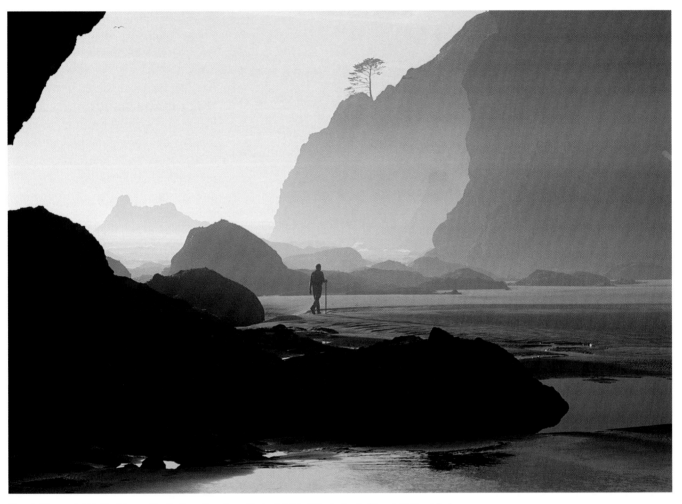

Dwarfed by coastal bluffs, this seaside stroller enjoys the solitude at Point of the Arches in Olympic National Park.

A glimpse of the ocean is a rare treat indeed for motorists wending their way along Washington's Olympic Peninsula coast. A long stretch of it is part of Olympic National Park, but only 12 miles of U.S. Highway 101 parallels the beach. Except for the southern coastline of the peninsula, from the resort community of Ocean Shores to Taholah, views of most beaches are rewards for the hardy, who are in for a bit of a hike before beholding dramatic and awe-inspiring ocean vistas.

Four Indian reservations are located along the Olympic coast. Members of the Quinault, Hoh, Quillayute, and Makah nations have inhabited this rich but craggy shore for thousands of years. From the forests they took materials for clothing, housing, canoes, and tools. The ocean was their hunting ground for whales, seals, salmon, and shellfish. Now the shore is popular with people fishing for perch, gathering smelt with nets, or digging for clams.

Short detours from the highway into the Quinault and Hoh rain forests lead to a completely different world. Even the

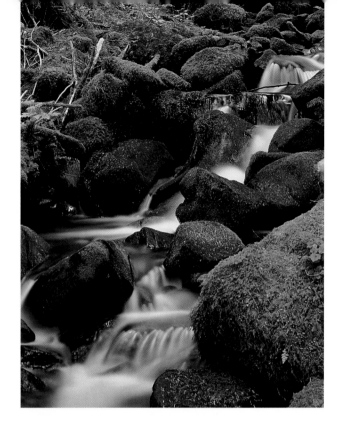

Moss-covered rocks line a feeder stream of the Soleduck River.

atmosphere changes from light mist to mossy dampness. Here, where the annual rainfall reaches 12 to 14 feet (by contrast, Seattle's rainfall is 36.16 inches), enormous trees of record-breaking girth and layers of moss, ferns, and lichens form lush carpets and canopies of green.

In the Slow Lane

Don't try to go from the tip of the Ocean Shores peninsula to Cape Flattery, the most northwestern point in the contiguous U.S., in one day; leave time to explore the beaches and forests. Also, there are two historic lodges along the way, beautiful Lake Quinault Lodge (built in 1926) and rustic, beachfront Kalaloch Lodge, built in the 1930s and used as a Coast Guard station in World War II.

You can reach Ocean Shores via Hoquiam and Aberdeen, on U.S. Highway 12 west from Olympia. This popular resort sits on a sandy peninsula at the mouth of Grays Harbor, named after Robert Gray, the U.S. ship captain who stopped here before discovering the Columbia River in 1792. Activities abound, from bird-watching to digging for razor clams, and you'll find restaurants and shops.

The beaches to the north, along State Highway 109, are not as busy but just as lovely. Pacific Beach has the small beach-town feeling that eludes Ocean Shores. In Taholah, where State 109 ends inside the Quinault Indian Reservation, visitors must get beach passes from the tribal office.

To return to U.S. 101, either head back to Hoquiam or follow the rough Moclips Highway to Neilton. Just 4 miles north of Neilton is beautiful Lake Quinault, where a sprawling lodge, with cedar shingles, green shutters, and white trim, overlooks a lush lawn leading to the lakeshore. Guests can relax in the period wicker furniture in front of the large, brick fireplace. The lodge's Roosevelt Dining Room is named after its most famous guest, FDR himself.

A short drive farther on South Shore Road stands the "World's Largest Sitka Spruce Tree." More than 200 feet tall and 58 feet around, it is thought to be nearly 1,000 years old.

To the Beach

The road jogs west again, and soon you are on the only part of U.S. 101 that affords a view of the northern peninsula coast. But the beaches are beautiful and, after a short hike from your parked car, accessible. Between South Beach and Ruby Beach, six beach trails from the highway lead to Beach 1, Beach 2, and so forth. Sturdy shoes are recommended for tidepool exploring and hiking in search of migrating whales.

Between Beaches 2 and 3 is scenic Kalaloch (pronounced kalay-lock) Lodge, built on a cliff above the ocean. At the north end of the stretch, Ruby Beach has the best view of sea stacks, offshore rocks, and islands. The

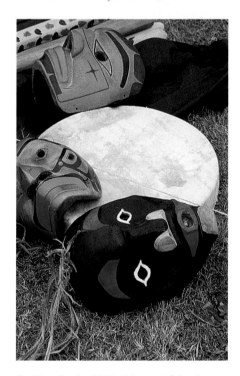

Brightly painted and intricately carved Quinault masks surround a ceremonial drum.

beacon from an 1891 lighthouse blinks from Destruction Island, 3 miles offshore.

After the highway turns inland again, watch for signs for the Hoh Rain Forest. The drive to the visitor center follows the beautiful Hoh River along a corridor of huge, moss-covered trees. Don't miss the 3/4-mile Hall of Mosses Trail, just behind the visitor center.

A trip back to the beach requires another detour off U.S. 101, heading west from Forks on State Highway 110 to Rialto Beach, just north of La Push. This wild and rugged beach is the start of the North Wilderness Coast Hike, which extends as far north as Cape Alava, north of Ozette Lake. But beware of high tides and shifting logs in the surf.

Meeting the Makah

Heading north from Forks, the town with the highest rainfall (162.14 inches in 1997) in the continental U.S., follow signs to Neah Bay on the Makah Indian Reservation. A remarkable museum tells the story of the Makah people through artifacts excavated from a 500-year-old village near Ozette Lake.

Follow the road through town to Cape Flattery. After a short hike, you'll find yourself overlooking the ocean and standing on the very tip of America, the northwestern corner of the contiguous United States.

TRIP PLANNER

Unless otherwise noted, area codes are 360. Lodging rates for two people range from $ (under $100) to $$$ (above $250) per night.

WHERE

Cape Flattery is about 145 miles northwest of Seattle; Ocean Shores is 132 miles to the southwest.

LODGING & DINING

Accommodations and restaurants are scarce on the west side of the Olympic Peninsula, so reservations are recommended.

Lake Quinault Lodge (P.O. Box 7, Quinault; 288-2900, 800/562-6672; $-$$$), on South Shore Rd., has 92 rooms with private baths, indoor swimming pool, sauna, and dining room.
Rain Forest Resort Village (516 S. Shore Rd., Quinault; 288-2535, 800/255-6936; $-$$) has been offering rustic lakeshore accommodations since 1923. Choose between cabins with fireplaces or motel-style rooms.
Kalaloch Lodge (157151 Highway 101, Forks, WA 98331; 962-2271; $-$$), has rooms in the lodge and cabins, with kitchens, along a bluff overlooking the ocean. Here too are a dining room and coffee shop.

MUSEUM

Makah Museum (Neah Bay; 645-2711) is open daily, 10-5, from Memorial Day to mid-September; closed Monday and Tuesday in winter. For a small admission charge, you'll see a giant whaling canoe carved from a cedar log, a replica of a longhouse, and artifacts excavated from an ancient Makah village.

FOR MORE INFORMATION

North Olympic Peninsula Visitor and Convention Bureau (338 W. First St., Port Angeles, WA; 452-8552). Olympic National Park Visitor Center (3002 Mt. Angeles Rd.; Port Angeles, WA; 452-0330). Ocean Shores Chamber of Commerce (120 W. Chance-a-la-Mer St.; 289-2451, 800/762-3224).

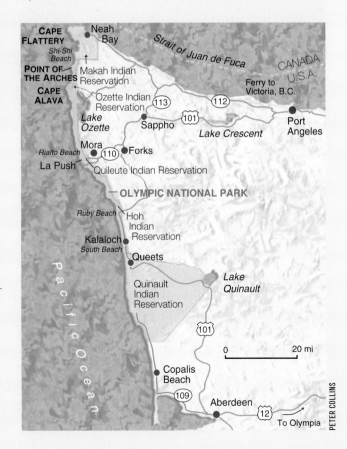

REGION	WASHINGTON
Where X	A ferry ride northwest of Seattle
When X	Spring, summer, and early fall

serene,
seafood-rich
Hood Canal

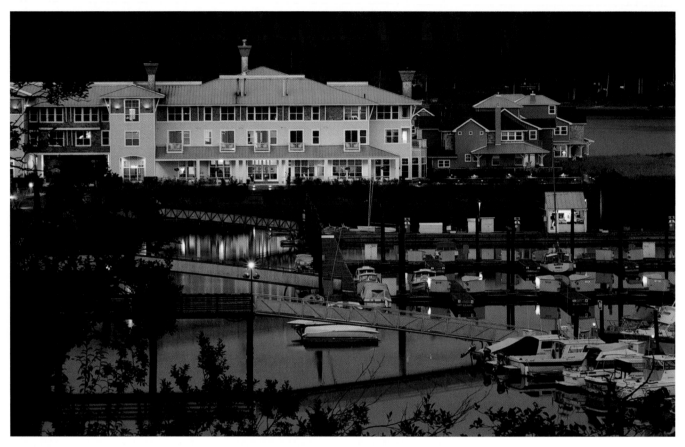

Aglow at dusk, Heron Beach Inn in Port Ludlow has water views from all guest rooms, attracting boaters and romantics.

In the spring of 1792, Captain George Vancouver and his crew sailed into Hood Canal. The shores of the 62-mile-long forested fjord were abloom with dogwood and wild rhododendron, its waters filled with oysters, spot prawns, and fish. To the west lay the snowcapped Olympic Mountains, monuments of serenity. Likely the only sounds to be heard were the creaking of the yawl, the soft splash of water, and bird calls—for even the most seasoned explorer had to be silenced by the beauty and bounty of this setting.

What's essential hasn't changed. Visit in spring or fall to find that same brand of calm. In summer, when the canal and its small shorefront communities buzz with activity, you must rise early to sample the silence. Come anytime to find rhododendrons and delicious seafood and take in inspiring views.

Our tour starts at the Kingston Ferry from Edmonds (you can also take the Bainbridge Island Ferry from Seattle and go north), where we visit two very different ports flanking the mouth of the canal.

Port Gamble & Port Ludlow

Port Gamble Historic Site lies 7 miles from Kingston, on State Highway 104. A lumber mill, built here in 1873, operated until the mid-1990s, and the town housed mill workers and their families. A church, fire station, and many fine old clapboard homes give it the air of a New England village. From the overlook, you may see a Trident submarine pass through the waters from the nearby base at Bangor. Stop at the historic general store for an ice cream cone or a deli sandwich or just to peruse their shell display. Before you leave town, pick up a map and ferry schedule at the visitor center, a few doors down from the store.

About a mile beyond Port Gamble, go right at Hood Canal Bridge (still State 104), crossing the north end of the canal. On a clear day, you'll have close-up views of the Olympic Mountains. Just beyond the bridge, take the Paradise Bay Road exit (the first right). About 4 miles from the highway you'll see signs to Port Ludlow Resort, a residential and vacation community for boaters and golfers. Water sports, golfing, and condominium rentals make this a popular spot for families. Nearby, on a small, flat peninsula, is Heron Beach Inn.

Back on State 104, continue west and take the turnoff to Quilcene, driving south through forested hills. You'll soon be on U.S. Highway 101, glimpsing

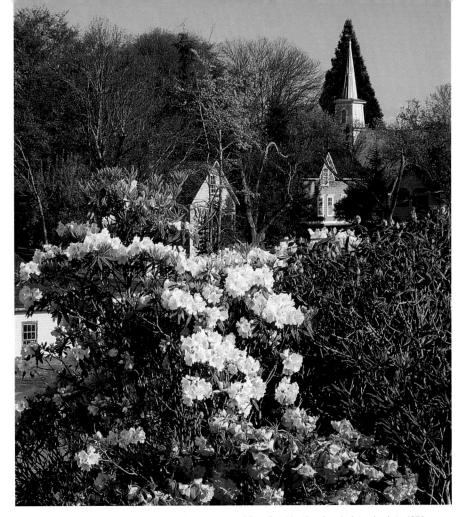

Flowers frame the prim and proper Americana beauty of Port Gamble; the church dates back to 1870.

water views through a thin border of trees.

Pristine Waters & Delicious Oysters

The clean waters of Hood Canal make it a perfect home for oysters. Many delicious bivalves, such as Quilcene, take their names from the rivers that start high in the Olympics and feed into the west side of the canal.

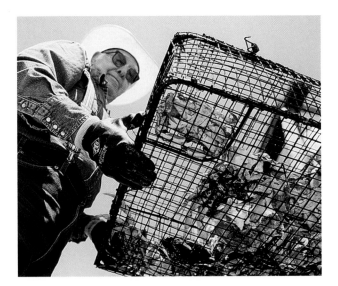

This fisherman hauls in a bounty of crabs at the Rest-A-While RV Resort boathouse in Hoodsport.

The marina and estuary of the Quilcene River is 2 miles from the highway, on Linger Longer Road. Here too is the area's largest oyster seed farm.

You'll see signs for oysters, crabs, clams, and other seafood in many places along U.S. 101, such as Hood Canal Seafood Marketplace in Quilcene (294963 U.S. 101; 765-4880; open 10 to 7 daily). Between mileposts 200 and 300 on U.S. 101 south of Quilcene, you'll see signs for Mt. Walker. A turnoff on the east side of the highway and a dirt road (open, weather permitting, in March or early April) lead to the 2,804-foot summit. Views of the canal, Seattle, and the Cascade Mountains to the east and the Olympics to the west are worth the drive; however, the steep route is not suitable for all vehicles.

Six miles south at Whitney Gardens and Nursery (306264 Highway 101; 796-4411) in Brinnon you'll find a seven-acre display garden (including native rhododendrons) to tour and plants for sale; it's open daily. Dosewallips State Park just beyond Brinnon has grassy campsites and beach access. It's fun to buy oysters and other seafood direct from the growers and hard to beat the selection at the Hama Hama Company (N. 35959 Highway 101; 877-5890), south of Eldon.

Hoodsport, 12 miles south of Eldon, is the largest community along the west side, with a marina, motels, and eateries. Several dive shops here hint at a little-known secret of the canal. Long underwater walls and ledges lead to a 500-foot-deep trench that provides a paradise of exploration for divers. Giant octopuses (the world's largest) share these ledges with wolf eels, rockfish, urchins, and anemones. You can taste a local vintage made from 'Island Belle' grapes at the Hoodsport Winery (N. 23501 Highway 101, 877-9894; open daily except for Christmas and Thanksgiving).

Potlatch State Park has water-front picnic sites near the Skokomish Indian Reservation. Watch for Joan's Smoked Salmon, (20031 N. Highway 101; 877-6737) owned and operated by Skokomish native Joan Pell; she sells and ships vacuum-packed smoked steelhead, salmon, and oysters, and frequently offers samples.

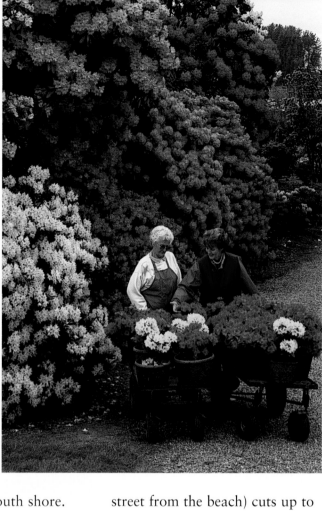

In Brinnon, Anne and Ellie Sather (shown here) run Whitney Gardens and Nursery, one of the Northwest's best specialty nurseries.

The South Shore

Take State Highway 106 as the canal sharply hooks east, and you'll follow the canal's gold coast, a mix of modest and grand vacation homes along the south shore. Victoria's Restaurant is a good reason to stop in Union for delicious seafood appetizers and entrées, including fried oysters from nearby Skokomish Bay and local fresh berries and chantrelle mushrooms in season.

Alderbrook Inn is a favorite of boaters and golfers; kayaks, paddleboats, and motorboats are available for rent. Their 18-hole golf course is away from the water, south of the resort.

Twanoh State Park lies about 6 miles east of Alderbrook, between mileposts 12 and 13. Most people flock to its shores for swimming and picnicking. A lower-key option is a short hike (2 miles round trip) along moss- and lichen-carpeted Twanoh Creek, through cedars, firs, madrones, hemlocks, and maples. The trail (which starts across the street from the beach) cuts up to the west wall of the quiet canyon, winding through evergreen huckleberries and pines on top, before dropping back to the road.

If you are returning east across Puget Sound, check your ferry schedule and give yourself plenty of time to reach Southworth, Bremerton, or Kingston sailings. You don't want to spoil the relaxed mood of your Hood Canal visit by making a frantic dash back to reality. However, if your schedule permits, take a couple of hours to explore Bremerton. The largest community on the Kitsap Peninsula, it is home to the Puget Sound Naval Shipyard and the U.S. Naval Museum. You can see dozens of modern and moth-balled navy ships through Kitsap Harbor Tours (377-8924).

Unless otherwise noted, all area codes are 360. Lodging rates for two people range from $ (under $100) to $$$ (over $250) per night.

WHERE

It's about 135 miles all the way around—starting and ending at Hood Canal Floating Bridge. To access the south end of the canal, via Belfair, from Seattle, take the Bremerton Ferry; from Tacoma, take State Hwy. 16. From Olympia to the south, take U.S. Hwy. 101.

LODGING & STATE PARKS

The **Heron Beach Inn** (1 Heron Rd., Port Ludlow; 437-0411; $$-$$$) is a romantic destination that mixes ease and elegance in an overgrown cottage-by-the-sea setting. **Port Ludlow Resort** (200 Olympic Pl., Port Ludlow; 800/732-1239; $-$$$) is a good family destination: 27-hole golf course; boat, kayak, and bicycle rentals; and a 300-slip marina. **Eldon Schoolhouse B&B** (N. 36840 U.S. 101, Eldon; 253/631-5109; $) is set back from the road; three units with baths have water views. **Alderbrook Inn/CRISTA Conference Center** (E. 7101 State 106; 800/622-9370; $-$$) has 78 recently renovated lodge rooms and 22 refurbished two-bedroom cottages on woodsy grounds

Half a dozen state park facilities along our route offer camping and/or picnicking close to the canal, including **Dosewallips State Park, Potlatch State Park, Twanoh State Park**, and **Belfair State Park**; for information call 800/233-0321; for reservations, call 800/452-5687.

DINING

The casually elegant dining room at the **Heron Beach Inn** (see Lodging above) focuses on Northwest cuisine; seafood dishes are a specialty. The restaurant at **Port Ludlow Resort** (see Lodging above) also features seafood of the area and water views. The **Hungry Bear Restaurant**, next to Eldon Schoolhouse B&B (see Lodging above; 877-5527), is a classic café that serves sandwiches, seafood, prime rib, and excellent pies. **Alderbrook Inn** (see Lodging above) has a restaurant with views of the water; Sunday brunch is special (the inn serves no alcohol). **Victoria's** (E. 6790 State 106; 898-4400) in Union offers hearty breakfasts on Sunday mornings; reservations suggested.

FOR MORE INFORMATION

Kitsap Peninsula Visitor and Convention Bureau (2 Rainier Ave., Port Gamble; 800/416-5615; open daily). In Belfair, stop at North Mason Visitors Information Center (Mary Theler Community Center, E. 22871 State Hwy. 3; 360/275-5548; open weekdays). For maps of the national forest land that parallels the canal's west shore, stop at the U.S. Forest Service office on U.S. 101 at the south end of Quilcene (765-2200). Rangers here can direct you to the best hikes and drives. The office in Hoodsport (N. 150 Lake Cushman Rd. State 119; 877-5254) provides information on Lake Cushman recreation area; there's an Olympic National Park information office here as well. For ferry information, call (800) 843-3779 in Washington, or (206) 464-6400 from out of state.

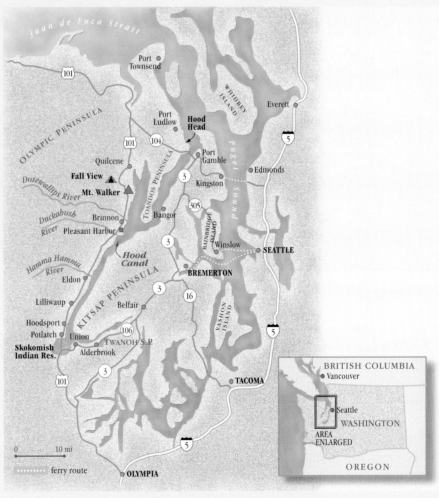

DEBRA LAMBERT

REGION	WASHINGTON
Where	X	226 miles east and north of Seattle
When	X	Spring, summer and fall trip

Grand Coulee
country

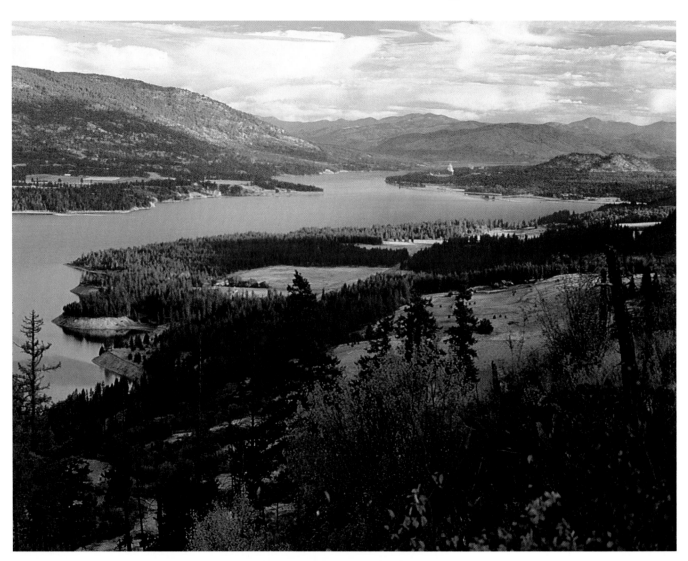

The sinuous blue ribbon of Franklin D. Roosevelt Lake bends eastward toward the mouth of Colville River.

Vast stretches of dry land and deep arid canyons—carved by centuries-old volcanic furor, ice ages, cataclysmic floods, and the meandering of one mighty river—shape Washington's Grand Coulee region. Signs of this dramatic story of fire and ice, water, and immense force can be readily seen in geologic landmarks that dot the area, such as Dry Falls, Banks Lake, Steamboat Rock, and Northrup Canyon. The largest and most impressive landmarks of all, though, are man-made: Grand Coulee Dam, a hydroelectric behemoth built in the 1930s, and the vast reservoir it created, 151-mile-long Franklin D. Roosevelt Lake.

Sparsely populated and bypassed by major roads, the region offers guaranteed hot summers and sparkling lakes for fishers, swimmers, and boaters. Cross-state travelers can leave Interstate 90 and detour here for

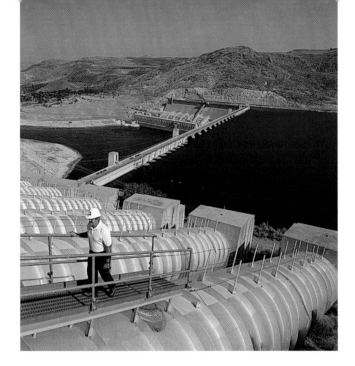

Grand Coulee Dam, a behemoth of concrete and power, has created a lake 400 feet deep at the dam base.

a true get-away-from-it-all experience.

From Seattle, take Interstate 90 east 137 miles to Vantage, where you'll get a stunning view of dry hills, rock, and the expansive Columbia River. About 14 miles northeast of Vantage, go northeast on State Highways 283 and 28, passing through the region's largest community, Ephrata. Six miles beyond, turn north onto State Highway 17 at Soap Lake, and you'll start your trek through the coulee's string of lakes.

Campers can overnight at Sun Lakes State Park, then visit the Dry Falls Visitor Center, where displays recount the history of the ancient floods that created the channel scablands. You'll have a dramatic view of the scant lake at the base of the falls, a favorite spot of fly fishers.

Steamboat Rock & an Original Back Road

Continuing north—following signs to Grand Coulee Dam on State Highway 155—the road skirts the east shore of Banks Lake, a favorite of bass fishers.

The lake's dominant feature is an 800-foot-high columnar basalt butte, Steamboat Rock, located about 20 miles from Coulee City. Once an island on the Columbia, it was left when the river changed its course.

Directly across from the entrance to the park is a short access road leading to historic Northrup Canyon. A trail—originally a narrow road traveled by stagecoaches and freight wagons—follows a small creek along the canyon floor. Columnar basalt buttes rise high on either side. In springtime, wildflowers, such as shooting stars, blue bells, and balsamroot, and flowering shrubs, such as purple sage and wild current, flank the trail. Here too fir, ponderosa pine, and alder trees mix with sagebrush, tumbleweed, and cattails to form Grant County's only natural forest. The 1½-mile trail leads to the 1890s homestead of John Northrup. A narrow side trail leads farther to a handful of small lakes; the largest, Northrup Lake, offers good trout fishing.

A Modern World Wonder

About 5 miles north of Steamboat Rock is Grand Coulee Dam. The third-largest producer of electricity in the world, Grand Coulee is almost a mile in length and rises 350 feet above the water level; 12 million cubic yards of concrete went into its construction.

The Visitor Arrival Center, just north of the dam (open daily except holidays), offers exhibits

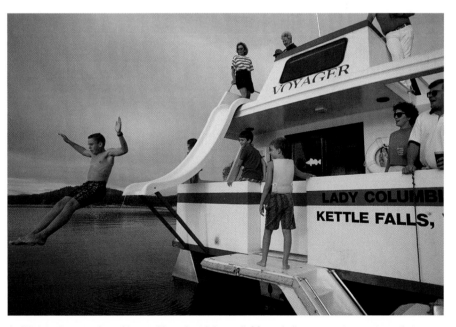

A slide into the water from this rental houseboat brings relief from sizzling summer temperatures that can easily hit 90°.

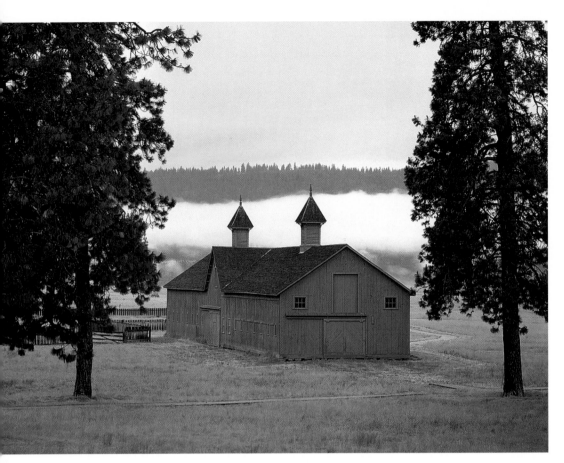

Built in 1884, the Quartermaster Stable at Fort Spokane once housed around 100 mules used to pull supply wagons.

and audiovisual presentations on how the dam was built. Allow two hours for a visit. Admission is free.

One of the most spectacular ways to see the dam is at night (hours vary according to season) when the Bureau of Reclamation's laser light show projects patterns and rich color onto the face of the dam, and an accompanying narration and music tell of the dam's history. Call (509) 633-9265 for schedule and details.

Houseboating on Lake Roosevelt

A 151-mile-long reservoir behind the dam, Lake Roosevelt extends clear to the Canadian border. Coulee Dam National Recreation Area, Colville National Forest, and the Colville and Spokane Indian Reservations surround the lake. Most of the hundreds of

miles of sandy beaches are public property open to visitors. Houseboating is fun—and a unique way to explore the lake. You can watch wildlife, find secluded spots for swimming and sunbathing, or check out old historic pioneer sites near the shore.

Historic Sites on Lake Roosevelt's Shores

To explore the east side of Lake Roosevelt by car, take State Highway 174 from Electric City (south of Coulee Dam) about 20 miles east to Wilbur, then follow U.S. Highway 2 about 12 miles, heading north to State Highway 25 and Fort Spokane.

Washington's last frontier outpost is now a historic site on the south shore of the Spokane River where it enters Lake Roosevelt. You can tour the handful of buildings erected in the 1880s.

About 35 miles north on State 25, you'll see signs for the Gifford Ferry, a tiny free ferry service that carries autos across the lake. However, to sample more of the region's history stay on the lake's eastern side and continue on State 25 to Kettle Falls, a pleasant small town with eateries and lodging. Just west of Kettle Falls, on U.S. Highway 395, stands the hand-crafted chapel of St. Paul's Mission, a reconstruction of the church built in the early 1880s on the shores of the upper Columbia. Nearby, the People of the Falls Interpretive Center depicts the area's history through clothing, artifacts, dioramas, and photographs. The center is open 11 to 5 Wednesday through Sunday, mid-May through mid-September.

From Kettle Falls, you can head west on State Highway 20, following it through the forested northern reaches of Washington, returning to the west side of the state via the beautiful North Cascades Highway (mountain pass closes in winter).

Unless otherwise noted, all area codes are 509. Lodging rates for two people range from $ (under $100) to $$$ (up to $250) per night.

WHERE

Grand Coulee Dam is 226 miles northeast of Seattle. Interstate 90 lies to the south, Canada's border to the north.

LODGING

The towns of Electric City, Grand Coulee, and Coulee Dam have motels, including the **Columbia River Inn** (10 Lincoln St., Coulee Dam; 800/633-6421; $), directly across the street from the dam's visitor center, and **Coulee House Motel** (110 Roosevelt Wy., Coulee Dam; 800/715-7767; $-$$), with a full view of the face of the dam. Both have swimming pools.

CAMPING

Two state parks and one national park offer resort-type settings. **Sun Lakes** (off State 17 near Coulee City) has 190 campsites, 18 hook-up sites. **Steamboat Rock** (near Electric City) has 100 hook-up sites and two boat launches. Call the Washington State Parks information line (800/233-0321) for details; for reservations—a good idea, especially on weekends—call (800/452-5687).

Spring Canyon Campground, a National Parks Service facility (about 5 miles east of Grand Coulee town on State 174; 633-9441), is an easy way to get to Lake Roosevelt from the dam. It has 87 campsites (available on a first-come, first-served basis), a boat launch, and a swimming beach.

HOUSEBOATING

Two concessions offer a variety of houseboat rentals (including power-boats and fishing skiffs) on Lake Roosevelt: **Lake Roosevelt Vacations** (Kettle Falls Marina, 2 miles south of Kettle Falls; 738-6121, 800/635-7585) and **Roosevelt Recreational Enterprises** (Keller Marina; 800/648-5253) on the south shore of the lake. Houseboats (sleeping 4 to 14 people) have a variety of layouts and amenities, including complete galleys, baths, comfortable beds (you provide bedding and towels), and gas barbecues. Some of the larger craft even have hot tubs. Summer rental rates (3 days and 2 nights) start around $1,500 (gasoline is extra). Attractive off-season rates start in early September, a month that's a good bet for those travelers seeking cooler temperatures.

FOOD

Rockin' Robin (121 Bridgeport Highway/State 174 at intersection with State 155, Grand Coulee; 633-1290) is a hamburger stop with nostalgic '50s jukebox tunes. **La Prasa** (515 East Grand Coulee Ave., Grand Coulee; 633-3173) offers Mexican food, and **Siam Palace** (Main St., Grand Coulee; 633-2921) serves Chinese-American cuisine. **The Melody** (next to Coulee House Motel, see Lodging; 633-1151) has outdoor seating and good views of the dam.

NATIVE AMERICAN CULTURE

The **Colville Tribal Museum and Gift Shop** (516 Birch St., Coulee Dam; 633-0751, 888/228-0546), in an A-frame structure near the Coulee House Motel, is operated by the Colville Federated Tribes, 11 native bands that unified in 1872. Exhibits look at 8,000 years of area Native American history; baskets and other artifacts are also on display. A gift shop offers an array of books and souvenirs.

FOR MORE INFORMATION

Contact Grand Coulee Dam Area Chamber of Commerce (306 Midway St., Coulee Dam, WA 99133; 633-3074, 800/268-5332).

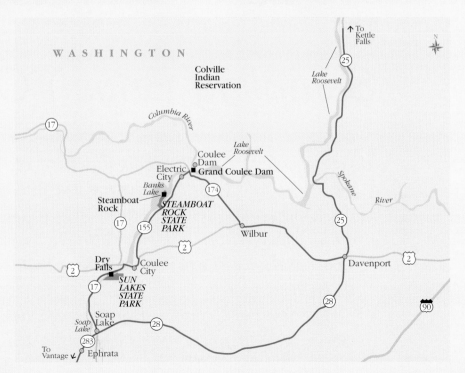

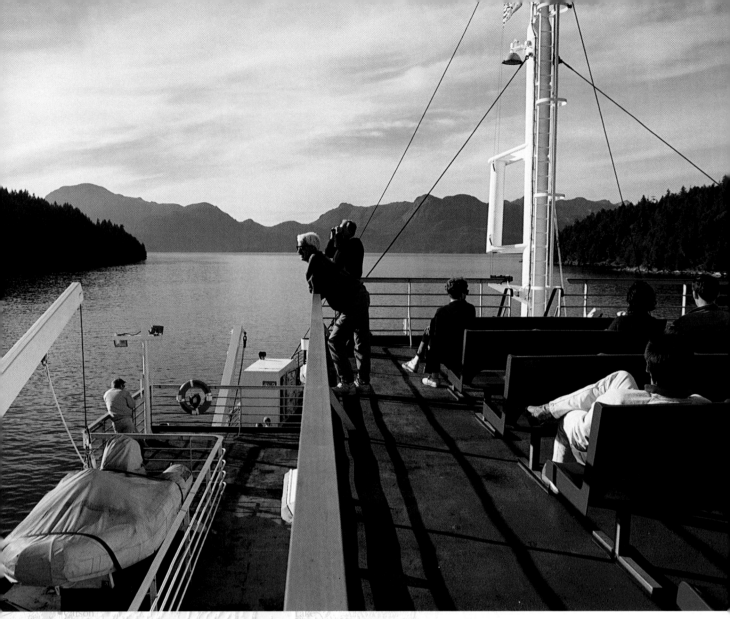

Topside passengers relax, taking in views as the ferry threads through forested shores between Earls Cove and Saltery Bay.

Sampling British Columbia

Getting to Vancouver Island via a leisurely circle of the Strait of Georgia offers a delightful dip into parts of British Columbia where you may want to linger for several days to take advantage of the scenery and activities. After you visit Vancouver Island's eastern side and Victoria's popular attractions, explore the quiet Sooke Coast to the west, a part of the island that locals prefer to keep to themselves.

The Strait of Georgia—Puget Sound's beautiful Canadian sister—is the centerpiece of this leisurely, water-oriented excursion.

It mixes scenic drives and restful ferry rides as you traverse mainland inlets as well as the broad strait separating British Columbia's tranquil Sunshine Coast from alluring Vancouver Island.

From Art Enclave to the End of the Road

The loop begins at Horseshoe Bay ferry terminal, 13 miles northwest of Vancouver. A 40-minute ferry trip takes you to Langdale and Provincial Highway 101. Gibsons, 3 miles from the ferry, has a marina, a seawall, shops, and galleries to explore. The larger village of Sechelt, 14 miles away, is a growing magnet for glass-blowers, potters, and other artists; the area can be jam-packed each August during jazz and writers' festivals. However, get-away-from-it-all lodging is nearby. Eye–popping views can be had from Four Winds Beach House's waterfront cliff site, and water views and total seclusion are yours at Halfmoon Bay Cabin.

From Sechelt, it's 34 miles to Earls Cove, every mile of road prettier than the one before as you pass good fishing and swimming lakes, resorts, and peek-a-boo views of water, mountains, and islands.

The second ferry run, from Earls Cove to Saltery Bay, takes 50 minutes and leaves you with a 22-mile drive to Powell River. Before you catch another ferry

from Powell River to Vancouver Island, you can follow Highway 101 north to the outskirts of town, where Powell Lake stretches into the evergreen-thick foothills of the Coast Mountains. Floatplanes carrying anglers to remote lakes in the British Columbia interior take off from the marina, just off the highway at the south end of the lake. Dine at the Shingle Mill Pub and you can watch.

Highway 101 ends 19 miles north at the tiny Scandinavian-style fishing village of Lund. Its equally diminutive harbor is filled with boats offering fishing and sight-seeing tours and charters to Desolation Sound, and a water taxi to small Savary Island, nearby. Kayaks are also available for rent. There's a small general store in the Lund Hotel. A grassy area offers prime waterfront picnicking overlooking the marina.

Just Beachy—Oysters & Sand Castles

Looking across the Strait of Georgia from Powell River on a clear day, you'll be flanked by breathtaking scenery—the snow–tipped peaks of the Coast Mountains

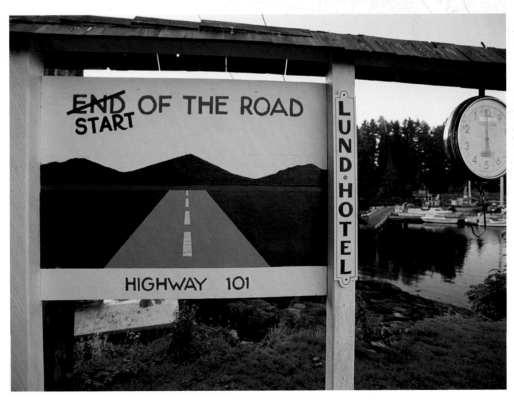

Lund's location on Provincial Highway 101 depends on whether you're coming or going.

to the north and the Vancouver Island Range to the south. The ferry, a 1¼-hour run, lands at Little River, near Comox and Courtenay in the Comox Valley, a verdant agricultural area. Follow Highway 19 south as it winds along the shellfish-rich shores of Baynes Sound. In some areas you can dig clams and pick oysters, or take it easy and stop at one of the seafood outlets along the road near Fanny Bay. This stretch of shoreline is dotted with small fishing resorts, cabins, and bed-and-breakfasts. Ships Point Beach House is a tranquil, beachfront hideaway spot, its garden packed with roses in summer.

Continuing south, you'll see signs for the new Island Highway. Unless you're hurrying to a ferry, stick to the coastal road. It winds past watery views and through the towns of Qualicum Beach and Parksville. Expect crowds in summertime, especially in late July when Parksville hosts its annual sand castle contest.

Just south of town, watch for signs to Rathtrevor Beach Provincial Park. Stop here on a pleasant day, and you won't want to leave. Grassy picnic areas, wide swaths of beach that grow enormous at low tide, and woodsy campsites make this large and beautiful park well worth a visit.

As you near Nanaimo, one of Canada's fastest-growing communities, you'll encounter increasing congestion, malls, and other marks of busy work-a-day life, a sign that you're leaving the back roads behind. However, Nanaimo is known for its harbors and for a water-front considered by many the most beautiful in Canada, so it's well worth a stop. You can buy fresh seafood at Fisherman's

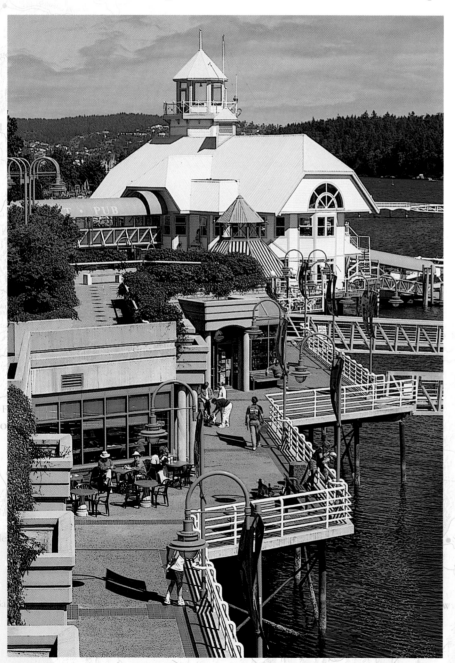

Nanaimo's Harbourside Walkway offers a 3-mile waterfront promenade with picturesque views of marina and boat activity plus grand vistas of Newcastle, Protection, and Gabriola islands.

Wharf, then stretch your legs and take in views along the Harbourside Walkway, a fishing and walking pier. If you prefer to return to Horseshoe Bay, catch a ferry from Nanaimo's Departure Bay, at the north end of the city, or travel south 8 miles to Duke Point Ferry Terminal to return to Tsawwassen Terminal on the mainland.

About 15 minutes south of Nanaimo on Provincial Highway 1, watch for the Cedar Road turnoff. Follow it and you will see signs for The Crow and Gate Pub (250/722-3731). An authentic English-style country pub on spacious, flower-filled grounds, it makes a great stop on a sunny day to enjoy a traditional ploughman's plate of cheese, bread, and condiments and a glass of ale on the outdoor terrace (open daily from 11 to 11).

Continuing south, plan to make at least a driving detour through the small town of Chemainus. One of the oldest European settlements on the island, it was home to loggers from the mid-1800s until the early 1980s, when the last sawmill closed. Then an artistic movement aimed at capturing the history of the area in murals began to revitalize the town; now dozens of murals give you a quick history lesson of the area.

South of here is the town of Duncan in the Cowichan Valley. Known as the "City of Totems" because of the many poles that dot the area, it is also home to the Cowichan Native Village (200 Cowichan Way; you'll see signs from the highway; 250/746-8119). The village shares the lifestyles, crafts, and legends of the Pacific Coast people with demonstrations on weaving and knitting—the Cowichan people are known for their knitted rustic sweaters—and totem-pole carving.

From Duncan, it's a 45-minute drive south to Victoria, where you can see beautiful gardens, visit the grand Empress Hotel, and take in the many other modern and historical attractions of the island's largest city. You can also take the tiny ferry

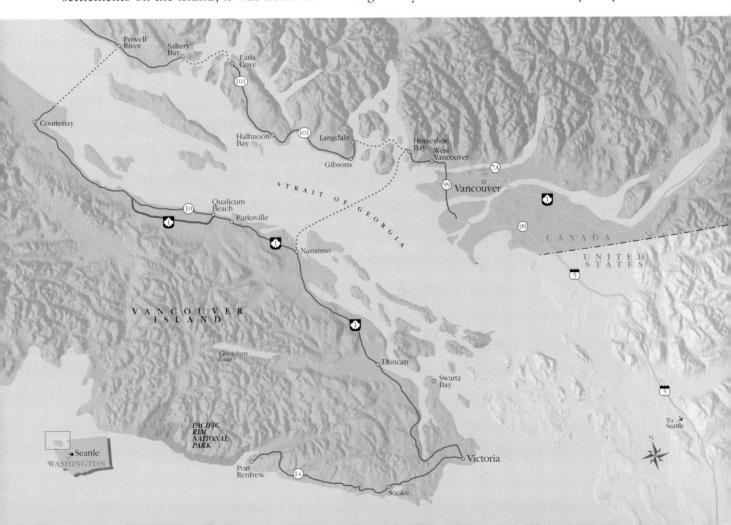

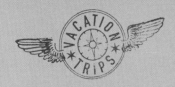

Ferry Facts

Ferry travel can be an idyllic way to get around, but there are a few things to consider before you set out on a British Columbia trip. Because some routes have only a few sailings a day, it's smart to plan your ferry connections well in advance. Travel is heavy in summer and on sunny weekends, so be prepared for delays; a savvy traveler brings a book. In the height of the season, check with the transportation line for current traffic reports.

To avoid long waits, consider traveling early or late in the day. Most ferry runs stop ticket sales 5 to 10 minutes before sailing time, so give yourself an extra hour to reach your point of embarkation.

B. C. Ferries (604/444-2890) provides transportation along the Sunshine Coast and to Vancouver Island; with their CirclePac fare you save 15 percent for combined travel on four routes.

from Mill Bay to Brentwood Bay. This watery detour puts you on the Saanich Peninsula north of Victoria and near the famous Butchart Gardens, a "must stop" for any first-time island visitor. From here your choice is to go south to Victoria, north to the Swartz Bay ferry terminal to catch a ferry back to Vancouver (Tsawwassen terminal) on the mainland, or southwest to the peaceful Sooke Coast.

Sooke Coast Getaway

The village of Sooke (rhymes with *spook*), 40 miles west of Victoria, looks quite ordinary. But beyond its innocent, leafy façade lies a stunning spread of rugged coastal wilderness—43 miles of rainforests and rocky driftwood beaches that stretch west to the tiny fishing village of Port Renfrew. The last 29 miles of the shoreline belong to the Juan de Fuca Marine Trail, which strings together a necklace of remote coves anchored at the western end by Botanical Beach, the Sooke Coast's crown jewel.

Exploring this wide expanse is easiest if you spend a few nights near Sooke, then move to lodging farther along the coast. Stop by the Sooke Region Museum/Visitor Information Centre on Highway 14, just

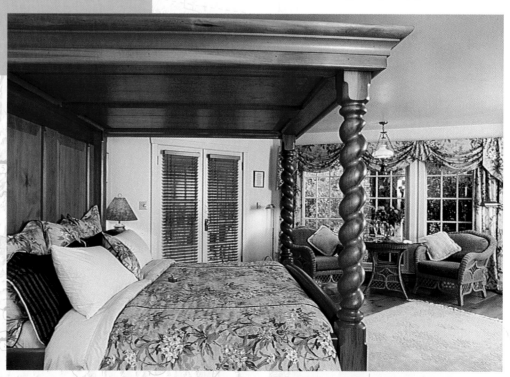

In the Honeymoon Suite at Hartmann House B&B, you can breakfast in the huge Edwardian-style cedar bed handcrafted by owner Ray Hartmann.

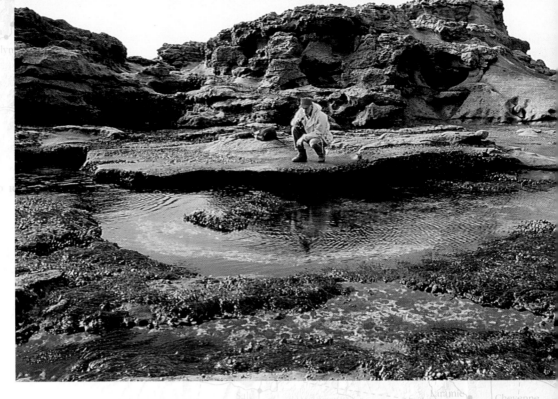

Botanical Beach's pitted sandstone shelf reveals pools of hardy marine life for study at low tide.

west of the Sooke River, to pick up a map and check tide times. (Botanical Beach should be seen at low tide. The center can tell you exactly when this occurs each day.) You can also visit the local history museum here and get information on area restaurants and lodging.

Ann and Ray Hartmann own Hartmann House B&B, one of the finest inns on the coast, complete with exquisite gardens and such handsome cedar furnishings as a 7¹/₂-foot-high, handcrafted Edwardian style canopy bed. Nearby, the Sooke Harbor House was recently named the world's best restaurant for authentic local cuisine by *Gourmet* magazine.

To reach Sooke Potholes Provincial Park, head north a few miles on Sooke River Road. Salmon spawn here mid-October through November. Rocky pools beneath a series of waterfalls provide excellent hiding places for their eggs—and afford a good view. From the pools, you can climb a steep hill to the top of the lower falls. In view is a wood trestle, part of Vancouver Island's Galloping Goose Trail, which runs through the park on its way from Victoria to the Cowichan Valley.

In and around the village, local artisan studios are open to the public. Pick up a list of them, published by the Sooke B&B Association, at the visitor center or from individual innkeepers. Exhibit Room III, located at Constable Matheson's B&B (2050 Drennan St.), features colorful fiber art by Sheila Beech, most notably her wool Gnomeknocker Slippers. Blue Raven Gallery (1971 Kaltasin Rd.) showcases the West Coast native art of the Newman family, which includes carved jewelry, masks, and original clothing designs.

When you get hungry, stop by GoodLife Restaurant and Bookstore or Mom's Café for lunch or dinner.

Back in town, stroll along Whiffen Spit to the mouth of Sooke Harbor, where seals stalk the salmon as they start their run upstream. Sooke Cycle (6707 West Coast Road/Highway 14) is a good place to rent mountain bikes and helmets for a spin on the Goose.

Early the next day, hike the seaside trail along the windswept bluff in East Sooke Provincial Park. Ancient Coast Salish people carved petroglyphs on some of the jagged outcroppings here. You might want to have lunch at historic 17-Mile House pub before driving west to Sheringham Point Lighthouse and the rustic Point-No-Point Resort.

There is a choice of trails leading down to the beach and out to Point-No-Point, named by early navigators who couldn't

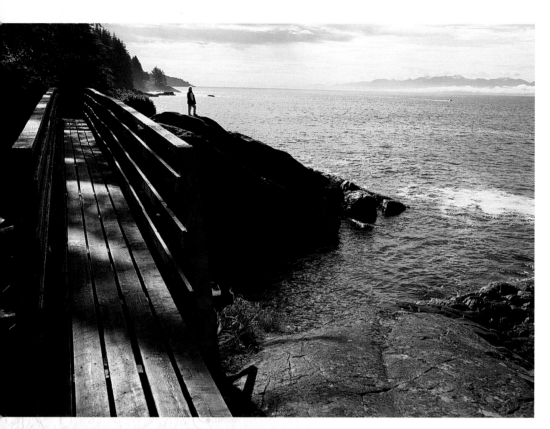

Before heading home, look for the barely marked access to Sandcut Beach. You may have to negotiate your way down this steep rainforest trail by holding onto Sitka spruce roots, but if you follow the roar of the waves, you reach a deserted beach in 15 minutes. There's no more fitting place to bid farewell to the Sooke Coast than in this hidden pocket of wild, fresh splendor.

agree on whether it was prominent enough for pointhood. Dinner in the resort's small dining room includes such exemplary wildlife viewing that binoculars are provided at each table. The food is impressive also.

Reserve a full day for "must see" Botanical Beach. At low tide, its sandstone bluffs and ledges form a natural laboratory for studying marine life. As myriad pools are exposed, you can peer into sea gardens populated by purple sea urchins, giant green anemones, button-shaped limpets, leathery chitons, and ocher sea stars.

Even if you don't have time to hike the entire Juan de Fuca Marine Trail, sample some of it from Botanical Beach. You can check out the east end of the trail at China Beach, one of the few spots along the coast that you can remotely describe as crowded. The trail down to this beach winds through a lovely stand of rust-skinned arbutus trees.

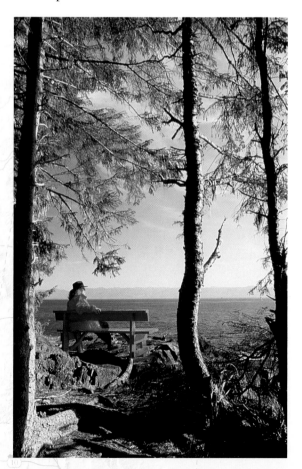

Solitude comes with a view of the Olympic Mountains at Point-No-Point, a short hike from a rustic resort overlooking the Strait of Juan de Fuca.

Unless otherwise noted, area codes on the mainland (Sunshine Coast) are 604; area codes on Vancouver Island are 250. Lodging rates for two people range from $ (under $100) to $$$ (over $250) per night.

WHERE

Vancouver, British Columbia, is 141 miles north of Seattle. Ferry terminals lie south and northwest of the city. Plan your ferry connections well in advance (there are only a few sailings a day on some runs).

The circle route takes in the southeastern mainland coast of B.C. (the Sunshine Coast) and the eastern coast of Vancouver Island. The Sooke Coast, 40 miles west of Victoria, is reached by following Hwy. 1 south to Hwy. 14 and heading west. From Sooke to Port Renfrew, Hwy. 14 is signed as both Sooke Rd. and West Coast Rd.

LODGING

On the Sunshine Coast, **Four Winds B&B** in Sechelt (5482 Hill Road; 885-3144; $$) has a resident massage therapist; views extend south across the strait to the night lights of Nanaimo. **Halfmoon Bay Cabin** (688-5058 for reservations and directions; $$) has a soaring fireplace and gardenlike private grounds. **Ships Point Beach House** (7584 Ships Point Road, Fanny Bay; 250/335-2200; $$-$$$) offers expansive views of beach, birds, and sea life. **Tigh-Na-Mara Resort Hotel** (1095 E. Island Hwy., Parksville; 248-2072, 800/663-7373; $-$$), a compound of woodsy log cabins and condominium units, is the pick of several resorts south of Rathtrevor Beach park.

The Sooke region offers everything from very expensive inns to roadside motels. **Hartmann House B&B** (5262 Sooke Rd.; 642-3761; $$, two-night minimum) has a sumptuous Honeymoon Suite, complete with whirlpool tub, that opens into exquisite gardens and a Garden Room with private bath. Breakfasts are laden with fresh flowers and garden-picked fruits. **Constable Matheson's B&B** (2050 Drennan St. at Hwy. 14; 642-7176; $$) offers a whimsical one-bedroom suite with double Jacuzzi. These quarters, transformed from a Royal Canadian Mounted Police depot and jail, come with a bulletproof front door. **Point-No-Point Resort** (1505 West Coast Rd./Hwy. 14; 646-2020; $$, 2-night minimum on weekends) has woodsy housekeeping cabins, some with hot tubs on decks with ocean views that extend across the Strait of Juan de Fuca to the Olympic Mountains.

DINING

The **Blue Heron Inn** (Porpoise Bay Road; 885-3847, 800/818-8977) restaurant in Sechelt has water views, linen napery, a relaxed atmosphere, and lots of seafood including B.C. oysters on the half shell. It's open Wed. through Sun., dinner only. Reservations are suggested. The **Shingle Mill Bistro and Pub** (6233 Powell Place, Powell River; 483-2001) serves chowder, pasta, burgers, or prime rib meals. It's a good family stop; reservations suggested. In Courtenay, The **Old House Restaurant** (1760 Riverside Lane; 338-5406), a riverfront English country house-style eatery, is also good for families. **Lefty's** (710 Memorial Ave.; 752-7530) in Qualicum Beach is a small bistro-style cafe; try their sweet/tart lemon meringue pie. **Tigh-Na-Mara's** (see Lodging above) log restaurant offers seafood, pasta, steaks, and more.

Don't miss **Sooke Harbour House** (1528 Whiffen Spit Rd.; 642-3421; open daily, dinner only) for award-winning fine dining centering around fish and shellfish. Most of the herbs and vegetables are culled from co-owner and chef Sinclair Philip's gardens. Another choice, **GoodLife Restaurant and Bookstore** (2113 Otter Pt. Rd.; 642-6821; lunch and dinner daily except Monday), lets you browse before dining on innovative cuisine. Locals favor the home cooking at **Mom's Café** (2036 Shields Rd.; 642-3314). For English pub fare and local seafood, stop by the **17-Mile House** (5126 Sooke Rd.; 642-5942; lunch and dinner daily), a historic roadhouse and stagecoach stop. The daily menu at **Two Bean Café** (Village Food Market Plaza, Hwy. 14 at Otter Pt. Rd.; 642-3088) features inexpensive low-fat muffins, bagels and toppings, and soups and sandwiches.

On the west side of the Sooke coast, the best dining is at **Point-No-Point Resort** (see Lodging above). **Country Cupboard Café** (402 Sheringham Pt. Rd. at Hwy. 14; 646-2323; lunch and dinner daily) offers hearty fare and picnics-to-go. For good food near Botanical Beach, stop at the **Lighthouse Pub Restaurant** (Parkinson Rd., Port Renfrew; 647-5543). They're open until midnight (lunch and dinner; closed Mon.).

FOR MORE INFORMATION

British Columbia (800/663-6000) provides information and reservation services. Sooke Region Museum/Visitor Information Centre (Hwy. 14 and Phillips Rd., just west of Sooke River; 642-6351; open daily in summer, closed Mon. rest of year).

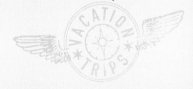

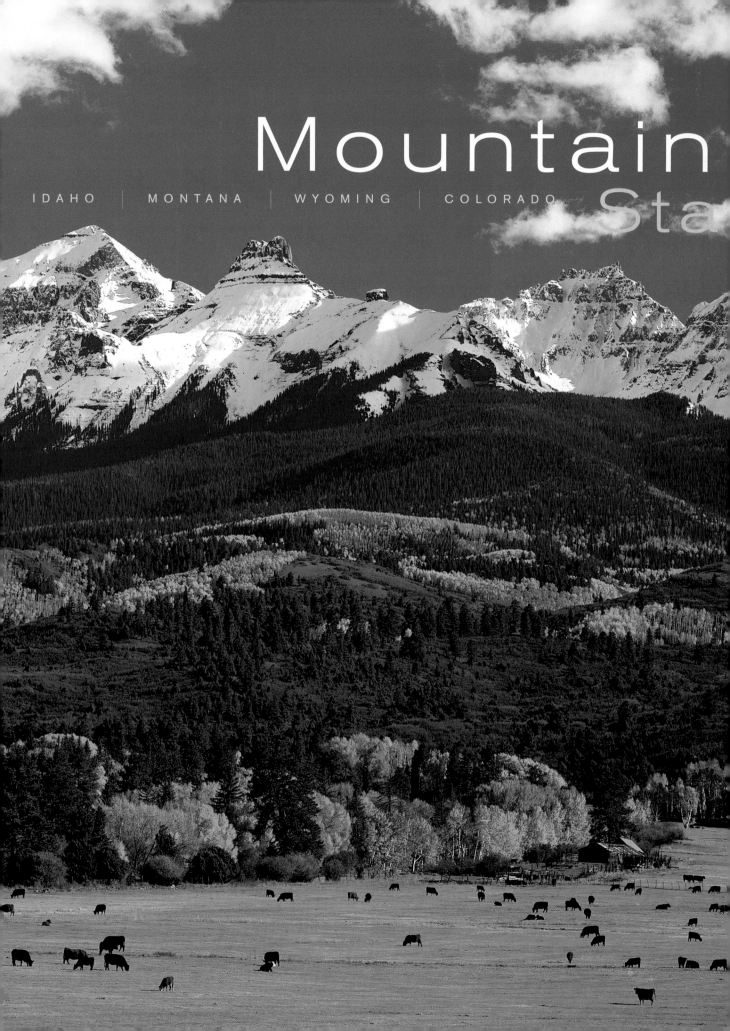

Mountain

IDAHO | MONTANA | WYOMING | COLORADO

Sta

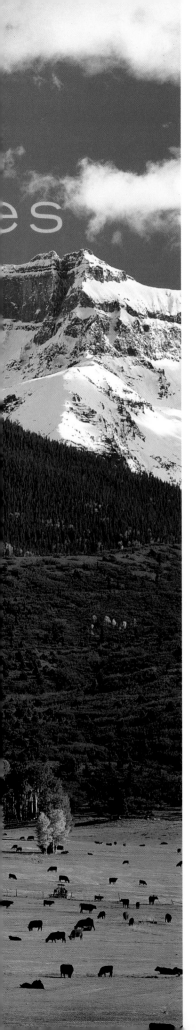

With vast expanses of unspoiled wilderness and captivating beauty, Idaho, Montana, Wyoming, and Colorado are true bastions of the Old West. Cowboys still ride the range, miners scratch the earth or pan the streams in search of gold, and Native Americans gather for powwows. The jeans, plaid shirts, and boots worn by the residents of this laid-back region boast no designer brand, and only vividly clad winter visitors stand out on the ski slopes.

United by the rugged Rocky Mountain range that spills across state boundaries, the landscape is both grand and diverse: towering peaks, crystal-clear alpine lakes, broad semiarid valleys, high desert plains, and deeply carved and intricate river gorges, buttes, and mesas. Back roads pass traces of old settlements and mining claims and venture into the fringes of wildlife refuges inhabited by mountain lions, bears, bighorn sheep, mountain goats, elk, deer, and even bison.

You'll discover these delights—along with shifting sand dunes, fossil fields, and hot springs—in the pages of this chapter.

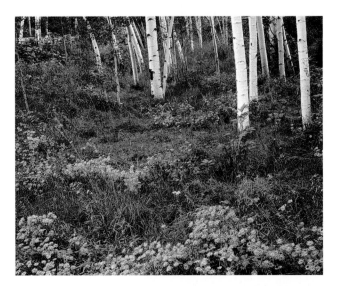

Contented cattle graze in a meadow below snow-capped Rocky Mountain peaks (far left).

Showy daisies (left) carpet the floor of an aspen forest in Colorado's Uncompahgre Primitive Area.

Idaho

When you visit Idaho, you get a feeling the frontier still exists, and, in fact, traces of the state's fur-trading, gold-seeking past are evident. But a large part of it is due to the vast, rugged wilderness that remains: dramatic river canyons, soaring mountain ranges, and more than 16,000 miles of rivers and streams. Such inspiring scenery, plus a wealth of recreational opportunities, attracts both summer and winter visitors.

Boise, the state's capital city and major population center, is the departure point for a look at three of the state's grand wild rivers and North America's deepest river gorge, spectacular 7,900-foot-deep Hells Canyon.

Montana

Lewis and Clark's footprints are all across the Big Sky State, which is not surprising when you realize that their 1805 expedition was the first U.S. incursion into the spacious land now known as Montana. A gold strike in 1858 brought prospectors and homesteaders searching for a better life. There is still plenty of room to roam; Montana is the third least densely populated of all of the contiguous 48 states. Helena, the state capital, looks back proudly to its pioneer beginnings.

Among Montana's scenic wonders are two of the country's most dramatic natural features—the northern rise of the Rockies, and the Great Plains, which roll across much of the state. The Rocky Mountain Front, a cascade of limestone and shale that tilts eastward to the plains, is the doorstep to millions of acres of mountain wilderness. Though it bears no physical resemblance to the savannahs of Africa, it's sometimes referred to as America's Serengeti because of its spectacular wildlife habitat.

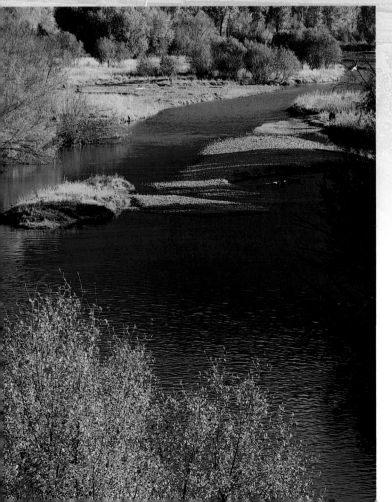

Autumn brightens the landscape along Clark Fork River near Milltown, Montana.

Wyoming

Wyoming's century-old history would make a great Western classic; it has all of the characters—Indians, trappers, cattlemen, farmers, and miners. Though all played roles in the growth of this colorful land, the best-known, and most enduring, cast member would have to be the cowboy, who arrived on the scene with the longhorns in the late 1800s. The cowhand is still much in evidence today—on the range, around the ranches, and coming out of chutes at dozens of rodeos.

Wyoming's landscape is grand. From the geysers of Yellowstone (the country's first national park) to the spectacular Grand Tetons, many of the state's renowned natural features have been preserved. A loop drive through the southern part of the state, west of Cheyenne and nearby Laramie, takes you over the Medicine Bow Range to the celebrated North Platte River and back through classic Old West towns.

Colorado

Maroon Bells, Longs Peak, Pikes Peak, and Sangre de Cristos—these are just a few of the prominences that make up Colorado's Rocky Mountains. Here the Continental Divide, in addition to being the source of several of the West's major rivers, clearly defines the state, separating the plains to the east from the high plateaus to the west. It was this stunning vista that inspired Katherine Lee Bates to write "America the Beautiful."

Although the region was explored earlier by such noted mountainmen as Jim Bridger and Kit Carson, it took a gold strike west of Denver to attract the attention of others. Central City, Colorado City, Leadville, and Georgetown quickly became legendary mining camps. Just when gold pickings became slim, silver was discovered, and the rush for fortune continued well into the 20th century.

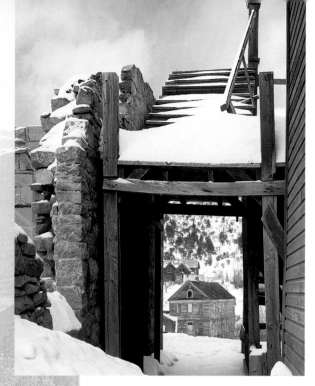

Snow covers buildings in historic Silver City, a former gold and silver mining camp high in the Owyhee Mountains of southwestern Idaho.

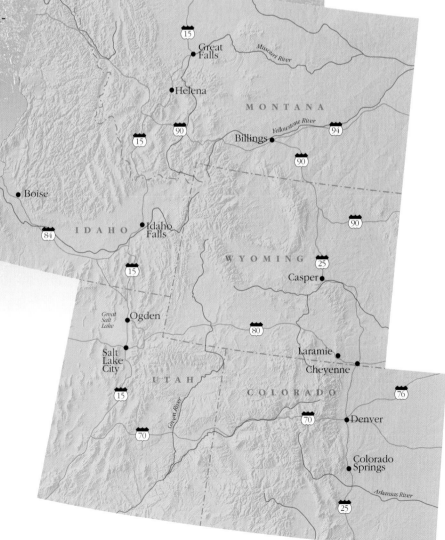

N

0   100   200   300 miles

Idaho's

surprising

Backcountry

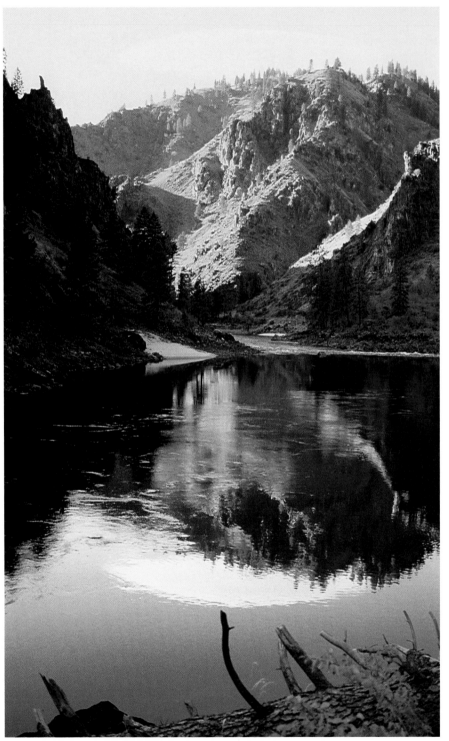

One of the most accessible stretches of Idaho's untamed Salmon River lies near the town of Riggins, in the rugged backcountry northwest of Boise.

Only two other canyons in the U.S. are deeper than that of the Salmon River: Arizona's Grand Canyon and Hells Canyon, into which the Salmon eventually flows. The Salmon, unlike the Colorado and Snake rivers, has never been tamed, and its wild beauty is one of Idaho's most valued treasures.

This slow backcountry route from Boise through western Idaho takes in more scenery than it does galleries, more wild-flower-filled meadows than it does museums. It also accesses stretches of three grand rivers—the Salmon, Snake, and Payette. It's a journey for those who enjoy a long weekend of outdoor fun and wilderness experiences. Campers find a wide choice of scenic sites, and those who prefer a more civilized setting will discover one of Idaho's best-kept secrets, a secluded—and upscale—resort.

North to Riggins

State Highway 55 winds through the breathtaking canyon of the Main and North Forks of the Payette River, a popular white-water rafting run. McCall, on the south shore of Payette Lake, has a choice of places to eat and sleep. Thickly forested Ponderosa State Park, which sits on a peninsula jutting into the lake, offers grand views of the deep, glacially carved lake from a bluff high above. Other good views come from nearby Brundage Mountain Ski Area, where, even in summer, chairlifts carry passengers high above the forested terrain. At a narrow gorge cut by Little Goose River, a turnoff to the Last Chance Campground leads to Krigbaum Hot Springs, often called a spa in the rough. Park by the bridge and follow a path along the right side of the creek to sit in the knee-deep waters.

En route to New Meadows and the junction of State 55 and U.S. Highway 95, you descend into a delightful green valley. Just north of town, look for the marker for the 45th Parallel—the halfway point between the North Pole and the Equator. Another 30 minutes on U.S. 95 brings you to the town of Riggins (population 443). Most of the year Riggins sleeps, but it bustles dur-

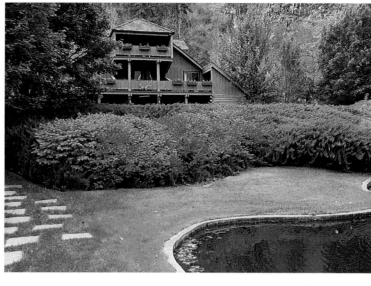

Manicured lawns front The Lodge at Riggins Hot Springs, a luxury resort built around hot springs once treasured by Native Americans.

ing the summer rafting season, the fall steelhead run, and on the first weekend in May, when cowboys congregate for one of the West's most authentic rodeos.

Turning east on Big Salmon Road at the south edge of town leads to one of the most accessible stretches of the Salmon and one of Idaho's best-kept secrets, The Lodge at Riggins Hot Springs. The hot springs, treasured for thousands of years by Native Americans and a welcome stop for early explorers and settlers, have been incorporated into a modern pool setting for lodge guests.

Upriver from the lodge you still see traces of old homesteads and mining claims; trails lead into the surrounding countryside. Along a 20-mile stretch of road you'll discover many porcelain-white sand beaches, some with adjoining campsites. You are on the edge of two large wilderness areas teeming with wildlife, including whitetail and mule deer, elk, mountain lions, black bears, mountain goats, and bighorn sheep.

Hells Canyon Overlooks

Far to the west lies Hells Canyon, North America's deep-

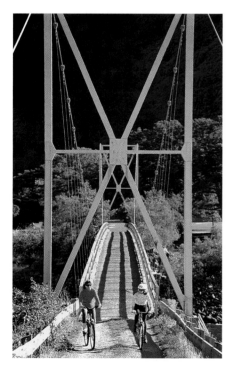

Cyclists head for Big Salmon Road and 20 miles of photogenic backcountry pedaling.

est gorge. You can pick up area maps and information from the ranger's office in Riggins. To get a good chasm view, take Forest Service Road 517 southwest of Riggins to Heavens Gate Lookout in the Seven Devils region. The sprawling vista of the gorge below makes the drive worthwhile. Pack a lunch, as it takes the better part of a day to make the round trip.

For a more up-close and personal canyon vista, follow U.S. 95 south to Cambridge and turn west on State Highway 71 for a 55-mile drive that eventually ends at Hells Canyon Dam, a launching site for white-water boaters, who make a 32-mile wilderness run to Pittsburg Landing. Again, the round trip takes a day.

Back to Boise

Rejoining U.S. 95, head south to Weiser, an old farming and ranching town that has been around long enough to have historic appeal. Among the town's turn-of-the-century buildings are the old Oregon Short Line Depot on State Street and the Pythian Castle (30 E. Idaho Street), a fairy-tale structure worthy of

Sleeping Beauty. The Snake Ridge Heritage Center (2295 Paddock Avenue) is rich in Native American and pioneer artifacts. If you're in the area the third week in June, don't miss the annual National Old Time Fiddlers Contest, where tiny tots scrape strings alongside bewhiskered oldsters.

Parma, another farming town, stands along the route of the Oregon Trail, near the site of Old Fort Boise, a Hudson's Bay Company outpost built in 1834. A reproduction of the fort east of town houses a pioneer museum, open summer weekends.

Caldwell and Nampa, the last two major towns before you return to Boise, were railroad towns in the late 1800s. In fact, Nampa's historical museum, appropriately housed in the Oregon Short Line Depot (1200 Front Street), is full of rail mem-orabilia. The region's annual Snake River Stampede rodeo takes place the third week in July.

South of Nampa and Caldwell lies Idaho's wine district and a major fruit-growing area. Most wineries offer tours and tasting; Ste. Chapelle Winery is noted for its Chardonnays. If you're in the area in harvest season, roadside stands offer baskets of fresh-picked fruit.

⇦ TRIP PLANNER ⇨

Unless otherwise noted, area codes are 208. Lodging rates for two people range from $ (under $100) to $$$ (above $250) per night.

WHERE

Riggins is approximately 3 hours north of Boise. Cycling is a good way to explore the terrain around Riggins, but you'll have to bring your own bike.

LODGING

Lucky guests at **The Lodge at Riggins Hot Springs** (P.O. Box 1247, Riggins, ID 83549; 628-3785; $$$) discover some of the most unique and comfortable accommodations in the state. The lodge has 7 rooms in the main building plus 3 cabins nestled up against a canyon wall and overlooking a trout pond.

Prices include 3 ample gourmet meals a day and all beverages. Advance reservations are required. The lodge is on Big Salmon Rd. 9 miles east of U.S. 95.

Other Riggins lodging choices include **Half Way Inn** (on Little Salmon River between Mileposts 182 and 183; 628-3259; $), **Riggins Motel** (615 S. Main St.; 628-3001, 800/669-6739; $), **Salmon River Motel** (1203 S. Hwy. 95; 628-3231, 888/628-3025; $), and **The Lodge Bed and Breakfast** (on Little Salmon River at U.S. 95; 628-3863; $).

The road to **Seven Devils Campground**, 17 miles west of Riggins, turns off just before you enter town. There are numerous smaller campsites upriver. Some secluded beach spots have no ameni-ties, but views and privacy may make up for it.

Bear Creek Lodge (3492 State 55; P.O. Box 8, New Meadows, ID 83654; 634-3551; $$) has 13 rooms and cabins on 65 acres along the Bear River 4 miles north of McCall. The **Hartland Inn & Motel** (211 Norris St., New Meadows, ID 93654; 347-2114; $) has 11 motel rooms and 3 rooms in a bed-and-breakfast.

DINING

Stream-fresh fish are featured at many area restaurants. The restaurant at **Bear Creek Lodge** (see Lodging above) offers continental dining most evenings and a Sunday brunch. Hours and days vary; call for reservations.

FOR MORE INFORMATION

Salmon River Chamber of Commerce (P.O. Box 289, Riggins, ID 83549; 628-3441). Idaho Travel Council (Box 83720, Boise, ID 83720-0093; 800/VISIT ID).

For a list of operators offering float and jet boat trips down the Snake River from Hells Canyon Dam, contact Hells Canyon National Recreation Area (P.O. Box 699, Clarkston, WA 99403; 509/758-0616).

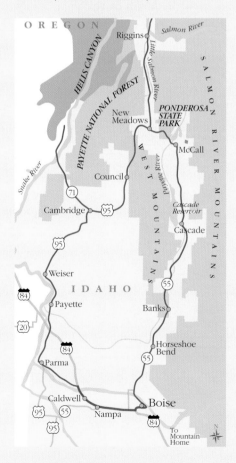

circling

Flathead Lake

REGION	MONTANA	
Where	X	80 miles north of Missoula
When	X	Most popular late spring through summer

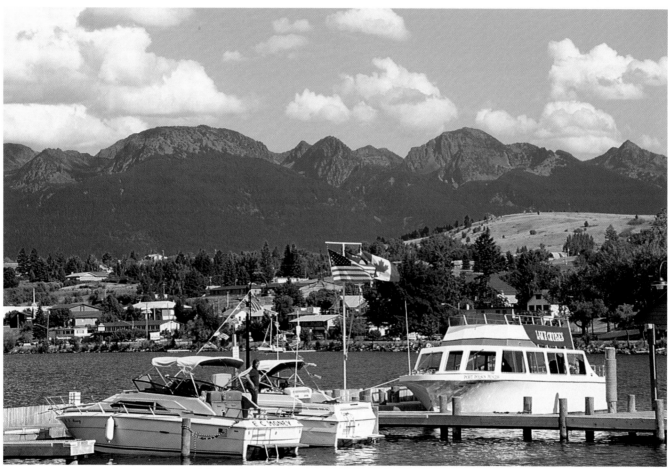

Flags whip in the breeze at Polson marina on a perfect day to cruise Flathead Lake.

From May to September, the exodus of cars towing boats, pickups, and RVs from Montana towns to Flathead Lake is proof of the area's appeal. But to boat, swim, fish, or skip rocks on the riffled blue waters of this large freshwater lake is to experience the essence of a Montana summer. On an 87-mile drive around the lake, you'll find luxurious resorts, excellent restaurants, award-winning theaters, and thriving art galleries, not to mention abundant cherry orchards and world-class hiking trails into the wilderness.

Stretching 30 miles north from Polson to Bigfork, Flathead Lake was created nearly 12,000 years ago when river water backed up behind a terminal moraine to fill a glacier-carved trench. Fed by the three arms of the Flathead River to the north and draining into the dam-controlled river to the south, Flathead Lake lies in the jagged Mission Mountains. It's the perfect setting for vacations ranging from active to relaxed.

Polson: Fiddlers, Musicals & White Water

As you descend into Polson (population 4,300), the lake's blue grandeur spreads out before you. Located at the tip of the 1.2-million-acre Flathead Indian Reservation, the town was established in 1840 by rancher David Polson, whose fiddling talents are

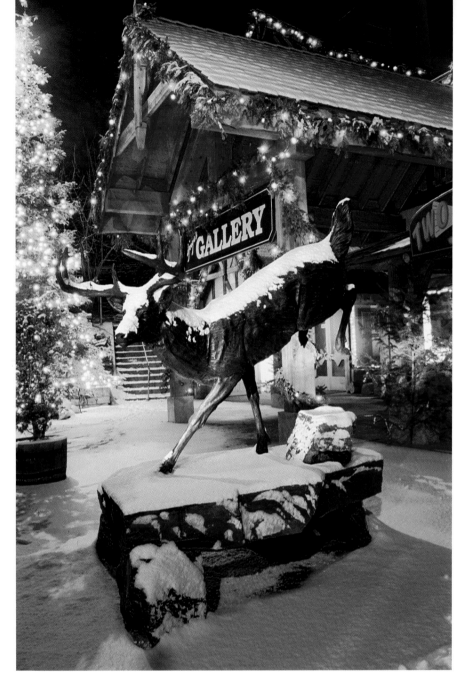

Bigfork's Electric Avenue lives up to its name at Christmastime when local residents decorate the town—and their work—with lights, pine boughs, and red bows.

way in spring, and orchards supply roadside stands with Bing cherries in late July. Nestled beneath towering larch trees at Yellow Bay, the University of Montana's 100-year-old Flathead Lake Biological Station is home to limnologists, who conduct studies of lakes and streams. Stop for a tour of the station or take a nature walk in the woods.

The lake's western side, bordered by the rolling Salish Mountains, is drier and more open. Watch for wild horses and bighorn sheep on Wildhorse Island. Farther north in the grain and cattle country lie the vineyards of Mission Mountain Winery. Try a glass of their Johannesburg Riesling or a blush wine called "Sundowner" at the tasting room in Dayton. For a treat, stop for buffalo jerky at Rollins M & S Meats. For an outstanding Italian meal, don't miss Rosario's at the Lakeside Marina.

Bigfork's Potters & Putters

Located on a sheltered bay where the Swan River pours into the lake's northern tip, Bigfork boasts a delightful setting and a temperate climate. Because artists tend to congregate in such places, finding a thriving artistic community here is no surprise. A sleepy village of 4,000 people in winter, Bigfork is transformed into a hive of activity in summer. Dip into one of 11 art galleries on Electric Avenue's geranium-festooned boardwalk for items ranging from buffalo bronzes to Chinese tapestries. Or line up at the Center for the Performing Arts to attend a performance by

honored each July when members of the Montana Oldtime Fiddlers Association tune up at the local high school. Across town at the golf clubhouse turned Polson Performing Arts Center, the Port Polson Players put on a mean musical.

Get out on the water on a lakeside cruise or take a knuckle-whitening trip down the Buffalo Rapids of the Flathead River. Anglers can try their hand at

catching mackinaw or lake trout. Those who prefer more sedentary pursuits might assemble a picnic to enjoy at Boettcher Park.

East Side, West Side

The east and west sides of Flathead Lake are quite distinct. Drive the narrow eastside highway, built by convicts in 1914, and you'll immediately notice the area's lushness. A pink profusion of cherry blossoms lines the high-

Bigfork Summer Playhouse, now in its 40th season.

If you crave outdoor activity, try the 27-hole Eagle Bend Golf Club or head for Jewel Basin Hiking Area, where 35 miles of trails offer shimmering lakes and wildflowers. To reach the area, take Echo Lake Road off State Highway 83.

Rapidly becoming a year-round destination, Bigfork at

Flathead Lake's rural east shore is prime cherry-growing country; in late July, orchard signs invite you to pick your fill.

Christmastime looks like a scene out of Currier and Ives. Streets are lined with hundreds of decorated and lighted pine trees and horse-drawn sleighs replace cars.

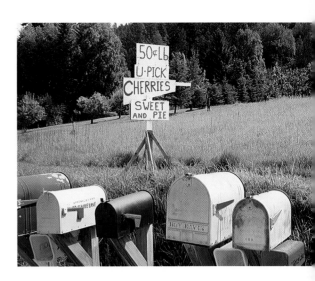

⋯ TRIP PLANNER ⋯

Unless otherwise noted, area codes are 406. Lodging rates for two people range from $ (under $100) to $$$ (above $200) per night.

WHERE

Polson is 70 miles north of Missoula on U.S. Hwy. 93. To reach Bigfork from the west side of the lake, take U.S. 93 north 40 miles to State Hwy. 82, head east 8 miles to State Hwy. 35, and go 4 miles south. From the east side, drive 33 miles north from Polson on State 35.

LODGING

Lodging varies from basic motels to well-appointed bed-and-breakfasts and lavish resorts.

The Best Western **KwaTaqNuk Resort** (303 U.S. 93 East; 883-3636; $), owned by the confederated Salish and Kootenai tribes, is a striking 112-room facility that combines traditional and contemporary Indian motifs. It offers indoor and outdoor swimming pools, a whirlpool, and the **Pemicin Restaurant**, where you can sample Indian tacos or prime rib.

In Bigfork, choices include the 125-room lakeside **Marina Cay** resort

(180 Vista Ln.; 800/433-6516; $-$$$), the quaint 3-room **Swan River Inn** (360 Grand Ave.; 837-2505; $$), or the spacious log home that houses the 5-room **O'Duachain Country Inn Bed and Breakfast** (675 Ferndale; 837-6851; $-$$). **Flathead Lake Lodge** (150 Flathead Lake Lodge Rd.; 837-4391; $$$$ a week) is a well-established lakeside dude ranch, with horseback riding, tennis, and windsurfing.

DINING

Bigfork is the place to venture away from standard burger-and-steak Montana fare. Downtown you can eat rack of lamb with a glaze of cherry port in **Showthyme Cafe**'s 1908 bank building or try New Orleans–style catfish at the **Bridge Street Gallery**. On the deck of the **Swan River Inn**, feast on salmon Wellington while you ponder the lake's blue expanse.

ACTIVITIES

At the **KwaTaqNuk Resort**, the Port of Polson Princess offers cruises three times a day. The resort also rents everything from canoes to jet skis. For float trips on the Flathead River, call **Flathead Raft Company** (800/654-4359). Two cruises are

offered at the lake's north end, one out of Somers and the other from Flathead Lake Lodge.

For tickets to the **Port Polson Players**, call 883-4691. Make **Bigfork Summer Playhouse** reservations early by calling 837-4886.

FOR MORE INFORMATION

Polson Chamber of Commerce (on State 93, Polson, MT; 883-5969). Bigfork Area Chamber of Commerce (on State 35, Bigfork, MT; 837-5888).

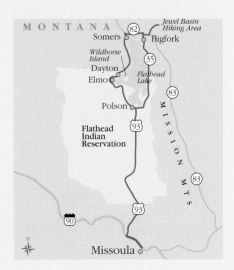

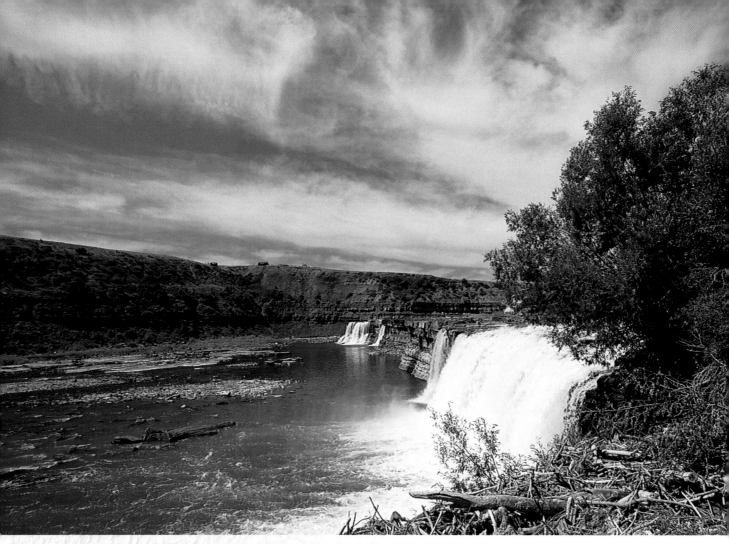

"The grandest sight I ever beheld," Lewis exclaimed of the cascade called Great Falls of the Missouri River.

Lewis and Clark's Montana

Almost 200 years after making their journey across North America, Lewis and Clark are hot. They were anointed by the Ken Burns PBS documentary The West, *and historian Stephen Ambrose's biography of Lewis,* Undaunted Courage, *became a bestseller a few years ago. Given such resurgent fame, it's small wonder many localities along their trail claim Lewis and Clark as their own. Montana's claim is the strongest. Lewis and Clark's journey was an epic one, and Montana is an epic landscape.*

In miles and travel days, the "Corps of Discovery," as it was termed by President Thomas Jefferson, spent about a quarter of their journey here, more than in any other state. And Great Falls, site of the $6 million Lewis and Clark National Historic Trail Interpretive

Center (built in 1998), is just about midway between the expedition's starting point near St. Louis and its westernmost camp, Fort Clatsop in Oregon.

Floating Down the Missouri

About 70 miles to the north of Great Falls, the tiny ranch town of Virgelle wasn't around when Lewis and Clark passed through, but Virgelle sits beside one of the few sections of the Missouri River that Lewis and Clark would still recognize. And it's one of only two upriver launching sites for canoe trips down the Missouri.

It's a gentle float, even in early summer when the current runs relatively fast. And paddling downstream certainly cannot approximate the struggles Lewis and Clark had as they moved in the opposite direction, poling, sometimes dragging, their boats up the river. You paddle past Judith River, which Clark named for his true love back East; farther upstream Lewis named the Marias River for his. Clark won his Judith. Lewis lost his Maria. Historians conjecture that a broken heart contributed to the captain's sad end.

You know the story. In 1803, President Thomas Jefferson chose Meriwether Lewis, a young Army captain from Virginia, to head an exploration of the Missouri River with the goal of finding a route to the Pacific Ocean. In turn, Lewis chose his former commanding officer, William Clark, to serve as his right-hand man. Their party set out in 1804 from Wood River, Illinois, and traveled up the Missouri in a keelboat and canoes. The trek took 28 months and was successful in many ways. Although they did not find a water route across the continent, they fulfilled Jefferson's second charge of mapping the area and reporting on the geography, geology, climate, botany, zoology, and native people of this vast tract of land acquired when Jefferson doubled the size of the U.S. with the Louisiana Purchase. By the time Lewis and Clark arrived in what is now Virgelle, they had been traveling more than a year. They had lost one man to appendicitis and gained a French interpreter, Charbonneau, his Shoshone wife, Sacagawea, and the couple's infant son.

A Legacy in Great Falls

Lewis and Clark's lengthy stay around Great Falls was not by choice. They had been advised by the Mandan Indians to expect a waterfall on the Missouri. When Lewis found it, he declared it "the grandest sight I ever beheld." His mood soon changed. He was expecting one waterfall; instead, above Great Falls roared four more cascades. The corps had to portage boats, food, and gear a brutal 18 miles. Their feet were bloodied by prickly pear spines. Lewis was attacked by a grizzly. And a trip they expected to take one day took a month.

The city of Great Falls hasn't always treated the Lewis and Clark legacy with respect. In the early 1900s, the city built a series of hydroelectric dams, earning Great Falls the nickname the "Electric City" but diminishing the cascades at which Lewis first marveled, then railed. Now it's making amends. The 5-mile paved River's Edge Trail allows pedestrians and cyclists handsome views out across the Missouri. Alongside it rises the bold, modern Lewis and Clark National Historic

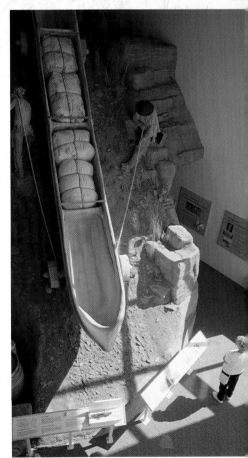

A life-sized canoe portage display dominates the entrance at Lewis & Clark National Historic Trail Interpretive Center.

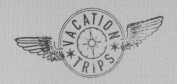

Sacagawea—A Shoshone Heroine

During their expedition, Lewis and Clark hired a French interpreter named Charbonneau, but he turned out to be haughty, querulous, and inept. It was his teenage Shoshone wife, Sacagawea (also spelled Sacajawea), who, though burdened with the couple's infant son, Jean Baptiste, proved to be an invaluable aide.

When the party met a band of Shoshone and made camp with them, she realized that their chief, Camaeahwait, was her long-lost brother. Lewis's journal records the scene: "She instantly jumped up, and ran and embraced him, throwing over him her blanket and weeping profusely...her new situation seemed to overpower her, and she was frequently interrupted by her tears."

Despite the lure of her homeland, Sacagawea remained with the expedition and helped Lewis and Clark trade with her brother for the horses required to travel into the Rocky Mountains.

A plaque in Sacagawea Park in downtown Three Rivers commemorates her contribution to the success of the Lewis and Clark expedition, and she is portrayed with Lewis and Clark in a statue in Fort Benton's river-side park. Her image will appear on the new gold-colored dollar coin to be produced by the U.S. Mint in the year 2000.

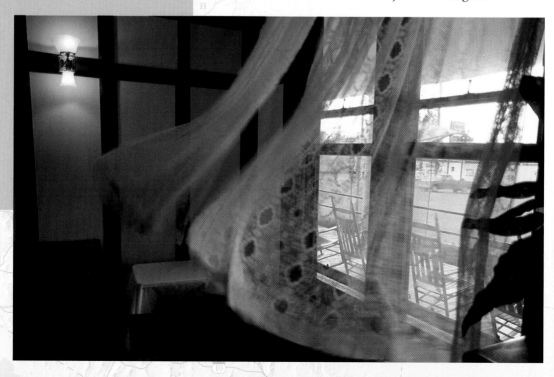

Curtains sway at the Sacajawea Inn, a Three Forks hostelry built in 1910.

Trail Interpretive Center which leads you on an interactive exploration of the corps's entire trek. An annual Lewis and Clark Festival gives local citizens a chance to fire rifles, build campfires, and parade around in elk-hide leggings.

To Lemhi Pass

South of Great Falls, the Missouri toys with the Rockies, acting as if it's going to climb straight up the mountainsides but instead sidling through a break in the peaks. In 1805, when Lewis came upon the river emerging from this stony portal, he named the region Gates of the Rocky Mountains. Today the base of the Gates is flooded by the waters of Holter Lake, and visitors glide in tour boats along the corps's route.

Much happened near Three Forks, southeast of Helena via U.S. Highway 287. Today Three Forks is on the fringe of the southerly valleys where movie stars and media moguls have bought million-dollar ranches. But back then, just north of town, Lewis and Clark achieved one of the main goals set out for them: they found the headwaters of the Missouri River. When you reach that area, now set aside as Missouri Headwaters State Park, you may be bemused that such a major river begins with three mild streams. Lewis named them after three expedition benefactors—Jefferson, Madison, and Gallatin, then secretary of the treasury.

From here, the corps traveled south through the Beaverhead Valley. Near Dillon, at the valley's head, the explorers had one of the major fortuitous encounters in American history. All through Montana they had not met a single Indian: historians are uncertain why, except that the Assiniboin and Atsinas may have been wary of white strangers. Now they were in Shoshone country, and Sacagawea, kidnapped from her tribe and taken to live with Mandans far to the east, recognized her homeland. When the explorers met a band of Shoshone and made camp with them, she realized that their chief was her long-lost brother. The corps traded with her brother for horses, essential now that they had to travel overland west up into

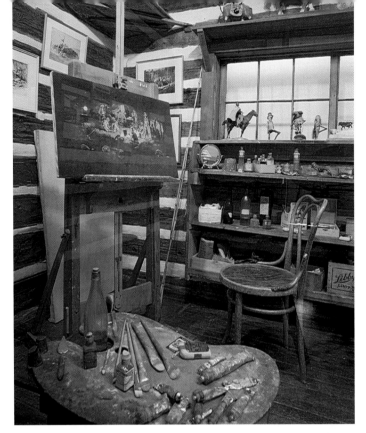

Built in 1903 from telephone poles, this cabin served as cowboy artist Charles M. Russell's studio in Great Falls; his home was next door.

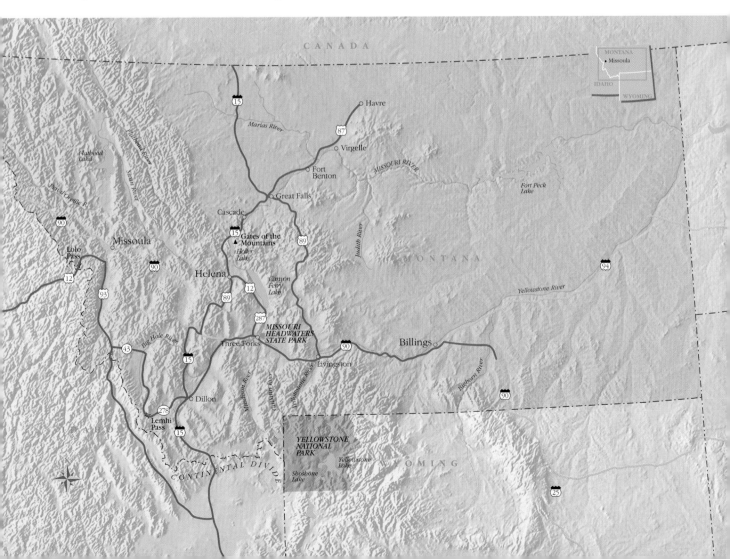

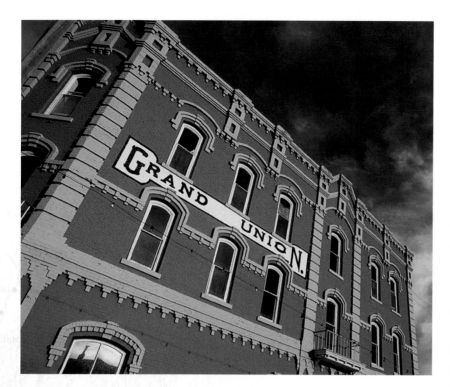

Fort Benton's Grand Union Hotel harks back to the days when the town was a bustling port for steamboats plying the Missouri.

the Continental Divide, you may identify with Lewis, who stood here for a while, knowing that he and the expedition had far to go but unable to contain his excitement at reaching this point.

The expedition itself was a mixed blessing, both for its members and for the people they encountered. More than a few historians note that for Sacagawea, the Shoshone, and all the other tribes in this new land, Lewis and Clark's journey marked the beginning of the end for an entire way of life. Nor did fate treat all members of the corps equally well.

They would reach the Pacific and they would return home to find they had been given up for dead. Clark would build a successful political career, but his friend Lewis would kill himself only three years after their return.

the Rocky Mountains. You can travel the same route.

South of Dillon, County Road 324 leads west, then a gravel road runs northwest, approximating the route the corps took. You climb past wheat fields and cattle ranches, gaining elevation as Montana spreads out behind you. As you climb the mountains, at last reaching Lemhi Pass and

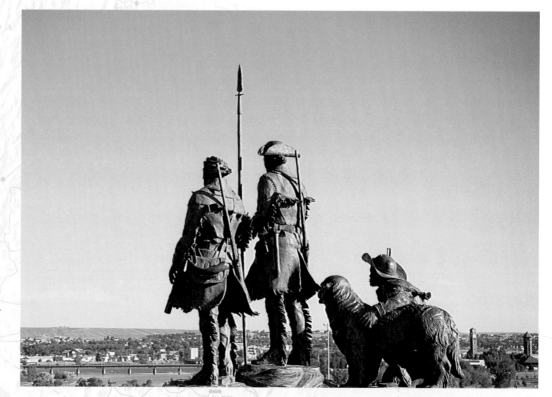

"Explorers at the Portage," a sculpture by Robert Scriver, overlooks the confluence of the Missouri and Sun rivers.

Unless otherwise noted, area codes are 406. Lodging rates for two people range from $ (under $100) to $$$ (above $250) per night.

GETTING THERE

Lewis and Clark took 133 days to cross Montana, 40 to return. You can follow much of their route in far less time, but plan on spending at least a week, particularly if you opt to float down the Missouri. Lewis and Clark traveled here in late spring and summer, a good choice for today's visitors. Most of the areas mentioned are easily accessible from the capital city, Helena, by interstate, but to retrace the trip, you'll also follow scenic state and county roads.

GREAT FALLS

Drivers can reach Montana's second-largest city from the south via Interstate 15, from Glacier National Park to the north via U.S. Hwy. 89. Lodging is mainly of the chain-hotel variety, comfortable but nothing extraordinary. The best restaurant in town is actually 20 miles east, in tiny Belt, Montana, on U.S. 89. It's called the **Black Diamond Bar & Supper Club** (277-4118), looks like a speakeasy, and serves superb steaks; it also boasts a good wine list.

Don't miss the bold **Lewis and Clark National Historic Trail Interpretive Center** (4201 Giant Springs Rd.; 791-7900). The center opens daily in summer from 9 to 8; admission tops out around $5 for adults. Nearby, stroll the **River's Edge Trail** to **Giant Springs Heritage State Park** for overlooks of the site where the corps had to portage. An even better view lies a few miles northwest (from downtown, take U.S. Hwy. 87 north, then turn east on Ryan Dam Rd.).

The annual **Lewis and Clark Festival** takes place in June. Events feature food, guided float trips, and living history demonstrations. For details, contact the Great Falls Area Chamber of Commerce (815 Second St. S., Great Falls, MT 59405; 761-4434) or Travel Montana (800/847-1868).

For information on other Great Falls attractions, which include the **Ulm Pishkin State Park** bison-killing site and the excellent **Charles M. Russell art museum and homesite**, contact Travel Montana.

UPPER MISSOURI

U.S. 87 runs parallel to the Missouri from Great Falls to Fort Benton to Virgelle.

Fort Benton, 44 miles northeast of Great Falls, is a drowsily charming town with a riverside park that features a noble statue of Lewis, Clark, and Sacagawea. In the mid-1800s, Fort Benton was a housing port for steamboats sailing up the river. The brick buildings lining Front Street were built during this era, and the **Museum of the Upper Missouri** (open daily mid-May–early Oct., by appointment rest of year; 622-5494; small fee) in Old Fort Oak Park details those days. Nearby stands the **Old Fort Benton Blockhouse**, which dates from 1850 and is said to be Montana's oldest building. Down the street is the stately **Grand Union Hotel**.

Fort Benton and Virgelle, about 25 miles northeast, are starting points for float trips along the Missouri. For river information (between May 15 and Sept. 30), stop by the **Visitor Center of the Wild & Scenic Upper Missouri** in Fort Benton (1719 Front St.; 622-5185).

Fort Benton is shy on places to stay, but the **Pioneer Lodge** (1700 Front; 622-5441; $) has adequate

rooms in a historic building. The tin-sided **Virgelle Mercantile** has been restored as a B & B (800/426-2926; $). Its modest rate includes an excellent breakfast.

NEAR HELENA

I-15 follows the Missouri southwest from Great Falls past Cascade and into the Rockies. On a bend of the river in Cascade is the **Fly Fishers' Inn** (2629 Old U.S. 91; 468-2529; $$). It caters to trout fishers and has comfortable rooms. Rates include great breakfasts and dinners.

Just north of Helena lies a major Lewis and Clark landmark, Gates of the Mountains. **Gates of the Mountains Boat Tours** (458-5241) offers inexpensive river rides in the area from Memorial Day through mid-Sept.

HEADWATERS AREA

From I-15 and Helena, U.S. Hwy. 287 leads south to Three Forks and Missouri Headwaters State Park. Dillon is south of Helena off I-15.

Three Forks is home to the broad-porched **Sacajawea Inn** (5 N. Main St.; 800/821-7326; $-$$), one of the nicest places to stay in Montana, with a fine restaurant to boot. Dillon has chain motels; call the Beaverhead Chamber of Commerce (683-5511) for a listing.

Missouri Headwaters State Park in Three Forks has fishing spots, historical displays, and campsites (994-4042). Dillon is a solid Western town with some fine turn-of-the-century architecture. Its **Beaverhead County Museum** (15 S. Montana St.; 683-5027) is worth a stop.

FOR MORE INFORMATION

Lewis and Clark Trail Heritage Foundation (Box 34334, Great Falls, MT 59403). **Travel Montana** (444-2654; out of state, 800/847-4868).

REGION	WYOMING
Where X	190-mile loop from Laramie
When X	Late spring through autumn drive

driving the
Snowy Range Road

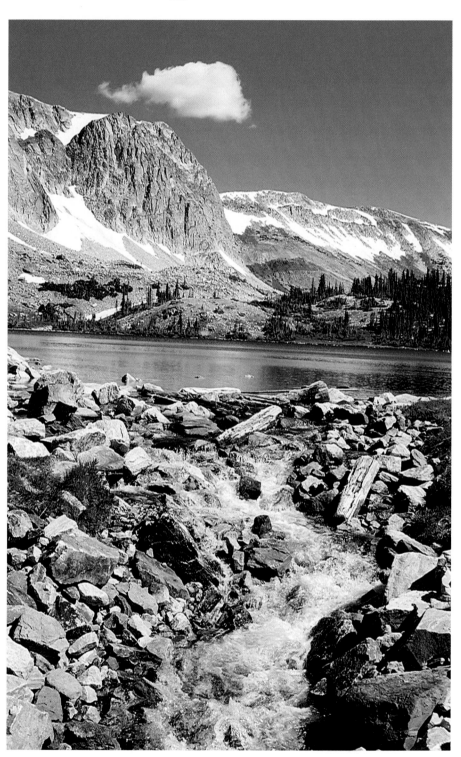

Lake Marie, only one of many lakes in Wyoming's Snowy Range, nestles at the foot of impressive quartzite peaks.

One of Wyoming's most spectacular drives takes you from the rolling plains around Laramie into the wildflower-dotted meadows, alpine lakes, and glaciated cliffs of the Medicine Bow Mountains before descending to a fishing haven on the North Platte River. You return by way of some classic Old West towns, rounding off your trip with a visit to one of the last territorial prisons.

When you start out on the Snowy Range Road (State Highway 130), telephone poles and fence posts are just about the only vertical growth you'll see as the plains stretch all the way to the base of the mountains. Then velvety foothills begin to rise, and clumps of trees define the course of the Little Laramie River. Along the way, watch for pronghorn antelope grazing unconcernedly as cars whisk by and hawks circling lazily overhead.

In 27 miles you reach Centennial, a would-be gold town founded in 1876 and the last town before you start your climb into the Snowy Range. About 10 miles farther, the impressive quartzite peaks come into view. Libby Flats lookout, at the summit of the 10,857-foot pass, provides panoramic views that, on a clear day, extend south as far as Rocky Mountain Park in Colorado. A helpful chart at the observation point locates peaks, including Medicine Bow, the highest at 12,013 feet. A succession of lakes laps at glacial scree beneath the white mountains. The area is peppered with hiking trails, campsites, and picnic areas. Activities match the season, but it is always a photographer's paradise.

A Town for All Tastes

After its descent from the mountainous heights, State 130 reaches Saratoga on the North Platte River. This recreational access point, named after New York's Saratoga Springs, boasts its own hot spas.

The free mineral springs called Hobo Pool are on Walnut Street (2 blocks off the highway). After luxuriating in the heat, you'll cool off quickly in the river just feet away.

Saratoga offers a variety of outdoor fun, from trophy fishing and white-water rafting to mountain biking and golf. An annual Arts Festival takes place over the July 4th weekend. A small museum, open afternoons from Memorial Day to Labor Day, contains a collection of historical and archaeological artifacts.

Along the UP Tracks

The first highway through Wyoming paralleled the original Union Pacific tracks. To follow a piece of it, continue on State 130 to Walcott Junction. Cross Interstate 80 onto U.S. Highway 30. Railroad buffs will notice almost omnipresent trains, as this is still one of the busiest rail corridors in America.

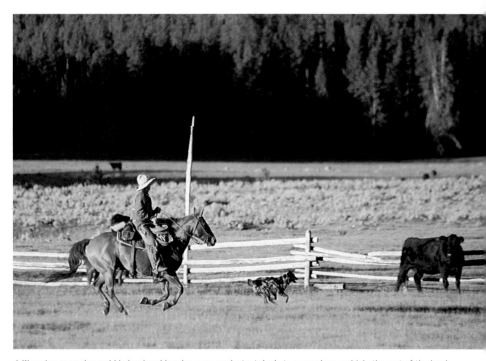

A Wyoming wrangler and his hardworking dog urge a reluctant dogie to move along and join the rest of the herd on the Wyoming plains.

The town of Medicine Bow down the tracks was thriving when U.S. 30 was the main highway. American author Owen Wister made the community famous in his classic Western, *The Virginian*. Though Wister never stayed at the hotel that took the name, the Victorian decor and Wister memorabilia are worth a stop. Peek upstairs; staying here isn't for everyone, but it could be fun for adventuresome spirits.

Across the highway, the old UP station is now a museum crammed with exhibits depicting the history of the town—and the West. Wister's cabin is here too.

Visible to the south is the world's largest wind turbine, part of Reagan-era energy experiments. Though it no longer works, newer models are producing energy nearby.

Jurassic Graveyard

U.S. 30 wends its way through some of the richest dinosaur fossil beds ever discovered. Como Bluff, to the north, has yielded specimens that are displayed worldwide. Digs are on private land and require permission to explore. To penetrate these 200-million-year-old burial grounds briefly, turn north on Marshall Road (a well-maintained dirt road 12 miles east of Medicine Bow). Go 7 miles to the turnoff for the state's Como Bluff Fish Hatchery, open year-round. Here thousands of fish are nurtured for Wyoming anglers.

A Wide Spot in the Road

Eight more miles on U.S. 30 is the wide spot called Rock River, another town changed by the rerouting of the main highway. The General Store is also the gas station, laundromat, and information center. In summer, crews of paleontologists working the digs rent the eight cabins. The small Rock River Museum has some excellent specimens from Como Bluff—plus the safe blown

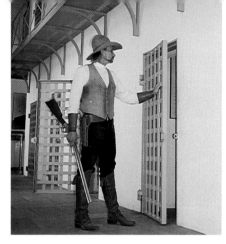

Guides in period dress lead tours of Wyoming Territorial Prison in Laramie.

up by Butch Cassidy in the infamous Wilcox Train Robbery.

More of the Old West

After you return to Laramie, take the time to visit the restored Wyoming Territorial Prison (exit 311 off I-80), one of only three still standing in the country. It's believed to be the only place where Butch Cassidy was ever incarcerated. A single admission fee includes a prison tour and a visit to the U.S. Marshals Museum from May to September. Here, too, the re-created Frontier Town offers activities and characters of the period. The park operates from Memorial Day through Labor Day. For more information, call 745-6166; 800/845-2287.

⋯TRIP PLANNER⋯

Unless otherwise noted, area codes are 307. Lodging rates for two people range from $ (under $100) to $$$ (above $250) per night.

WHERE

The loop trip begins and ends in Laramie and follows Snowy Range Rd. (State 130) to U.S. 30 (also U.S. 287). U.S. 30 is a year-round highway, but it's wise to check weather advisories. State 130 is closed at the summit in winter.

LODGING

A ranch stay adds to any western trip. Rates include lodging, meals, and activities. Call for reservations and detailed directions. **Vee Bar Guest Ranch** (2091 State 130; 6 miles west of Laramie; 745-7036, 800/483-3227; $-$$) offers both a riverside lodge and cabins. **Snowy Mountain Lodge** (742-7669; $-$$) lies 30 miles west of Laramie at the top of Snowy Range. **Medicine Bow Guest Ranch** (326-5439, 800/409-5439; $-$$) is 49 miles west of Laramie, and **Brush Creek Ranch** (327-5241; 800/726-2499; $-$$), on County Rd. 203, is another 15 miles.

Lodging in Saratoga includes **Hotel Wolf** (101 E. Bridge St.; 326-5525; $), established in 1893; cozy **Far Out West B&B** (304 N. 2nd St.; 326-5869; $-$$); and **Saratoga Inn and Resort** (601 E. Pic Pike Rd.; 326-5261, 303/825-2779; $-$$). In Medicine Bow, **The Virginian** (U.S. 30; 379-2377; $) offers turn-of-the-century décor. Laramie offers a number of chain motels.

DINING

In Laramie, **Jeffrey's Bistro** (123 Ivinson Ave.; 742-7046) is popular with locals for its healthy food. **Overland Fine Eatery** (100 Ivinson Ave.; 721-2800) calls its cuisine "creative." **Coal Creek Coffee** (110 Grand Ave.; 745-7737) is a favorite for freshly prepared light meals, specialty coffees, and dessert.

Both Saratoga's **Hotel Wolf** and **The Virginian** in Medicine Bow have restaurants.

SHOPS & MUSEUMS

Most worthwhile browsing will be in Laramie and Saratoga shops. Most small towns along this route have interesting museums. **Laramie Plains Museum** (603 Ivinson Ave., Laramie; 742-4448) houses an exquisite turn-of-the-century collection in a restored Victorian mansion. The grounds include a carriage house and a one-room schoolhouse. The **University of Wyoming**'s various museums are well worth seeing; for information, call 766-3160 or stop by the visitor center (1408 Ivinson Ave.).

FOR MORE INFORMATION

Laramie Chamber of Commerce (800 S. Third St., Laramie, WY 82070; 745-7339, 800/445-5303). Medicine Bow–Routt National Forest Service (2468 Jackson St., Laramie, WY 82070; 745-2300).

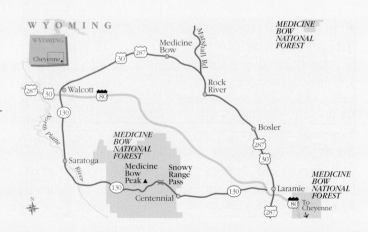

an old west
Ski Resort

REGION	COLORADO
Where	X	160 miles northwest of Denver
When	X	Winter and summer fun

Although Steamboat Springs is best known as a ski resort, at heart it's still a laid-back ranch town and quite different from Aspen and Vail, its higher-profile, celebrity-filled neighbors. Visit for a long winter weekend and you'll find that, after days of skiing, soothing dips in hot mineral springs, and some cowboy fun, you'll start feeling a little laid-back too. What really sets the town apart is the Old West hospitality and casual style you find here.

The historic ranch town tantalizes visitors with a mountain of powder in winter and a variety of outdoor fun in the lovely Yampa River Valley in summer. Victorians and brick-front shops on the town's main street provide a fitting backdrop for Levi-clad locals. In fact, cowboys have been gazing longingly at a wall of new Stetsons in F.M. Light & Sons Western shop (830 Lincoln Avenue) since the store opened in 1905. The Tread of Pioneers Museum, at 6th and Oak streets, displays antiques dating back to early pioneers as well as Native American artifacts.

Colorado's "White Gold"

Carl Howelsen, best known as the Flying Norseman, introduced skiing to the townspeople in 1913. The single ski jump he built then turned the town into a world-class ski resort by the 1930s. Since snowfall in this area

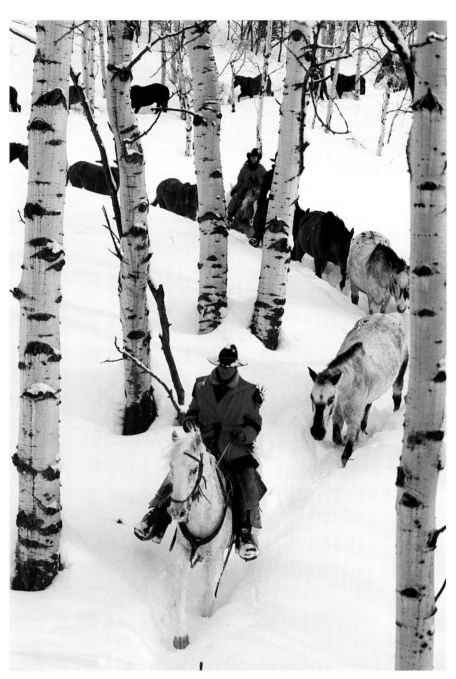

Roaming in Colorado's cowboy country: At the ski resort of Steamboat Springs, a downhill run sometimes happens in the saddle as well as on the slopes.

often produces powder so light it bubbles up under skis like champagne, it's no surprise the resort has been the training grounds for over 40 Olympic contenders and has earned the nickname Ski Town U.S.A. Former Olympic athletes and coaches provide skiing clinics; novices can watch interactive videos before heading for easy runs like Headwall near the base area. Cross-country enthusiasts will find miles of trails into the surrounding Routt National Forest. Other options include ice skating, snowshoeing, ice fishing, and sleigh riding.

Après Ski

Legend has it that mountain trappers in the early 1800s named the town after mistaking a pulsating thermal spring that shot 15 feet into the air for a

Another mode of transportation: rodeo riders at the raucous Cowboy Downhill swap broncs for skis.

chugging steam engine. While that spring no longer makes its rhythmic music, the area around Steamboat Springs boasts over 150 medicinal and recreational spas. A good way to end your day is with a soothing soak at Strawberry Park Hot Springs,

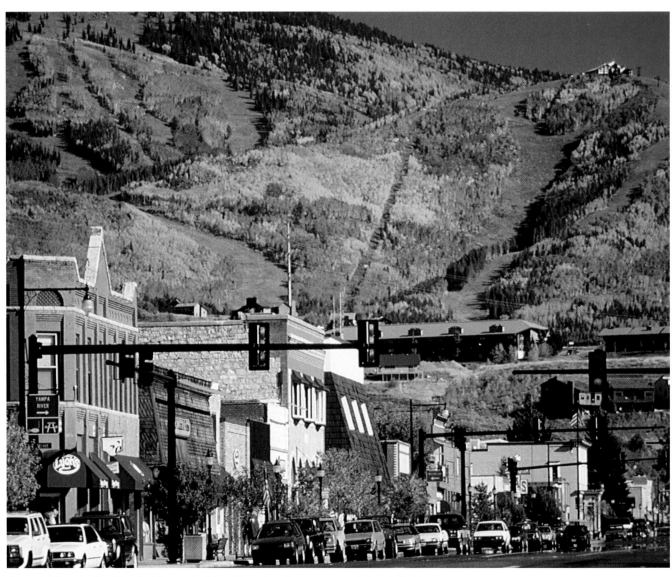

A crisp fall day in bustling Steamboat Springs; in winter, skiers schuss down snow-covered slopes behind town.

7 miles north of town. On a chilly night, plumes of steam rise in the air as the heated water hisses into a chain of deep pools.

Warming Up

Steamboat Springs is popular in warmer weather as well. Events such as musical concerts, rodeos, and hot air balloon races attract many visitors. In summer, the Silver Bullet Gondola up Mt. Werner makes it easy to spend a day hiking or just leisurely sunning from the deck of the mountaintop cafe. From downtown, walkers and skaters take the 4-mile Yampa River Trail into the countryside or follow a footpath leading to spectacular Fish Creek Falls. The more energetic try white-water rafting, and kayaking or mountain biking on more than 100 miles of trails. A number of old ghost towns lie within easy driving distance.

TRIP PLANNER

Unless otherwise noted, area codes are 970. Lodging rates for two people range from $ (under $100) to $$$ (above $250) per night.

WHERE

Steamboat Springs is three hours west of Denver off Interstate 70. After you pass through the Eisenhower Tunnel, take State Hwy. 9 north to U.S. Hwy. 40, which proceeds west over Rabbit Ears Pass (chains required in winter).

LODGING

Though the area has plenty of places to stay in all price ranges, it fills up fast during ski season, so reserve rooms well in advance. **Sheraton Steamboat Resort** (2200 Village Inn Ct.; 800/848-8878; $$-$$$) at the base of the downhill skiing action has a variety of rooms and condos. A dude ranch in summer, **Vista Verde Ranch** (call 800/526-7433 for information and road directions; $$$), 26 miles north of Steamboat Springs, becomes a cross-country ski resort in winter, with trails and knowledgeable backcountry guides. The lodge has 8 cabins and 3 lodge rooms, rustic-looking outside, handsome and well appointed inside. The cost includes all meals and activities, including horseback riding.

In town, **Steamboat Valley Guest House** (1245 Crawford Ave.; 870-9017; $-$$) offers 4 rooms with baths and an outdoor hot tub that overlooks the town. Some of the rooms at **Rabbit Ears Motel** (201 Lincoln Ave.; 879-1150; $-$$) have river views.

DINING

Popular **Antares Restaurant** (57½ 8th St.; 879-9939), set in a 1906 livery stable, serves a cuisine described as New American. A few blocks away, **Riggio's Fine Italian Food** (1106 Lincoln Ave.; 879-9010) lives up to its name with large portions of classic Italian fare. Closer to the mountain, locals flock to **La Montaña** (Après Ski Way and Village Dr.; 879-5800) for mouth-watering Southwestern and Tex-Mex food.

SKIING, SOAKING & MORE

For all winter activities, contact **Steamboat Ski & Resort Corporation** (879-6111). For the latest snow report, phone 879-7300. Access to **Strawberry Park Natural Hot Springs** (879-0342) is from a steep, rugged road open only to four-wheel-drive vehicles in winter. Local tour companies provide van transportation.

A popular **Cowboy Downhill** event, in which bowlegged and hilariously inept skiers in chaps, parkas, and cowboy hats wrangle their way down the slopes, takes place in mid-January. One of the West's oldest **Winter Carnivals** is held the first weekend in February. A series of pro rodeos enliven weekends from mid-June through Labor Day.

Three scenic drives around the area, ranging from 1 to 3 hours, show off peak aspen color. Check with the city's visitor center for routes and local maps.

FOR MORE INFORMATION

Steamboat Central Reservations (Box 774728, Steamboat Springs, CO 80477; 800/922-2722) books lodging and vacation packages. Steamboat Springs Chamber Information Center (1255 S. Lincoln Ave., Steamboat Springs, CO 80477; 879-0880) is centrally located between downtown and the ski area.

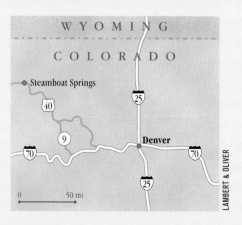

REGION		COLORADO
Where	X	160 miles west of Denver
When	X	A year-round spa

Glenwood Springs—

a thermal tonic

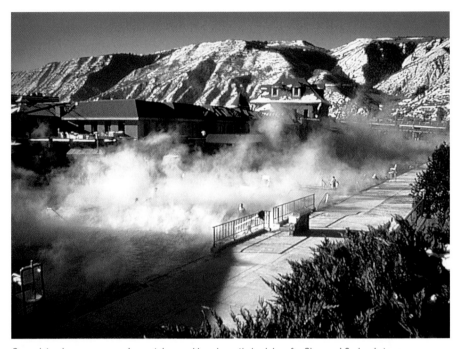

On a winter day, snow-covered mountains provide a dramatic backdrop for Glenwood Springs' steamy, spring-fed mineral pools.

While back roads often lead travelers toward secluded getaways, it's wise not to overlook what lies just off a main highway. When you need to be pampered, you can't beat Glenwood Springs off Interstate 70 near Denver. This pleasant town is known primarily for its underground steam baths and the world's largest outdoor hot springs pool. But it offers much more.

Dubbed Colorado's Spa in the Rockies, Glenwood Springs makes a good base for day trips to the ski capitals of Aspen and Vail or scenic backcountry jaunts to wineries and historic mining towns. Lying at the confluence of the Colorado and Roaring Fork rivers, the town's idyllic location makes it a mecca for year-round recreation. Best of all, after enjoying a full day of skiing or fly fishing, you can sooth weary muscles in mineral-rich waters.

Teddy Bears & Spas

Centuries ago, Ute Indians believed the ancient Yampah Hot Springs possessed curative powers. Before battle, warriors took dips in heated pools and sniffed vapors from underground caves to strengthen body and spirit. Years later, weary miners discovered the waters' relaxing powers.

In the 1880s, mining baron Walter Devereux sank a fortune into building the eight-story Hotel Colorado, a lavish spa modeled after an Italian Renaissance castle. Touted as Colorado's answer to Bath, England, and Germany's Baden-Baden, the luxurious spa soon attracted the rich and famous.

Among the prestigious guests was President Theodore Roosevelt, who referred to the elegant hotel as "The Summer White House" and used it as a base camp during a bear-hunting expedition in 1905. Legend has it that when the president returned empty-handed after a disappointing day of hunting, hotel maids presented him with a small bear stitched from rags. Thus was born the teddy bear.

Today, the outdoor spring-fed pools—a 90° pool the length of a football field and a smaller 104° therapy pool—continue to offer a relaxing, detoxifying experience. Nearby, the steam-filled caverns of the Yampah Spa and Vapor Caves provide further stress relief.

Before the Plunge

To help you appreciate the heated pools, the area around Glenwood Springs offers many ways to use the muscles you plan to soak later. The Glenwood Canyon Recreation Path winds for 16 miles along the Colorado River, its paved surface maintained for walkers, bikers, and skaters. This scenic trail offers prime picnic spots and side trails leading to secluded creeks.

Closer to town, the Glenwood Caverns and Historic Fairy Caves, closed for more than 80 years, reopened in 1999. In the 1890s, the subterranean grottoes filled with colorful geological formations were considered "The Eighth Wonder of the World."

When the day is too pleasant to spend underground, hike up Jasper Mountain to pay your respects to gunslinger Doc Holliday, who came here to treat his consumption. Sadly, Doc arrived too late.

Not even mineral-rich waters could cure gunslinger Doc Holliday, but he rests in peace in a cemetery overlooking town.

Making the Rounds

For a day trip that combines small town charm, historic sites, and scenic vistas, head south on State Highway 82 about 10 miles to Carbondale, where you can wander into quaint shops and galleries or hike to Thomas Lakes. Continue south on State Highway 133 15 miles for lunch at Redstone Inn and a tour of Redstone Castle.

TRIP PLANNER

Unless otherwise noted, area codes are 970. Lodging rates for two people range from $ (under $100) to $$$ (above $250) per night.

WHERE

Glenwood Springs lies off I-70 between Denver and Grand Junction. Amtrak trains from Denver or Salt Lake City make daily stops, and rental cars are available.

LODGING

Hotel Colorado (526 Pine St.; 800/544-3998; $-$$$), the grande dame of Glenwood Springs hostelries, has changed since the days when Presidents Roosevelt and Taft, "The Unsinkable" Molly Brown, Al Capone, and Clark Gable were guests. Both lobby and gardens have been restored and suites are charming; rooms vary in size and style. Built in 1906, the **Hotel Denver** (402 7th St.; 800/826-8820; $-$$) has been renovated in a sleek 1930s Art Deco style. To be closer to the heated pools, try **Hot Springs Lodge** (415 E. 6th St.; 945-6571; $-$$), a modern motel.

DINING

The lobby restaurant in the **Hotel Colorado** (945-6511) receives high marks for its food and setting. Similar marks go to **Florindo's** (721 Grand Ave.; 945-1245), with its homemade Italian cuisine. Five miles south of town on State 82, the **Sopris Restaurant** (945-7771) may look like a cowboy roadhouse, but it serves continental fare. For more casual dining, the **Glenwood Canyon Brewing Company** (945-1276) in the Hotel Denver features handcrafted beers.

OTHER ATTRACTIONS

The **Hot Springs Pool** (401 N. River St.; 945-7131; fee) is open daily until 10 P.M. The **Yampah Spa and Vapor Caves** (709 E. 6th St.; 945-0667; fee), open daily, offers full spa and salon services. Reservations are required for spa treatments.

The **Glenwood Canyon Recreation Path** begins near the Yampah Spa and runs east along the north bank of the Colorado River. A few blocks south of the river, the 1/2-mile hiking trail up Jasper Mountain to the **grave of Doc Holliday** starts at

12th St. and Bennett Ave. For bike rentals and river rafting, contact **Canyon Bikes** (945-8904) and **Blue Sky Adventures, Inc.** (945-6605), both in the Hotel Colorado. Reservations are suggested for **Glenwood Caverns and Historic Fairy Caves** (508 Pine St.; 945-4228). Call for the tour schedule at **Redstone Castle** (0058 Redstone Blvd.; 963-3463).

FOR FURTHER INFORMATION

Glenwood Springs Chamber Resort Association (1102 Grand Ave., Glenwood Springs, CO 81601; 945-6589).

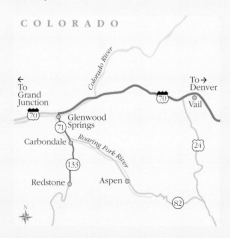

into the

San Juans

REGION		COLORADO
Where	X	About 4 hours southwest of Denver
When	X	Best from late spring through autumn

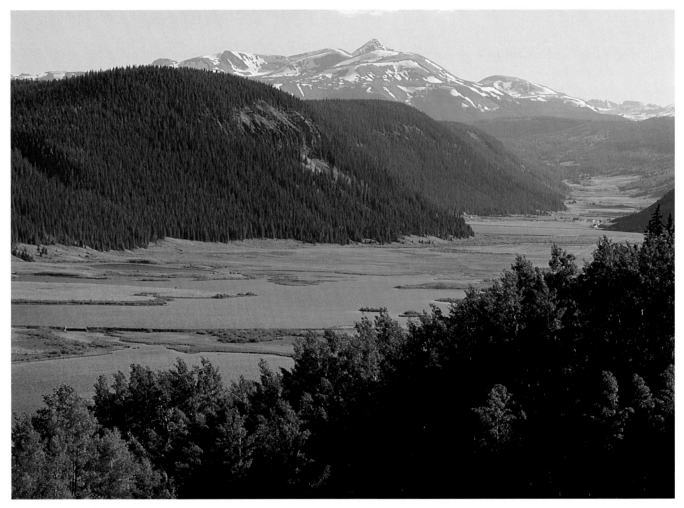

A scenic drive through Colorado's majestic San Juan Mountains rewards with dramatic vistas that include the headwaters of the Rio Grande.

One of southwest Colorado's loveliest byways wanders among the spires of the grand San Juan Mountains, exploring the headwaters of the Rio Grande and Arkansas rivers and winding through the area's small towns—unspoiled Salida, the trout-fishing capital of Lake City, and the old gold community of Creede. Along the way, it climbs over three mountain passes and cruises across the broad plains of the San Luis Valley toward the unexpected Great Sand Dunes National Monument.

Historic Salida

One of the last of Colorado's unspoiled towns, this Victorian-era community of 6,000 strung along the Arkansas River and surrounded by the 14,000-foot peaks of the San Juan and Sangre de Cristo ranges has been drawing visitors since the railroad arrived in 1880. Its comfortable summer weather and relatively mild winters attract backcountry guides specializing in rafting, fly-fishing, mountaineering, and cross-country skiing. Rock-hounds search for aquamarines, garnets, sapphires, topaz, turquoise, and Indian arrowheads around the area.

The well-kept downtown is also Colorado's largest historic district, and though its streets today are lined with art galleries, coffee shops, and fine restaurants (try Il Vicino for luscious pizza with innovative toppings), it retains touches of its wilder days as an outpost for carousing miners and lumberjacks.

Trout in Lake City

Head west over Monarch Pass (11,312 feet) on the road that is Salida's main drag (U.S. Highway 50), stopping for gas and an ice cream cone in Gunnison, gateway to Curecanti National Recreation Area, a boating and fishing haven.

Turn south on State Highway 149 for the scenic drive into Lake City along the Lake Fork of the Gunnison River. Skirting the west edge of Powderhorn village, State 149 winds through rock formations, alpine valleys, and flower-filled meadows before descending into the small town of Lake City.

With its high-mountain setting (8,671 feet), spring arrives late in Lake City, and it's not uncommon to see lilac bushes blooming well into July—or snowfalls in early September. Come the warm days of summer, this town of 350 residents explodes in size, with visitors filling up campgrounds, fishing for rainbow trout, and four-wheeling along old mining roads leading to several nearby ghost towns.

Lake City is surrounded by 14,000-foot mountains that locals refer to as "Fourteeners," and two (Redcloud Peak and Sunshine Peak) provide the snowmelt that helps fill Lake San Cristobal, a famous trout-fishing destination. Lakeview Resort, a family-owned seasonal resort on the shores of this crystal-clear,

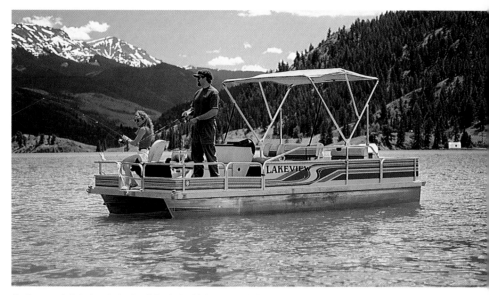
Anglers try their luck at Lake San Cristobal, which supposedly harbors a number of gullible trout.

high-country lake, offers everything from fishing boats to mountain cabins and four-wheel-drive vehicles. And for those who don't care to catch their dinner, there's always Charlie P's Mountain Harvest Restaurant (if you're feeling adventurous, try the enchiladas chipotles).

To Creede & Beyond

Continuing southeast on State 149, the road out of town passes Starvation Gulch, site of the Alfred Packer massacre. Hired as a guide to lead gold prospectors across the San Juans during the winter of 1874, Packer and his five employers became stranded in what was then a desolate mountain valley. When a well-fed Packer wandered out of the San Juans alone the next April, he soon became part of Wild West legend and lore. Convicted of cannibalism, he was confined briefly in nearby Saguache before escaping to Wyoming, where he was arrested nine years later.

Moving from gore to glory, a gorgeous vista of the headwaters of the Rio Grande is less than an hour away. The ribbon of black-

top first crosses Slumgullion Pass (11,361 feet) and Spring Creek Pass (10,901 feet) before revealing a breathtaking view of Rio Grande Pyramid, a 13,580-foot peak. Snowmelt to the north of this symmetrical mountain is destined for the Rio Grande and the Gulf of Mexico, while waters from its eastern and southern flanks eventually flow into the

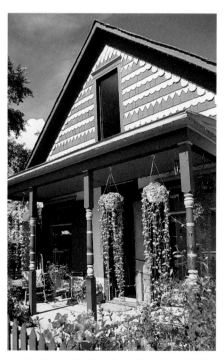
A colorful coat of paint enlivens this old house in the former mining town of Creede.

Gulf of California via the Colorado River.

Fields of wild blue irises (in bloom from May through July) line sections of the road as it wends its way into the Victorian town of Creede, a former mining community now filled with art galleries, craft stores, and a highly regarded repertory theater.

The Rio Grande, a popular trout-fishing stream area, offers prime terrain for mountain biking and alpine hiking.

Wind alongside the Rio Grande away from Creede and aim for the Great Sand Dunes National Monument. You're on your way across the broad and verdant San Luis Valley. State 149 ends at State Highway 160.

⁝⁝⁝TRIP PLANNER⁝⁝⁝

Unless otherwise noted, the area code is 719. Lodging rates for two people range from $ (under $100) to $$$ (above $250) per night.

WHERE

Less than 4 hours from Denver and about 1 hour north of New Mexico, the San Juan Mountains of south-central Colorado are sprinkled with small towns whose economies are thriving and whose residents are friendly. Agriculture still rules some regions; in others the emphasis has shifted from mining to cultural tourism and outdoor recreation. This route is all smooth sailing on two-lane blacktop, with passing lanes on steepest mountain roads—ideal for everything from Harleys to Winnebagos.

LODGING

In Salida, **Gazebo Country Inn** (507 E. Third St.; 800/ 565-7806; $) is near the historic district. **Tudor Rose Bed & Breakfast** (6720 Paradise Rd.; 539-2002, 800/379-0889; $) is another cozy, rural retreat. In Lake City, the **Lakeview Resort** (800/456-0170; $) has cabins, lodge rooms, hotel suites, and RV sites. The **Creede Hotel** (120 N. Main St., Creede; 658-2608; $) includes a full breakfast, while **Old Firehouse Bed & Breakfast** (121 N. Main St.; 658-0212; $) inhabits the town's original firehouse.

DINING

Il Vicino Pizzeria & Brewery (1136 E. Second St., Salida; 539-5219) is a pizza haven, while **Laughing Ladies Restaurant** (126 W. First St.; 539-6209), housed in a turn-of-the-century charmer, serves a more varied lunch, dinner, and Sunday brunch. **Charlie P's Mountain Harvest Restaurant** (951 N. Hwy. 149, Lake City; 970/944-2332) specializes in Mexican food. **Café Olé** (112 N. Main St., Creede; 658-2608) is open until 11 during theater season.

RECREATION

Headwaters Outdoor Equipment/American Adventure Expeditions (228 No. F St., Salida; 539-4680, 800/288-0675) offers half-day to overnight whitewater rafting trips. **Henson Jeep Rental** in Lake City (970/944-2394) has full-day rentals for exploring the surrounding countryside, and **Lakeview Outfitters** (800/456-0170 for reservations and directions) provides 2-hour guided horseback trips and morning-long, guided fishing trips for two adults. The **Creede Repertory Theatre**'s (121 N. Main St.; 658-2540) season usually runs from mid-June to late August.

FOR FURTHER INFORMATION

For a free vacation planner, call the Colorado Travel and Tourism Authority (800/265-6723). Heart of the Rockies Chamber of Commerce (406 W. U.S. 50, Salida, CO 81201; 539-2068), Lake City Chamber of Commerce (3rd and Silver Sts., Lake City, CO 81235; 970/944-2527, 800/569-1874), and Creede/Mineral County Chamber of Commerce (1207 N. Main St., Creede, CO 81130; 719/658-2608, 800/327-2102) are helpful resources.

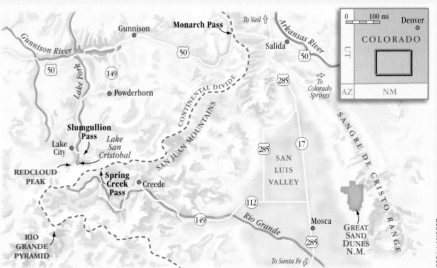

if this be
Purgatory...

REGION	COLORADO	
Where	X	7 hours southwest of Denver
When	X	Year-round destination; spectacular fall color

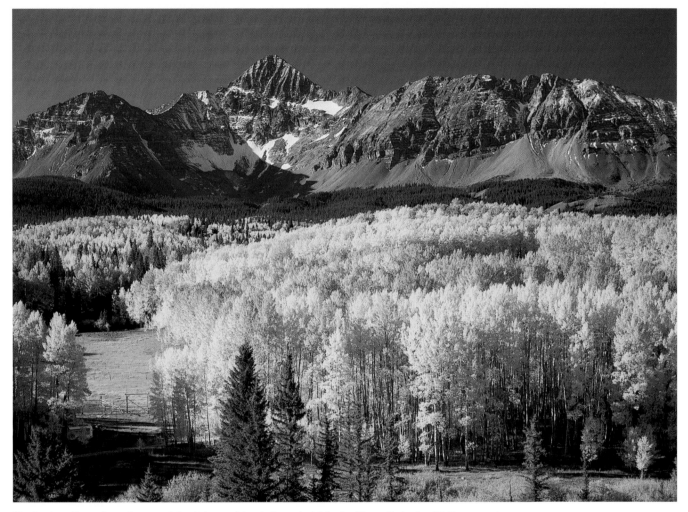

The San Juan Skyway in southwestern Colorado is one of America's greatest fall-color drives, offering breathtaking aspen views.

Known for its legendary snow conditions, Purgatory Ski Resort in the southern San Juan Mountains enjoys a different reputation in autumn, when the countryside resembles an impressionistic painting. Rustling groves of shimmering aspens set against majestic peaks and lapis lazuli skies make this region a prime destination for fall color.

Purgatory is only one stop on the 236-mile San Juan Skyway, which ranks among the West's most spectacular drives. Looping north from Durango, the road rings the rugged edges of the San Juan Mountains, a wild profusion of jagged, snow-etched peaks that pierce the clouds floating at 13,000 feet. Steep, winding, and narrow in places, the Skyway rambles well above 7,000 feet for most of its length, with no shortage of rangetop views as it climbs over four 10,000-foot-plus passes. Besides stunning scenery and plenty of pullouts for picnicking, hiking, and exploring, the Skyway connects a string of old mining towns, each offering its own brand of historic charm.

Durango to Silverton

Durango makes a good starting point for the drive. Heading north on U.S. Highway 550, you pass the Purgatory Ski Area,

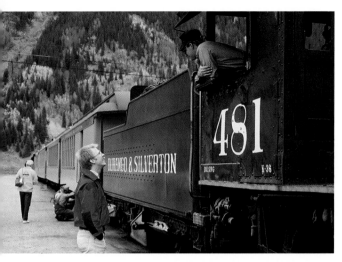

Passenger gets the inside track on popular Durango & Silverton Narrow Gauge Railroad excursion.

where you can ride the chairlift up the mountain to drink in the fresh air and vertical views. Past Purgatory, the road climbs over 10,640-foot Coalbank Pass. Three miles beyond the pass is a turnoff to Old Lime Creek Road, a graded dirt road most cars can negotiate if it's dry.

This detour (which loops 11 miles back to the Skyway above Purgatory) winds down through aspen stands on open hillsides to Lime Creek, where you can spread out a picnic lunch and even get in some fishing. Once you rejoin the highway, it's 21 more miles to Silverton.

Tucked into a high mountain valley surrounded by aspens, this 1875 mining town, with its preserved and restored false-front buildings, is the most genuinely historic stop on the loop. The last of the silver mines closed just 10 years ago; Silverton now survives on tourism, much of it generated by its being the terminus of the Durango & Silverton Narrow Gauge Railroad. If time permits, walk around the historic

district, visit a saloon dating from the 1880s, or tour a mine.

On to Ouray & Telluride

Ten miles beyond Silverton, U.S. 550 tops 11,075-foot Red Mountain Pass, then narrows to a twisting ribbon of asphalt that clings to the craggy shoulders of mine-pocked peaks until it plunges into the gorge of the Uncompahgre River. This tortuous stretch has been dubbed the Million Dollar Highway, most likely a reference to the cost of its construction in the mid-1920s. But that sobriquet as readily reflects the aesthetic value of the cliff-hanging views the road affords—views that change around each bend all the way to Ouray (YOU-ray), a photogenic mining town.

Gold and silver lured miners here in the 1870s, but Ouray really boomed after the founding of the Camp Bird Mine. Between 1896 and 1910, it yielded $26 million, the highest return of any mine in the state. Today, a walking tour through the nine-block-long historic district takes you past structures built in the late 1800s with all that wealth.

Leaving Ouray, the highway heads north to Ridgway, then climbs to the turnoff for Telluride. Nestled in a box canyon surrounded by majestic peaks, Telluride was once a lawless mining camp; in 1889, Butch Cassidy began his career with an unauthorized withdrawal from the town's bank. Today, the village of restored Victorian-era buildings is a trendy ski resort.

The heart of some of the best fall color is found as the Skyway climbs toward Lizard Head Pass. Once over the pass, The Skyway passes ancient cliff dwellings and other attractions as it loops back to Durango.

Nestled in a box canyon and surrounded by soaring peaks, once-lawless Telluride has become a trendy ski resort and summer vacation village.

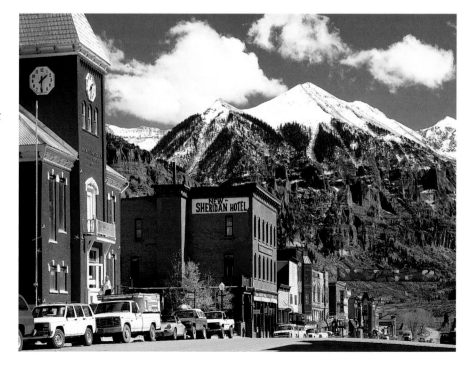

Unless otherwise noted, area codes are 970. Lodging rates for two people range from $ (under $100) to $$$ (above $250) per night.

WHERE

You can drive the San Juan Skyway as a long day loop from Durango, but allowing at least two full days gives you time to stretch your legs on aspen-lined hiking trails, get in some late-autumn fishing, and explore historic mining camps.

LODGING

Ouray and Telluride provide the best spots to overnight among the aspens. In Ouray, the **St. Elmo Hotel** (426 Main St.; 325-4951; $-$$) is a restored period piece with 9 rooms. In Telluride, check into the latest luxury resort, 32-room **Inn at Lost Creek** (119 Lost Creek Ln., Mountain Village; 728-LOST, 888/601-LOST; $$-$$$) or spend the night in vintage surroundings at the **New Sheridan Hotel** (231 W. Colorado Ave.; 728-4351; $-$$ includes complimentary appetizers and wine). The charming **Strater Hotel** (699 Main Ave.; 247-4431; $-$$) in Durango offers Victorian-era elegance and complimentary breakfast.

DINING

The region incorporates a wide variety of dining choices, from fine restaurants with wild game specialties to lighter saloon fare in vintage honky-tonks. In Ouray, the **Outlaw Steakhouse** (610 Main St.; 325-4366) offers rustic Western ambience and a look at the hat John Wayne wore in *True Grit*. In Telluride, ascend via a free gondola ride up to Mountain Village for a view of the sunset from the **Peaks'** bar (136 Country Club Dr.; 728-6800), then sample Northern

Italian cuisine at **La Piazza** (117 Lost Creek Ln.; 728-8283). In Durango, popular **Season's** (764 Main Ave.; 382-9790) offers patio seating and microbrews, while **Old Tymer's** (1000 Main Ave.; 259-2990) is famous for hamburgers and green chile.

ATTRACTIONS

Reserve seats well in advance to take a trip aboard the **Durango & Silverton Narrow Gauge Railroad** (888/872-4607). Five miles east of Silverton on State Hwy. 110, the **Old Hundred Gold Mine** (800/872-3009) is open for tours and free gold panning from mid-May to mid-Oct.

To reach not-to-be-missed **Bridal Veil Falls** in Telluride, continue on the

dirt road at the east end of State Hwy. 145. Park your car at the base of the falls and walk 1.8 miles along an old mining road to the head of the 365-foot waterfall, the state's longest free-fall waterfall. The private residence at the top of the falls was formerly a power plant.

FOR MORE INFORMATION

Durango Chamber of Commerce (111 Camino del Rio, Box 2587, Durango, CO 81302; 800/525-8855). Ouray Chamber Resort Association (1222 N. Main St., Box 145, Ouray, CO 81427; 800/228-1876). Telluride Visitor Services (666 W. Colorado Ave., Box 653, Telluride, CO 81435; 888/355-8743).

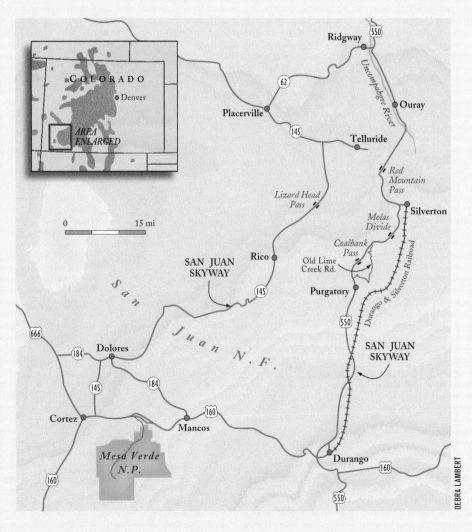

Southwest

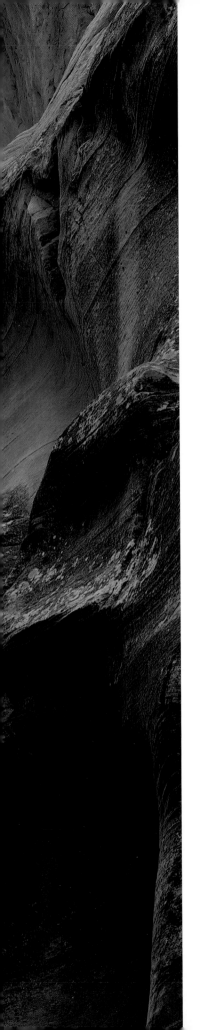

Lofty mountain peaks; high plateaus pungent with the aroma of pine, sage, and juniper; multicolored arches, spires, and buttes; deep, tortuously carved canyons; and sweeping desert punctuated by sentinel saguaros—the scenic offerings of the Southwest have no equal. But the history and cultural diversity are what attract many visitors.

The nation's two oldest continually occupied villages are here: Acoma, atop a high mesa in northwestern New Mexico, and Old Oraibi, on a mesa top in northeastern Arizona. Here, too, are centuries-old Spanish churches, reminders that the conquistadors arrived in the 16th century searching for gold and attempted, unsuccessfully, to subjugate the indigenous people they encountered. Deserted ghost towns testify to a later boom-and-bust era, a time when prospectors dug for lodes of silver and gold.

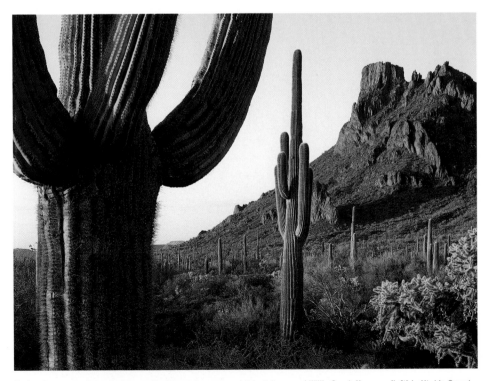

National monuments protect some Southwest treasures—intricately carved Willis Creek Narrows (left) in Utah's Grand Staircase—Escalante and starkly beautiful cactus country (above) in southwestern Arizona.

New Mexico

Blessed with a varied landscape that includes lush forests, sandy deserts, high plateaus, and soaring mountains, New Mexico is known as the Land of Enchantment. But as enchanting as the scenery is the state's rich heritage, a colorful mosaic of Native American, Hispanic, and Anglo cultures unmatched by most states. Sky-high Santa Fe, the state's capital, is a happy blend of the best scenery and culture. When you throw in its temperate climate and the magical light and intense colors that have enthralled artists for so long, it's easy to see why visitors gravitate here. The Turquoise Trail, a back road between Albuquerque and Santa Fe, highlights old mining camps given new life by artisans. Other roads lead to ancient Indian pueblos and colonial Spanish villages. We also journey to the state's southwest corner, where the Silver City area would be the perfect setting for a Western movie.

Arizona

From the heights of the San Francisco Peaks to the depths of the Grand Canyon, Arizona's terrain is spectacular and diverse. Diverse, too, are its Native American tribes, whose reservations cover one-quarter of the state's total land area. In this chapter you will sample some of that diversity—the vast Navajo reservation and mesa-top Hopi villages, Canyon de Chelly's ancient cliff dwellings, and the surprising Sonoran desert. Visit old copper towns and dude ranches, sample vintages in a vinous valley, and tour a verdant valley by rail. All trips are within easy driving distance of sun-drenched resorts in Phoenix and Tucson.

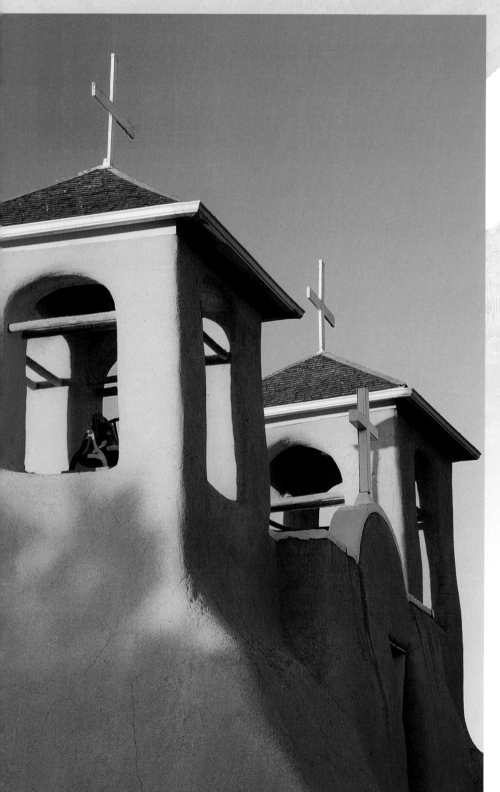

Painters and photographers have immortalized San Francisco de Asis Church in Ranchos de Taos, New Mexico.

Utah

It's not surprising that Zane Grey used southern Utah as a setting for so many of his novels. This is where the state's bountiful geologic formations present a unique and colorful showcase of canyon and rock wilderness. So varied and unbelievable is the stunning scenery that four national parks and one state park were created to preserve the weirdly eroded landscape. This is also the location of a new national monument, Grand Staircase–Escalante, with 1.7 million acres of multicolored cliffs and mesas extending from Bryce Canyon to Grand Canyon. These pages take you on a delightful scenic loop through this exciting country south of Salt Lake City.

Nevada

Most Nevada visitors head for the gaming tables of Las Vegas and Reno, with perhaps a peek at mighty Boulder Dam on the Colorado River or a short stay on Lake Tahoe's east shore. But it's the state's hidden interior that can enliven a visit. One of our back-road loops takes you out of Las Vegas to the state's only winery, to a refuge sheltering several dozen endangered plants and animals, to a ghost town enlivened by a whimsical sculpture garden, and to a one-woman performance for an audience that's been there 30 years. Another drive leads along "the loneliest highway" to almost-ghost towns and the skeletal remains of gigantic seagoing dinosaurs.

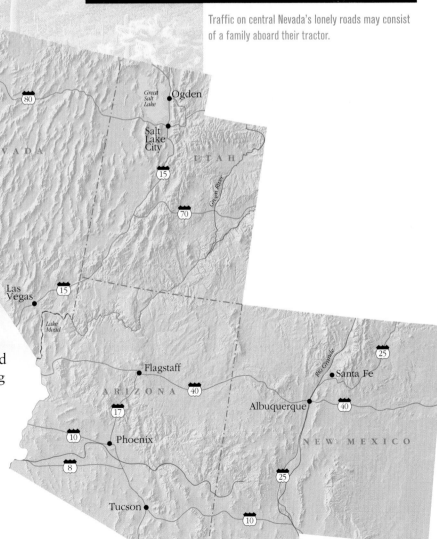

Traffic on central Nevada's lonely roads may consist of a family aboard their tractor.

Silver City
& beyond

REGION	NEW MEXICO	
Where	X	200 miles southwest of Albuquerque
When	X	Best in late spring and early autumn

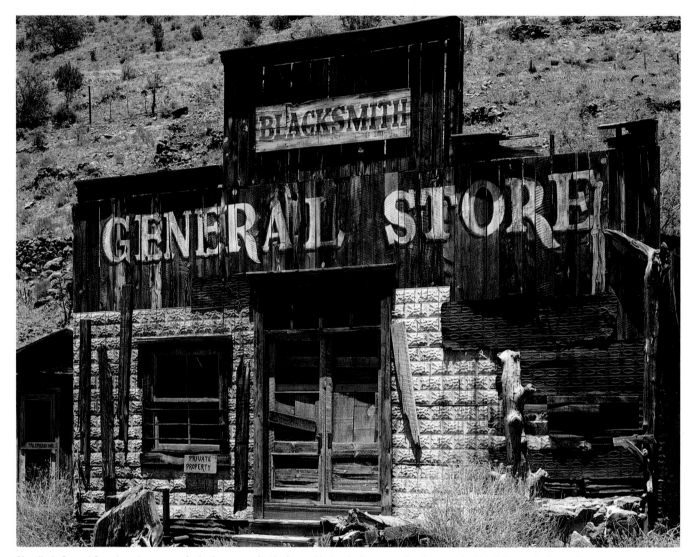

Mogollon's General Store is no longer open for business, even for the few residents who live among the ghost town's old buildings and mine shafts.

Silver City in the southwest corner of New Mexico has an aura that comes across as Old West rather than Spanish. A pretty little hillside town bisected by a steep canyon, it easily could be a setting for a Western movie and was, in fact, the boyhood home of William Bonney (later known as the notorious outlaw Billy the Kid). Signs point out the cabin where Bonney and his family lived and the old jail from which he made his first escape at age 15, while under arrest for robbing a Chinese laundry. His mother is buried on the town's east side.

A classic boom town, Silver City grew rapidly when silver was discovered in the 1860s. It became the county seat of Grant County in 1871 and home to Western New Mexico University in 1893 (the same year the bottom dropped out of silver). Now it's copper that fills the area's coffers. And the latest boom is in tourists and new residents, many of the latter students.

Silver City's historic downtown is alive and bustling with new restaurants, art galleries, and student-oriented stores. The entryways of old buildings are inlaid with mosaic tiles that bear the names of their original businesses. Some storefronts face Big Ditch Park, a tree-lined arroyo running through the center of town, rather than the street. Big Ditch was the original main street, until floods in the 1890s eroded it to its present depth.

Silver City makes a good base for day trips to outlying Indian ruins, ghost towns, wilderness areas, mines, and ranches. To learn a little about area history first, stop by the handsome mansard-style mansion at 312 West Broadway, which houses the free Silver City Museum (open Tues.-Sun.). Also don't miss the university's extensive collection of prehistoric Mimbres pottery and other artifacts in

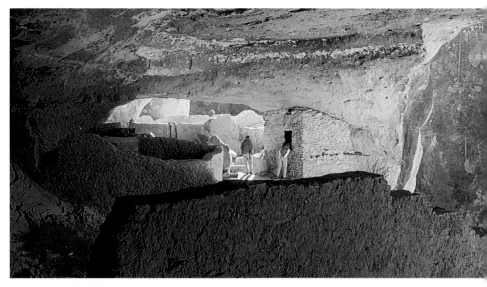

Visitors inspect the Gila Cliff Dwellings, a well-preserved collection of 14th-century apartments 44 miles from Silver City. You might stop at Buckhorn Saloon on your way through Pinos Altos.

Fleming Hall (open daily; donations accepted), at 10th and West streets.

Into Gila Country

About 44 miles north of Silver City on State Highway 15 lies Gila Cliff Dwellings National Monument. (Because of the serpentine roads, allow 2 hours for the drive.) A 1-mile loop walk leads through a lovely canyon (especially nice in fall) to a collection of well-preserved Mogollon ruins. With several other longer trails into the Gila Wilderness, you could easily spend a day up here.

En route up to the cliff dwellings, State 15 passes through Pinos Altos, where gold was discovered in 1860. Pinos Altos is famous today for the landmark Buckhorn Saloon, a typical Western oasis, but it's also an interesting town to explore. A small adobe church built by the Hearst family in 1898 is now home to the Grant County Art Guild (open 10-5 summer weekends). Nearby stands a 3/4-scale reproduction of

the Santa Rita del Cobre Fort and trading post (open summer only). The log cabin on Main Street that houses Pinos Altos Museum (open year-round; small admission charge) was built in 1866 by the grandfather-in-law of the present owner. The town's little cemetery reveals how tough and random life here once was: one child died at 3 years, another at 3 days. Their brother lived to be 87.

To Glenwood & Mogollon

Another trip out of Silver City heads 65 miles up U.S. Highway 180 to the small community of Glenwood and the ghost town of Mogollon beyond. (To reach Mogollon, you make a 9-mile side trip off the highway via a road that has more than its fair share of twists and turns.) Though the road is open year-round for the few residents who live there, the ghost town is most inviting from late spring to early autumn, when museums and shops are open. (The dirt road heading northeast out of town closes in winter.)

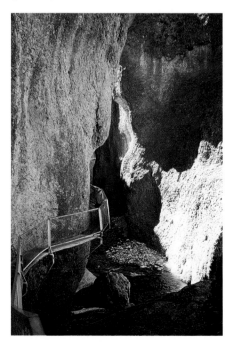

The Catwalk, east of Glenwood, clings to a rocky wall, affording viewer a bird's-eye view of Whitewater Creek cascading into the canyon below.

Don't miss walking along the Catwalk, which lies a few miles outside Glenwood. Part trail and part metal walkway, a short but beautiful stroll takes off from Whitewater Picnic Area (no drinking water), 5 miles down Catwalk Road.

The walkway runs alongside canyon walls and above the rushing waters of Whitewater Creek for about a mile before connecting to a network of backcountry trails. It follows the route of two pipelines that once supplied water and power to the turn-of-the-century gold- and silver-mining town of Graham.

Whitewater Canyon was used as a hideout for Indians and desperados alike, including Geronimo and Butch Cassidy. For a great late-season hike, continue up Whitewater Canyon on Trail 207 beyond the end of the Catwalk Trail.

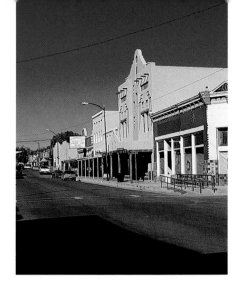

Art galleries, restaurants, and shops line the streets in Silver City.

⁙TRIP PLANNER⁙

Unless otherwise noted, area codes are 505. Lodging rates for two people range from $ (under $100) to $$$ (above $250) per night.

WHERE

To reach Silver City from the east, take U.S. 180 north from Interstate 10 at Deming; from the west, take State Hwy. 90 north from I-10 at Lordsburg.

LODGING

For overnighting in Silver City, try the **Palace Hotel** (106 W. Broadway; 388-1811; $ includes continental breakfast) in the historic district, first opened to guests in 1892. Its Victorian-style rooms aren't spacious, but they do make you feel as if you've just come in from the range, stabled your horse, and settled in for the night.

More rustic is the **Bear Mountain Guest Ranch** (3 miles north of Silver City off U.S. 180; 2251 Cottage San Rd.; 538-2538; $ includes all 3 meals). Owner Myra McCormick is a dedicated birder and can help arrange tours that emphasize nature and archaeology, both as day trips and as part of her 6-day Lodge and Learn program. Another good choice is **Bear Creek Motel and Cabins** (88 Main St., Pinos Altos; 388-4501; $-$$) about 6 miles north of Silver City. The beautiful two-story cabins, nestled in the trees and standing on hillsides overlooking the Gila National Forest, afford lots of quiet privacy.

If you are looking for a place to spend a few nights near Glenwood, try **Los Olmos Guest Ranch** (U.S. 180 and Catwalk Rd. just north of Glenwood; 539-2311; $ includes breakfast). Rustic stone cabins stand in a quiet wooded setting with dining room, pool, spa, and recreation facilities. With advance notice, they make arrangements for horseback riding.

DINING

A haven in Silver City for green-chili lovers is the **Jalisco Café** (106 S. Bullard St.; 388-2060). **Diane's Bakery & Café** (510 N. Bullard St.; 538-8722) has homemade baked goods and soups plus salads, sandwiches, quiches, and pastas. Across the street, **Higher Grounds Coffee Shop** (501 N. Bullard St.; 534-0966) also offers fresh baked goods as well as soups, homemade pizzas, and salads. Set in a classic old Route 66-style motel is **Adobe Springs** (1617 Silver Heights Blvd.; 538-3665), which serves delicious breads and a menu ranging from Americana to New Mexican.

In Pinos Altos, don't miss the highly regarded **Buckhorn Saloon** (538-9911), with great steaks and seafood.

FOR MORE INFORMATION

Grant County Silver City Chamber of Commerce (1103 N. Hudson, Silver City, NM 880061; 538-3785, 800/548-9378). Southern Catron County Chamber of Commerce (P.O. Box 183, Glenwood, NM 88039; 539-2711). The Glenwood Ranger Station (539-2481) has a wealth of maps, travel guides, and brochures.

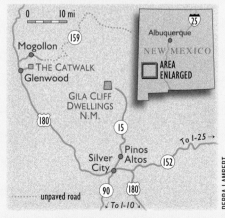

REGION	NEW MEXICO
Where X	160-mile loop from Santa Fe
When X	Year-round; crowds in summer, snow in winter

High Road *to* Taos

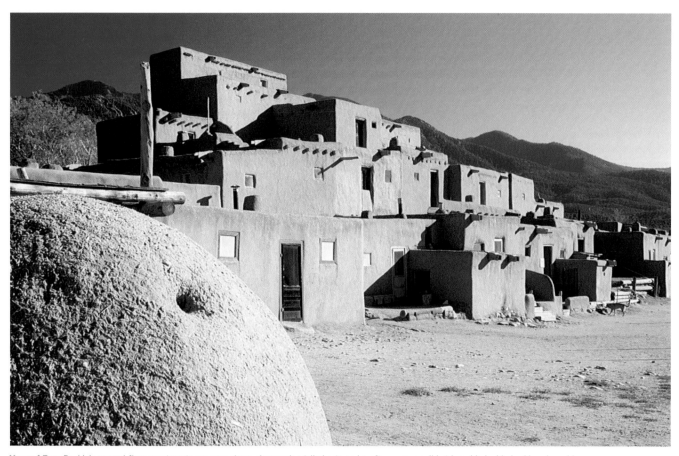

Many of Taos Pueblo's ground-floor apartments are now shops showcasing tribal arts and crafts; women sell hot bread baked in beehive-shaped hornos.

This meandering back-road loop from Santa Fe takes visitors into mountain villages founded by Spanish colonists hundreds of years ago, through pristine ponderosa forestland, and then into Taos and the multistoried Taos Pueblo. The "low road" return follows the Rio Grande valley, with stops at two more traditional New Mexico pueblos.

Although all the driving could be done easily in one day, tempting stops abound, so an overnight stay in Taos makes the trip more leisurely.

Food, Crafts & Miracles

Begin your journey north from Santa Fe, turning east at Pojoaque onto State Highway 503, a road flanked by cottonwoods and small farms, into Nambe. Then, as the road climbs into the hills, take County Road 520 left to Chimayó, a village known for its adobe chapel, colorful restaurant, and generations of weavers.

Before the Spanish founded the town in the 1700s, there were Tewa-speaking Indians in the area, and, according to their legends, there was a pool here with water—or mud—that could effect healing. A private shrine, erected here in 1816, was turned over to the Archdiocese of Santa Fe in 1929. Some 300,000 pilgrims come to the Santuario de Chimayó annually. The walls inside the chapel are covered with crutches, canes, and other testimonials of miraculous cures. Believers often leave with a scoop of healing dirt from a back room.

The Rancho de Chimayó restaurant nearby has its own

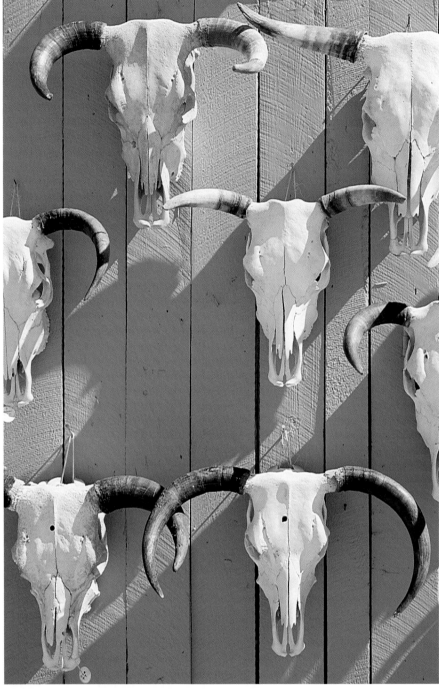

The wall of skulls outside Featherston Trading Company in Ranchos de Taos achieves its goal—to catch the eyes of those passing by.

woodcarvers such as the Lopez family. Then proceed along a narrow ridge that rises to 8,000 feet at the village of Truchas, where the jagged Truchas Peaks form a spectacular backdrop. Here, and elsewhere along the route, visitors are welcome to view local crafts in shops and home display rooms.

Watch for the turn to Las Trampas. Where the graceful restored church of San Jose de Gracia exemplifies Spanish Colonial architecture of the mid-1700s. Note that area houses often have pitched tin roofs, an advantage over flat roofs during heavy mountain rains and snows.

Three Faces of Taos

After leaving the town of Peñasco, follow State Highway 518 through Carson National Forest, passing wild green meadows and stands of ponderosa, fir, and aspen. (The grand mountain views often call for off-road photography.) At the settlement of Ranchos de Taos, the oft-painted and much-photographed adobe bulk of the mission church San Francisco de Asis firmly anchors the southern end of town.

The town of Taos, a few miles north, is packed with enticing museums, galleries, shops, restaurants, inns, and bed-and-breakfasts. The Harwood, Millicent Rogers, and Kit Carson museums are good places to start. Then browse through galleries such as the Stables or Fenix before dining at Apple Tree, Doc Martin's, Bent Street Deli & Café, or another restaurant.

About 2 miles to the north stands another adobe landmark, Taos Pueblo. Nearly 1,000 years

attractions—from mouth-warming enchiladas or carne adovada (meat marinated in red chile) to airy "little pillow" sopaipillas—all served in rustic rooms or in the garden outside.

At the other end of town, Ortega's Weaving Shop and the Galeria Ortega showcase the Ortega family's muted-color weavings as well as works in wood, metals, and pottery by other artisans. They also have a supply of dried Chimayó red chile on hand.

Continuing north on State Highway 76, visit the compact village of Cordova, known for

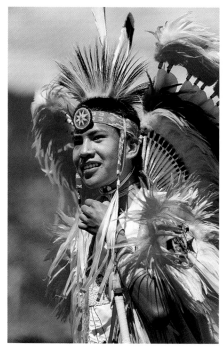

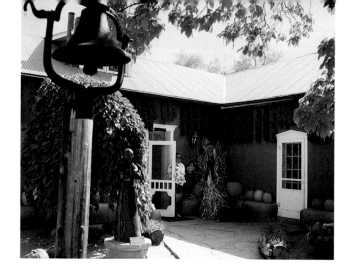

Traditionally garbed Pueblo dancer (left) pauses during ceremonial festivities.

Pumpkins (right) provide colorful accents in the courtyard of Restaurante Rancho de Chimayó, a local favorite.

old, it remains one of the most conservative of the state's 19 Indian pueblos. In the two multi-storied adobe complexes, residents have opted for traditional ways over electricity and running water.

Most days, visitors are welcome at the pueblo's central plaza, the small church, and home shops. When there are ceremonies, such as the corn dances in June and July, the deer or *matachines* dances at Christmas, and the San Geronimo races and pole-climb in late September, visitors may watch quietly. Guides from the Taos Indian Horse Ranch also offer trail rides year-round.

To Santa Clara & San Ildefonso Pueblos

After a good night's sleep in Taos, begin the return trip south on State Highway 68, stopping for a look back at Taos Mountain and the dark slash cut

across the plain by the Rio Grande. The road descends into the river canyon, passing orchards and fruit stands near Velarde where chile *ristras* and wreaths of dried herbs and flowers are sold year-round, and where white-water rafts ride the rapids in spring.

At Espanola, turn west onto State Highway 30 to Santa Clara Pueblo. Signs in the village indicate the shops and homes where

visitors are welcome to meet residents and shop for crafts—pottery, in particular—made famous by generations of accomplished artisans such as the Tafoya and Naranjo families. Among the village's colorful ceremonies are the corn dances in June, its feast day (August 12), and Christmas dances.

The tribe's ancient summer home at Puye Cliffs lies 3 miles south on State 30 and 11 miles

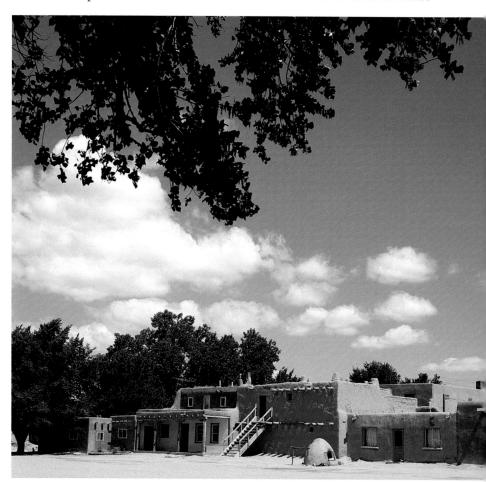

Well known for its fine pottery tradition, San Ildefonso Pueblo welcomes tourists to its visitor center and mission church.

west on a dirt road. Here you can explore abandoned cliff dwellings and kiva on foot, using pole ladders to reach the rim, or drive around and up for the sights and impressive views.

San Ildefonso Pueblo is near-by, off State Highway 502. Note the squared-off hump of Black Mesa jutting from the plain. A sacred site, the mesa is off-limits to outsiders, although they may drive into the village below it. After registering at the visitor center, you may visit the small church and informal craft shops.

Indian pottery was rejuvenated here in the mid-1900s when Maria Martinez began reworking old designs. Her famous black-on-black pots became collector's items.

⇇ TRIP PLANNER ⇉

Unless otherwise noted, New Mexico area codes are 505. Lodging rates for two people range from $ (under $100) to $$$ (above $250) per night.

LODGING

In Taos, **Casa Benavides** (137 Kit Carson Rd.; 758-1772, 800/552-1772; $-$$ includes bountiful breakfasts), a compound of older, carefully renovated adobes about a block from the plaza, has been transformed into a 31-room bed-and-breakfast. **Casa de las Chimeneas B&B** (405 Cordoba Rd.; 758-4777; $$), a 8-room inn about 3 blocks from the plaza, has formal gardens, hot tub, sauna, and massage and fitness rooms. Massages, facials, and herbal steam treatments are extra. The **Fechin Inn** (227 Paseo del Pueblo Norte; 751-1000, 800/811-2935; $$-$$$ includes breakfast buffet), behind the historic home of artist Nicolai Fechin, has 85 rooms and suites, a well-decorated lobby and lounge, a fitness center, and a large open-air hot tub. For other suggestions, call **Taos Central Reservations** (800/821-2437) and **Taos Bed and Breakfast Association** (800/976-7857).

In Santa Fe, the **Hotel Santa Fe** (1501 Paseo de Peralta; 982-1200; $$) is a beautifully furnished retreat with a strong Native American influence, which is not surprising as it is partially owned by the Picuris tribe.

Large rooms (most have extra-long king beds), a delightful restaurant showcasing regional specialties, and a hot tub are only some of the amenities.

DINING

Taos dining: the **Apple Tree Restaurant** (123 Bent St.; 758-1900) serves elegantly prepared meals in comfortable rooms of an old house; **Bent Street Deli & Café** (120 Bent St.; 758-5787) is a casual setting for soup, sandwiches, and daily specials; and **Doc Martin's** (in the Taos Inn, 125 Paseo del Pueblo Norte; 758-1977) offers an historical ambience along with an extensive wine list and fine contemporary Southwestern cuisine.

Restaurante Rancho de Chimayó (300 County Rd. 98, Chimayó; 984-2100; open daily 11:30-9:30, weekend breakfast 8:30-10:30; closed Mondays in winter) is well worth a trip just for the northern New Mexico cuisine, but the hacienda setting is another plus.

INDIAN PUEBLOS

Taos Pueblo (758-9593): Parking and entry fees. Call ahead to confirm visitor days and festival dates. No photography is permitted during ceremonies. **Santa Clara Pueblo** (455-3549); photography at ceremonies by permit only. **San Ildefonso Pueblo** (753-7326); photography by permit only.

SHOPS & ACTIVITIES

In Chimayó, **Ortega's Weaving Shop** (351-4215) and **Galeria Ortega** (351-2288), intersection of State 76 and Rte. 98, are well worth a stop. Browsing at **Fenix Gallery** (2288 Paseo del Pueblo Norte, Taos; 758-9120) and **Stables Art Center** (133 Paseo del Pueblo Norte, Taos; 758-2036) gives you an idea of the area's wealth of artistic talent.

Taos Indian Horse Ranch (Taos Pueblo and off State Hwy.150; 758-3212, 800/659-3210) offers two-hour or longer trail rides from $85. **Puye Cliff Dwellings** (near Santa Clara Pueblo; 753-7326) are open Mon.-Fri. 9-6, Sat.-Sun. 8-8; entry fee to visit.

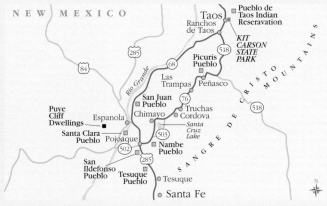

along the
Turquoise Trail

REGION	NEW MEXICO	
Where	X	83 miles between Santa Fe and Albuquerque
When	X	Year-round destination

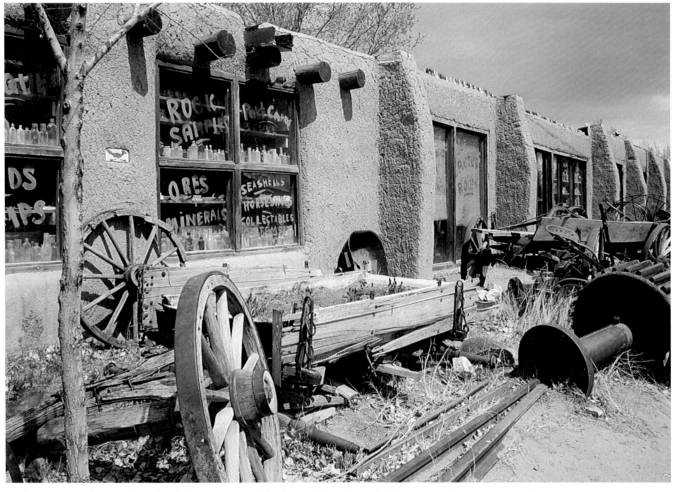

A relic from the past fronts the Turquoise Mining Museum, one of the shops that transformed tiny Cerrillos from ghost town to tourist haunt.

The Turquoise Trail, a scenic back road linking Albuquerque and Santa Fe, offers an adventurous—albeit somewhat longer—alternative route to the 60-mile cruise along four-lane Interstate 25. This two-lane, paved road winds through the scenic high desert past old mining towns that today are havens for some of New Mexico's finest artists and craftspeople. Along the road you see old buildings that have been converted into galleries and studios, and mining relics of a bygone era dot the hillsides.

The route could be driven in a couple of hours, or it could be slowly savored by stopping to poke around shops, eat at good-smelling restaurants, enjoy grand views, and spend a night at a picturesque inn. Though the trail (State Highway 14) can be driven in either direction, we started at the southwestern edge of Santa Fe, taking the exit south from I-25.

Note the panoramic views as you head south. The Cerrillos hills were once mined for turquoise and minerals. Looming behind them are the Sandia Mountains and, to the left, the Ortiz Mountains. Past the state penitentiary, look for the San Marcos Café (noted for breakfast burritos), where peacocks might greet you out front and baking odors flourish inside. Just north

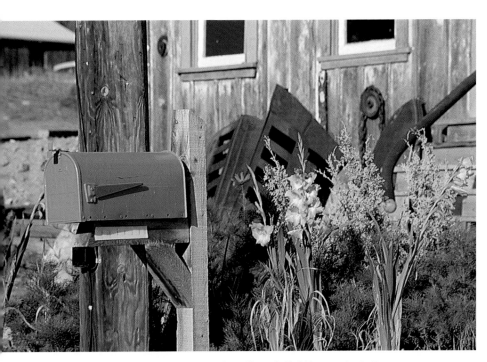

Everything is colorful along Highway 14; even the mailboxes in Madrid are no standard hue.

is a bed-and-breakfast, Open Sky, located in a renovated adobe.

Cerrillos—One-time Boom Town

Continue into Cerrillos, a boisterous mining mecca in the 1800s, with eight newspapers, 21 saloons, and four hotels. No longer a ghost town, Cerrillos has been revitalized by merchants who set up shops in storefronts of old buildings. The What-Not Shop on First Street is stuffed with a variety of curiosities old and new; the Casa Grande Trading Post, located in an old adobe at the other end of town, contains turquoise mining items and other souvenirs.

Cerrillos is a good place get into the countryside on horseback, heading out to overlooks above Devil's Canyon and Madrid, another old mining town down the trail. Both beginners and experienced riders will find suitable mounts at the Broken Saddle Riding Co. (see Trip Planner).

Madrid & More

Farther south, State 14 becomes the main street of Madrid (pronounced MAD-rid), a former coal mining town that flourished into the 1950s, then declined to near-ghost status. Today it is home to some 300 residents, and has a new lease on life with whimsically renovated houses, galleries, shops, and eateries vying for attention from visitors.

Many restored buildings are incorporated in the Old Coal Mine Museum, including the locomotive repair shop and the town's original jail. The 3-acre museum contains an exposed coal seam, a turn-of-the-century steam locomotive, and mining tools. At the Mine Shaft Tavern, travelers can fortify themselves with a meal before venturing farther. If you decide to spend the night, two bed-and-breakfast inns are nearby.

From Madrid, the road winds south into the foothills of the Ortiz Mountains, which bristle with cholla cactus, scrub oak, and juniper trees. Views extend as far as Estancia Basin and the Sandia Mountains. Golden, another former mining town along the trail, was the site of an 1825 gold rush. You'll learn more of its history at La Casita, a shop at the north end of the village.

A Detour to Sandia Crest

Twelve miles south, a turn onto State Highway 536, a national scenic byway, leads 14 miles up to Sandia Crest, the mountains' high point at 10,678 feet. From a viewing platform, you look down over the city of Albuquerque immediately below. On clear days, Mt. Taylor, some 75 miles to the west, is visible. The crest-top gift shop and snack bar are open daily, and you can stretch your legs on several trails that

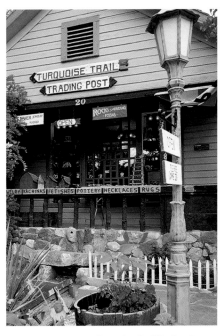

Flowers bloom outside Turquoise Trail Trading Post; the building is painted to match its name.

lead along the crest and into the Sandia Mountains Wilderness.

On the drive down, note the Sandia Peak Ski Area, which Albuquerque skiers can also reach by taking the aerial tramway up the mountain's west side. In summer, mountain cyclists take bikes up the chairlift for thrilling rides down 15 miles of ski trails.

Near the beginning of State 536, the privately owned

Tinkertown Museum is a good stop for restless children. It has a walk-through display of 22 rooms of fascinating animated miniatures, including an intricately carved Old West town and a three-ring circus. A pottery studio and gift shop will appeal to adults.

Cedar Crest Stop

At Cedar Crest, a bustling mountain community near the junction

of the Turquoise Trail and Interstate 40, travelers will find several options for dining or overnighting before heading into Albuquerque, including a bed-and-breakfast with a grand view. The town also has a fascinating Museum of Archaeology & Material Culture, which displays a 12,000-year time line depicting the story of North America's earliest inhabitants.

⇉TRIP PLANNER⇉

Unless otherwise noted, area codes are 505. Lodging rates for two people range from $ (under $100) to $$$ (above $250) per night.

LODGING

If you'd like to stay longer in this rugged country, **Open Sky B&B** (on State 14 south of Santa Fe; 471-3475; $-$$) has grand views from its 4 rooms, patios, and an open-air hot tub. Another good choice is the spotless **Heart Seed B&B and Spa** (5 miles east of State 14 on County Rd. 55; 471-7026; $) near Cerrillos. Breakfast is included with the price of your room; spa packages with massages and health and beauty treatments are extra. Guests are also welcome to roam the trails on the 80-acre property.

In Madrid, both **Madrid Lodging B&B** (nicely decorated suite in private home; 471-3450; $) and **Java Junction B&B** (second floor of a restored mining house; 438-2772, 474-8359; $) offer rooms. The 3 rooms in **Elaine's B&B** (72 Snowline Rd., Cedar Crest; 800/821-3092; $) are not only comfortable but also offer fine mountain views, particularly from

the large upstairs room. Breakfasts are tasty.

DINING

San Marcos Café outside Santa Fe (3877 State 14; 471-9298) is open 8-2 daily and 5:30 to 8 p.m. Thurs.-Sat. The **Whispering Dove Restaurant** (3810 State 14 at Lone Butte; 474-3486) serves hearty meals, including vegetarian fare daily 7–8 (Sun. 9–8). Dine on the patio when weather is warm.

Madrid's **Mine Shaft Tavern** (on State 14; 473-0743) is open daily (to 8 on Wed., Fri.-Sun.). **Sandia Crest's** snack bar and visitor center lie at the top of State 536 (243-0605). A good place for an informal meal in Cedar Crest is the **Cedar Point Grill** (12124 State 14; 281-2534), open Tues.-Sun.

The Place to Eat (12019 State 14, Cedar Crest; 281-1060) serves imaginative cuisine (dinner only) with perhaps a glass of wine to celebrate the end of the trail.

ACTIVITIES

In Cerrillos, the What-Not Shop and Rio Grande Trading Post tempt travelers; the **Broken Saddle Riding Co.** (470-0074) offers rides by appointment. In Madrid, stroll into **Maya**

Jones for Central American crafts; **Primitiva** for folk art, furniture, and pottery; **Tapestry Gallery** for handwoven wearable art; **Woofy Bubbles Woowear** for fanciful clothing; and the **Red Rail Car Trading Post** for antiques. Or step into the Old West at **Old Coal Mine Museum, Engine House Theatre & Mine Shaft Tavern**. From Memorial Day through Labor Day, hoot and hiss at the weekend melodrama (Sat. 3 and 8 p.m., Sun. 3 p.m.). **Tinkertown Museum** on State 536 (281-5233; small fee) is open daily Apr.-Oct.

FOR MORE INFORMATION

Turquoise Trail Association (P.O. Box 1335, Cedar Crest, NM 87008; 281-5233).

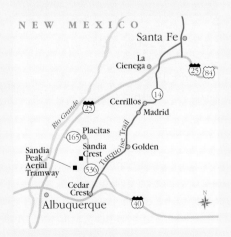

REGION		ARIZONA
Where	X	110 miles northwest of Phoenix
When	X	Drive best in spring and fall

back road
to Prescott

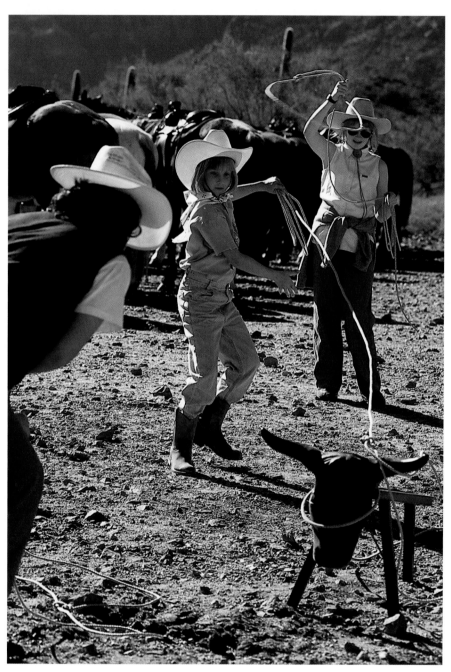

Beginning cowpunchers practice their roping skills at Rancho de los Caballeros in Wickenburg.

From Phoenix there's the quick way to get to Prescott. Then there's the other way, the road that winds up some 3,200 feet in elevation—from the desert floor through boulder-strewn grasslands into pine-scented forests. You'll pass through small towns, old mining centers, and ranches that leap straight from the pages of Arizona's Wild West past.

Wickenburg's Western Flavor

Pick up this back road, U.S. Highway 89, in Wickenburg, about an hour's drive northwest of Phoenix. Wickenburg, built along the banks of the Hassayampa River, sprang to life in the 1860s with the discovery of gold. By the turn of the century, scores of mines dotted the surrounding desert hills. Ranching also grew to be a mainstay in this area.

Wickenburg still has many reminders of its colorful past. The Vulture Mine, site of the first gold strike, is open for self-guided tours; just outside town, Robson's Arizona Mining World is a detailed re-creation of an 1890s mining camp. Cowboy wannabes can sample life in the saddle at one of Wickenburg's many guest ranches, where accommodations range from homey to downright luxurious. Downtown Wickenburg still maintains its Old West feeling with false-front buildings that house antique shops, galleries catering to cowboy art, and home accessories boutiques.

You can learn more about the local environment with a stop at the Nature Conservancy's Hassayampa River Preserve, where the river, which runs underground most of its 100-mile course through the desert, emerges into a lush, riparian zone. Trails lead along the river and around a small lake where waterfowl abound. Local legend has it that if you drink water from the Hassayampa, you'll never tell the truth again.

On the Road

Heading north 16 miles out of Wickenburg on U.S. 89, you'll pass through Congress, a still-active mining community. About a mile out of town, on the west side of the road, you'll see the landmark "frog," a boulder that has been painted amphibious green by locals since 1928.

The road climbs about 2,000 feet in elevation in the 9 miles toward Yarnell, the next town. Stop at the scenic overlook and you can look back to the vast desert valley and Wickenburg in the distance.

Yarnell, a quiet community that was founded as a ranching and mining center, has undergone somewhat of a renaissance since the late 1980s, with Phoenix resi-

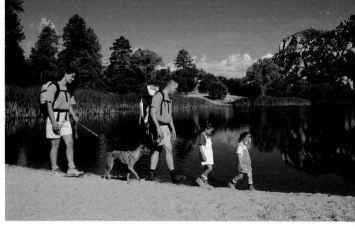

Granite Basin Lake is one of the lures of Granite Mountain Wilderness, just minutes from downtown Prescott.

dents renovating old homes and building new ones to use as weekend retreats amid the town's landmark granite boulders. Even the shops along the highway have attained a nouveau attitude, offering cappuccinos, crystals, and other New Age accessories.

Yarnell's most noted attraction is the Shrine of St. Joseph of the Mountains, a nondenominational grotto built in 1939 by a Tucson sculptor. Statues depicting St. Joseph and the Way of the Cross dot a wooded trail through large rock formations; benches offer spots for quiet contemplation. It draws thousands of visitors during Easter week. About 3 miles north of Yarnell is Peeples Valley. The area's rolling grasslands are home to vast cattle and

horse ranches, a serene contrast to urban Arizona's booming growth.

Continuing north past the minute village of Wilhoit, the highway begins a series of twists and turns through the pines and canyons of the Prescott National Forest. Those last 15 miles into Prescott itself are best done during dry weather. Snow and heavy rain can make some of the hairpin turns hairy indeed.

Prescott—A Hometown

Despite Prescott's gold rush and boomtown history, the town has a calming effect on visitors. Maybe it's the mile-high altitude. More likely, though, it's Prescott's reputation as "everyone's hometown."

A grand courthouse stands guard over a welcoming town square—so "American Pie" that many a movie has been filmed there. Old-fashioned shops and restaurants (many now fully restored) flank the square, offering antiques, art, books, and decent eats. The buildings on the

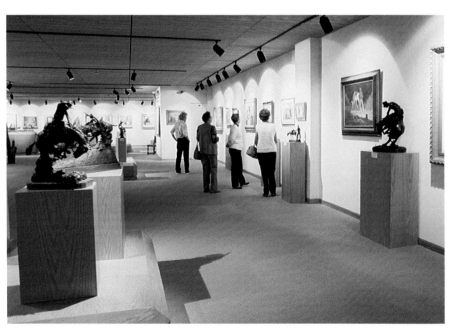

Russells, Remingtons, and works of other famous artists are represented in Wickenburg's Desert Caballeros Western Museum.

west side of the square make up the infamous Whiskey Row, once home to several dozen rough-and-tumble saloons where miners and cowboys blew their Friday wages. There are still several "old-timey" saloons that will serve you a mug of suds along with a whiff of former danger.

Adjacent residential neighborhoods are filled with restored Queen Anne and other Victorian houses. Porch swings and rockers abound.

Swings and rockers have limited use, though, in an area brimming with trails, lakes, mountains, and campgrounds.

The Prescott National Forest has a downtown office where you can pick up maps and guides to outdoor activities.

It's no wonder, then, that Prescott has grown with urban refugees looking for just the right combination of scenery and small-town atmosphere.

TRIP PLANNER

Unless otherwise noted, area codes are 520. Lodging rates for two people range from $ (under $100) to $$$ (above $250) per night.

WHERE

The back road to Prescott is U.S. 89. To get there from Phoenix, take Interstate 17 north to State Hwy. 74. Go west 30 miles to the junction of U.S. Hwy. 60, then head northwest 10 miles into Wickenburg. U.S. 60 turns into 89 in Wickenburg; watch for signage pointing you northeast toward Prescott. A quick way back from Prescott is to head east on State Hwy. 69 approximately 30 miles to I-17, then south to Phoenix.

LODGING

If you're hankerin' for a Western experience, spend the night at a Wickenburg guest ranch, and join in on horseback riding, cookouts, and family-style meals. Many Wickenburg guest ranches are only open mid-autumn to late spring. Prescott offers a wide variety of lodging choices, including hotels and bed-and-breakfasts with history.

Rancho de los Caballeros (1551 S. Vulture Mine Rd., Wickenburg, AZ 85390; 800/684-5030; $$$ includes meals) has horseback riding, golf, tennis, and children's programs in

an elegant Southwestern setting. The **Kay El Bar** (P.O. Box 2480, Wickenburg, AZ 85358; 800/684-7583; $$$ includes meals), operating since 1926, welcomes guests with genuine adobe buildings, tall trees, and plenty of saddle horses. The **Hassayampa Inn** (122 E. Gurley St., Prescott; 800/322-1927; $$) was built in 1927 as the town's grand hotel. Now restored, it has cozy rooms and a complimentary breakfast served in the signature dining room. **The Marks House** bed-and-breakfast (203 E. Union St., Prescott; 800/370-6275; $-$$) is one of many restored Victorians that dot the residential area near downtown. Feather beds, private baths, and a full breakfast add comfort to the inn. **Hotel Vendome** (230 S. Cortez St., Prescott; 888/468-3583; $-$$) boasts a resident ghost along with its historical ambience.

DINING

Stock up on chocolate chip cookies for the road at the **Cornerstone Bakery** (22773 U.S. 89, Yarnell; 427-9558). Order something more substantial, like bangers and mash and a locally brewed beer at **Prescott Brewing Company** (130 W. Gurley St., Prescott; 771-2795). **Murphy's Restaurant** (201 N. Cortez St., Prescott; 445-4044) serves fish and prime rib in a restored, turn-of-the-century store.

MUSEUMS

Desert Caballeros Western Museum (21 N. Frontier St., Wickenburg; 684-2272; small fee) houses a fine collection of Western art, history, and culture, including works by Cowboy Artists of America. **Phippen Museum of Western Art** (4701 Hwy. 89 N., Prescott; 778-1385; small fee) also features Western art, while **Sharlot Hall Museum** (415 Gurley St., Prescott; 445-3122; donations) has a collection of houses and a museum center that trace Prescott's history.

FOR MORE INFORMATION

Wickenburg Chamber of Commerce (216 N. Frontier St., Wickenburg, AZ 85390; 684-5479). Yarnell/Peeples Valley Chamber of Commerce (P.O. Box 275, Yarnell, AZ 85362; 427-3301). Prescott Chamber of Commerce (117 W. Goodwin St., Prescott, AZ 86302; 800/266-7534).

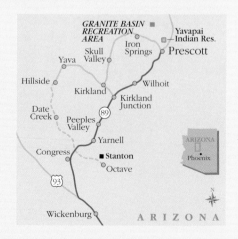

the
Verde Valley

REGION	ARIZONA	
Where	X	About 1½ hours north of Phoenix
When	X	Year-round destination

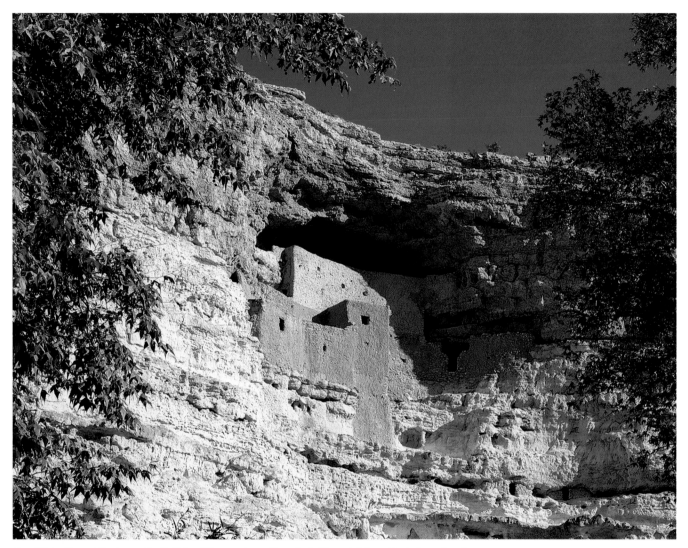

The cliff dwellings at Montezuma Castle National Monument near Camp Verde fit snugly into a niche in the rock wall.

Much ink has been splashed across the red rock formations of Sedona. Indeed, the town and surrounding area do offer plenty of travel-related opportunities. But less known (and less crowded) is Sedona's neighbor to the south, the Verde Valley.

Set at the base of the ocher- and rust-colored cliffs of the Mogollon Rim, the Verde Valley counts history, nature, pastoral scenery, and lively small towns among its many virtues. Bisected by the Verde River, the valley was first settled by Native Americans, who farmed the fertile soil as early as A.D. 600 to 700. The area's modern communities, including Camp Verde, Cottonwood, Clarkdale, and Jerome, sprang to life in the late 1800s as ranching, farming, and mining centers.

A Valley Loop

To make what roughly amounts to a loop tour through the Verde Valley, take the Camp Verde exit off Interstate 17 and head 3

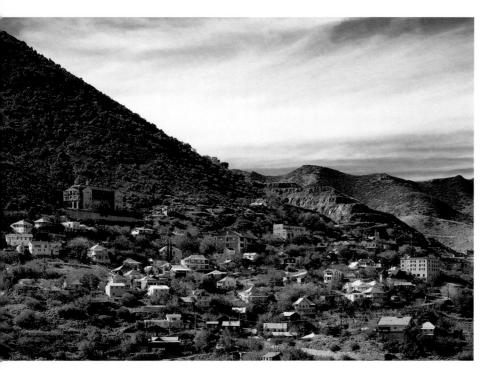
The photogenic ghost town of Jerome tumbles down Cleopatra Hill high above the Verde Valley.

Tuzigoot National Monument, another 12th-century Sinaguan village, crowns a hill about 2 miles north of Old Town Cottonwood. Dead Horse Ranch State Park nearby provides a shady, cool spot to picnic, hike, and fish along the Verde River.

Two miles north of Tuzigoot is Clarkdale, built in 1912 as a company town for the United Verde Copper Company. The town's more recent claim to fame was the 1990 reincarnation of the Verde Canyon Railroad (300 N. Broadway) as an excursion train. Built in 1911 to serve mining and ranching needs, the railroad goes into the canyon and along the river, winding by pristine wilderness, Indian ruins, and eagle-nesting aeries. Passengers can soak up the scenery during a four-hour trek. For information on schedules, prices, and reservations, phone 639-0010 or 800/293-7245.

miles east into town on Yavapai County Road 35. Historic Fort Verde, located just off Camp Verde's Main Street, is a good place to learn the lay of the land and area history. The fort, established in 1865, was abandoned by the early 1880s. Today the old administration building houses a museum detailing military life at the outpost on the river. Other buildings, all part of a state park, are also open. Fort Verde is also a starting point for the General Crook National Recreation Trail, a 138-mile-long hiking and equestrian route that retraces an old military road between forts.

To step back even further in time, head northeast out of Camp Verde several blocks on Main Street, then north again on Montezuma Castle Highway for about 5 miles to Montezuma Castle National Monument. The monument, misnamed by early settlers, consists of two 12th-century Sinagua Indian cliff dwellings. You can walk past the ruins and check out exhibits at the visitor center. About 8 miles northeast of Montezuma Castle lies Montezuma Well, a natural limestone sinkhole, whose springs once irrigated Sinaguan crops.

From Montezuma Well, head west on Forest Route 119, also called the Cornville Highway, for approximately 11 miles to Cornville. The bucolic farming and ranching community straddles Oak Creek and has, in recent years, become popular with urban refugees and retirees.

Follow Cornville Highway 4 miles west to State Highway 89A, and turn southwest for 2 miles to reach Cottonwood, the valley's commercial center. Just behind the strip malls and fast-food emporiums, Old Town Cottonwood—along North Main Street—has been experiencing a renaissance. The ambience is still decidedly late-Sixties Psychedelia, but galleries, eateries, and boutiques are cropping up.

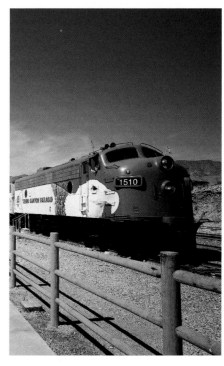
The Verde Canyon Railroad takes visitors into a canyon wilderness area.

To Photogenic Jerome

Lying 4½ twisting miles up State Highway 89A from Clarkdale is Jerome, a thriving arts community and National Historic Landmark. The town, perched precariously on Cleopatra Hill high above the valley floor, is Swiss-cheesed with tunnels and mines that attest to its heyday at the turn of the century as a big copper camp. Saloons, brothels, churches, and shops once stood side by side along the town's sloping streets. At one time, 15,000 called the place home; when the mines closed in 1953, only a handful of hardy souls remained. By the 1970s, the town had reestablished itself as a mecca for artists, writers, and tourists.

Visit Jerome State Historic Park, housed in a 1916 mansion, to learn about the town's copper-laced past, then head up the hill to wander through art galleries, boutiques, and restaurants. Before you leave, take a snapshot of the Verde Valley spread out below. At 5,200 feet in elevation, Jerome overlooks it all.

TRIP PLANNER

Unless otherwise noted, area codes are 520. Lodging rates for two people range from $ (under $100) to $$$ (above $250) per night.

WHERE

To get to the Verde Valley from Phoenix, take I-17 north about 70 miles to the Camp Verde exit (Exit 285). Head east on County 35 into Camp Verde to begin the loop tour. If you end your trip in Jerome, take State Hwy. 260 southeast for approximately 18 miles to return to I-17.

LODGING

Though the valley has plenty of moderately priced lodging, particularly in Cottonwood, and Jerome has a handful of bed-and-breakfast inns. the widest choice of accommodations is in Sedona, a 30-minute drive to the north.

To spend more time in Jerome, try **Ghost City Inn** (541 N. Main St.; 888/63GHOST; $), housed in a circa 1898 residence with a view-grabbing veranda. **The Surgeon's House** (P.O. Box 998, Jerome 86331; 800/639-1452; $-$$) bed-and-breakfast was once the private residence for the chief surgeon at the nearby hilltop hospital.

In Sedona, **Briar Patch Inn** (3190 N. Highway 89A; 282-2342; $$-$$$) offers creekside cabins; healthy breakfasts are served in the garden. **Enchantment** (525 Boynton Canyon Rd.; 800/826-4180; $$-$$$) features tennis, golf, and other full-service resort amenities.

DINING

The name might raise eyebrows, but **Gas Works** (1033 N. Main St., Cottonwood; 634-5283) serves spicy New Mexican-style cuisine in a colorful, funky setting; afterward, cool your taste buds with an ice cream soda at old-fashioned **Clarkdale Antique Emporium** (907 Main St.). **Flatiron Cafe** (416 Main St., Jerome; 634-2733) features espresso drinks, breakfast, and creative lunches, all served in a teeny, wedge-shaped building. Just down the street, **House of Joy** (416 N. Hull Ave.; 634-5339) is as well known today for its reservations-only continental cuisine as it was a century ago for its painted ladies.

SHOPPING

Pick up produce—organic and otherwise—from **Maxfield's Produce** (9655 Cornville Hwy., Cornville). In Jerome, visit **Sky Fire** (140 Main St.) for artsy home accessories. For pure art, head to **Jerome Artists Cooperative Gallery** (502 Main St.), which exhibits sculpture, painting, jewelry, and other works by local artists.

FOR MORE INFORMATION

Cottonwood-Verde Valley Chamber of Commerce (1010 S. Main St., Cottonwood, AZ 86326; 634-7593). Jerome Chamber of Commerce (310 N. Hull Ave., Jerome, AZ 86331; 634-2900). Camp Verde Chamber of Commerce (P.O. Box 3520, Camp Verde, AZ 86322; 567-9294).

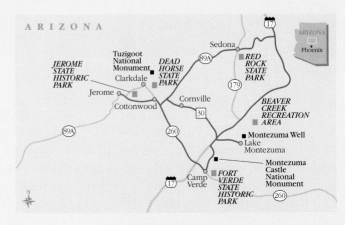

REGION	ARIZONA
Where X	About 90 miles southeast of Tucson
When X	Autumn through spring delightful

deep into Copper Country

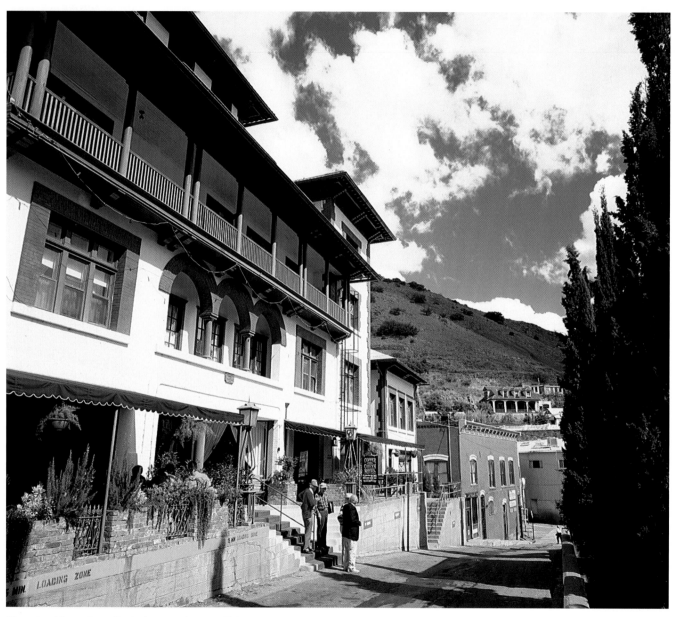

The restored Copper Queen Hotel reigns over downtown Bisbee, a one-time mining mecca and now an enclave for artists and artisans.

The Old West towns of southeastern Arizona were once the center of a bustling commercial region where outlaws and entrepreneurs flocked in the 1880s and where fortunes were won and lost in a matter of weeks or even days. Over $6 billion worth of minerals was mined in these rugged hills, and, at one time, the historic town of Tombstone was larger than San Francisco.

We remember the outlaws, gambling halls, saloons, and houses of prostitution that followed in the wake of the riches, but what drew everyone here in the first place were the rich veins

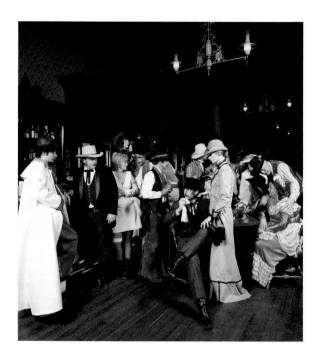

of silver and copper—particularly the latter. A quick tour of Copper Country begins in Tombstone, the town called "too tough to die," then climbs 1,000 feet to the turn-of-the-century boom town of Bisbee and ends in the border town of Douglas, where a grand old hotel, built in 1906, is a lasting testament to the region's heyday.

Exploring Tombstone's Legendary Past

Legend has it that when Ed Schieffelin decided to prospect in the rugged hills of southeastern Arizona, he was warned that the only thing he'd find was his own tombstone. Instead, he came upon a mountain of silver and, in a bit of irony, named the town that grew around him Tombstone.

Most of the sights in town these days focus on the lawless cottage industries that followed Schieffelin's discovery. The O.K.

Corral, a block south of U.S. Highway 80 on Allen Street, was the setting for the infamous gun battle between the Earp brothers and the outlaw McLaury boys. If you wonder who lost, mosey on over to the Boot Hill Graveyard, just off U.S. 80, where you'll find the graves of the McLaurys and other outlaws and gunfighters.

To get a sense of what the town used to be like in the late 1800s, when some $37 million worth of silver was extracted from the hills in less than 10 years, stop by the imposing Tombstone Courthouse State Historic Park. For a more engaging setting, drop by the Rose Tree Inn Museum, formerly a boardinghouse for miners.

Mine Tour in Bisbee

Continue south on U.S. 80 for 24 miles to Bisbee. Unlike Tombstone, which pretty much died when the silver played out, Bisbee continued to pull riches out of the region until 1975. In this case, it wasn't silver but copper. Stop by the chamber of commerce offices, 7 Main Street, for a free historical walking tour that will lead you to the Bisbee Mining and Historical Museum, housed in the old red brick building that was once the general offices of the town's biggest mine

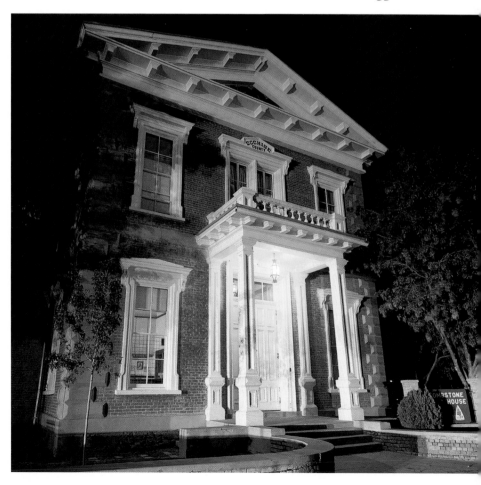

operator. Several dozen giftshops have sprung up in the old downtown area, designed to garner still more silver—from visitors.

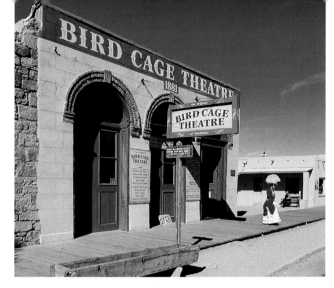

Looking as if she had stepped from the past, a lady strolls along a Tombstone street.

After getting a sense of the town's history, you may want to take the Copper Queen mine tour. Bring a jacket since it's a brisk 47° below ground. If you'd rather stay above ground, there is also a surface tour of the nearby Lavender Mine by van.

A Grand Hotel in Douglas

Most of the copper ore from Bisbee was processed in giant smelters in Douglas, a border city another 24 miles southeast on U.S. 80 Visit the historic Gadsden Hotel and marvel at its vaulted stained-glass skylights, white marble staircase, and decorative mezzanine. Ask at the Chamber of Commerce offices, 1125 Pan American Avenue, for directions to the many ghost towns and mining camps in the vicinity.

TRIP PLANNER

WHERE

To reach the heart of Copper Country, take Interstate 10 east from Tucson 45 miles to Benson, then pick up U.S. 80 and drive 24 miles south through easy rolling hills to Tombstone. The total trip is about 47 miles.

LODGING

The **Best Western Lookout Lodge** (U.S. 80 West, Tombstone; 457-2223; $) will get you in the mood with its Victorian-style lamps and Western furnishings. But to really sample turn-of-the-century life, try the **Copper Queen Hotel** (11 Howell Ave., Bisbee; 432-2216; $-$$), which played host to Teddy Roosevelt when it was owned and run by the Copper Queen Mining Company, or the **Gadsden Hotel** (1046 G Ave., Douglas; 364-4451; $), built in 1906

and declared a National Historic Monument in 1976.

DINING

They say Tombstone's oldest dining establishment is **The Nellie Cashman Restaurant** (117 S. 5th St.; 457-2212), housed in a historic building near the Rose Tree Inn Museum. There's nothing old-fashioned about **Café Roka** (35 Main St., Bisbee; 432-5153), which might be the best restaurant in southeastern Arizona. In Douglas, try **The Grand Café** (1119 G Ave.; 364-2344), with its Mexican menu favorites such as chicken mole enchiladas.

ATTRACTIONS

The **Tombstone Courthouse State Historic Park** (219 E. Toughnut St.; 457-3311; open daily) reflects the days when Tombstone was the county seat. The **Rose Tree Inn Museum** (Toughnut and 4th sts.; 457-3326; open daily) houses furnishings from the town's heyday; outside you'll find the world's largest rose bush, which gives the old hotel its name. Exhibits

reflecting the region's mining past can be seen in the **Bisbee Mining and Historical Museum** (5 Copper Queen Plaza; 432-7071; tours offered daily), but to really find out what life was like down in the mines, take the **Copper Queen Mine Tour** (118 Arizona St., Bisbee; 432-2071; daily tours).

FOR MORE INFORMATION

Tombstone Office of Tourism (P.O. Box 917, Tombstone, AZ 85638; 800/457-3423). Bisbee Chamber of Commerce (7 Main St., Bisbee, AZ 85603; 432-5421.

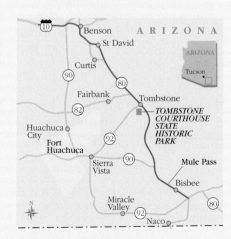

along the
Coronado Trail

REGION	ARIZONA
Where	X	220 miles east of Phoenix
When	X	Summer and fall destination

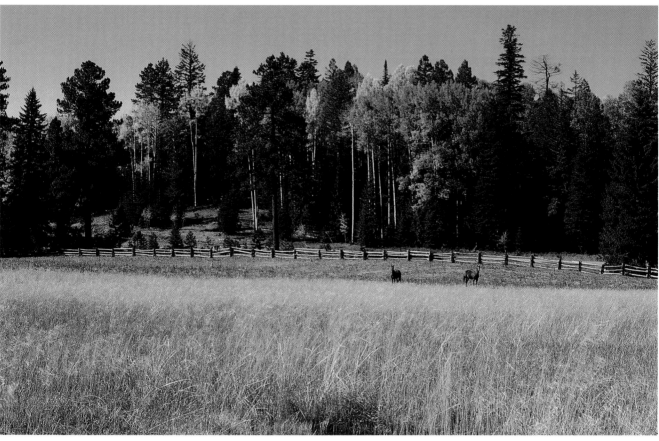

Hannagan Meadow in the White Mountains lies at a cool 9,100 feet elevation, making it a popular summer retreat for low-desert dwellers.

Told that cities paved in gold could be found in the mountainous country of what is now eastern Arizona, Francisco Vásquez de Coronado led 300 Spaniards and several hundred Indians through the high peaks of the White Mountains in 1540. Instead of the mythical Seven Cities of Cibola, he found a number of Indian pueblos and provided us with the earliest records of the inhabitants.

The Coronado Trail Scenic Byway (State Highway 191) tra-verses areas that remain much as they were 460 years ago. Today the treasures to be found along the 127-mile-long stretch of winding highway lie in the wealth of scenic wonders along the route. These mountains are a summer playground for Phoenicians, who enjoy everything from the shimmering forests of aspens around Alpine to the impressive mountain peaks that appear as majestic backdrops to the mining towns of Clifton and Morenci.

Prehistoric Indian Ruins

Start your trip in the trading-post community of Springerville, at the junction of U.S. highways 60 and 180, a popular gateway to the mountains to the west. Until recently, the biggest attraction in town was the giant, domed high school football stadium, the only one of its kind in the country. The Round Valley Ensphere, as it's called, is still worth a look, but even more inspiring are the prehistoric ruins of the ancient Mogollon people at Casa

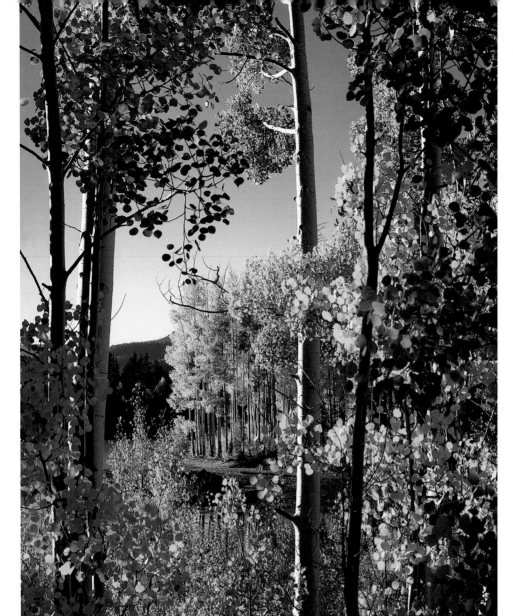

Autumn adds splashes of gold to eastern Arizona's Apache-Sitgreaves National Forest.

red in fall, and the sparkling meadows of summer wildflowers do make for majestic scenery. To find the best displays of aspens in the autumn, try one of the hiking trails into the Escudilla Mountain Wilderness just outside of town.

From Mountain Peaks to Mines

If you need gas or supplies, stock up in Alpine as there are no towns on the dizzying stretch of State 191 south to Morenci. There are, however, lots of mountainous curves and a number of splendid spots for mountain biking, hiking, or picnicking. One of the best is the Hannagan Meadow area, 22 miles south of Alpine. In winter, this area

Malpais Archaeological Park. These impressive burial catacombs and ceremonial sites, presumably built over 600 years ago, can be visited on a 90-minute guided tour.

From Springerville, take U.S. 180 south for 28 miles to Alpine, a small picturesque hamlet originally dubbed Frisco by the Mormon settlers who founded the area in 1879. It was later renamed because settlers thought the high mountain valley resembled the Alps. That may be stretching things, but the forests of aspens, which turn gold and

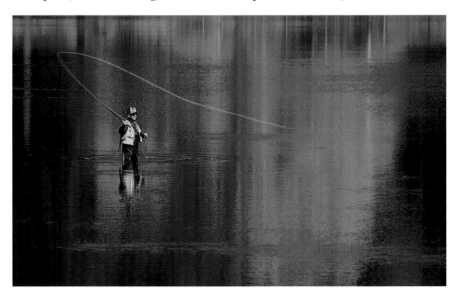

An angler tries his luck in the waters of A-1 Lake, east of McNary.

becomes a popular cross-country skiing area. In summer and fall, it attracts outdoor lovers to its splendid forests of aspen, spruce, and fir. If you haven't packed a lunch, you can enjoy a meal at the log building housing Hannagan Meadow Lodge.

From here, the road begins its descent, threading its way south past a series of impressive mountain peaks, each more than 7,500 feet high, eventually ending in the mining towns of Morenci and Clifton. There's a modest historical museum in the latter town, that explains a bit about the town's prospecting days, a time when Mexican miners discovered gold in the same hills Coronado's expedition had marched through some 300 years earlier. Exhibits and artifacts document these strikes.

TRIP PLANNER

Unless otherwise noted, area codes are 520. Lodging rates for two people range from $ (under $100) to $$$ (above $250) per night.

WHERE

The Coronado Trail Scenic Byway (State Hwy. 191) runs along the eastern edge of Arizona through the Apache-Sitgreaves National Forest, a hub for outdoor enthusiasts with hundreds of miles of trout streams and several campgrounds around Alpine and Hannagan Meadow. To reach Springerville from Phoenix, take U.S. Hwy. 60 east through Globe and Show Low; to return to Phoenix, take U.S. Hwy. 70 west to Globe and rejoin U.S. 60.

LODGING

The adjacent towns of Springerville and Eager have a number of inexpensive family hotels. Just a few miles west of Eager is the **South Fork Guest Ranch** (P.O. Box 627, Springerville, AZ 85938; 333-4455; $-$$), with creekside cabins. There are campgrounds at **Luna Lake**, just east of Alpine on U.S. 180, or try the rustic **Tai-Wi-Wi Lodge** (P.O. Box 169, Alpine, AZ 85920; 339-4319; $), popular with sportsmen. The **Hannagan Meadow Lodge** (P.O. Box 335, Alpine, AZ 85920; 339-4370; $) offers rustic cabins in a gorgeous setting.

DINING

Most of the places you're likely to stop for lunch or dinner keep it simple. **Ms. Ellie's at South Fork Guest Ranch** (see Lodging above) serves a little bit of everything, from barbecued ribs to hearty pasta dishes. The dining room at the **Tai-Wi-Wi Lodge** (see Lodging above) likes to stick to country roots, with breakfast plates big enough to get you through lunch and simple but filling dinners.

ATTRACTIONS

The **Casa Malpais Archaeological Park** (318 Main St., Springerville; 333-5375; open daily summer through fall) is a good place to learn about the first people who lived here. The **Escudilla Mountain Wilderness Area** is a popular spot for wildlife viewing; black bears, elk, and deer roam the hillsides. For a sparkling view of the surrounding countryside, hike the 3.3-mile **Escudilla National Recreation Trail**, which climbs through lovely groves of aspens and conifers to a high lookout. To learn more about the area's mining days, stop at the **Greenlee Historical Museum** (317 Chase Creek St., Clifton; call 865-3115 for hours).

FOR MORE INFORMATION

Round Valley Chamber of Commerce (418 N. Main St., Springerville, AZ 85938; 333-2123). Apache-Sitgreaves National Forest (309 S. Mountain Ave., Springerville, AZ 85938; 333-4301).

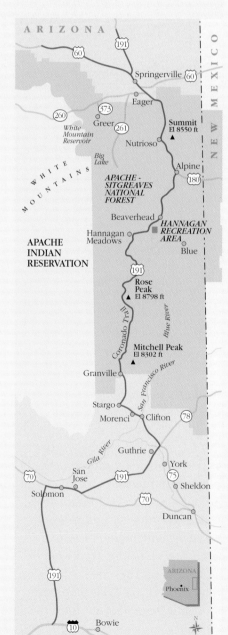

REGION	ARIZONA
Where X	145-mile loop southeast of Tucson
When X	Year-round destination, but hot in summer

Arizona's
Wine Country

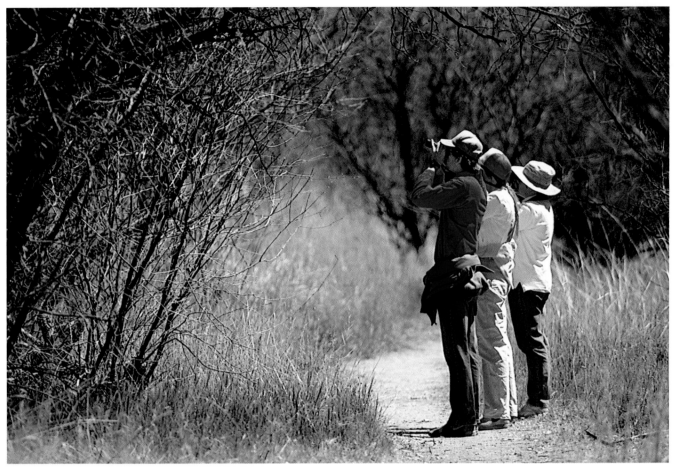

With binoculars raised, birdwatchers at Sonoita-Patagonia Creek Preserve sneak peeks at some of the region's nearly 300 avian species.

An oasis in the Sonoran Desert that spreads across most of southern Arizona, sleepy Santa Cruz County surprises visitors with its lush river valleys, craggy pine-dotted peaks, and mile-high golden grasslands. Missionaries, ranchers, miners, and, more recently, winemakers have all been drawn to this fertile patch southeast of Tucson—as have migrating birds, who stop here en route from Mexico for a drink of water before heading north for the summer.

From Wineries to Ghost Towns

Once an important cattle-shipping depot and now the gateway to the state's wine country, tiny Sonoita looks more like a crossroads than a town. Don't be put off, however. The strip shopping centers that line the intersection of State highways 83 and 82 host several interesting Western boutiques as well as a number of excellent restaurants.

Napa Valley needn't start worrying just yet, but some of the wineries in the Santa Cruz Valley, which didn't get serious about grapes until the 1980s, have already produced award-winning vintages. In Elgin, a picturesque ghost town a few miles east of Sonoita where scenes from films such as *Oklahoma*

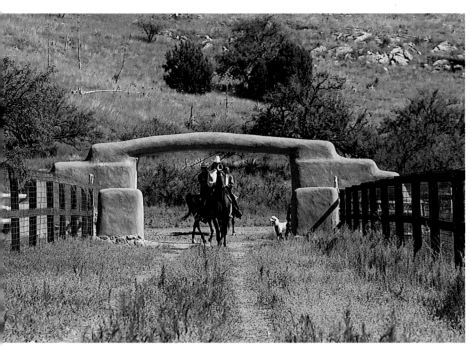

After a morning gallop, riders return their mounts to an Arabian horse ranch near Sonoita in southern Arizona.

The scenery on the back roads leading from Patagonia to the San Rafael Valley's abandoned mining enclaves is breathtaking. Duquesne, the most intact of these ghost towns, is also the most difficult to find. Don't set out without a good Forest Service map (get one at Patagonia's visitor center); a high-clearance vehicle is helpful, too.

Patagonia is 19 miles from Nogales, Mexico, via State 82. If you want to cross the border, park in one of the many inexpensive guarded lots on the U.S. side and walk.

Missionaries, Shoppers & Stargazers

It's a straight shot north 67 miles via Interstate 19 to return to Tucson from Nogales. The route along the Santa Cruz River was followed first by Jesuit missionary Eusebio Kino at the end of the 17th century and later by conquistador Juan Bautista De Anza. Now paved, it's still scenic and endearingly quirky. I-19 is

and *Red River* were shot, The Village of Elgin Winery occupies a former (1895) bordello. Three miles southwest of Sonoita, the Sonoita Vineyards is the domain of winemaker Gordon R. Dutt, credited with discovering the oenological potential of this area. Less than a mile farther south, Callaghan Vineyards has garnered the greatest national acclaim.

Other area wineries include R.W. Webb, off Interstate 10 en route to Sonoita. Arizona's oldest winery, Webb recently opened the Dark Mountain Brewery, the Southwest's only microbrewery in a winery. In Patagonia, the Santa Cruz Winery produces the only kosher wine between New York and California under its Naveh Vineyards label.

Like Sonoita, Patagonia used to be a cattle center, and the adjacent ore-rich Patagonia Mountains also made it a magnet for miners. These days, Patagonia attracts mostly crafts

shoppers and nature lovers, but its old railroad depot (now the town hall) and walnut-lined main street—not to mention the occasional cowhand seen trotting on horseback alongside car traffic—help maintain its Old West aura.

Avid birders make a beeline for the Nature Conservancy's Sonoita-Patagonia Creek Preserve at the edge of Patagonia, where nearly 300 avian species have been spotted, and for the Roadside Rest (a little over 4 miles south of town on State 82), famed for sightings of the rare violet-crowned hummingbird and rose-throated becard. To get there, go right on 4th Avenue until it dead-ends, then left about a mile.

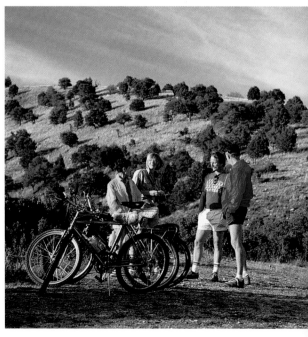

Bikers in Santa Cruz County discuss their route for the day's outing.

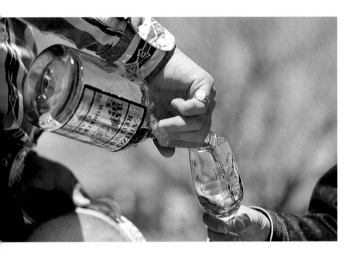

one of the few U.S. highways marked in kilometers, not miles, and it's an "interstate" that never leaves southern Arizona.

One of the missions Father Kino established in southern Arizona, the ruined Tumacacori (Exit 29 off I-19), retains a beautiful, brooding presence. Two other nearby missions, Guavavi and Calabazas, also fall under the aegis of Tumacacori National Historical Park.

Tubac (Exit 40 off I-19), the presidio built in 1752 to protect the Spanish priests and their peaceable Pima and Tohono O'odham Indian converts from Apache raids, is the oldest European settlement in Arizona. Before he embarked from Tubac on his historic 1775 journey to found San Francisco, De Anza served as the presidio's captain. Now a state park and museum, Tubac is adjoined by a thriving artisan's colony with more than 70 craft shops. A self-guided tour includes the church, cemetery, mortuary, chapel, and visitor center.

If you're more interested in the future than the past, Mt. Hopkins, the second-highest peak of the Santa Rita Mountains (on your right as you head north), is home to the Smithsonian Institution's Fred Whipple Observatory (Exit 56 off I-19), renowned for its innovative Multiple Mirror Telescope. The visitor center is open year-round, but guided tours to the top of the mountain are offered

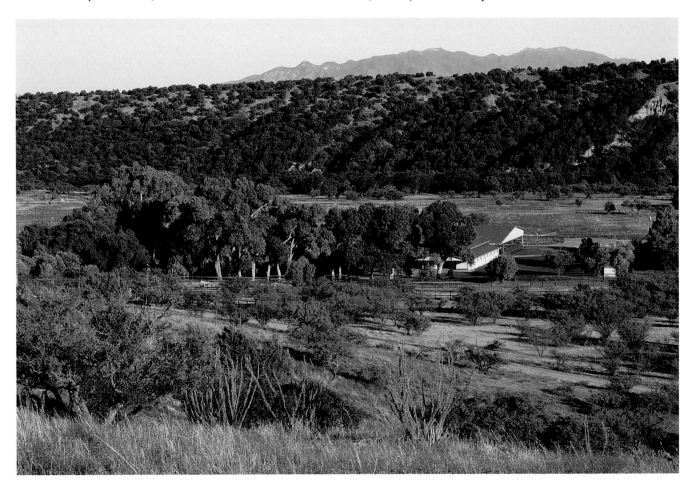
Canyons near Sonoita make tranquil settings for the region's large cattle and horse ranches.

March through November only.

To fill in some more blanks on your bird list, take Exit 63 off I-19 to Madera Canyon, a verdant mecca for more than 400 feathered types. Even Tucsonans who don't know a cockatiel from a cuckoo flock here in summer to enjoy the higher elevations and the shade of the Coronado National Forest. Bring a picnic lunch.

⇐ TRIP PLANNER ⇒

Unless otherwise noted, area codes are 520. Lodging rates for two people range from $ (under $100) to $$$ (above $250) per night.

WHERE

Sonoita is 44 miles southeast of Tucson via Interstate 10 east and State 83 south; to reach Elgin, drive a few miles southeast of Sonoita on State 83. Patagonia lies 12 miles south of Sonoita on State 82.

LODGING

Around Sonoita: At **Vineyard Bed & Breakfast** (92 Los Encinos Rd.; 455-4749; $), you sleep in an antique-filled 1916 ranch house or a Southwestern-style casita. Live oaks, a swimming pool, and a resident burro are among the perks. The 3 rooms at the **Yee Haa Guest Ranch** bed-and-breakfast (8 miles southeast of Sonoita; 455-9285; $), set on 120 acres of rolling grassland, are Western-themed but boast TVs, VCRs, and Jacuzzi-style tubs.

In & around Patagonia: All accommodations in the artsy **Duquesne House B&B** (357 Duquesne St.; 394-2732; $), a former miners' boardinghouse, have private entrances and access to a pretty conservatory. Arizona's oldest continuously operating dude ranch, the 5,000-acre **Circle Z Ranch** (4 miles southwest of Patagonia off State 82; 394-2525, 888/854-2525; $$$ includes meals and trail rides) sits in the foothills of the Santa Rita Mountains. A cantina and a lodge add to the Western ambience.

DINING

Though there are a surprising number of high-quality restaurants in this low-key area, hours are often erratic. Always call ahead.

Sonoita: A pretty patio, a select wine list, and entrees like honey-jalapeño glazed chicken are among the reasons to visit **Karen's Wine Country Café** (3266 State 82; 455-5282). The menu at the cheerful **Grasslands Restaurant & Bakery** (3119 S. State 83; 455-4770) runs the gamut from light, eggless quiches to stick-to-the-ribs bratwurst with sauerbraten. Though **Café Sonoita** (3280 State 82; 455-5278) looks modest, its creative soups, pastas, and fish preparations are anything but.

Patagonia: **Marie's** (340 Naugle Ave.; 394-2812; dinner only) dishes up creative Mediterranean fare in intimate, casually elegant rooms. **Velvet Elvis** (292 Naugle Ave.; 394-2102) is a combination pizza place and art gallery. The deliciously sophisticated prix fixe Italian dinners at **CoseBuone** (436 Naugle Ave.; 394-2366; dinners only) meet big-city standards at small-town prices.

WINERIES

Winery hours vary; call ahead for schedules and precise directions. **R. W. Webb** winery (Exit 279 off I-10; 762-5777) is in Vail. The **Callaghan Vineyards** (455-5650; open Sunday only), **Sonoita Vineyards** (455-5893), and **The Village of Elgin Winery** (455-9309) are all in Elgin. **Santa Cruz Winery** (154 McKeown Ave.; 394-2888) is in Patagonia.

SHOPPING

With its concentration of craft boutiques, most with a Southwestern flair, **Tubac** is the prime stop for shoppers. Still, there are enough galleries and shops in **Patagonia** and **Sonoita** to endanger any credit card balance.

FOR MORE INFORMATION

Patagonia Visitor Center (305 McKeown Ave., in Mariposa Books; 394-0060, 888/794-0060). Sonoita Chamber of Commerce (3123 State 83, Unit C, in Carnevale Travel; 455-5844, 800/659-8808).

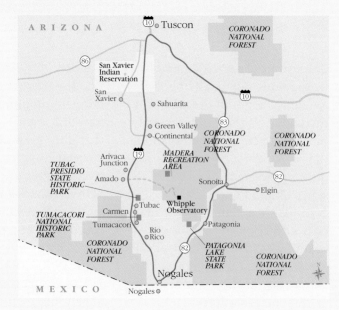

REGION	ARIZONA
Where X	130 miles west of Tucson
When X	February through June best for wildflowers

land of the Organpipe

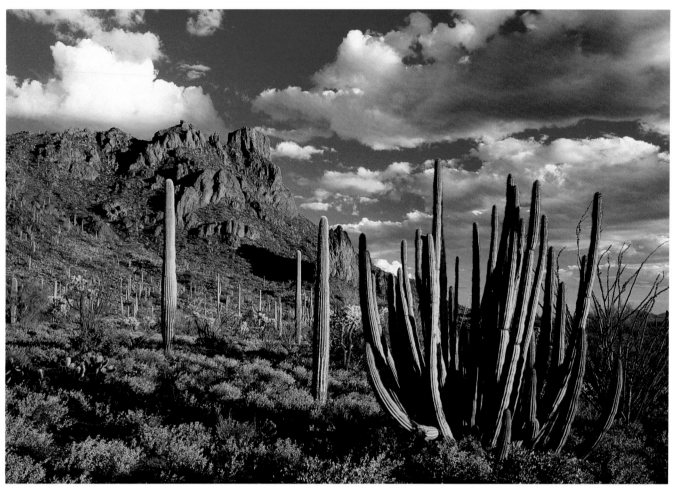

Ribbed stems of many-armed organpipe cactus stretch skyward. The treelike cactus normally grows 8 to 10 feet tall and lives as long as 100 years.

The towering saguaro cactus may be the most popular symbol of Arizona's Sonoran desert, but it's the saguaro's shorter and skinnier-armed cousin, the organpipe, that grabs visitors' attention in the southwestern part of the state. Organ Pipe Cactus National Monument is not the only attraction in this starkly beautiful, wide-open land—a gaping mine pit, a wildlife preserve, and a state-of-the-art observatory are among other lures.

Garlic & Copper

The town of Ajo, gateway to the national monument, was possibly named for garlic (*ajo*, in Spanish) that once grew wild here—or, alternatively, for *au-auho*, a red paint pigment used by early Native American inhabitants. It was a mineral, however, that spurred the town's growth. Copper was king in Ajo from the early 1900s to 1985, when Phelps Dodge shut down its hugely successful New Cornelia

Mine. Chances are good that it will reign again soon. With new ecological surveys and permits in place, Phelps Dodge is just waiting for copper prices to rise before it brings its gigantic earthmovers back to the enormous open mine pit.

In the meantime, Ajo's stillsleepy central plaza is worth exploring. Designed in 1917 by Isabella Greenway, wife of the original mine manager and a friend of Eleanor Roosevelt, the

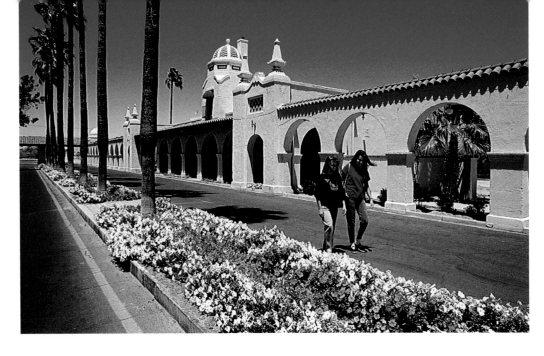

A whitewashed arcade and a domed church overlook the palm-lined plaza in downtown Ajo.

palm-lined square is highlighted by two Spanish Revival churches, small but well proportioned.

The Mine Lookout on Indian Village Road, which features a small historical mining museum, is another key attraction. It's hard not to be impressed by the gigantic stepped chasm below, the former—and maybe future—source of millions of dollars of ore. Nearby, the one-time St. Catherine's Mission (160 Mission Street) is home to a mélange of artifacts from the town's past, collected by the Ajo Historical Society.

An Animal Haven

You need a permit and a high-clearance, four-wheel-drive vehicle to enter the 860,000-acre Cabeza Prieta Wildlife Refuge (1611 N. Second Avenue), about 10 minutes from Ajo. The preserve's rugged terrain, set aside to protect animals such as the desert bighorn sheep, intersperses craggy peaks with spreading valleys punctuated by sand dunes and lunarlike lava floes. The Barry M. Goldwater Air Force Range shares airspace with this vast, isolated refuge; visits are banned when practice missions are under way.

A Cactus Collection

Ten miles south of Ajo, State Highway 85 meets State Highway 86 at Why, a crossroads originally named for its "Y" shape. When the post office gave out zip codes in 1950, it insisted that town names have at least three letters, thus the quizzical appellation.

It's another 26 miles from Why via State 86 to the Organ Pipe Cactus National Monument visitor center. Be forewarned: you won't see huge concentrations of the spiky plant for which this desert preserve is named. These cactus, which resemble the pipes of a church organ, grow taller and in denser stands south of the border; indeed, you'll find more saguaros here than organpipes. That said, the 516-square-mile monument is the best place in the U.S. to view the spindly limbed cactus, along with a rich mix of other desert flora and fauna.

Two graded dirt drives cut through the park; if you only have time for one, the 21-mile Ajo Mountain Drive is by far the more interesting, winding among foothills lush with a vast variety of desert vegetation. The 53-mile Puerto Blanco drive is flatter and less eye-catching, but it has one major draw: shady Quitobaquito Springs, a desert oasis and birder's mecca.

It's only 4 miles from the park entrance to Mexico. There are some souvenir shops in Sonoita, but lots of people just pick up perfume or liquor at the duty-free store in Lukeville on the U.S. side and walk back and forth across the border to legitimize the tax break.

Starry, Starry Night

Arrange to arrive at sunset on your way back to Tucson, and you can take in dinner and a stargazing session at Kitt Peak National Observatory. Managed by a consortium of more than 20 prestigious universities, the observatory has the world's greatest concentration of optical telescopes, including the world's largest asteroid hunter. (If a huge chunk of space debris is going to crash into Earth, the folks at Kitt Peak will be the first to know.)

You won't see stars if you come during the day, but you can watch the high-desert scrub at the base of the 6,875-foot peak change to piñon pines as you ascend to the top. You can also peruse the intricately woven Tohono O'odham baskets sold in the observatory's gift shop.

Kitt Peak leases its lofty 200 acres from the tribe, whose reservation encompasses most of the land you'll be driving through en route to Ajo. Ask someone at the visitor center to point out imposing Baboquivari Peak, sacred to the Tohono O'odham people, who believe it to be the home of their deity I'itoi (Elder Brother).

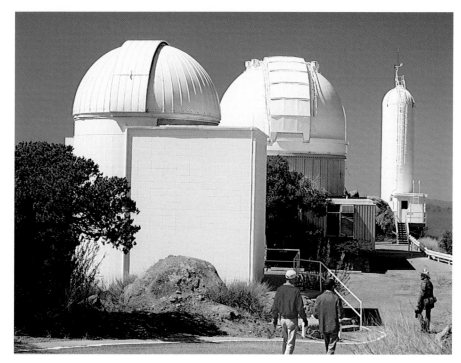

Kitt Peak National Observatory offers nightly Stargazing programs with advance reservations.

TRIP PLANNER

Unless otherwise noted, area codes are 520. Lodging rates for two people range from $ (under $100) to $$$ (above $250) per night.

WHERE

To reach Ajo from Tucson, take State 86 west to its junction with 85 at Why and head north. Kitt Peak National Observatory lies 56 miles southwest of Tucson, at the junction of State 86 and State Hwy. 386; drive south 12 miles up the mountain.

LODGING

Ajo offers three motels and two appealing bed-and-breakfasts: The 5,000-square-foot **Mine Manager's House** (601 W. Greenaway Dr.; 387-6505; $), dating back to 1919, has an aerie on Ajo's highest hill. The 1925 **Guest House Inn** (3 Guest House Rd.; 387-6133; $), built to accommodate mining executives, is now run by a former company employee who is

happy to point out the birds in the region.

DINING

Ajo's several restaurants satisfy diners with down-home, filling fare. **Señor Sancho** (663 N. 2nd Ave.; 387-6226) is the place to go for hearty plates of enchilada suizas and chicken mole. Locals gather at the **Copper Kettle** (23 Plaza; 387-7000) for eggs,

biscuits, and gravy in the morning, and burgers at lunch.

FOR MORE INFORMATION

Ajo Chamber of Commerce (321 Taladro St., Ajo, AZ 85321; 387-7742) is open weekdays. The visitor center at Organ Pipe Cactus National Monument (387-6849; small vehicle fee) is open daily 8-5. For stargazing on Kitt Peak, call 318-8726.

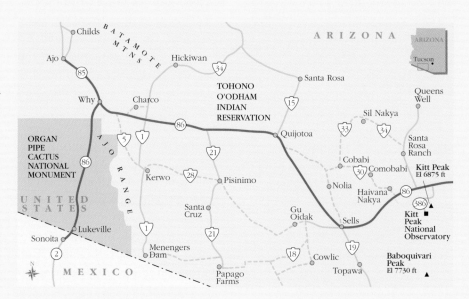

REGION	UTAH	
Where	X	300 miles south of Salt Lake City
When	X	Spring and fall trip

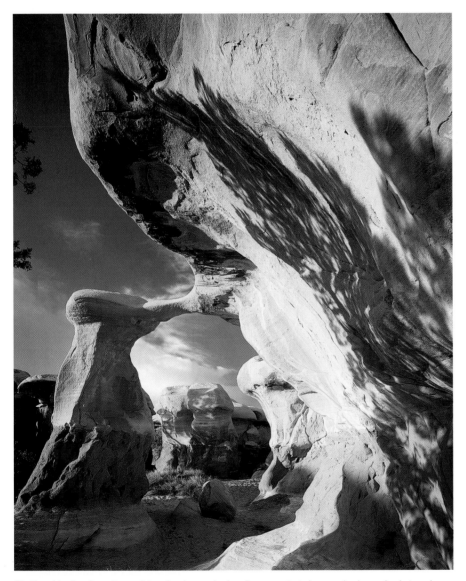

Weathered by the elements, sandstone hoodoos and spires form a contorted canyon landscape in photogenic Devil's Garden along Hole-in-the-Rock Road.

munities of Boulder and Escalante make convenient bases for exploration, and Hell's Backbone Road offers a dramatic loop off State 12 between the two towns. This 44-mile gravel and dirt route (closed in winter) crosses high above Box Death Hollow Wilderness Area in a spectacular feat of engineering.

Stretching between Bryce Canyon National Park and Glen Canyon National Recreation Area, Grand Staircase-Escalante includes multicolored cliffs and mesas, natural bridges and arches, and major prehistoric dwellings and rock art. The Escalante and Paria rivers have carved dramatic valley and canyon landscapes deep into the sandstone. These intricate formations share space with petrified wood deposits, a free-roaming buffalo herd, and other animals and birds.

Sampling Escalante Canyons

Branching off State 12 at Boulder, Burr Trail Road, a back door to Capitol Reef National Park, is the only other paved road on the north side of the monument. The turnoff is next to the Burr Trail Café; look for a sign that reads "Boulder/Bullfrog Scenic Drive."

Eleven miles south of Boulder, a trailhead leads to Lower Calf Creek Falls, the monument's only

It's hard to go anywhere in southern Utah without being on federal lands: the state has five national parks and seven national monuments. But Grand Staircase-Escalante, America's newest national monument, is certainly the biggest and, arguably, the best. Most of its 1.7 million acres of magnificent and rugged natural beauty remains hard to visit, but its northeastern reaches can be sampled from one of the country's most scenic byways, State Highway 12. The pioneer com-

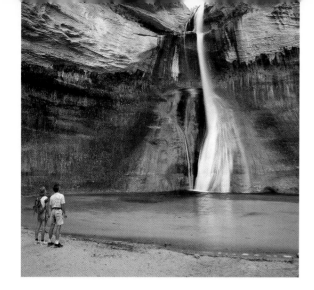

An easy hike from the trailhead leads visitors to Lower Calf Creek Falls, a 126-foot cascade.

officially marked interpretive trail. An easy 5.5-mile round-trip hike, the trail ends at falls that cascade 126 feet into a tree-lined pool. The trailhead for an extended hike to the Escalante River lies 1 mile beyond Calf Creek.

Back on State 12, stop at the pullout 18 miles beyond Boulder for an expansive view that takes in the Aquarius Plateau to the north and the sacred hump of Navajo Mountain in Arizona to the south.

Hole-in-the-Rock Road, a 57-mile dirt and gravel road off State 12, begins 5 miles east of Escalante. On a 30-minute drive, you have time to reach the maze of sandstone hoodoos and spires in Devil's Garden, also a good place to picnic and take photos. In good weather with a four-wheel-drive, you can head all the way down to Hole-in-the-Rock, following the trail taken by Mormon settlers on their journey south to the Colorado River. At the trail's end, they cut a passage to lower their wagons over a 1,200-foot cliff.

Smoky Mountain Road, a 78-mile dirt road from Escalante, winds south through the monument to Big Water on U.S. Highway 89 near Lake Powell.

The trip demands careful navigation, with several sections requiring high-clearance vehicles, but the plateau-top route provides breathtaking vistas. The road is named for the often visible smoke from a coal mine fire that has been smoldering underground for over a century. In the Burning Hills area, fires oxidized the soil, giving the hills a red cast.

The South Side

The Grand Staircase and other southwestern sections are best dipped into from U.S. 89 along the monument's southern edge. Kanab makes a good base.

One way to reach U.S. 89 is via Cottonwood Canyon Road, a 46-mile road off State 12, which slices through the monument from the farming community of Cannonville. Paved only as far as picturesque Kodachrome Basin State Park (known for its intensely colored spires and chimneys), the route hugs a striking

A few old buildings are all that remain of Old Paria, a 19th-century settlement about 30 miles east of Kanab.

south-to-north sandstone formation called the Cockscomb that forms a ridge separating the Grand Staircase from the Kaiparowits Plateau region. Highlights include hidden gems like Hackberry Canyon and Round Valley, Castle Rock's massive turrets, and towering Grosvenor Arch, an impressive rock formation named in honor of the founder of the National Geographic Society.

Unpaved Paria River Valley Road, 30 miles east of Kanab off U.S. 89, offers a short excursion to a 19th-century ghost town and a cinema set that has served as a backdrop for Western movies since 1961. Beyond the set lie the tumbledown rock-and-log remains that make up Old Paria, a farming and cattle town settled in 1870. Drought and a failed gold-mining operation closed the town by the 1920s. To reach the ruins, drive past the Paria Cemetery and wade across the Paria River.

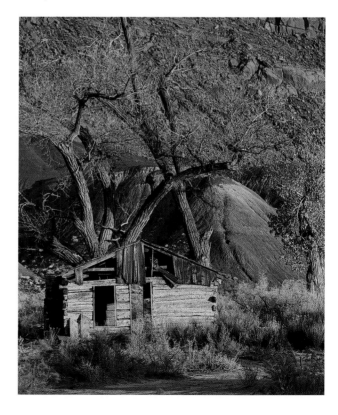

⠿TRIP PLANNER⠿→

HOW & WHEN TO VISIT

The monument is open year-round, but weather extremes make spring and fall the best times to explore. Check current road and weather conditions and buy maps and guidebooks at the Escalante Interagency or the BLM office in Kanab.

LODGING

In Boulder, the **Boulder Mountain Lodge** (20 N. Hwy 12; 800/556-3446) arranges hikes. **Boulder Mountain Ranch** (Salt Gulch/Hell's Backbone Rd.; 335-7480) is a working cattle ranch. Escalante's **Prospector Inn** (380 W. Main; 826-4653) is a comfortable motel. B&Bs include **Rainbow Country Tours Bed and Breakfast** (586 East 300 South; 800/252-8824) and **Grand Staircase B&B/Inn** (280 W. Main; 826-4890). **Escalante Outfitters** (310 W. Main; 826-4266) operates a hostel-style bunkhouse.

Kanab's **Parry Lodge** (89 E. Center St.; 644-2601) is a popular way station for Hollywood casts filming at Old Paria. **Best Western Red Hills** (125 W. Center St.; 800/830-2675) offers comfortable rooms. For campers, **Calf Creek** (13 sites next to State 12) and **Deer Creek** (5 sites along the Burr Trail; no water) are primitive year-round sites.

DINING

Both **Hell's Backbone Grill** (335-7460) and **Boulder Mesa Restaurant** (355-7447) in Boulder offer informal dining. Escalante eateries, include the **Ponderosa Restaurant** (826-4658), **Prospector Inn** restaurant (826-4653), **Esca-Latte Gourmet Coffee and Pizza Parlor** (826-4266), **Kanaf's Fernando's Hideaway** (644-3222), **Parry's Lodge Restaurant** (644-2601), and **Houston's Trail's End Restaurant** (644-2488).

OTHER ATTRACTIONS

Anasazi Indian Village State Park (335-7308) in Boulder is the site of one of the largest prehisoric Native American communities west of the Colorado River. **Escalante State Park**, 1 mile west of Escalante on State 12, showcases petrified wood and dinosaur bones.

FOR MORE INFORMATION

Escalante Interagency Office (755 W. Main St., P.O. Box 225, Escalante, UT 84726; 826-5499); Bureau of Land Management, Kanab Field Office (318 North First East, Kanab, UT 84741; 644-2672).

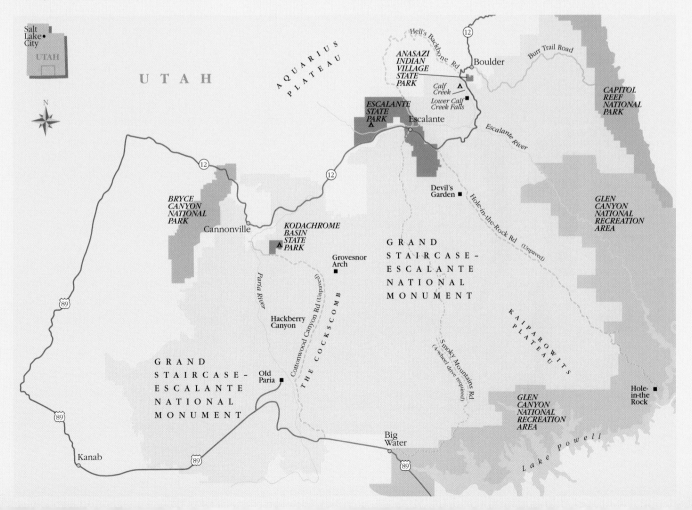

REGION	NEVADA	
Where	X	350-400 mile loop from Las Vegas
When	X	Spring or fall best weather

gateway to

Death Valley

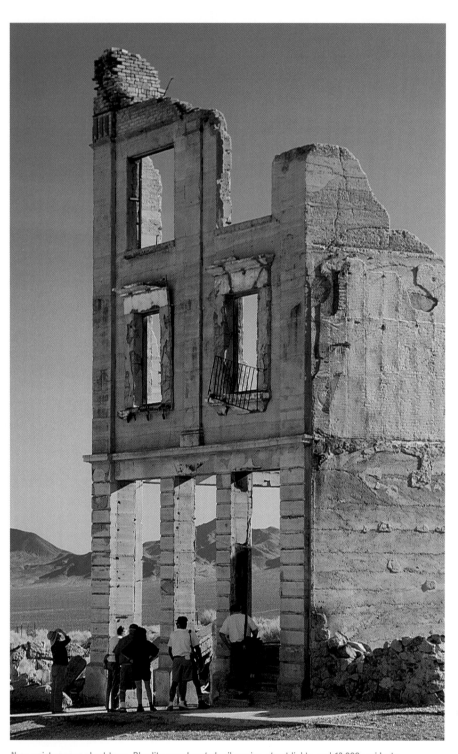

Now a picturesque ghost town, Rhyolite once boasted rail service, street lights, and 12,000 residents.

Between the glitter of Las Vegas and the magnificent, though stark, landscape of Death Valley National Park lies a stretch of high desert that holds Nevada's only winery, a reserve for Ice Age fish, a picturesque ghost town, a ballerina's theater, and other hidden oases. Our suggested drive dips into California for a peek at Death Valley before crossing back into Nevada.

Pahrump Valley & Beyond

Unincorporated Pahrump, about an hour west of Las Vegas on State Highway 160, is one of Nevada's fastest-growing areas. Unregulated expansion is largely fueled by Las Vegas workers looking for inexpensive housing and retirees searching for places to park mobile homes. Along the highway are several large casinos and motels; nearby lie RV parks and two golf courses.

Nevada's only winery, Pahrump Valley Vineyards, is an island of inspired architecture in this otherwise unsettled-appearing region. White stucco buildings with blue-tiled roofs and arched doorways top a landscaped slope facing 1,919-foot Mt. Charleston. Though the elegant restaurant (lunch and dinner) is worth a stop on its own, the large tasting room has a

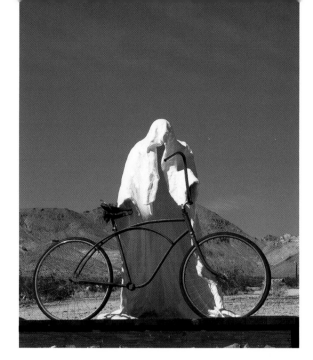

pleasant ambience. All of its vinous offerings are presently pressed from California grapes (wild horses trampled the winery's vineyards a few years ago), but new rootstock is taking hold.

Into Amargosa Valley

Leaving Pahrump on State 160, turn north on Bell Vista Road (about 22 miles) to reach Ash Meadows National Wildlife Refuge. These 22,117 acres of spring-fed wetlands and alkaline desert uplands, managed by the U.S. Fish and Wildlife Service, provide sanctuary for several dozen plants and animals found nowhere else in the world, including two species of endangered pupfish. A quarter-mile-long boardwalk leads from refuge headquarters to Crystal Spring, one of 30 springs and seeps that transform the desert scrubland into lush, marshy wetland. The inch-long, silvery pupfish (colorful only during spring spawning) look insignificant until you remember they were around during a time when mastodons roamed the earth. Nearby Crystal Reservoir is a refuge for herons, egrets, coots, and dozens of other species of waterfowl thankful for a drink in an otherwise arid landscape.

A few miles from the reservoir, Devils Hole, an underground seep that is home to another pupfish species, is a remote outpost of Death Valley National Park. The tiny pupfish here are even more difficult to spot because the water is deep and murky blue. It's also fenced off to keep people from illegally diving into it.

If you leave the refuge from the other end, Longstreet Inn & Casino appears in about 8 miles. The inn provides the valley's only nightlife, especially on weekends, when live music and the Nebraska Steakhouse attract both visitors and locals. From here, head north on State Highway 373 to the town of Amargosa Valley and then west 30 miles on U.S. Highway 95 to Beatty, a Nevada gateway to Death Valley.

West to Death Valley

En route to Death Valley on State Highway 374, turn onto a dirt road 2 1/2 miles west of Beatty to view the remnants of Rhyolite, a one-time prosperous mining camp and now a picturesque ghost. In 1907, the town boasted 12,000 residents, hundreds of homes, saloons, an opera house, telephone service, and electric street lights. An elaborate train depot and the well-known Bottle House are two of the few surviving structures.

As you approach Rhyolite, notice the collection of sculpture rising from the base of chaparral-covered Bonanza Mountain. These are works of two Belgian artists, sculptor A. Szukalski and expressionist Fred Bervoerts.

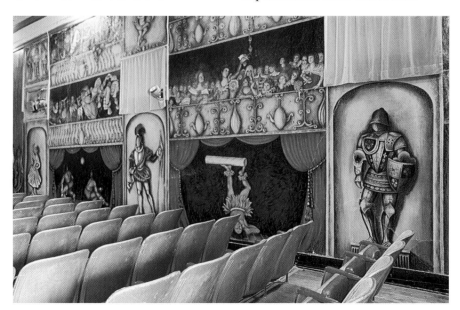

Painted audience at Marta Becket's Amargosa Opera House outside Death Valley awaits dancer's performance.

Subjects range from a plaster rendition of the Last Supper to a whimsical metal silhouette of a miner and his pet penguin.

You enter Death Valley about midway between Furnace Creek, center for park activities, and Scotty's Castle, an isolated (still furnished) mansion built in the 1920s as a vacation retreat (tours offered by park rangers). The grand Furnace Creek Inn (now open year-round) is a good spot to linger for lunch or longer. For park information, suggested

drives, and other activities, stop by the nearby visitor center and museum.

Heading southeast on State Highway 190, you leave the park a few miles before reaching Death Valley Junction, home of Marta Becket's Amargosa Opera House. Over 30 years ago, Marta, a New York ballerina, defected to the desert and bought a place in which to stage a one-person ballet. In case nobody attended her performances, she painted a permanent audience,

with brilliant murals depicting gypsies, cherubs, nuns, monks, royalty, and other figures. Marta is in her 70s now—and still dancing. A few years ago, she also restored rooms at the adjoining hotel so live theatergoers could spend a night. For an unforgettable experience, time your visit to see Marta perform with partner Tom Willett; call (760) 852-4441 for performance times and room reservations.

To return to Las Vegas, take State 127/373 north to U.S. 95.

⇇ TRIP PLANNER ⇉

Unless otherwise noted, area codes are 775. Lodging rates for two people range from $ (below $100) to $$$ (above $250) per night.

LODGING

Pahrump's accommodations include **Saddle West Hotel & Casino** (1220 S. Hwy. 160; 727-1111; $), a two-story motel. **Longstreet Inn & Casino** (Amargosa Valley; 372-1777; $-$$) is an oasis on the California-Nevada state line, complete with pool, two restaurants, and RV park (51 hookups). **Beatty's Exchange Club** (U.S. 95; 553-2333; $), established in 1906, and the **Burro Inn** (U.S. 95; 553-2892; $) both have restaurants.

In Death Valley, the **Furnace Creek Inn** (1 mile south of the visitor center; 760/786-2345; $$-$$$) has 66 rooms, a restaurant, tennis courts, and pool; the golf course is nearby. **Furnace Creek Ranch** (760/786-2345; $-$$), a motel next to the visitor center, has a pool, tennis courts, and a playground.

DINING

Pahrump Valley Vineyards (3810 Winery Rd., Pahrump; 727-6900) includes a handsome restaurant serving creative cuisine (open daily for lunch and dinner). The winery also offers tours and wine tasting. The **Nebraska Steakhouse** (see Longstreet Inn & Casino above), open weekends only, is the valley's best. Furnace Creek's elegant **The Inn Dining Room** (see Lodging above) is

open for breakfast, lunch, dinner, and Sunday brunch. At Death Valley Junction, almost everyone in town congregates at **Serendipity Ice Cream Parlor & Sandwich Shop**.

FOR FURTHER INFORMATION

Ash Meadows National Wildlife Refuge (P.O. Box 2660, Pahrump, NV 89041; 372-5435). Death Valley National Park (P.O. Box 579, Death Valley, CA 92328; 760/786-2331).

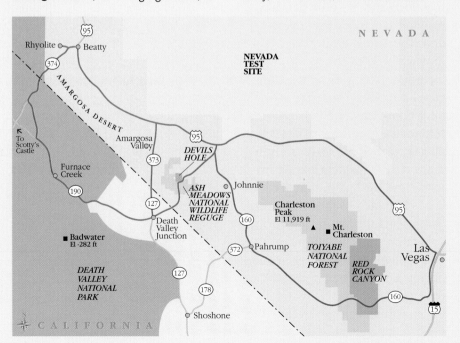

Nevada's
Pioneer Territory

REGION	NEVADA
Where	X	A 500-mile loop from Reno
When	X	Best from spring to early summer

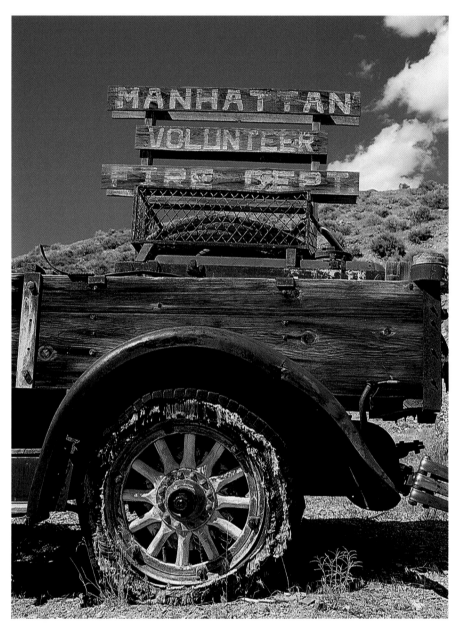

Central Nevada's boom-and-bust towns shelter many relics: this antique truck will put out no more fires in Manhattan, one of many almost-ghost towns south of Austin.

The country's loneliest highway, ghost towns with real spirit(s), and gigantic fossilized fish—these are just some of the discoveries you'll make on a weekend loop trip through central Nevada. Visit in late spring, when the land is at its most colorful; midsummer sizzles, and winter can close high desert roads.

The Lonely Road to Austin

Road signs along U.S. Highway 50 boast that this route across Nevada is "the loneliest road in America." They aren't far wrong: you can look ahead to where distant mountain peaks rise above the desert floor and never see a car. The ribbon of road parallels the route Pony Express riders took across the state; about midway between Reno and Austin lie the remains of one of their way stations, Cold Springs. A sign near the highway marks the spot, and a short trail leads to the former station site.

If you leave Reno in the morning, Austin is a good lunch spot. The town perches at the place where the steep sides of Pony Canyon empty into the Reese River Valley.

One story goes that the old mining town sprang up in 1862 after a Pony Express rider's horse kicked over a rock that covered the mouth of a cave laden with silver. At any rate, within two years this high-desert town had a population of 10,000, and gold and silver poured from nearly a dozen mills. In its heyday, it was the biggest town between Virginia City and Salt Lake City.

Though today's population is less than 400, Austin never really died. Many of the original buildings still stand, including three

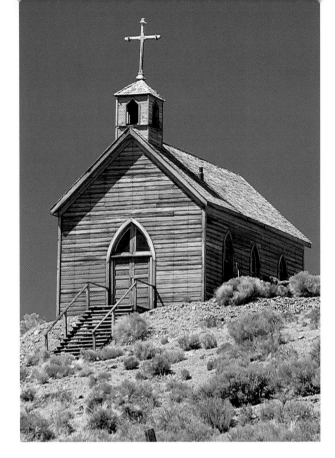

steepled churches. One of the strangest structures is a three-story stone tower perched on a bluff southwest of town. Built as a summer home by mining tycoon Anson Stokes, it was used only a month or so in 1897. In town, the second-story balcony of Lander County Courthouse served as a gallows for vigilantes. The town's cemetery has some colorful inscriptions on its tombstones.

Austin was once home to the Sazarac Liars Club, named after a tavern where some of the West's tallest tales were told. If you go into the International Café for a meal or drop by the adjoining saloon, you may hear a few tales yourself, such as the one about a former roomer who still watches over the pool table.

Big Smoky Valley's Ghosts

About 10 miles east of Austin, turn onto State Highway 376,

A state park protects Berlin's photogenic ruins.

which leads south through Big Smoky Valley. The valley, prime alfalfa-growing land, lies between two of Nevada's highest mountain ranges, the Toiyabes and the Toquima Range. You'll pass the turnoff to Round Mountain, where modern mining equipment has dug well over a mile into the ground in search of gold.

To reach Manhattan, an almost-ghost town, detour onto State Highway 377. The town boomed in 1906, after gold was discovered at April Fool Hill, but eventually faded. With a population of 60, the town today is mainly a collection of old buildings, including two saloons and a picturesque church.

Belmont, one of Nevada's most photogenic ghost towns, lies in a canyon setting among rock outcroppings and piñon pines. Though it's only 12 miles east of Manhattan by dirt road, it's best to take the long (and paved) way around, heading south on State 376 until you see a spur road to the north.

A silver-mining town that boomed around 1865, Belmont was the seat of Nye County until the silver played out. Now fewer than a dozen people live here, and the Belmont Saloon (open occasional weekends) is the town's only business. The entire area is a national historic district, with picturesque ruins extending well over a block. Don't miss the old courthouse, still remarkably preserved.

It's another 40 miles south on State 376 to the junction with U.S. Highway 95. Tonopah, 5 miles to the west, offers hotels with casinos, motels, and RV facilities. Wyatt Earp and Jack Dempsey were only two of the colorful characters who lived here. For an in-depth look at the history of this "Queen of the Silver Camps," visit the free Central Nevada Museum on Logan Field Road.

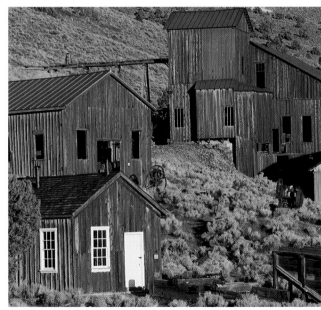

Berlin-Ichthyosaur State Park

Nobody lives in Berlin anymore except the park rangers who look after this unusual site. Unique among Nevada's ghost towns, Berlin is protected as a state park.

You can wander through town, visiting the stamp mill and peeking into the windows of an assay office, a doctor's office, a rooming house, and several miners' cabins. Many of the cabins look as if the resident just stepped out for a moment. That might be due to the "cleaning ghost," who seems insistent on rearranging the furniture and keeping things tidy in two of the tightly locked cabins.

The park ranger leads tours through town on weekends from Memorial Day through Labor Day. He is also responsible for a different—and somewhat older—attraction about a mile up the hill. Here, in 1955, an excavation yielded the fossilized remains of 40 ichthyosaurs, 60-foot-long fish-lizards. These giant seagoing dinosaurs, swam in the ocean that covered this area 240 million to 90 million years ago.

The major fossil beds are protected inside a building and may be toured only with a ranger. Tours are offered on weekends. A nicely kept campground with 14 sites lies along the road between Berlin and the fossil beds.

To get to Berlin from Tonopah, follow U.S. 95 northeast to State Highway 361. Berlin lies in the foothills about 23 miles east of Gabbs. To return to Reno, take State 361 north to U.S. 50 and head west. If time permits, return to U.S. 95 and follow it through Hawthorne and past 24-mile-long Walker Lake, a remnant of the large lake that once covered this area.

⌗TRIP PLANNER⌗

Most of this circle route is on lonely roads with few places to eat or buy gas, so fill up in major towns and carry plenty of water. Unless otherwise noted, all area codes are 775. Lodging rates for two people range from $ (under $100) to $$$ (above $250) per night.

LODGING

If you linger in Austin, two places to stay along U.S. 50 are the **Lincoln Motel** (964-2698; $) and the **Mountain Motel** (964-2471; $). Look at your room before checking in; sizes vary, but none are fancy. In downtown Tonopah, the **Best Western Hi Desert Inn** (320 Main St.; 482-3300; $ includes continental breakfast) and the **Jim Butler Motel** (on U.S. 95; 482-3577; $) are good for families. The historic **Mizpah Hotel and Casino** (100 Main St.; 482-6202; $) is registered as a state monument.

RVers in Austin can stay at the **Baptist Church RV Park** for a moderate fee. Tonopah has RV facilities at the **Tonopah Station House**, **Lambertucci Roma**, **Twister Inn**, and **Joshua Tree**.

DINING

The **International Bar & Café** (Cedar and Main sts.; 964-9905) is the place the Austin locals eat, drink, and chat. The two-story wooden building was built in Virginia City in 1860, then dismantled and moved in its entirety to Austin in 1863. Tonopah's restaurants include the Pittman Room in the **Mizpah Hotel** (see Lodging above), open 24 hours a day, and the Whistle Stop in **The Station House** (1100 Erie Main St.; 482-9777), which serves "down home food at down home prices."

FOR FURTHER INFORMATION

Austin Chamber of Commerce (Austin, NV 89310; 964-2200). Tonopah Chamber of Commerce (P.O. Box 869, Tonopah, NV 89049; 482-3859).

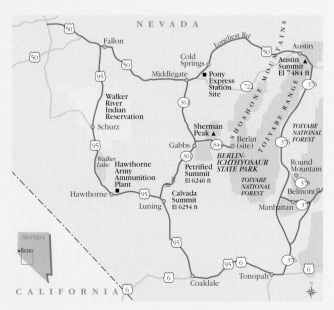

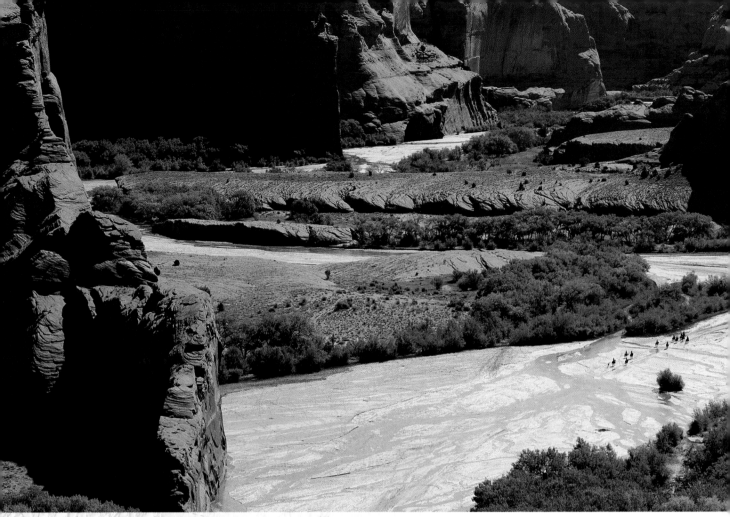

From the rim of Canyon de Chelly National Monument, horseback riders on the valley floor resemble tiny ants.

Navajo & Hopi Lands

The Navajo Indian Reservation, the nation's largest (around 27,000 square miles), spills across state boundaries in northeastern Arizona, southeastern Utah, and northwestern New Mexico. The Hopi Indian Reservation and surrounding former Hopi-Navajo joint holdings are an "island" within the Navajo lands.

Part of the vast Shonto Plateau, this is high country, ascending from 3,500 feet to over 10,000 feet at Navajo Mountain. Hopi villages cling to the slopes of Black Mesa, a tableland that rises over 6,200 feet above sea level.

There are at least three good reasons to visit this land: to absorb its dramatic, sculptured sandstone scenery; to inspect its archaeological relics, evidence of an advanced civilization from a thousand years ago; and to learn a little about its present occupants, whose distinctive cultures survive long after those of many other North American tribes have all but disappeared.

Visiting in spring means you'll gamble on the weather, as you would on any high-country trip. But the region is at its best from mid-April through May—a time when grass covers valley floors, wildflowers carpet hills, and spindle-legged lambs join flocks roaming the reservation. Summer heat descends around mid-June and is punctuated at fairly regular intervals by short, violent, traffic-stopping thunderstorms that continue through early September. Late September and October again bring ideal travel weather (warm, clear, sunshiny days and chilly nights). By November, winter—and with it snow and cold—begins to close in.

The Navajo Nation

Navajos traditionally have been semi-nomadic, following their flocks, living in simple hogans of logs and earth in winter and in more simple shade ramadas in summer. Seldom did you see more than two or three hogans together, and the only towns grew up around governmental or industrial centers. But housing patterns are slowly changing.

The pickup truck (jokingly referred to by the Navajo as their "convertible") has replaced the horse as the principal mode of transportation in most areas, and modern dress has replaced traditional attire for most young Navajos. Tribal members, however, still wear the fine turquoise and silver jewelry for which they are famous.

For nearly 100 years after they signed a treaty with the government in 1868 and returned home from four years of exile at Fort Sumner, New Mexico, the Navajo livelihood depended principally on sheep raising. But growth of the tribe (now around 165,000) and its herds increased the demands on overgrazed ranges. Fortunately, new sources of income emerged. Uranium, oil, coal, and gas discoveries brought lease bonuses and royalty payments, and Congress voted for long-range rehabilitation funds.

These efforts have resulted in a slow but steady broadening of the tribe's economic base.

Window Rock—Seat of Navajo Government

Window Rock, a once-sleepy town near the intersection of Navajo Route 12 and State Highway 264, has turned into a busy place. At the highway intersection stands a metropolitan-style shopping center. Just beyond the northeast corner of the intersection is the Navajo Arts and Crafts Enterprise, the largest tribally owned craft shop on the reservation. Browse awhile in the display room; even if you aren't planning to buy, you'll enjoy comparing quality and prices. Much of the Navajos' best work is here: weaving, silver, leather, painting, and carving.

The Navajo Museum, Library, and Visitors Center, housed in a huge hogan-shaped building, is on State 264 near the Navajo Nation Zoological Park. The excellent museum traces the tribe's history and provides a feeling for its culture. West of the intersection lie the fairgrounds,

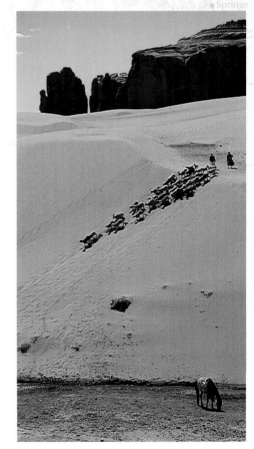

Shepherds herd their flock over the sands of Navajo National Monument as they have done for centuries.

setting for the lively Navajo Nation Fair held the second weekend in September.

The road north leads to tribal headquarters, where buildings blend with the massive red sandstone shapes around them. The large, round window in the rock—for which the town was named—overlooks the complex. Of particular interest is the Navajo Tribal Council building, shaped like a hogan and containing murals depicting the tribe's history.

The tribe owns the town's small motor inn, a good place to stay on this side of the reservation. Several cafés right across the street offer options to the motel's fine restaurant.

Hubbell Trading Post

In 1876, Juan Lorenzo Hubbell founded his trading post at Ganado (4 miles east of the junction of State 264 and U.S. Highway 191), and it's still doing business in the old reservation tradition. Here Navajos visit with friends and trade their wool, rugs, and jewelry (and paychecks) for groceries and supplies. But today the trading post is a national historic site operated by a nonprofit proprietor.

More than just a trader, Hubbell was the Navajos' friend, settling family quarrels, explaining government policy, and helping the sick. When he died in 1930, he was buried next to his family and his longtime Indian friend Many Horses on a small hill above the trading post.

Don't overlook the rug room; it's crammed with one of the area's best selections. At the small museum, you can watch local Navajo women weaving on traditional looms. Rangers also conduct scheduled tours of Hubbell's home, which contains a fine collection of paintings and artifacts.

The neighboring town of Ganado was named for Ganado Mucho, one of the chiefs who signed the 1868 treaty between the Navajos and the U.S. It has a

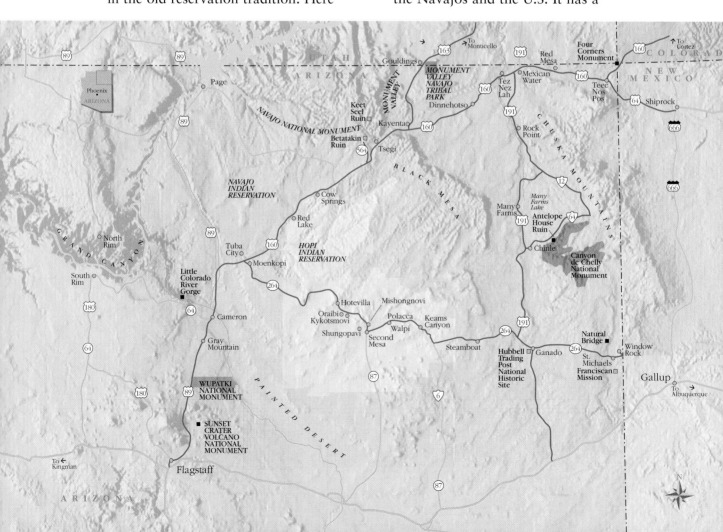

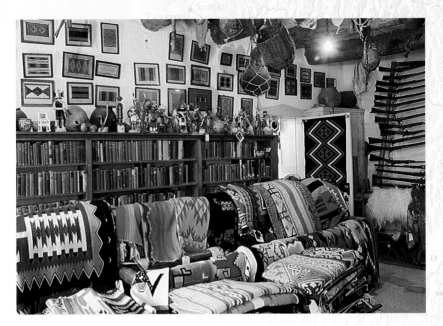

Presbyterian mission and hospital and several schools.

Canyon de Chelly

Nestled in a magnificent canyon setting, prehistoric dwellings resembling toy villages draw visitors to Canyon de Chelly National Monument. The Navajos call it Tsegi, "rock canyon." For more than 300 years, its fortresslike walls provided a sanctuary against enemy forces that, at times, threatened to subdue or destroy the Navajo people. Canyon de Chelly (pronounced "shay") still offers sanctuary to those who prefer the old ways. Each spring they return to plant their crops, tend their orchards, and graze their sheep in the quiet manner of their forefathers.

Unlike the Grand Canyon, this beautifully proportioned canyon complex is a size to which humans can relate. On its 100-plus-mile course, the canyon plunges from a depth of 30 feet to a depth of over 1,000 feet; it contains over 100 prehistoric sites, most dating from the 11th and 13th centuries.

The canyon entrance is on Navajo Route 64 just past the town of Chinle, a few miles east of U.S. 191. Scenic drives along both rims allow access to spectacular overlooks. With one exception, visitors are not allowed into the canyon unless accompanied by a Navajo guide. The exception is the 2 1/2-mile hike from the south rim of the canyon down to White House Ruin, one of the unique cliff dwellings of the Anasazi— the "ancient ones"—who built their multistoried apartment houses in open caves on the canyon floor and along its walls.

Concern for preservation of the unique cliff dwellings prompted a joint arrangement between the government and the Navajo tribe in 1931. The agreement established the 130 square miles of the Canyon de Chelly-Canyon del Muerto complex as a national monument, but stipulated that administration of the area would not interfere with the rights or privacy of the Navajos who lived there.

Four Corners Area

In Tsaile, east of Canyon de Chelly (intersection of Navajo routes 64 and 12), sprawls the nation's first Native American college. A free museum makes it worth a stop.

Some 63 miles north of Canyon de Chelly, U.S. 191 meets U.S. Highway 160. A short drive east on U.S. 160 takes you through Teec Nos Pos, where a well-known trading post displays the region's intricately designed rugs. Just beyond lies the turnoff to Four Corners, the only place in the country where four state boundaries converge.

U.S. 160 continues northeast toward Mesa Verde National Park in Colorado. At Teec Nos Pos, U.S. 64 heads eastward to Shiprock, the gigantic rock formation in New Mexico that was a landmark to pioneers. At Shiprock, the highway intersects with U.S. Highway 666, the north-south route through New Mexico, Colorado, and Utah.

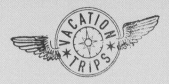
The Kachina Cult

To the Hopis, kachinas represent ancestral deities who dwell in the San Francisco Peaks near Flagstaff and return each year to the mesas, bringing rain. Every member of the tribe is involved in the cult in some way. Hopi children are initiated by a ritual held between the ages of 6 and 10. During ceremonial dances in the village plaza, they receive dolls to help them identify the distinctive mask and costume of each of the kachina spirits.

The pantheon of kachina spirits includes some 250 to 300 deities, ranging from a gift-bearing Santa Claus type to a ferocious black ogre who disciplines disobedient children. Others may represent an animal, plant, flower, heavenly body (sun, moon, or stars), or legendary figure from Hopi history.

Many kachinas are identified only by their particular ceremonial roles (runners, clowns, or escorts) or by some idiosyncrasy in costume or behavior. There is no fixed number of accepted kachinas; new ones are introduced almost every year during ceremonies but return the next year only if they develop a popular following or bring about some beneficial effect.

Authentically carved kachinas are prized by collectors as some of the most meaningful and colorful examples of Native American art.

Monument Valley

The most famous section of the entire Navajo reservation, Monument Valley is a land of fantastic buttes and spires of colorful rock that rise from the 5,000-foot desert floor. It's also a good place to catch glimpses of the traditional Navajo way of life: women and children tending flocks of sheep and goats, riders racing bareback across the plains, and weavers designing rugs in front of their hogans.

Now a Navajo Tribal Park, the area lies astride the Arizona-Utah border on U.S. Highway 163, which leads north from U.S. 160 at Kayenta. Just a few miles north of Kayenta, huge red rock pillars loom into view. The impressive landscape may look familiar—this remote area has been the setting of many Western movies. About 24 miles north of Kayenta, you pass through Mystery Valley and cross the New Mexico-Utah border.

A half-mile north of the state line is a crossroads. To the left lies Goulding's Ranch, a famous former trading post and now a lodge. Here, too, are a museum and a craft store. Oljeto, nearby, is another old trading post and museum. To the right the road leads to the visitor center. The center has a restaurant and small shop that sells some local crafts. This is also the place to

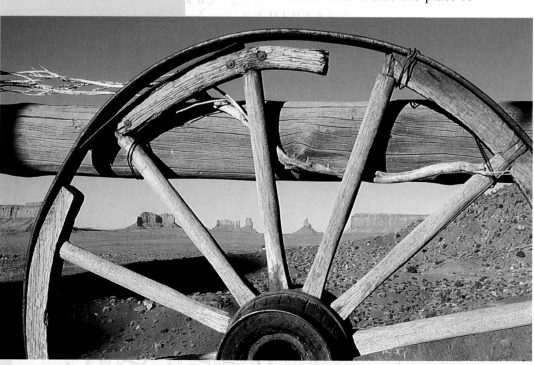

Wagon wheel marks the site of Goulding's Ranch, a former trading post and now a lodge, on the Utah side of Monument Valley.

get information on guided and self-guiding tours. A picnic area and a public campground are nearby.

For a small fee, you can drive into the park on a 17-mile signed road to see some of its famous landmarks: the tall, slender Three Sisters spires and the Totem Pole and Yei-Bi-Chei group. A 15-minute round-trip walk from North Window around Cly Butte rewards with panoramic views. To explore the valley more thoroughly, you can arrange for guided horseback and four-wheel-drive tours.

Navajo National Monument

Another group of prehistoric cliff dwellings—Betatakin, Keet Seel, and Inscription House—is preserved in Navajo National Monument, about 20 miles south of Kayenta. You can see Betatakin, which rests inside a great cave in the canyon wall, from monument headquarters, but it's a grueling 4- to 5-hour round trip and a tough climb back to the canyon rim. To reach Keet Seel, Arizona's largest cliff dwelling, you must make, and confirm, reservations well in advance and spend a day traversing a primitive trail on foot or on a horse; hikers usually spend the night at the ruins (no potable water). Inscription House, 25 miles to the northwest, is closed indefinitely for preservation.

To reach the monument (7,268 feet in elevation), follow State Highway 564 west from its junction with U.S. 160. The road climbs through juniper and piñon forests to the visitor center and Betatakin. You'll find a well-stocked crafts store and a Navajo hogan exhibit. A small campground is nearby.

Tuba City

Capital of western Navajoland, Tuba City lies just north of the junction of U.S. 160 and State Highway 264. The busy town has a trading post dating from 1880, a motel, large grocery stores, and several restaurants offering the Navajo version of a taco—on fry bread. The town hosts the

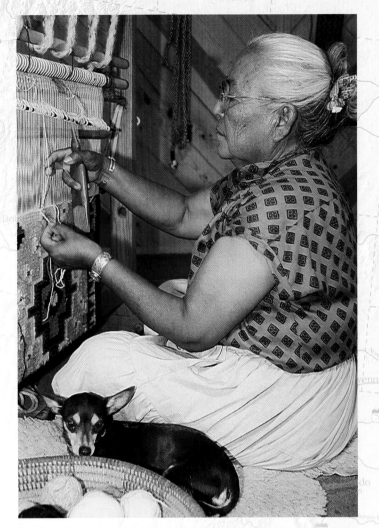

You can watch Navajo weavers like Sarah Natani demonstrate their craft on traditional looms in many places on the reservation.

annual Western Navajo Fair the second or third weekend in April.

The Hopi Reservation

Surrounded on all sides by the vast Navajo lands, the Hopi Reservation lies astride State 264, about midway between U.S. 89 on the west and U.S. 191 on the east. Related culturally to the Pueblo people of northern New Mexico, the Hopis, unlike the Navajos, live in fixed locations. Their villages are the focal points of their lives, and they have dwelt atop Black Mesa for centuries. (The village of Oraibi has been inhabited since about A.D. 1150, probably longer than any community in the nation.

From the time of their participation in the Pueblo Revolt of 1680, during which the Spanish were ejected from Indian lands, the Hopi people have remained culturally independent. Later Spanish conquests did not include the Hopis, and most of the tribe today continues to resist the influence of modern civilization. Religion plays a predominant role in their culture. Nowhere is this more evident than in their many colorful ceremonial dances, usually held from late December through July. Many dances are held on weekends, but dates and locations are not publicized; seeing them is usually a matter of luck. If you plan to be on the reservation, inquire at the Hopi Indian Agency in Keams Canyon (734-2441) or at the Hopi tribal headquarters in Kykotsmovi (734-2441).

Hopi Villages

By comparison to the Navajo's colorful landscape, the Hopi's mesa-top villages—dry, sunbaked, and often treeless—may seem desolate; when there's not a dance, very little attracts visitors. Even the residents are less colorfully adorned than the Navajos. But there's a certain mystique that intrigues even the most casual visitor.

Traveling west to east across the land of the Hopi, you'll pass by 12 villages. One of the largest, Moenkopi, dates from the late 1800s. Because it's situated near Tuba City, along U.S. 160, the village is one of the least traditional.

The road climbs gradually up to Third Mesa, about 45 miles from Moenkopi. Side roads lead to Bacabi and Hotevilla, both founded in the 20th century, and Old Oraibi. Kykotsmovi is a modern settlement, with tribal office, trading post, gas stations, and a grocery store, at the base of Third Mesa.

Though it's only 5 miles from Third Mesa, Second Mesa appears very remote. Three venerable villages occupy this thin mesa projection. Shungopovi, regarded as the religious heart of the Hopi world, is the site of many dances, the center for all the traditional Hopi crafts, and the best place for visitors to peek into tribal culture. Beside the highway on Second Mesa stands the Hopi Cultural Center, a complex that includes a motel, museum, restaurant, campground, and fine crafts shops.

It's a descent of about 8 miles from Second Mesa to the modern village of Polacca, today a center for Hopi potters, on First Mesa. Its convenient location attracts residents from the villages of Sichomovi, Hano, and Walpi. Walpi, which dates from the late 1600s, is considered the most visually stunning of the villages; its unpainted rock buildings seem to grow out of the ground.

Keams Canyon, about 11½ miles east of Polacca, is primarily a government town. The Keams Canyon Trading Post, Café, and Arts and Crafts Store displays some of the Hopis' finest work.

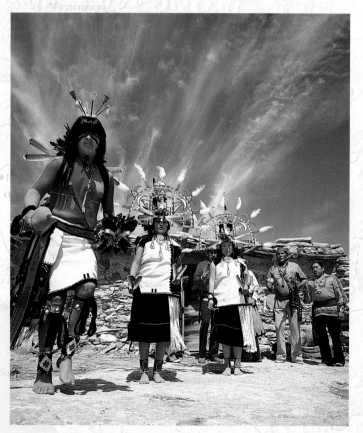

Hopi Butterfly Dancers perform ceremonial rites on their reservation at Second Mesa.

TRIP PLANNER

Unless otherwise noted, all area codes are 520. Lodging rates for two people range from $ (under $100) to $$$ (above $250) per night. The Navajo Indian Reservation goes on Mountain Daylight Time in summer, while the Hopis and the rest of Arizona remain on Mountain Standard Time.

WHERE

This journey covers the region's major attractions from east to west. If you start your trip in Flagstaff, northern Arizona's largest city, stop first at the Museum of Northern Arizona (3101 N. Fort Valley Rd.; 774-5211) to take a look at the best examples of Navajo and Hopi handicrafts.

TRIBAL PROTOCOL

Alcoholic beverages are not allowed on Indian reservations.

Visitors should not photograph Indians without permission; a gratuity is usually expected if permission is granted. Cameras, recording equipment, and even sketchpads are strictly forbidden at Hopi ceremonials.

LODGING

Navajo Nation Motor Inn (P.O. Drawer 2340, Window Rock, AZ 86515; 871-4108, 800/662-6189; $) has 56 air-conditioned rooms, a heated pool, and a café on the premises. At Canyon de Chelly, **Thunderbird Lodge** (P.O. Box 548, Chinle, AZ 86503; 674-5841; $-$$), with a cafeteria and Rug Room and Craft Shop, is located right at the canyon, just east of the visitor center. The area's other motor inns, **Best Western Canyon de Chelly Inn** (P.O. Box 295, Chinle, AZ 86503; 674-5875; $-$$) and **Holiday Inn Canyon de Chelly** (P.O. Box 1889, Chinle, AZ 86503; 674-5000; $-$$) are only a couple of miles away.

The only accommodation inside Monument Valley is **Goulding's Trading Post & Lodge** (Box 36001, Monument Valley, UT 84536; 435/727-3231; $$), just across the Arizona-Utah state line. Other lodging is in Kayenta, near the junction of U.S. 160 and 163.

The comfortable **Tuba City Quality Inn** (Box 247, Tuba City, AZ 86045; 283-4545; $) lies just behind the Tuba Trading Post next to the Hogan Restaurant. The centrally located **Hopi Cultural Center Motel** (P.O. Box 67, Second Mesa, AZ 86043; 734-2401; $) is the mesa's only accommodation. If the motel is full, drive 20 miles east to the very modest **Keams Canyon Motel** (Box 545, Keams Canyon, AZ 86043; 738-2297; $), with 18 rooms.

CAMPING

Cottonwood Campground (Canyon de Chelly; 674-5500), with 94 tent and RV sites, is well located in the trees at the mouth of the canyon. The Navajo-operated **Spider Rock RV and Camping Too** (South Rim Dr., Canyon de Chelly; 674-8261) has no hookups.

Goulding's Monument Valley Good Sam Park (see Lodging above) has full hookups on 50 sites, restrooms, showers, and a nearby store with gas pumps. **Navajo National Monument Campground** (672-2366) has 30 free tent and RV sites (no hookups or showers) near the Betatakin visitor center

Best bet for **camping on Black Mesa** is the campground adjacent to the Hopi Cultural Center and Motel on Second Mesa.

DINING

In Window Rock, the restaurant at the **Navajo Nation Motor Inn** (see Lodging above) has tribal specialties on the menu as well as other choices. The idea of a handsome cafeteria at

Canyon de Chelly's **Thunderbird Lodge** (see Lodging above) is a good one, particularly for families.

The **Holiday Inn Monument Valley** (Kayenta; 697-3221) restaurant serves some of the best food in this area. The **Stagecoach Dining Room** at Goulding's Lodge (see Lodging above) features American food with a few Navajo dishes. **Hashke Neiniih Restaurant** (Monument Valley Visitor Center; 435/727-3287) features Navajo food. Locals at the **Navajo Market Place** (U.S. 163 at Monument Valley turnoff) offer samples of their traditional food.

The **Hogan Restaurant** (Tuba City; 283-5260) sits between the trading post and the motel. For the best Navajo tacos, head for the **Tuba City Truck Stop Café** (U.S. 160 and 164; 283-4975). The **Hopi Cultural Center Restaurant** (see Lodging above) is one place you'll find Navajos as well as Hopis. It offers friendly service and interesting Hopi-American food, such as blue cornmeal pancakes, lamb stew, and posole (a corn dish).

TOURS

For close-up looks at the bottom of Canyon de Chelly, join one of the Navajo-led four-wheel-drive tours. Full- and half-day tours leave from the **Thunderbird Lodge** (see Lodging above). You may hike, ride horseback, or drive your own four-wheel-drive into the canyon, but you must be accompanied by a guide; check with the visitor center (674-5841).

FOR MORE INFORMATION

Navajo Tourism Department (P.O. Box 663, Window Rock, AZ 86515; 871-6436). Navajo Parks and Recreation Hopi Cultural Center (P.O. Box 67, Second Mesa, AZ 864043; 734-2401). Hopi Tribal Office of Public Relations (734-2441).

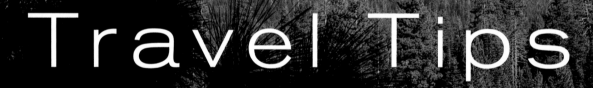

Travel Tips

SEASONAL TRAVEL   LONELY SUMMER PARKS

WINTER BEACHES & OCEAN RESORTS   SKI RESORTS

DUDE RANCHES   100 BEST CAMPGROUNDS

WEST'S BEST FESTIVALS & MORE

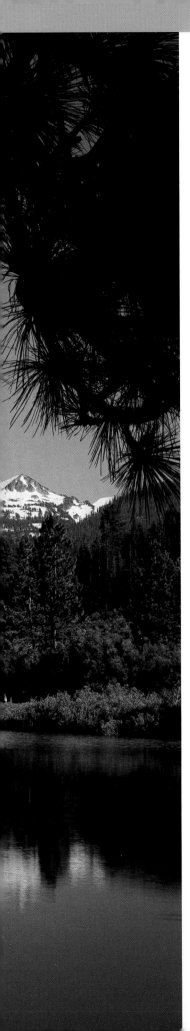

To help you get the most out of your travels throughout the West, our trips mention the best time to visit. Some are year-round destinations; others are best enjoyed in summer or winter. Many suggest spring or autumn as the optimum time of the year in terms of weather and seasonal color.

This chapter takes a closer look at seasonal travel in the West and highlights additional destinations for impromptu getaways—summer parks without crowds, the best beaches and ocean resorts for winter visits, good choices for skiing, and marvelous sites for viewing nature's displays of spring flowers and fall foliage. It also offers some of the West's top campgrounds, dude ranches, and regional festivals.

No matter when or where you travel, it's important to remember basic road and safety information. You'll find a few good ideas for desert and mountain driving and some sage advice for making the most of any travel with children or pets. For more information on state attractions, turn to the list of state tourist offices on page 237, a good resource for any Western adventure.

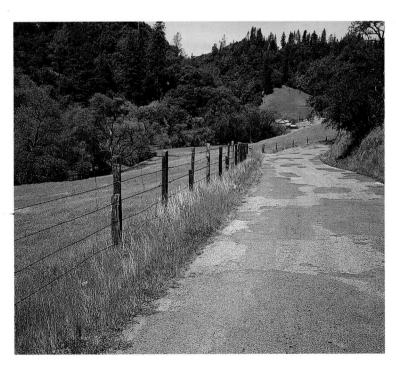

Our natural wariness of volcanoes has kept Lassen Volcanic National Park (left) unspoiled and beautiful.

Sheep Ranch Road (right) wanders through the Sierra Nevada foothills near Murphys.

SEASONAL TRAVEL

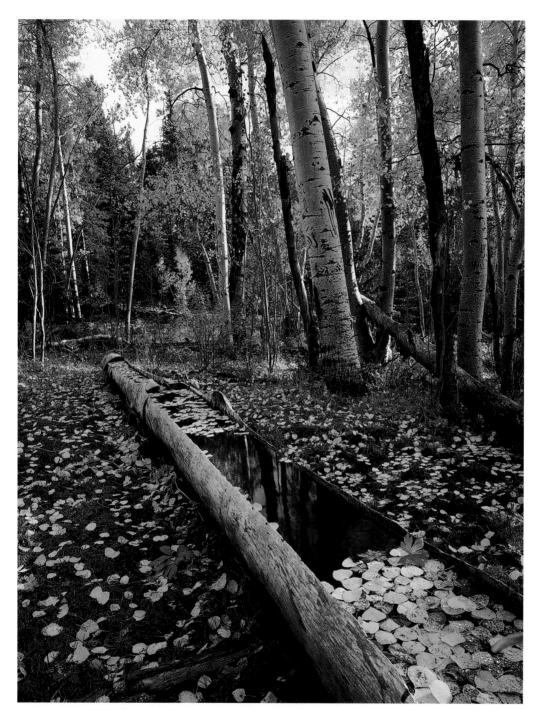

Golden aspen leaves float on the water in an old wooden watering trough in the White Mountains west of Alpine, Arizona.

Mother Nature puts on her best shows in spring and fall, adding vivid bursts of color to desert floors and mountain meadows in spring and illuminating high plateaus and mountainsides with scarlet and gold in autumn. These suggestions will help travelers enjoy these performances. Phone numbers are included for more information on areas and attractions.

Fall, a Golden Time of Year

In autumn, aspens splash their golden hue across mountainsides, maples tint forests with orange and red, and cottonwoods set canyons aflame. An area's peak color, however, depends on the weather and its elevation. When days shorten and the temperatures drop, trees go dormant, leaf chlorophyll diminishes, and the residual pigment shines forth. The high country of the Colorado Rockies will see color long before California's Sierra foothills, and the valleys throughout the West will be the last touched by Mother Nature's wand. You'll need to check locally to find out when color will be at its best for a particular region.

Arizona

From late September through mid-October, big-tooth maples, scarlet sumac, Virginia creeper, and aspens color the **Arizona Snowbowl** ski area near Flagstaff. Other leaf-peeping sites include the **White Mountains**, the **Mogollon Rim**, Sedona's **Oak Creek Canyon, Madera Canyon** near Tucson, and the **Chiricahua Mountains**. (For more information on state sites, call 888/520-3444) For a special fall treat, take the four-hour **San Pedro & Southwestern Railroad** excursion from Benson in southeastern Arizona (520/586-2266).

California

Any of the back roads in the **Sierra Nevada** foothills leads to spectacular fall color. Particular favorites for aspen viewing are State 4 into **Bear Valley** and State 88 into **Hope Valley** (209/795-1381). Don't want to drive? Take a 4-mile train ride aboard the **Yosemite Mountain–Sugar Pine Railroad** (209/683-7273).

Colorado

Trains are a popular form of leaf-peeping in this state. You might want to try a 45-minute trip on the **Cripple Creek & Victor Narrow Gauge Railroad** (719/689-2640) out of Cripple Creek into aspen country. The **Durango & Silverton Narrow Gauge Railroad** (970/247-2733) makes a nine-hour trip through the Animas River Valley into the San Juan Mountains. The **Georgetown Loop Railroad** (800/691-4386, 303/670-1686 or 569-2403) takes you over aspen-cloaked Clear Creek Canyon on the 95-foot-high Devil's Gate Bridge on a 70-minute trip to Silver Plume.

If you prefer driving, the following are some good bets for fall color: **Cottonwood Pass,** west of Buena Vista; **Guanella Pass Scenic & Historic Byway**, in Pike and Arapaho national forests; **McClure Pass**, outside of Carbondale; and **Independence Pass**, connecting Twin Lakes with Aspen.

Idaho

Two favorite foliage sites are the **White Pine Scenic Byway** (208/245-2531), which cuts through forests of larches, cottonwoods, and aspens east of Coeur d'Alene, and the **Cub River Canyon** (208/847-0375), with its fiery maples near Preston, south of Pocatello.

Montana

Beautiful **Flathead Lake valley** (406/644-2211) is noted for stands of cottonwoods. Another favorite is the mid-October show of larch at **Seely Lake** (406/677-2233), tucked between the jagged peaks of the Swan and Mission mountains, 59 miles northeast of Missoula.

Nevada

A 12-mile road snakes through **Lamoille Canyon** (800/715-9379), a glacier-carved gorge known as "the Yosemite of Nevada" by locals. It's located on the western side of the Ruby Mountains near Elko.

New Mexico

Enjoy great fall color on the 64-mile route of the **Cumbres & Toltec Scenic Railroad** (505/756-2151); the train climbs from 7,000 feet to 10,015 feet between Chama, New Mexico, and Antonito, Colorado.

Oregon

On a four-hour ride in October, **Mount Hood Railroad** (800/872-4661 or 503/386-3556) takes you through the Hood River Valley's pear and apple orchards and offers good views of bigtooth and vine maples and cottonwoods.

Utah

Two of this state's parks are prime spots for fall color. For maples, journey along the Ridgeline Loop Trail in **Wasatch Mountain State Park** (801/654-1791). The four-month fall color season at Zion National Park (801/772-3256) starts in the high country in mid-September and travels into the low country as late as mid-October and even early November, sometimes lasting into December.

For a leaf-viewing train trip, take the 3 1/2-hour **Heber Valley Railroad** (801/654-5601) excursion to Vivian Park.

Washington

In the **Okanogan Highlands** (509/486-2186), larch trees, the West's only deciduous conifer, line State 20 between Wauconda Pass and Sherman Pass near Republic, a 2 1/2-hour drive from Spokane.

Wildflowers: Spring's Colorful Show

The beginning of spring is heralded by a spectacular show of color that turns normally drab landscapes into a multihued floral festival. Taking time to savor this springtime beauty adds a special dimension to any Western vacation. Though the prime time for wildflower bloom is generally March to May, weather makes a difference in the timing and magnitude of a wildflower show. It's wise to call ahead to get the latest bloom information for the region you plan to visit.

Arizona

Lupine, owl's clover, Mexican gold poppies, and cactus flowers paint the desert of **Organ Pipe Cactus National Monument** (520/387-6849) in early April. (For cactus bloom times, contact the Desert Botanical Garden (602/941-1225.)

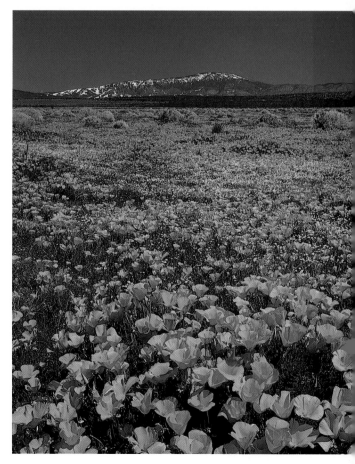

Acres of California poppies are preserved in Antelope Valley; Southern California's snow-covered Tehachapi Mountains rise in the background.

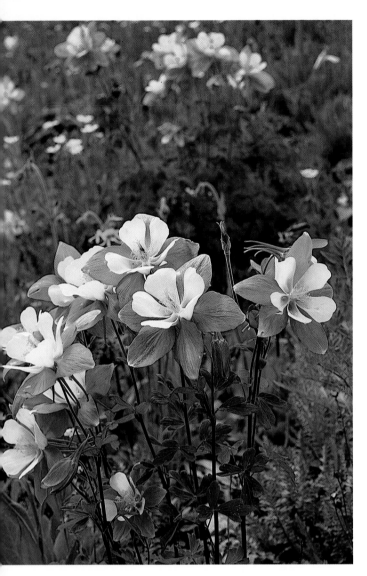

Popping up in late spring throughout Colorado's mountainous reaches, the delicate blue columbine is the state flower. Here it grows at Yankee Boy Basin, near Ouray.

California

Brilliant orange poppies are a mainstay in the **Antelope Valley California Poppy Reserve** at the edge of the Mojave Desert. The **Anza-Borrego** desert floor east of Julian offers primroses, sunflowers, and verbena. **Bear Valley** near Los Angeles boasts fields of blue lupines mixed with orange poppies, and the **Carrizo Plain** near San Luis Obispo puts on a wildflower show that includes goldfields, larkspur, and tidytips.

In the northern part of the state, **Mt. Diablo** in the San Francisco Bay area features classic natives like California poppies and Indian paintbrush, while **Pope Valley** near Napa is dotted with meadowfoam, owl's clover, and pink phlox. Other California wildflower sites include **Table Mountain** north of Oroville, **Toro County Park** west of Salinas, **Lower McGee**

Canyon south of Mammoth Lakes, and **Kern River Canyon** on State 178 between Bakersfield and Lake Isabella. (For general information on California wildflower bloom periods, contact the Theodore Payne Foundation, 818/768-3533.)

Colorado

Thanks to varying elevations, this state's bloom period stretches from late May through August. The blue columbine, Colorado's state flower, is the star of the show, and **Yankee Boy Basin** in southwestern Colorado is a favorite viewing stage. Other spots include **Maroon Creek Road** south of Aspen; the glacer-carved

One of the Northwest's most colorful spring destinations is Washington's Skagit Valley when the tulips are in bloom.

valleys above **Telluride, Silverton**, and **Ouray**; the meadows below **Crested Butte**; and **Rocky Mountain National Park**. (For more information on these and other wildflower-viewing sites, call 970/586-1206.)

Idaho

A variety of alpine flowers brightly color the high meadows and mountainsides in **Sawtooth National Recreation Area** (208/727-5013) from June through August.

Oregon/Washington

Spring blossoms are profuse along the **Columbia River Gorge**, where flowers bloom on both sides of the Columbia River from mid-April into June. Good viewing areas off State 14 (Washington side) include **Table Mountain, Dog and Wind mountains** near Home Valley, and **between Bingen and Lyle**. On the Oregon side of the river, the **Nature Conservancy's Tom McCall Preserve** in Rowena offers self-guided hikes.

Yellow John Day chaenactis, balsam root, and penstemon bloom on the flats and in the dry ravines creasing the usually barren sides of the **Painted Hills, John Day Fossil Beds** in eastern Oregon. Although not wildflowers, Washington's **Skagit Valley** is noted for its bountiful fields of blooming tulips in April. (For wildflower bloom information, contact 800/366-3530 in Oregon, 360/569-2211 in Washington.)

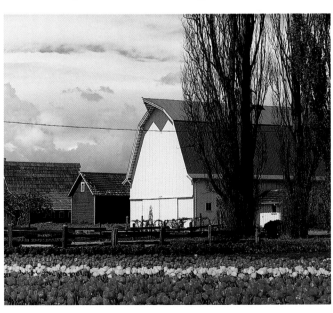

LONELY SUMMER PARKS

If you are seeking a place to soak up some of nature's grandeur undisturbed, you may be looking for a one of the West's less crowded parks. The following national parks and Bureau of Land Management holdings have yet to be discovered by hordes of people. Certainly none lacks for scenic splendor, so enjoy them while they are still lonely—and don't tell a soul.

Arizona

A 40-mile stretch of the San Pedro River, 65 miles southeast of Tucson, encompasses the **San Pedro Riparian National Conservation Area** (520/458-2266). It is home to some 80 percent of Arizona's bird species. A good way to view the region is on a four-hour **San Pedro & Southwestern Railroad** excursion out of Benson (520/586-2266).

California

The **Algodones Dunes** (760/337-4400), also known as the Imperial Sand Dunes, is a Sahara-like expanse of shifting sand east of Brawley, 150 miles from San Diego. Be sure to visit the 1/2-mile section of Plank Road, a reconstruction of what an earlier generation built to get across this inland sand sea

King Range National Conservation Area (707/986-7731) is a remote stretch of shoreline in Humboldt and Mendocino counties, with driftwood-strewn beaches, pounding surf, barking sea lions, and mountains with ferny dells touched by fog and dew. It's 230 miles north of San Francisco off State Highway 1.

Maybe it's the thought that Lassen Peak is one of the most volatile volcanoes in the lower 48 states; maybe it's the location in sparsely populated northeastern California, 250 miles from San Francisco. Whatever the reason, you can hike trails at **Lassen Volcanic National Park** (916/595-4444) undisturbed, enjoying the beauty of its craggy peaks, wildflower-painted meadows, and steaming thermals. Take scenic State 89 through the park,

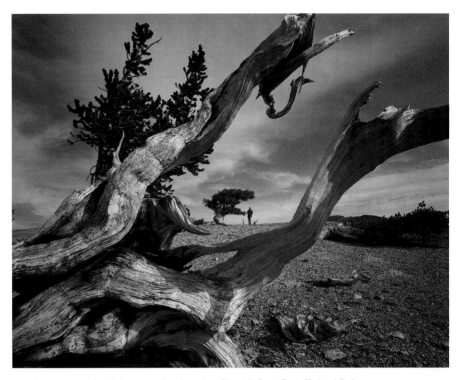

Traveler surveys ancient bristlecone pines in eastern Nevada's Great Basin National Park.

and don't miss Loomis Museum and Reflection Lake.

Redwood National Park (707/464-6101) encompasses three California state parks and half of the world's remaining stands of old-growth coastal redwoods. Don't miss Lady Bird Johnson Grove and Stout Memorial Grove, and drive along Davison Road, Coastal Drive, and Howland Hill Road. U.S. 101 runs through the park, located 300 miles north of San Francisco.

Colorado

Some 37,000 acres of spectacular alpine valleys are included in the **Redcloud Peak Wilderness Study Area** (916/595-4444), 320 miles southwest of Denver. Hike or take the Alpine Loop National Back Country Byway, an unpaved road. Cars can negotiate the south leg of the loop to the American Basin turnoff.

Nevada

Great Basin National Park (702/234-7331), in eastern Nevada just west of the Utah border, is an island of snow-capped green at the edge of the arid landscape of the Great Basin. Take the 12-mile

Wheeler Peak Scenic Drive; Nevada's only glacier is at the base of the peak. Don't miss limestone Lehman Caves either. The park is 200 miles southwest of Salt Lake City and 300 miles north of Las Vegas.

Utah

Anasazi Indian ruins lie throughout the tangle of canyons that make up the 37,580 acres of **Grand Gulch Primitive Area** (435/587-1500), located 350 miles southeast of Salt Lake City and 224 miles northeast of Flagstaff. In fact, the Cedar Mesa region, of which Grand Gulch is the centerpiece, is one of the nation's richest archaeological troves. The best way to explore is on foot. There are a number of full-day hikes.

Washington

In northern Washington, only 120 miles from Seattle, vast **North Cascades National Park** (360/856-5700, ext. 515) includes 318 glaciers and huge old forests of cedar and fir. You can cover the park by car in just a day, and, amazingly, it's one of the West's least-visited national parks.

WINTER BEACHES & OCEAN RESORTS

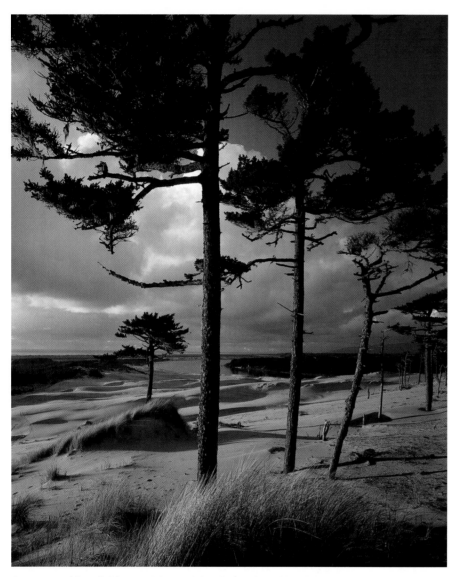

Oregon coast visitors find dunes and darn good chowder from Oceanside to Brookings.

The Pacific Ocean washes 7,863 miles of coastline in California, Oregon, and Washington. In winter, beaches are often lonely or dotted only with sparse crowds. If you like to run or walk along sandy shores, watch booming breakers, search for driftwood and shells, and cook a meal outdoors, head for the beach in winter. From north to south, the following collection surveys favorite stretches of sand and grand sites from which to enjoy a panoramic ocean view.

California Beaches

MacKerricher State Park (Fort Bragg; 707/964-7669; horseback riding). **Gualala Point Regional Park** (Gualala; perfect picnic spot). **Sonoma Coast State Beach** (707/875-3483; dozens of intimate sandy strands separated by rocky headlands dot 16 miles of coast stretching from Russian Gulch south to Bodega Head; popular family beaches include Goat Rock and Salmon Creek). **Drakes Beach** (Pt. Reyes National Seashore,

north of San Francisco; 415/663-1092; popular with hang gliders). **Cowell Ranch Beach** (off State 1, 2 miles south of Half Moon Bay; hidden sandy cove backed by steep cliffs). **Santa Cruz** (800/833-3494, Santa Cruz visitor information; 408/426-7433, Santa Cruz Boardwalk; great beach town with boardwalk, amusement park with roller coaster, municipal wharf). **Sand Dollar Beach** (Los Padres National Forest; 805/995-1976; wide, flat, gray sand beach on Big Sur coast 9 miles south of Lucia). **Jalama Beach** (20 miles southwest of Lompoc; 805/736-6316; one of the area's least crowded beaches). **El Capitan State Beach** (15 miles west of Santa Barbara; 800/444-7275 for reservations, 805/968-1033 for information; great campground). **Marina del Rey Swimming Beach** (310/305-9545; quiet cove with no waves, safe haven for toddlers). **Cabrillo Beach** (San Pedro; 310/548-7562; great tide pools, Cabrillo Marine Aquarium). **La Jolla Cove** (edge of San Diego–La Jolla Underwater Park, off Coast Blvd.; spiny lobsters and orange garibaldis thrive in sheltered cove).

California Beach Resorts

Stanford Inn by the Sea (Mendocino; 707/937-5615; rooms with fireplaces overlooking the bay). **Harbor House** (Elk; 707/877-3203; Craftsman-style 1916 redwood inn 17 miles south of Mendocino). **Whale Watch Inn by the Sea** (Gualala; 800/942-5342; rooms with decks, ocean views, fireplaces). **Spindrift Inn** (Monterey; 800/841-1879; fireplaces, window seats, feather beds). **Green Gables Inn** (Pacific Grove; 800/722-1774; 1888 inn with Victorian decor overlooking Monterey Bay). **The Inn at Spanish Bay** (Pebble Beach; 800/654-9300; posh resort on famed 17-Mile-Drive). **Lodge at Pebble Beach** (17-Mile-Drive; 800/654-9300; longtime favorite stop). **Mission Ranch** (Carmel; 800/538-

8221; country casual rooms in former 1850s dairy ranch). **Cliff House Inn** (Mussel Shoals, 10 minutes south of Santa Barbara; 800/892-5433; waves break within 20 feet of ocean-facing guest rooms). **Mandalay Beach Resort** (Oxnard; 800/362-2779; ocean views out to Channel Islands from upper-floor room balconies). **Malibu Beach Inn** (Malibu; 800/462-5428; oceanfront rooms just steps away from the pounding surf). **Shutters on the Beach** (Santa Monica; 800/334-9000; circa 1920s beach house set on liveliest section of beach in Southern California). **Surf and Sand Hotel** (Laguna Beach; 800/267-4378; soak up winter sunsets on private balconies). **Crystal Pier Hotel** (Pacific Beach, San Diego; 800/748-5894; circa 1930s blue-trimmed, white cottages on the pier with picket-fenced decks leaning over the Pacific). **Hotel Del Coronado** (Coronado; 800/468-3533; largest West Coast beachfront resort; circa 1888).

Oregon Beaches

Cape Lookout State Park (Tillamook; 800/452-5687, reservations; 800/551-6949, information; nestled between Netarts Spit and jutting Cape Lookout, it's a great place to pitch a tent). **Nye Beach** (Newport; perfect to stroll, particularly by moonlight). **Oregon Dunes National Recreation Area** (541/271-3611; 40 miles of incredible sand dunes stretching from Florence to Coos Bay). **Sunset Bay State Park** (541/888-4902; state's best swimming beach; small, shallow bay protected from big breakers with no riptides). **New River** (between Bandon and Cape Blanco; 541/274-7074; miles of uninterrupted beach backed by grassy dunes and shore pines). **Brookings** (800/535-9469; this stretch of coast boasts sunshine and warm temperatures).

Oregon Beach Resorts

Hallmark Resort (Cannon Beach; 800/345-5676; wood-shingled resort clings to a bluff above Haystack Rock beach). **House on the Hill** (Oceanside; 503/842-6030; popular place with down-home charm and dynamite vistas). **Channel House Inn** (Depoe Bay; 800/447-2140; many rooms with spas

and fireplaces overlooking Depoe Bay Channel). **Salishan Lodge** (Gleneden Beach; 800/452-2300; one of the state's best beach retreats; memorable dining). **Cliff House** (Waldport; 541/563-2506; four-room B&B perched on a cliff at Alsea River's mouth). **Heceta Head Lighthouse** (Yachats; 541/547-3696; rooms in a 104-year-old lightkeeper's quarters). **Overleaf Lodge** (Yachats; 800/338-0507; views of waves shooting up through holes in an eroded basalt ledge). **See Vu Motel** (Yachats; 541/547-3227; unassuming spot to suit any budget). **Sea Quest Bed & Breakfast** (Yachats; 541/547-3782; 5 rooms with ocean views, spas, private entrances). **Sunset Oceanfront Accommodations** (Bandon; 800/842-2407; self-proclaimed storm-watching capital of the world).

Washington & British Columbia Beaches

Spencer Spit State Park (Lopez Island; 800/452-5687, camping reservations; 800/233-0321, information; spit grows or shrinks depending on the tide; walk-in campsites and picnicking). **Alki Beach** (West Seattle; 2-mile stretch of beach with picnic tables and knockout views of downtown Seattle). **Ozette Loop Hike** (Olympic National Park; 360/452-0300, camping reservations; 360/452-0330, information; it's a long drive and hike to

this beautiful wilderness beach on the Olympic Peninsula). **Long Beach** (800/451-2542; kite flying is king on 28 miles of sandy beach at the state's oldest coastal resort). **Fort Canby State Park** (800/452-5687, cabin and yurt reservations; 800/233-0321, information; storms dump driftwood on Benson and Waikiki beaches where ocean and Columbia River meet at Cape Disappointment).

Washington & British Columbia Beach Resorts

Sooke Harbor House (Whiffen Spit, Vancouver Island; 250/642-3421; internationally known retreat with water-view rooms and gourmet dining). **Wickaninnish Inn** (west side of Vancouver Island; 800/333-4604; with fireplaces, views, and yellow rain slickers). **Inn at Semi-Ah-Moo** (Blaine; 800/770-7992; spa treatments and golf at a resort just this side of the Canadian border). **Roche Harbor Resort** (San Juan Islands; 800/451-8910; a boaters' haven; condo units sport fireplaces, water views). **Langley** (Whidbey Island; 360/221-6765; shop for art on town's cliff-hugging main street; overnight at Inn at Langley; 360/221-3033). **Kalaloch Lodge** (Olympic Peninsula; 360/962-2271; rustic cabins for romantic getaways on beach). **Iron Springs Resort** (Copalis Beach; 360/276-4230; homey cottages overlooking beach).

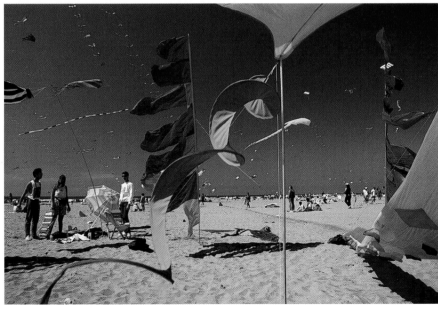

Kites play at Washington's Long Beach, an old coastal resort that is home to the World Kite Museum and Hall.

SKIING IN THE WEST

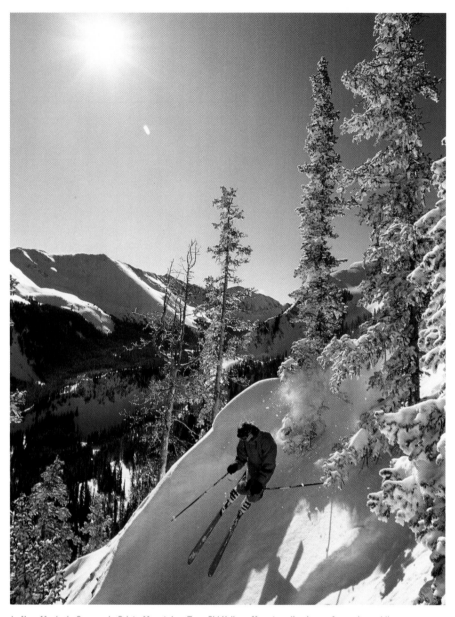

In New Mexico's Sangre de Cristo Mountains, Taos Ski Valley offers tree-lined runs for serious skiing.

As soon as mountain peaks wear their first dusting of snow, avid skiers are ready to schuss down slopes. The resorts below are a sampling of the West's best ski centers.

Arizona

Skiing may not leap to mind when you think of Arizona, but the state has several sites. In the San Francisco Peaks north of Flagstaff lie **Arizona Snowbowl** and **Flagstaff Nordic Center** (520/779-1951). **Mt. Lemmon Ski Valley** (520/576-1321) is just outside Tucson. **Sunrise Park Resort** (602/735-7600), run by the Apache Indians, is in the White Mountains east of Phoenix.

California

The Sierra Nevada offers a host of skiing opportunities. Lake Tahoe's ski resorts include **Alpine Meadows** (916/583-4232; 100+ runs), **Boreal** (916/426-3666; 41 runs), **Diamond Peak** (702/832-1177; 30 runs; cross-country; children's center), **Donner** (916/426-3635; 45 runs), **Heavenly** (702/586-7000; ski in two states), **Mt. Rose** (702/849-0704; 43 runs; highest Tahoe base elevation), **Northstar-at-Tahoe** (916/562-1010; 63 runs; cross-country), **Ski Homewood** (916/525-2992; 57 runs; children's day care), **Squaw Valley** (916/583-6985; wide-open skiing), **Sugar Bowl** (916/426-9000; 79 runs), and **Tahoe Donner** (530/587-9444; 14 runs; cross-country).

To the south lie **Kirkwood** (209/258-6000; 68 runs; cross-country), **Bear Valley** (209/753-2301; 60 runs; cross-country), **Dodge Ridge** (209/965-3474; 42 runs), and **Badger Pass** (Yosemite National Park; 209/372-1000; 9 runs; cross-country).

Southern Californians head for **Mt. Baldy** near Los Angeles (909/982-0800; 26 runs) or drive to **Mammoth Mountain** (760/934-2571; 150 runs) and **June Mountain** (619/648-7733; 35 runs) on the Sierras' eastern flank.

Colorado

Colorado's magnificent Rockies offer great snow, packed-powder runs, open bowls, and forested glades. Aspen, Telluride, and Vail are household words to skiers. Aspen, 220 miles from Denver, is a playground for the rich and famous, with elegant shops, hostelries, and restaurants. Ski areas include **Aspen Buttermilk** (970/925-1220; 43 runs; a good place to learn), **Aspen Highlands** (970/925-1220; 98 runs; stunning views; cross-country), **Aspen Mountain** (970/925-1220; 76 runs; cross-country), and **Aspen Snowmass** (970/925-1220, 83 runs; cross-country).

Other famous resorts include **Beaver Creek** (110 miles west of Denver; 970/949-5750; 146 runs; outdoor escalator transports skiers from parking lot to lifts; cross-country), **Breckenridge** (101 miles west of Denver; 800/789-7669; 139 runs; cross-country), **Purgatory** (150 miles from Grand Junction; 970/247-9000; 75 runs; cross-country),

Steamboat Springs (157 miles northwest of Denver; 970/879-6111; 140 runs; cross-country), **Telluride** (100 miles west of Denver; 800/801-4832; 65 runs; cross-country), and **Vail** (140 miles east of Grand Junction; 970/476-5601; 174 runs; cross-country).

Idaho

According to ads, the state offers skiers some of the longest runs, deepest powder, most exciting backcountry trails, and fewest crowds. **Sun Valley** (800/634-3347; 78 runs) is the most famous of the state's ski areas. Others include **Bogus Basin** (16 miles from Boise; 208/332-5151; 49 runs), **Brundage Mountain** (8 miles north of McCall; 800/888-7544; 36 runs), **Lookout Pass** (two hours from Spokane and 12 miles west of Wallace; 208/744-1301; 12 runs; affordable for families; cross-country), **Pebble Creek** (just south of Pocatello; 208/775-4452; 25 runs), **Pomerelle** (in Sawtooth National Forest, 75 miles from Pocatello; 208/638-5599; 22 runs; caters to families; cross-country), **Schweitzer Mountain Resort** (86 miles northeast of Spokane, near Sandpoint; 800/831-8810; 55 runs; cross-country), and **Silver Mountain** (on north-facing slope of Bitterroot Range at Kellogg; 208/783-1111; 50 runs).

Montana

The nation's fourth-largest state boasts more than 14,000 acres of skiing, 548 runs, 65 lifts, and 15 downhill ski areas. Among them are **Big Mountain** (8 miles north of Whitefish; 800/858-3913; 67 runs; cross-country), **Big Sky** (43 miles south of Bozeman; 800/548-4486; 75 runs; cross-country), **Bridger Bowl** (16 miles northwest of Bozeman; 800/223-9609; 60 runs), **Discovery Basin** (23 miles west of Anaconda at Georgetown Lake; 406/563-2184; 40 runs; cross-country), **Lost Trail Powder Mountain** (90 miles south of Missoula; 406/821-3211; 18 runs), **Montana Snowbowl** (12 miles northwest of Missoula; 800/728-2695; 35 runs), **Red Lodge** (1 hour southwest of Billings; 800/444-8977; 70 runs), and **Showdown Ski Area** (1 hour southeast of Great Falls; 800/433-0022; 34 runs; cross-country).

Nevada

(Nevada shares California listing for Lake Tahoe.)

New Mexico

Sandia Peak (505/856-6419; 25 runs), a short drive from Albuquerque, offers the world's longest tram and sports great views. Most of New Mexico's other ski resorts lie around Taos, including **Angel Fire** (22 miles east of Taos; 800/633-7463; 69 runs; good value for families), **Red River Ski Area** (45 minutes north of Taos; 505/754-2223; 58 runs), and **Taos Ski Valley** (Sangre de Cristo Mountains, about a half-hour northeast of Taos; (505/776-2291; 72 runs). Just two hours from El Paso on State 532 is **Ski Apache** (505/336-4356; 55 runs), owned and operated by the Mescalero Apache tribe.

Oregon

Mt. Hood, looming above the Columbia River east of Portland, is Oregon's main ski area. Mountain resorts include **Cooper Spur** (northeastern slope; 503/352-7803; gentle runs; affordable prices), **Mt. Hood Meadows** (sunny east side; 800-754-4663; 87 runs; varied terrain; cross-country), **Mt. Hood SkiBowl** (closest to Portland; 800/754-2695; 34 runs; extensive night skiing), **Summit Ski Area** (mountain's oldest ski area; (503/272-0256; 10 runs; ideal for families; cross-country), and **Timberline** (503/272-3311; 31 runs; Oregon's only "ski in, ski out" resort).

Utah

Many downhill ski centers are located in the northern mountains, many a short drive from Salt Lake City: **Alta** (Wasatch/Cache National Forest, 33 miles from Salt Lake City; 801/359-1078; 40 runs), **Brighton** (top of Big Cottonwood Canyon, 30 minutes southeast of Salt Lake City; 800/873-5512; 64 runs; family friendly; good value), **The Canyons** (32 miles east of Salt Lake City; 888/226-9667; 100 runs; 2,700 acres of varied terrain), **Deer Valley** (Park City, 36 miles from Salt Lake City; 800/558-3337; 84 runs), **Park City** (800/222-7275; 97 runs), **Powder Mountain** (55 miles north of Salt Lake City; 801/745-3772; 72 runs; deep powder; varied terrain; family

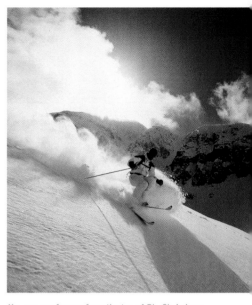

You can see forever from the top of Big Sky's Lone Peak; your descent starts from 11,150 feet, well above tree line.

fun), **Snowbird**; (29 miles from Salt Lake City; 800/385-2002; 66 runs; diverse terrain), **Solitude** (28 miles from Salt Lake City; 800/748-4754; 63 runs; cross-country), and **Sundance** 55 minutes from Salt Lake City; 800/892-1600; 41 runs).

Washington

Because many of the state's ski resorts are less than a two-hour drive from metropolitan areas, night skiing programs are among the country's best. Ski areas include **White Pass** (3½-hour drive from Seattle and Portland; 509/453-8731; 32 runs; laid-back; family place) and **49 Degrees North** (1 hour north of Spokane; 509/935-6649; 35 runs).

Wyoming

Wyoming's average snowfall ranges between 200 and 500 inches per winter. Enjoying this bountiful harvest are **Hogadon Ski Resort** (on Casper Mountain, 11 miles south of Casper; 307/235-8499; 19 runs), **Grand Targhee** (42 miles northwest of Jackson near Alta; 307/353-2300; 63 runs), **Jackson Hole Ski Resort** (Teton Village, 12 miles northwest of Jackson; 800/443-6931; 75 runs; continuous vertical drop of 4,139 feet), **Antelope Butte** (60 miles west of Sheridan; 307/655-9530; 19 runs), and **Snowy Range** (32 miles west of Laramie; 800/462-7669; 25 runs).

SADDLE UP!

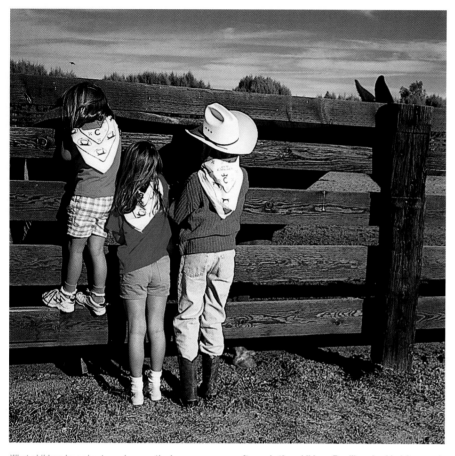

What children love about ranches are the horses, games, crafts, and other children. Families should pick a ranch with a well-organized kids' program.

This roundup of Western ranches is a sampling of what's available. Ranch vacations, including meals, range from $1,000–$2,000/person/week, $200–$300/person/day for ranches accepting guests for less than a week. Southwestern dude ranches are generally open from fall through early spring; summer is prime time for ranches farther to the north. Some ranches welcome guests year-round.

For more listings, contact the following: Arizona Dude Ranch Association, Box 603, Cortaro, AZ 85652; British Columbia Guest Ranch Association (800/663-6000); Colorado Dude & Guest Ranch Association (970/887-3128); Idaho Guest and Dude Ranch Association (208/633-3217); Wyoming Dude Ranchers (307/455-2584); and Dude Ranchers' Association (970/223-8440).

Ranches with History

Rancho de los Caballeros, Wickenburg, Arizona, has been entertaining families since 1947 (60 miles northwest of Phoenix; 520/684-5484; horseback riding, tennis, golf, skeet and trap, square dancing; children's program). **Bar Lazy J Guest Ranch, Parshall, Colorado**, opened its doors to well-heeled Eastern anglers in 1912 (110 miles northwest of Denver, near Grand Lake; 970/725-3437; heated pool/whirlpool, horseback riding, fly-fishing, square dancing, children's games). **63 Ranch, Livingston, Montana**, is listed on the National Register of Historic Places (12 miles southeast of Livingston; 406/222-0570; horseback riding, fly-fishing, square dancing, pack trips, chance to work cattle for experienced riders). **Eaton's Ranch, Wolf, Wyoming**, is where the social elite flocked in the

1920s (18 miles west of Sheridan; 800/210-1049, 307/655-9285; horseback riding, fly-fishing, hiking, cookouts, swimming; children's program).

Good Value Ranches

Coulter Lake Guest Ranch, Colorado, is an old-fashioned ranch (85 miles northeast of Grand Junction, near Rifle; 800/858-3046; horseback riding, relaxed schedule). **Sundance Trail Guest Ranch, Red Feather Lakes, Colorado**, is a family ranch with a wide array of activities (35 miles northwest of Fort Collins; 800/357-4930). **Beartooth Ranch, near Nye, Montana**, is adjacent to the Absaroka-Beartooth Wilderness Area (90 miles southwest of Billings; 406/328-6194; trail rides, square dancing, horseshoes, cookouts, hiking, fishing). **G Bar M Ranch, near Clyde Park, Montana**, invites guests to join in chores (26 miles northeast of Bozeman; 406/686-4423; fishing, hiking, trail rides). **Sweet Grass Ranch, near Big Timber, Montana**, offers day rides and pack trips around the area (115 miles northeast of Bozeman; 406/537-4477; horseback riding, ranch chores). **Hartley Guest Ranch, near Roy, New Mexico**, has guests participate in ranch life (220 miles northeast of Albuquerque; 800/687-3833). **Bar M Ranch, near Adams, Oregon**, lies along the Umatilla River and has pools fed by hot springs and a trout-stocked pond for kids (30 miles east of Pendleton; 541/566-3381; basketball, square dancing).

For a Learning Experience

Tanque Verde Guest Ranch, Tucson, Arizona (800/234-3833; bird-watching, nature walks in the Sonoran Desert, nightly lectures). **Lone Mountain Ranch, Big Sky, Montana** (45 miles south of Bozeman; 406/995-4644; luxury plus bird walks, fly-fishing program, classes in medicinal plants, orienteering). **Pine Butte Guest Ranch, near Choteau, Montana** (90 miles northwest of Great Falls; 406/466-2158; horseback riding, visits to Egg Mountain dinosaur dig with paleontologist, nature workshop series). **Breteche Creek Ranch, near Cody, Wyoming** (100 miles south of Billings; 307/587-3844; wildlife biology, photography, writing, geology, and horsemanship programs). **T-A Ranch, Buffalo, Wyoming** (30 miles south of Sheridan; 800/368-7398; fly-fishing; Bozeman Trail and Women in the West seminars).

Deluxe Ranch Resorts

Merv Griffin's **Wickenburg Inn & Dude Ranch, Wickenburg, Arizona** (60 miles northwest of Phoenix; 800/942-5362; swimming pool, spa, tennis, horseback riding, hiking, rodeos, cattle drives). **Echo Valley Resort, British Columbia** (30 miles northwest of Clinton; 800/253-8831; luxurious log cabins, fully equipped exercise room with massage and spa facilities). **C Lazy U Ranch, near Granby, Colorado** (95 miles west of Denver; 970/887-3344; cookouts, square dancing, swimming, massage, nearby golf). **Home Ranch, near Clark, Colorado** (18 miles north of Steamboat Springs; 970/879-9044; luxurious log cabins; hiking, horseback riding, barn dances, cookouts, guided fishing). **Wit's End Guest Ranch & Resort, Vallecito Lake, Colorado** (25 mile northeast of Durango; 800/236-9483, 970/884-4113; stylish cabins; tennis, swimming, hayrides, fly-fishing). **Mountain Sky Guest Ranch, near Emigrant, Montana** (60 miles south of Bozeman; 800/548-3392; luxurious lodging, gourmet meals; tennis, swimming; well-organized children's program). **Triple Creek Ranch, near Darby, Montana** (70 miles south of Missoula; 406/821-4600; log cabins; hiking, fishing, tennis, swimming, horseback riding; must be 16 or older). **Lodge at Chama, New Mexico** (90 miles north of Santa Fe; 505/756-2133; upscale hunting and fishing retreat; no families).

Short-Stay Ranches

Flying E Ranch, Wickenburg, Arizona (60 miles northwest of Phoenix; 520/684-2690; began as fly-in ranch with its own airstrip in 1940s; genteel Western ambience; horseback riding). **Rancho de la Osa, Sasabe, Arizona** (67 miles southwest of Tucson; 520/823-4257; elegant, but friendly; horseback riding, cooking demonstrations, cycling, birding, stargazing, fiestas, swimming pool). **Highland Ranch, near Philo, California** (125 miles north of San Francisco; 707/895-3600; horseback riding, fishing, tennis; two-night minimum). **Idaho Rocky Mountain Ranch, near Stanley, Idaho** (130 miles east of Boise; 208/774-3544; classic hand-hewn cabins and lodge, gourmet meals; pool fed by hot springs, horseback riding, mountain biking, fishing). **Hidden Valley Guest Ranch, near Cle Elum, Washington** (95 miles east of Seattle; 800/526-9269; family-run, low-key; horseback riding, fishing, mountain biking, bird-watching, pool/hot tub; two-night minimum, weekends). **Spear-O-Wigwam Ranch, Wyoming** (in Bighorn National Forest, 30 miles southwest of Sheridan; 888/818-3833; Ernest Hemingway stayed here in the 1920s; informal riding program, cookouts, swimming, boating; three-night minimum).

Working Ranches

Horseshoe Ranch, Bloody Basin Road, Arizona (65 miles north of Phoenix, near Mayer; 520/632-8813; experienced riders 12 and over help work cattle on 75,000-acre ranch; hearty family-style meals; three-night minimum). **Hunewill Circle H Guest Ranch, near Bishop, California** (foot of the eastern Sierras, about 120 miles south of Reno, Nevada; 702/465-2201, Oct.15–May 15, 760/932-7710; May 15–Oct. 15; horseback riding, campfire sing-alongs, hayrides, horseshoes; cattle roundup in September, 60-mile cattle drive in November, and cattle working in June and September for intermediate to advanced riders). **Vista Verde Guest Ranch, Colorado** (25 miles north of Steamboat Springs; 800/526-7433; old homestead ranch with luxury log cabins; fly-fishing, rafting, hot tubs, spa, gourmet meals;

optional cattle work, with two cattle drives a year). **Schively Ranch, near Pryor, Montana** (50 miles south of Billings; 307/548-6688; you feel more like a ranch hand than a dude; no organized programs; plenty of cattle work all summer, roundups in spring and fall). **Spur Cross Ranch, Golconda, Nevada** (18 miles east of Winnemucca; 800/651-4567; working ranch in the high-desert sagebrush; simple, clean accommodations). **Hideout at Flitner Ranch, Wyoming** (65 miles east of Cody; 800/354-8637; work cattle, brand, and join in other ranch activities; three-night minimum).

Children's Programs

Big Bar Guest Ranch, British Columbia (30 miles northwest of Clinton; 250/459-2333; casual atmosphere with boating, fishing, gold panning, river rafting, wilderness tours). **Rankin Ranch, California** (in Walkers Basin in the Tehachapi Mountains, 45 miles northeast of Bakersfield; 805/867-2511; working ranch with great children's programs, petting farm, treasure hunts, arts and crafts, swim meets). **Spanish Springs Ranch, near Ravendale, California** (160 miles east of Redding; 800/272-8282; varied horseback riding programs for ages 5 and up, weekly rodeo). **Lost Valley Ranch, Sedalia, Colorado** (65 miles southwest of Denver; 303/647-2311; families design a brand to burn onto the dining room's pine walls; excellent teen program). **Wilderness Trails Ranch, Colorado** (35 miles northeast of Durango; 800/527-2624, 970/247-0722; solid riding program, rafting, pack trips, cattle drives). **Nine Quarter Circle Ranch, Montana** (on Taylor Fork River, 60 miles south of Bozeman; 406/995-4276; for families with children, from infants to high schoolers; horseback riding, square dancing, nature talks, star walks). **Rock Springs Guest Ranch, Oregon** (10 miles northwest of Bend; 800/225-3833; great meals; special touches for kids, hayrides, talent shows, youth counselors). **Paradise Guest Ranch, Buffalo, Wyoming** (33 miles south of Sheridan; 307/684-7876; good food; horseback riding; children's program with arts and crafts, ice cream socials, kids' rodeo).

WEST'S 100 BEST CAMPGROUNDS

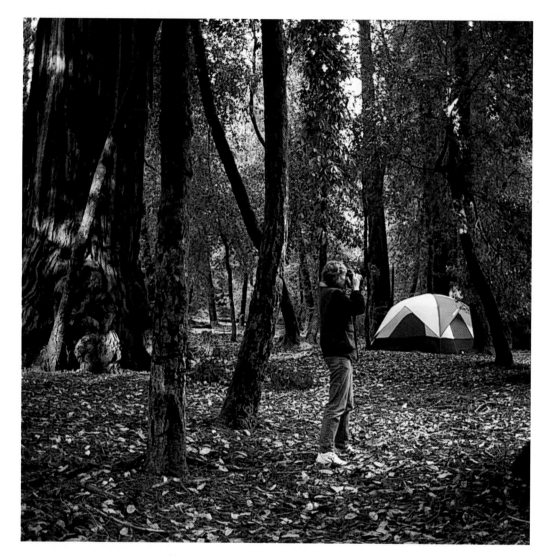

Camp among the redwoods at Big Basin State Park, one of Northern California's most popular getaways.

Camping is a good way to experience the West's great outdoors for a weekend getaway or longer. The following list of public campgrounds features places to pitch your tent or park your RV far from the bright lights. Campgrounds fill up quickly, particularly on weekends and during peak seasons. Some facilities may be closed in the off-season, so call ahead. Water, picnic tables, fire rings/grills, and toilets are included, except where noted. Some sites have RV dump stations.

ARIZONA

Bonito (10 miles north of Flagstaff off U.S. 89; 43 campsites; 800/280-2267 for reservations, 602/526-0866 for information). **Cholla** (off State 188 on Roosevelt Lake, 40 miles north of Globe; 206 campsites; no reservations; 602/467-3200). **Dead Horse Ranch State Park** (20 miles southwest of Sedona; 45 campsites; no reservations; 602/634-5283). **Hawley Lake** (on State 473, 8 miles south of State 260; 200 campsites; no reservations; 520/335-7511). **Picacho Peak State Park** (35 miles northwest of Tucson; 109 campsites; no reservations; 602/466-3183). **Pineflat** (12 miles north of Sedona off State 89A; 58 campsites; 800/280-2267 for reservations, 602/282-4119 for infor-

mation). **Roper Lake State Park** (5 miles south of Safford; 71 campsites; no reservations; 602/428-6760). **Tuweep** (North Rim of the Grand Canyon, 55 miles by graded dirt road from State 389 at Colorado City; 11 campsites; no water, gas, or RVs; free; no reservations; 520/638-7888).

CALIFORNIA

(Unless otherwise noted, call 800/444-7275 for campground reservations.) **Albee Creek** (40 miles south of Eureka just west of U.S. 101, in Humboldt Redwoods State Park; 39 campsites; 707/946-2409). **Big Basin State Park** (25 miles southwest of San Jose, off State 9 on State 236; 145 campsites, 35 tent cabins; 800/874-8368 for tent cabin reservations, 408/338-8860 for information). **Burnt Rancheria** (9 1/2 miles north of I-8 near Mt. Laguna; 110 campsites; 800/280-2267 for reservations, 530/445-6235 for information). **Castle Crags State Park** (45 miles north of Redding off I-5; 64 campsites; 530/235-2684). **Del Valle Regional Park** (8 miles south of Livermore off I-580; 150 campsites; 510/562-2267 for reservations, 510/373-0332 for information). **D. L. Bliss State Park** (13 miles north of U.S. 50 off State 89 at Lake Tahoe; 168

campsites; 530/525-7277). **Doheny State Beach** (Dana Point Harbor; 121 sites; 949/496-6172). **El Capitan State Beach** (20 miles north of Santa Barbara on U.S. 101; 140 campsites; 805/968-1033). **Gold Bluffs Beach** (Prairie Creek Redwoods State Park, about 4 miles north of Orick; 25 campsites; no reservations; 707/445-6547, ext. 10). **Grover Hot Springs State Park** (west of Markleeville in the Sierras off State 89; 76 campsites; 530/694-2248). **Hole-in-the-Wall** (Mojave National Preserve, 20 miles north of Essex Road exit off I-40; 35 campsites; no reservations; 760/733-4040). **Idyllwild** (Mt. Jacinto State Park, less than 1 mile north of Idyllwild off State 243; 33 campsites; 909/659-2607). **Indian Well**, (Lava Beds National Monument, 25 miles south of Tulelake and State 139; 40 campsites; no reservations; 530/667-2282). **Jalama Beach County Park** (20 miles southwest of Lompoc; 110 campsites; no reservations; 805/736-6316). **Kirk Creek** (off State 1 on the Big Sur coast, 4 miles south of Lucia; 33 campsites; no reservations; 805/995-1976). **Lake Almanor** (40 miles southeast of Lassen Peak off State 89; 101 campsites; 800/280-2267 for reservations, 916/258-2141 for information). **Lake Mary** (8 miles west of Mammoth Junction; 48 campsites; no reservations; 760/924-5500). **Lions Canyon** (15 miles northwest of Ojai; 30 campsites; no reservations; 805/646-4348). **MacKerricher State Park** (3 miles north of Fort Bragg; 142 campsites; 707/937-5804). **McArthur-Burney Falls State Park** (65 miles northeast of Redding off State 89; 128 campsites; 530/335-2777). **Montana de Oro State Park** (7 miles south of Morro Bay; 50 campsites; 805/528-0513). **New Brighton State Beach** (8 miles south of Santa Cruz; 112 campsites; 408/464-6330). **Paso Picacho** (11 miles south of Julian on State 79, in Cuyamaca Rancho State Park; 85 campsites; 760/765-0755). **Pfeiffer Big Sur State Park** (25 miles south of Carmel off State 1 in Big Sur; 218 campsites; 408/667-2315). **Plumas-Eureka State Park** (about 45 miles north of Truckee off State 89; 67 campsites; no reservations; 530/836-2380). **Portola**

Redwoods State Park (9 miles southeast of La Honda off State 35; 60 campsites; 650/948-9098). **Quaking Aspen** (45 miles east of Porterville off State 190; 32 campsites; 800/280-2267 for reservations, 209/539-2607 for information). **Rock Creek Lake** (7 miles southwest of Tom's Place, off U.S. 395; 28 campsites; no reservations; 760/873-2500). **Salt Point State Park** (20 miles north of Jenner; 139 campsites; 707/847-3221). **Wildrose** (30 miles south of Stovepipe Wells off State 190; 30 campsites, no fire rings/grills; free; no reservations; 760/786-2331). **William Heise County Park** (2 miles south of Julian; 103 campsites; 760/565-3600 for reservations). **Woods Lake** (in El Dorado National Forest, about 2 miles west of Carson Pass, off State 88; 25 campsites, hand-pumped water, no fire rings/grills; no reservations; 916/644-6048).

COLORADO

Avalanche Creek (3 miles east of State 133 on the edge of the Maroon Bells Wilderness Area; 13 campsites; no reservations; 970/963-2266). **Cayton** (43 miles northeast of Dolores off State 145; 27 campsites; no reservations; 970/882-7296). **Lost Park** (25 miles east of Jefferson off U.S. 285; 10 campsites; no reservations; 719/836-2031). **Moraine Park** (5 miles west of Estes Park off U.S. 36 in Rocky Mountain National Park; 247 campsites; 800/365-2267 for

reservations, 970/586-1206 for information). **Steamboat Lake State Park** (from U.S. 40 in Steamboat Springs, take County 129 north about 25 miles; 183 campsites; 800/678-2267 for reservations, 970/879-3922 for information). **Stillwater** (9 miles north of Granby off U.S. 34 at Granby Reservoir; 127 campsites; 800/280-2267 for reservations, 970/887-4100 for information).

IDAHO

Alturas Inlet (39 miles north of Sun Valley, off State 75 in the Sawtooth National Recreation Area; 32 campsites; no reservations; 208/774-3000). **Hells Gate State Park** (4 miles south of Lewiston and U.S. 12 on the Snake River; 93 campsites; 208/799-5015). **Henry's Lake State Park** (15 miles west of Yellowstone National Park off State 87; 48 campsites; 208/558-7532). **Heyburn State Park** (5 miles east of Plummer off State 5; 132 campsites; no reservations; 208/686-1308). **Ponderosa State Park**

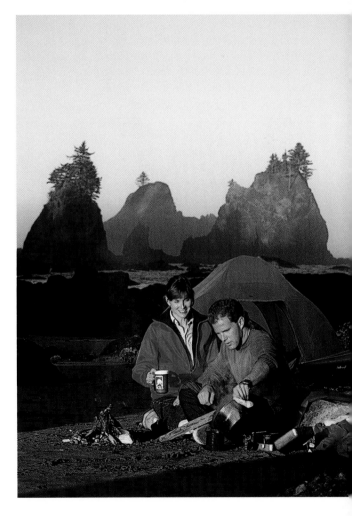

A romantic meal for two on the Washington coast at Point of Arches in Olympic National Park.

(on Payette Lake in McCall; 138 campsites; 208/634-2164).

MONTANA

(None of these campgrounds take reservations.) **Cromwell Dixon** (12 miles west of Helena off U.S. 12; 15 campsites; 406/449-5490). **Lake McDonald** (Glacier National Park on Lake McDonald's southwest shore; 180 campsites; 406/888-7800). **Seeley Lake** (16 miles north of State 200 off State 83; 29 campsites; 406/677-2233). **Swan Lake** (16 miles southeast of Bigfork off State 83; 36 campsites; 406/837-5081). **Upper Red Rock Lake** (Red Rock Lakes National Wildlife Refuge, 33 miles east of Monida and I-15; 7 campsites; no pets; free; 406/276-3536). **Yaak River** (6 miles west of Troy off U.S. 2; 44 campsites; 406/295-4693).

NEVADA

(Except where noted, none of these campgrounds take reservations.) **Cathedral Gorge State Park** (2 miles north of Panaca off U.S. 93; 22 campsites; 702/728-4460). **Temple Bar** (Lake Mead, 28 miles northeast of U.S. 93; 166 campsites; 702/293-8990). **Topaz Lake Park** (20 miles south of Gardnerville off U.S. 395; 70 campsites; 702/266-3343 for reservations). **Valley of Fire** (55 miles northeast of Las Vegas, east of I-15 on State 169 in Valley of Fire State Park; 53 campsites; 702/397-2088). **Wheeler Peak** (68 miles southeast of Ely in Great Basin National Park; 36 campsites; no pets; 702/234-7331).

NEW MEXICO

(None of the campgrounds listed take reservations.) **Dipping Vat** (25 miles east of U.S. 180 off State 159, on Snow Lake; 40 campsites; 505/533-6231). **Jemez Falls** (35 miles from State 44 on the south side of State 4, in Santa Fe National Forest; 52 campsites; 505/829-3535). **Juniper** (45 miles from Santa Fe in Bandelier National Monument; 94 campsites; 505/672-3861, ext. 517). **Silver** (off State 244, 2 miles north of U.S. 82 at Cloudcroft; 32 campsites; 505/682-2551). **South Fork** (14 miles northwest of Ruidoso off State 37 near Bonito Lake; 60 campsites; 505/257-4095). **Wild**

Rivers Recreation Area (30 miles north of Taos off State 522; 20 campsites; 505/758-8851).

OREGON

(Unless otherwise noted, call 800/452-5687 for campground reservations.) **Ainsworth State Park** (35 miles east of Portland off I-84; 45 campsites; no reservations; 503/695-2261). **Cape Blanco State Park** (10 miles northwest of Port Orford off U.S. 101; 58 campsites; no reservations; 541/332-6774). **Collier Memorial State Park** (30 miles north of Klamath Falls off U.S. 97; 68 campsites; no reservations; 541/783-2471). **Fort Stevens State Park** (7 miles west of Astoria off U.S. 101; 253 tent sites, 343 RV sites, 9 yurts; 503/861-1671). **Honeyman State Park** (about 3 miles south of Florence off U.S. 101; 381 campsites; 541/997-3851). **Humbug Mountain State Park** (6 miles south of Port Orford on U.S. 101; 108 campsites; no reservations; 541/332-6774). **LaPine State Park** (30 miles south of Bend; 145 campsites; 541/536-2428). **Memaloose State Park** (11 miles west of The Dalles off I-84; 110 campsites; 541/478-3008). **Silver Falls State Park** (26 miles east of Salem; 104 campsites; 503/873-8681). **Timothy Lake** (39 miles from Portland off U.S. 26; 170 campsites; 800/280-2267 for reservations, 503/622-3360 for information). **Tumalo State Park** (5 miles northwest of Bend; 88 campsites; 541/388-6055). **Wallowa Lake State Park** (6 miles south of Joseph at the end of State 82; 210 campsites; 541/432-4185).

UTAH

(Except where noted, none of these campgrounds take reservations.) **Escalante State Park** (1 1/2 miles west of Escalante off State 12 in Escalante Petrified Forest State Park; 22 campsites; 800/322-3770 for reservations, 435/826-4466 for information). **Fruita** (just south of State 24 in Capitol Reef National Park; 70 campsites; 435/425-3791). **Little Mill** (east of Timpanogos Cave National Monument off State 92; 79 campsites; 800/280-2267 for reservations, 801/785-3563 for information). **Point Supreme** (6 miles north of State

14 in Cedar Breaks National Monument; 30 campsites; 435/586-0787). **Sunset** (off State 63 in Bryce Canyon National Park; 104 campsites; 435/834-5322). **Watchman** (off State 9 just inside the southwest entrance to Zion National Park; 228 campsites; 435/772-3256).

WASHINGTON

Beacon Rock State Park (35 miles east of Vancouver off State 14; 33 campsites; no reservations; 509/427-8265). **Deception Pass State Park** (10 miles south of Anacortes off State 20; 246 campsites; no reservations; 360/675-2417). **Fort Canby State Park** (3 miles southwest of Ilwaco, off U.S. 101; 250 campsites; 800/452-5687 for reservations, 425/642-3078 for information). **Hoh Rain Forest** (western edge of Olympic National Park, 11 miles south of Forks off U.S. 101; 88 campsites; no reservations; 206/374-6925). **Joemma Beach State Park** (30 miles due west of Tacoma near Longbranch; 19 campsites; no reservations; 206/884-1944). **July Creek** (Olympic National Park, on Lake Quinault off U.S. 101; 29 walk-in campsites; no reservations; 360-452-0330). **Palouse Falls State Park** (60 miles west of Pullman; 10 campsites; no reservations; 509/646-3252). **Rainbow Falls State Park** (17 miles west of Chehalis off State 6; 50 campsites; no reservations; 253/291-3767). **Rockport State Park** (7 miles east of Concrete off State 20; 58 campsites; no reservations; 360/853-8461). **Steamboat Rock State Park** (12 miles south of Grand Coulee off State 155; 126 campsites; 800/452-5687 for reservations, 509/633-1304 for information). **Washington Park** (3 miles west of downtown Anacortes; 75 campsites; no reservations; 206/293-1927).

WYOMING

Hoop Lake (50 miles south of I-80 off State 414; 44 campsites; no reservations; 307/782-6555). **Jenny Lake** (25 miles north of Jackson, in Grand Teton National Park; 49 campsites; no reservations; 307/739-3399). **Sugarloaf** (40 miles west of Laramie off State 130; 16 campsites; 800/280-2267 for reservations, 307/745-2300 for information).

TRAVELING WITH CHILDREN & PETS

Going on vacation with children or pets lets you see the world at a slightly different pace. Their company needs only a little more planning.

Family Travel

Driving vacations can be a challenge with fidgety passengers in the backseat. The following tips will help the miles roll by more smoothly.

Let children help plan the trip. Pull out the maps and talk about what there is to see and do. Older children can write or call for travel brochures. Let each child choose a destination or activity and make that part of your travel itinerary. Also, do call ahead for reservations and be sure your planned lodging welcomes children.

Don't overschedule activities. Start early, and don't drive too long. Allow time for children to relax. Evenings are great times to read aloud; check with your local library or bookstore to find literature that relates to your trip.

When driving, stop every couple of hours for short breaks. Find places where you can all stretch your legs—a nature trail or a park. Rather than going to a restaurant for lunch, pack a picnic. After being confined in the car, children enjoy a chance to be active outdoors.

In addition to picnic supplies, be sure to carry along water, drinks, and non-messy snacks; moist towelettes facilitate cleanups. A small first-aid kit is a must. Other useful supplies include pillows, blanket, Swiss army knife, towels, and plastic bags.

Car activities can help while away the hours. Have each child bring along a small knapsack with a few favorite toys. Good choices might include small figures, toy cars, magnetic games, activity books, personal tape players with tapes and headsets, and playing cards. A well-prepared parent will have a stash of small surprises

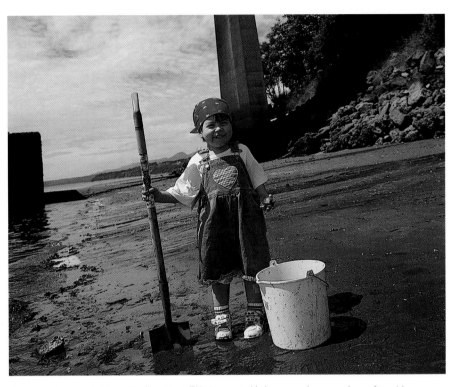

Children enjoy participating in family outings. This two-year-old clammer welcomes a chance for outdoor activity, and looks delighted with her results.

to pull out when old favorites begin to lose their appeal.

Encourage children to keep trip journals with words and/or drawings. Give each child a disposable camera to record favorite sights. They can also collect free or inexpensive memorabilia—postcards, brochures, stickers, patches, maps, and tickets. Trip memories and memorabilia will provide hours of enjoyment long after the trip is over.

Bringing Rover & Fluffy

If you want to bring your pet along on your back-road adventure, be sure it is obedient. If your animal takes off at every rest stop, your vacation could become a nightmare. Try it out on a few test drives.

A pet's traveling papers should include proof of a current rabies inoculation and a health certificate from a veterinarian, which should be enough for most state borders. Immunization requirements vary from state to state, however, so it's wise to check with the agriculture department in the states in which you will be traveling.

Make sure your dog is licensed in your home state. A license and pet ID tag should be attached firmly to a collar and the collar left on at all times. You might also want to carry along a photo to show people in case your pet strays.

Don't leave your animal unattended in a parked car. On an 85° day, a parked car even with its windows partly open can reach 102° in just 10 minutes. When traveling in warm weather, it's also important to keep your pet from being overheated, so don't forget that cool supply of water or ice cubes. Take frequent breaks from driving so both of you can stretch your legs. Always have animals on a leash.

You'll need to find a place you both can stay on the road. More and more places are taking well-behaved pets. Many Books list pet-friendly hostelries.

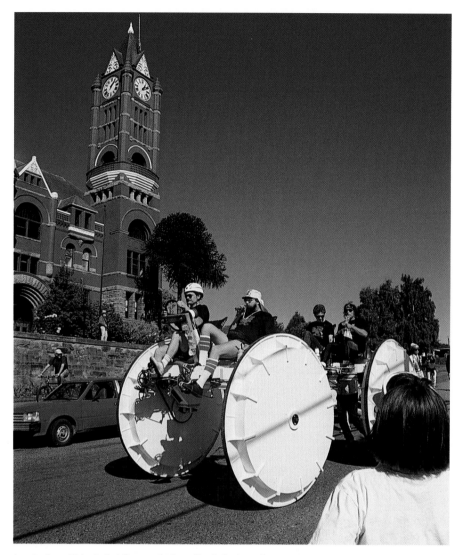

Imaginative vehicles in Port Townsend's Great Kinetic Sculpture Race must run on land, through mud, and over water. The zany Washington event takes place in October.

Travelers will find colorful festivals and events galore throughout the West. Here is a sample of what's available; for more complete listings of activities, contact state tourist offices (see page 237).

Arizona

Gold Rush Days, February, Wickenburg. Celebrates the town's gold-mining heritage—parades, dances, rodeo, gold panning, gem show, arts and crafts. **O'Odham Tash Indian Pow Wow**, February, Casa Grande. Ceremonial dances, rodeos, arts and crafts. **Ostrich Festival**, March, Chandler. Ostrich races, musical performances for every taste.

Navajo Nation Tribal Fair, September, Window Rock. Traditional singing and dancing, arts and crafts, rodeo. **Pueblo Grande Indian Market**, December, Phoenix. More than 450 Native American artists from 60 different tribes gather to sell their creations.

California

National Date Festival, February, Indio. Elaborate outdoor Arabian Nights pageant, daily camel and ostrich races. **Cinco de Mayo**, May 5, Los Angeles Old Town. Colorful Mexican holiday celebrates the 1862 victory in the fight for independence from France. **Dixieland Jazz**

Jubilee, Memorial Day weekend, Sacramento. Bands from around the world. **California Rodeo**, mid-July, Salinas. One of the country's largest rodeos. **Garlic Festival**, July, Gilroy. Garlic foods from appetizers to desserts, crafts, and entertainment. **Danish Days**, September, Solvang. Town celebrates its heritage with costume, food, and activities.

Colorado

Avon Winter Carnival, January, Avon. Colorado Snow Sculpting Championships, dog sledding, ice skating, and more. **Western Colorado Heritage Days**, April, Grand Junction. Dutch oven cook-off, Ute dancers, rodeo, mountain men rendezvous, cowboy dance. **Burro Days**, July, Fairplay. World championship pack burro races, llama races, arts and crafts. **Fiddlers on the Gorge**, August, Canon City. World-class fiddling competition at Royal Gorge Bridge. **Festival of Mountain and Plain: A Taste of Colorado**, Labor Day weekend, Denver. Free outdoor festival with four days of food and entertainment.

Idaho

Winter Carnival, January, McCall. World-class ice sculptures, sled dog races, fireworks, wine tasting. **Western Days**, May, Twin Falls. Week-long event with shootouts, BBQ, parade, and chili cook-off. **Timberfest**, June, Sandpoint. Idaho's timber heritage honored with logging competitions, log rolling, axe throwing, pole climbing. **National Oldtime Fiddlers Contest**, June, Weiser. The nation's best country fiddlers compete. **Oregon Trail Rendezvous Pageant**, July, Montpelier. Relives the history of the Oregon Trail.

Montana

Miles City Bucking Horse Sale, May, Miles City. Here's where rodeo operators buy their stock. See cowboys try to ride some of the country's wildest. **Custer's Last Stand Reenactment**, June, Hardin. Historical re-creation of the Battle of the Little Big Horn at its original site. **Bannack Days**, July, Bannack. Stagecoach rides, mock gunfights, old-time dancing in Montana's first territorial capital, now a living ghost town. **Flathead Festival**, mid-July to early August, in Kalispell, Whitefish, Columbia Falls. Top-name musical and dance performances in Montana's premier music festival. **Threshing Bee and Antique Show**, September, Culbertson. Antique farm equipment parade, grain-threshing demonstrations, tractor races.

Nevada

Las Vegas Helldorado Days, June, Las Vegas. Parades, carnival, rodeo, street dance, chili cook-off. **National Basque Festival**, July, Elko. Largest gathering of Basque Americans in U.S., sheep-dog trials, wood chopping, sheep hooking, bread baking. **Jim Butler Days**, July, Tonopah. Old mining camp hosts competitive mining contests. **Reno National Championship Air Races**, September, Reno. Air racing's Indianapolis 500 with the best in aerobatic flying, formula planes, and more. **National Finals Rodeo**, December, Las Vegas. Premier event of PRCA Circuit featuring bronco riding, roping, barrel racing, and bull riding.

New Mexico

Gathering of the Nations Powwow, April, Albuquerque. More than 5,000 costumed native dancers compete for prize money in one of the largest Indian events staged anywhere. **Eight Northern Indian Pueblos Arts and Crafts Fair**, July, various Indian pueblos. Two-day arts and crafts market, Indian dances. **Indian Market**, August, Santa Fe. World's largest Native American market, with 1,200 tribal artists from the U.S., Canada, and Mexico displaying crafts in Santa Fe Plaza. **Inter-Tribal Indian Ceremonial**, August, Gallup. Some 50 Indian tribes participate in ceremonial dances, all-Indian rodeo, arts and crafts, and Native American food booths. **Kodak International Balloon Fiesta**, October, Albuquerque. More than 900 balloons take to the skies at sunrise, with special shapes rodeo and more.

Oregon

Newport Seafood & Wine Festival, February, Newport. Seafood, wine, arts and crafts. **Northwest Cherry Festival**, April, The Dalles. Parade, food court, crafts. **Chief Joseph Days**, July, Joseph. Nez Perce/Umatilla Indian encampment, parades, and rodeos. **Pendleton Round-Up**, September, Pendleton. Famous rodeo, traditional Indian powwow. **Oktoberfest**, September, Mt. Angel. Arts and crafts, Bavarian food, biergarten, street dances.

Utah

Sundance Film Festival, late January, Park City. Premieres works of independent filmmakers. **Utah Shakespearean Festival**, June-Sept., Cedar City. Live performances, renaissance festivities. **Utah Pioneer Days**. July, statewide. Street festivals and rodeos. **Festival of the American West**, July, Wellsville. Great West Fair, military encampment, re-created Frontier Street, heritage crafts, Dutch oven cook-off, cowboy poetry. **Temple Square Christmas Lights**, November/December, Salt Lake City. Historic square is decorated with more than 250,000 lights.

Washington

Deer Park Winter Festival, January, Deer Park. Bonfire, fireworks, dogsled pulls, ice sculptures. **Celebration of Chocolate &**

Red Wine, February, Yakima Valley. Pair chocolate with valley wines for a Valentine treat. **Sandhill Crane Festival**, March, Othello. View migrating sandhill cranes in Columbia National Wildlife Refuge. **Sand Castle and Sculpture Contest**, September, Pacific Beach. Structural dreams rise from the sand. **Great Kinetic Sculpture Race**, October, Port Townsend. Imaginative vehicles that will run on land, through mud, and over water.

Wyoming

Cowboy Ski Challenge, February, Teton Village. Novelty ski races, rodeo, Dutch oven cook-off, poetry, barn dance. **Old West Days**, May, Jackson. Parades, rodeo, mule show, Indian dancers, cowboy poetry, mountain man rendezvous. **Woodchoppers Jamboree & Rodeo**, June, Encampment. Loggers vie for the championship title in timed events from tree cutting to log chopping. **Cheyenne Frontier Days**, July, Cheyenne. Ten-day event with world's largest outdoor rodeo, bull riding, roping, horse-drawn carriage parade, and chuck wagon, barrel, chariot, and wild horse races. **Mountain Man Rendezvous**, September, Fort Bridger State Historic Site. Mountain men encampment, crafts, music, Indian dancing, black powder shoots.

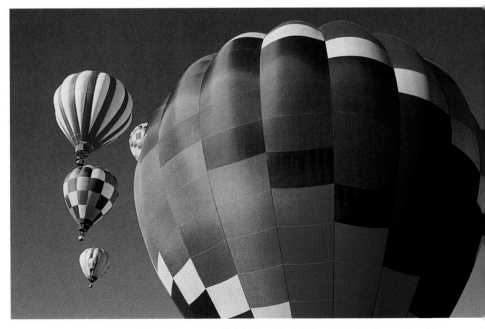

Up, up, and away! A mass ascension at Albuquerque's Kodak International Balloon Fiesta fills the morning skies with more than 900 balloons of all shapes and colors.

ROAD SAFETY TIPS

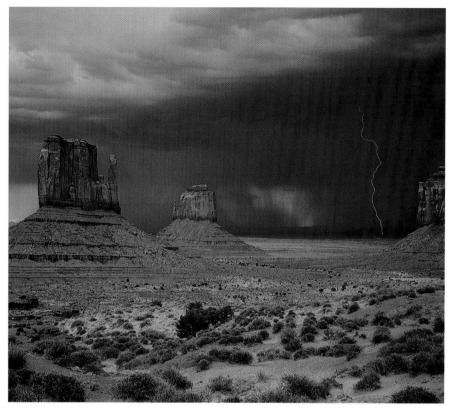

Quick-moving storms roll across the Southwest in summer; when rain impairs visibility, drivers may be wise to pull off the road and wait until the downpour is over.

Scenic byways can provide countless hours of pleasure if you follow a few simple suggestions before setting out on your back-road adventures.

Preparation

Service stations and garages may be few and far between on some back roads, so give your car a thorough check before leaving home—battery, lights (including emergency flashers), windshield wipers and washer, horn, tires, drive belts, fluid levels, spark plugs and ignition wires, radiator, and hoses. Make sure that your air conditioner is in working order for summer travel and that you have antifreeze for winter sojourns. Chains are a must if you travel in winter or in mountainous terrain where fall or spring snowfalls may be a surprise. Depending on weather, even a 4-wheel drive vehicle may require chains.

Take drinking water, plenty of it. Many travelers also pack an ice chest with snacks and cold drinks. A first-aid kit is also a good idea, along with an emergency car kit containing a reliable flashlight, tow rope, tire pump, air pressure gauge, shovel, paper towels, booster cables, flares, extra window-washing solvent, and sacks for traction in case you get stuck in sand, mud, or snow.

Make sure you have a good map of the area before you leave. Automobile clubs such as AAA are good resources.

Gasoline & Water

Because gas stations are few and far between in some areas, fill your tank before you set out and in large towns along the way. The same thing applies to water. It's also smart to carry extra water for your radiator.

Livestock

When driving through open range, watch out for cattle and sheep on the road. Also look out for other wildlife such as deer, especially at dawn and dusk. Slow down when you approach a rise or a blind curve, and scan the sides of the road. Generally, where there's one deer, there are others.

Desert Driving

Thunderstorms, particularly prevalent in summer, can quickly cause local flooding. Be alert in low-lying areas where signs warn that dry washes can quickly fill bank to bank with rushing water during heavy rains. You might want to pull off the road and wait out sudden and quick-moving storms.

Breakdowns

If your car breaks down and leaves you stranded in the middle of nowhere, stay inside the car and wait for help. If you are a member of an automobile club and have your cell phone, use the emergency number on your card. You may be tempted to leave your car and start walking, but unless you know help is nearby, it's best to stay put. Searchers can spot a vehicle long before they can spot a lone walker. If you feel you must go for help, insist other family members stay behind. Take water with you, but leave some for others. Head back in the direction you came from; don't try a shortcut.

Important Phone Numbers

Here is a list of places to call for road and travel conditions:

Arizona: 888/411-7623
California: 916/445-1534
Colorado: 303/639-1234
Idaho: 208/336-6600 (winter)
Montana: 800/226-7623
Nevada: 775/888-7000
New Mexico: 800/432-4269
Oregon: 800/977-6368
Utah: 801/964-6000
Washington: 888/766-4636 (winter)
Wyoming: 307/635-9966

STATE TOURIST OFFICES

Most of our trips include names and addresses of local tourist offices that can provide you with additional information. The following is a list of state tourist offices that can help you even further in obtaining travel information. When requesting travel planners and maps from these tourist offices, allow at least 4 to 6 weeks lead time.

Arizona

Arizona Office of Tourism
2702 North 3rd Street, Suite 4015
Phoenix, AZ 85004
602/230-7733
Internet address: www.arizonaguide.com

California

California Division of Tourism
P.O. Box 1499
Sacramento, CA 95812-1499
800/862-2543
Internet address: http://gocalif.ca.gov

Colorado

Colorado Travel & Tourism Authority
P.O. Box 3524
Englewood, CO 80155
800/265-6723
Internet address: www.colorado.com

Idaho

Idaho Travel Council
P.O. Box 83720
Boise, ID 83720-0093
800/635-7820
Internet address: www.visitid.com or www.visitid.org

Montana

Travel Montana
1424 9th Avenue
P.O. Box 200533
Helena, MT 59620-0533
800/847-4868 (outside MT) or 406/444-2654
Internet address: http://travel.mt.gov

Nevada

Nevada Commission on Tourism
Capitol Complex
Carson City, NV 89710
800/638-2328
Internet address: www.travelnevada.com

New Mexico

New Mexico Department of Tourism
491 Old Santa Fe Trail
Santa Fe, NM 87501
800/733-6396
Internet address: www.newmexico.org

Oregon

Oregon Tourism Commission
775 Summer Street, N.E.
Salem, OR 97310
800/547-7842
Internet address: www.traveloregon.com

Utah

Utah Travel Council
Council Hall/Capitol Hill
Salt Lake City, UT 84114
801/538-1030
Internet address: www.utah.com

Washington

Travel Development Division
Department of Commerce and Economic Development
General Administration Bldg.
Olympia, WA 98504
360/586-2088 or 586-2102
Internet address: www.tourism.wa.gov/001.htm

Wyoming

Wyoming Division of Tourism
I-25 at College Drive
Cheyenne, WY 82002
307/777-7777
Internet address: Wyoming Electronic ScouT(WEST) at
http://commerce.state.wy.us/west